Fireworks 4
Expert Edge

About the Authors

Jeffrey Bardzell is the cofounder of allecto.net (www.allecto.net), an e-learning consulting and multimedia instruction development company in Bloomington, Indiana; and a founding partner of Flash-Guru (www.flash-guru.com), a comprehensive Flash resource site. During the day, he develops web-based learning applications at Indiana University, where he is also a Ph.D. Candidate in Comparative Literature.

Jeffrey's other publications include several Flash courses and tutorials, which can be found at both Flash-Guru and ehandson.com. He is both a contributor and technical editor for the *Flash 5 Bible* by Robert Reinhardt and Jon Warren Lentz, and he has authored several academic and education policy articles on topics that include early literacy instruction, school finance reform, and epic poetry.

Before moving to web development full time, he was an education policy analyst and also taught ancient and medieval literature, composition, and English as a second language at Indiana University, Mary Washington College, Ignatius University, and the Taipei Language Institute.

Lisa Lopuck is an award-winning visual and user interface designer, a regular speaker at web design conferences around the world, and a best-selling author, whose books include *Web Design for Dummies, Adobe Seminars: Web Page Design*, and *Designing Multimedia*. She has been on Macromedia's Fireworks advisory board since the product's inception, and has consulted as an Internet designer for companies such as eBay, Inktomi, National Geographic, Twentieth Century Fox, and Microsoft.

She is the founder of eHandsOn (www.ehandson.com), a company that provides high-quality online training, taught by the world's leading experts, and helps other companies create their own expert training products.

Lisa holds a BA in Communication Design from UCLA.

Fireworks 4
Expert Edge

Jeffrey Bardzell
and **Lisa Lopuck**

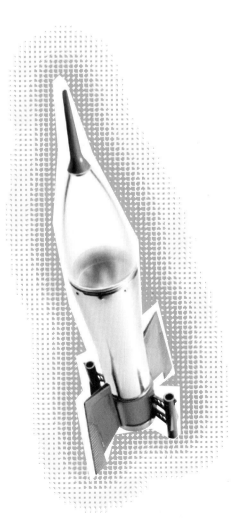

Osborne/McGraw-Hill

New York   Chicago   San Francisco
Lisbon   London   Madrid   Mexico City   Milan
New Delhi   San Juan   Seoul   Singapore   Sydney   Toronto

Osborne/**McGraw-Hill**
2600 Tenth Street
Berkeley, California 94710
U.S.A.

To arrange bulk purchase discounts for sales promotions, premiums, or fund-raisers, please contact Osborne/**McGraw-Hill** at the above address. For information on translations or book distributors outside the U.S.A., please see the International Contact Information page immediately following the index of this book.

Fireworks 4 Expert Edge

1234567890 QPD QPD 01987654321

ISBN 0-07-213146-2

Publisher Brandon A. Nordin
Vice President & Associate Publisher Scott Rogers
Editorial Director Roger Stewart
Project Editor Jody McKenzie
Acquisitions Coordinator Alissa Larson
Technical Editor Brian Baker
Copy Editor Jan Jue
Proofreaders Marian Selig, Stefany Otis
Indexer Jack Lewis
Computer Designers Jean Butterfield, Melinda Moore Lytle
Illustrators Beth E. Young, Lyssa Sieben-Wald, Michael Mueller, Alex Putney
Series Designer Jean Butterfield
Cover Designer Ted Holladay
Series Illustrators Beth E. Young, Lyssa Sieben-Wald

This book was composed with Corel VENTURA™ Publisher.

I dedicate this book to Shaowen, who made the sacrifice that triggered it all—I owe everything to that sacrifice. Today, you and I till the earth for two goddesses, a witch, and a grammarian. And tomorrow, I hope, for Madeleine.

Wo yongyuan ai ni; wo shi ni de.

—*Jeffrey Bardzell*

For my family, Matt and Jasmine, and my sister, Gina—my three favorite people in the universe. Thanks for all your individual support and encouragement through the years. I also want to thank my parents for all their glowing pride, and my parents-in-law—especially Marilyn, who is thankfully still with us despite incredible odds.

—*Lisa Lopuck*

Contents at a Glance

Contents

Acknowledgments

This book has been a lot of fun to write, and I have collaborated with many bright and hard-working people. I am grateful for this opportunity to extend my warm thanks to the following friends and collaborators.

Most of the credit is due to those who collaborated directly in the making of the book. To my coauthor, Lisa Lopuck, thanks for a great collaboration—I love your work and this has been a lot of fun. Thank you, Mark Grilli, for so many different things in the past year; and all the great people at eHandsOn, in particular Natalie Muldaur. Chris Van Buren, our agent: thanks for the timely problem solving and the smooth ride! To all of you at Osborne—Alissa Larson, Jody McKenzie, Roger Stewart, and others—I am grateful for your patience and hard work—and sorry for giving you cause to nag so much! Special credit is due to our Technical Editor, Brian Baker— you were both eminently qualified and quite conscientious. I am also grateful to our contributors—Adam Bell, Nik Schramm, and Stephen Voisey—for your excellent sidebars—in some cases on rather short notice!

To my partners at Flash-Guru—Jon Warren Lentz and Nik Schramm—thanks for your patience and guidance. I understand the sacrifices you made for this project. Jon, your mentoring and, yes, let it be said, nurturing belies the "madman" exterior. All for one, guys! In addition, I appreciate the flexibility and indulgence afforded me by the management at my day job at Indiana University's Financial Management Services—especially Harriet Fierman, who has been a more positive force in my life than she will ever realize or acknowledge. You resuscitated my career *and* introduced me to Harry Potter—I'll never get over that combination!

Behind the work, the phone calls, the e-mail, and the attachments stand your family and closest friends, who hold you up when you would fall, and who make you who you are. Thank you Malcolm Airst and V. Kessler, for bringing out the geek within and making him want to write about it, too. To my family—on both sides of the Pacific—your ongoing love and support means everything to me.

Finally, a hearty thanks to the cross-check "therapy" of the Driveway Hockey League—Chris, Jim, Kate, Kim, Kim, Pallas, and sometimes Meg—you keep me sane and give me something to look forward to.

—*Jeffrey Bardzell*

I'm so pleased to be a part of this new Expert Edge series that combines high-level concepts with hands-on, real-world application—there are so many books that present one without the other. I attribute this book's success to many people who worked as hard as Jeffrey mentioned, but I especially want to point out Jeffrey himself, whose work ethic and dedication made this book happen. Thanks, Jeffrey, for an excellent book!

—Lisa Lopuck

Introduction

How to Use This Book

One common dilemma that writers of computer books face is the choice to write a book that serves primarily as a *reference*, a handy document to keep nearby for when you have esoteric questions; or a *training document*, which teaches the reader how to use the software. While the reference book is systematic and comprehensive, it tends not to teach all that well—you kind of have to know the software at some level before you can benefit from it. Likewise, while the training document teaches well, it does not always provide systematically ordered content comprehensively.

Our goal in creating this book was to provide a middle path. Each chapter is broken down into several parts:

1. Basic concepts, tasks, and dialogs, to provide an orientation.

2. Advanced tasks, combinations of features, and real-world ideas.

3. A step-by-step tutorial, in most cases with an online version hosted by ehandson.com, which exemplifies in project form many of the tasks and features covered in the main chapter.

While each of the tutorials is mostly self-contained, they are all intended to follow up and provide experience with the tasks covered in the chapter. For that reason, we generally recommend that you at least familiarize yourself with the chapter's main contents before you work through the tutorial.

What You Should Know Coming In

Fireworks 4 Expert Edge is not a beginner's book. That doesn't mean this book is all that hard, either. What it means is that we assume you have access to (and roughly understand) the basic operations of the program—how to draw a square, how to add a drop-shadow to text, how to draw a slice. These issues are covered quite well in the *Using Fireworks 4* manual that ships with Fireworks. Once you've gotten the gist of that, you'll want to move on to bigger and better things. That's where we fit in.

And What You Should Get Out of It

Rather than providing the same information that you probably already have, this book was written to serve two primary purposes:

1. **To Serve as a Reference and Inspiration for Intermediate and Advanced Users**   The book is organized around the web design and building *workflow* (initial design, creating development templates and teams, building art, optimizing art, integrating Fireworks files with other programs, creating animation and interactivity, and extending Fireworks). As you reach each successive stage of the workflow, keep the book by your side as you go.

2. **To Provide Real-World Training to Ambitious Learners**   The chapters cover increasingly harder topics as they go along. If you are new to Fireworks or to one or more advanced techniques, use this book as an intermediate to advanced course—read through the chapters in order, and you will find yourself building great-looking, interactive web designs in no time!

Above all, we hope this book will help you learn Fireworks and (more importantly) learn how to use Fireworks to build beautiful sites in conjunction with other programs. We hope that the book will do more than help you solve immediate problems—we hope it will draw you into new territory and serve as your companion as you explore techniques and create web art today that was inaccessible to you yesterday.

Setting the Foundation

Part

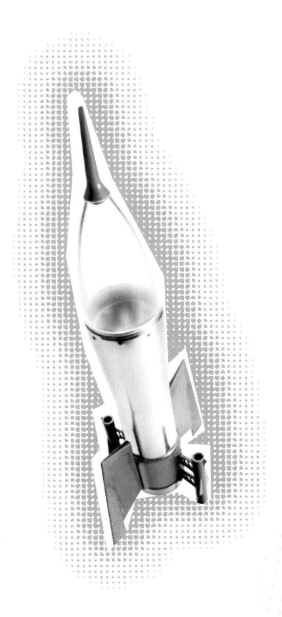

1 Fireworks' Place in the Web Design Workflow

If you've been designing web sites for some time with Photoshop, you may wonder why you need Fireworks. After all, Photoshop is fairly adept at building graphics from scratch, and ImageReady is right there to add interactivity. But Fireworks has several features and advantages that make the creation, modification, and deployment of lean web graphics and sophisticated interfaces powerfully fast. Chief among them are its heavy use of vector graphics and its multifaceted integration with Dreamweaver. We will discuss the how-tos and benefits of both of these features in the course of this book.

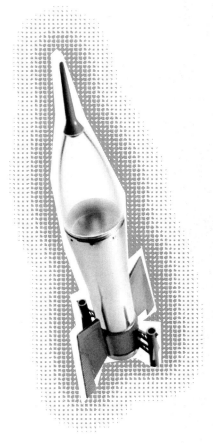

L ike illustration tools such as Adobe Illustrator and Macromedia Freehand, Fireworks is an object-oriented, vector-based program. When you build web graphics in Fireworks, you are building individual objects with standard Bezier curves, paths, and shapes. This gives you infinite control. One of the earliest (and most alluring) claims Macromedia made of Fireworks is that everything is editable, all the time, even months after you create the file. Whether the secondary color needs to be changed throughout a banner, a textual drop-shadow needs to be deepened, or the beveling of a button needs to be less pronounced, Fireworks allows you to make the change instantly. You are forever liberated from the single Undo of yesteryear.

While Fireworks does have tools that allow you to create and edit bitmap graphics, you can also use Fireworks to build complex and textured vector illustrations and logos that you can then export to illustration tools (such as Freehand) or bitmap tools (such as Photoshop) for further refinements or print preparation. The beauty of vector-based web graphics is that they afford you infinite control and flexibility—imagine sweeping image-editing being as easy as changing text in a word processor! Once you build your web graphics with Fireworks, the fun really begins. Unlike Photoshop, Fireworks is a dedicated web graphics program, and extensive built-in tools allow you to add interactive links, animation, complex rollover buttons, and even drop-down menus to your designs.

In this book, we take you on a real-life journey of building a professional web site for Habitat for Humanity using Fireworks in conjunction with other tools from Photoshop to Dreamweaver and Flash. The book assumes you have some basic familiarity with Fireworks' tools; it will not cover each of the drawing tools in turn, for example. We will not have you create widgets—useless graphics just for the sake of showing you how to use, say, the Pen tool. Instead, after covering several new features and providing a general overview, we will jump right into creating and refining a professional site. Thus, the book will devote considerable attention to using Fireworks in conjunction with other software—particularly Dreamweaver and Flash. Along the way, you will master the entire workflow of producing professional web sites with Fireworks, from comps and storyboards through optimization, publication, and post-publication maintenance.

Understanding Vector Graphics

When you first open Fireworks, you'll see a familiar interface—complete with a Layers panel—that might remind you of other programs like Photoshop. Stop right there! Fireworks is a very different graphics program, functioning more like Illustrator or Freehand. The distinction between these two types of programs that we have mentioned—bitmap- and vector-based graphics—governs the strengths and limitations of the software, the nature of the design process, and the qualities of the resulting artwork. Understanding these two graphic types is fundamental to working in Fireworks.

To a computer, a *bitmap graphic* consists of a large table, or *matrix,* of pixels. The graphic might, as shown in Figure 1-1, have 100 rows and 100 columns, and

Figure 1-1   A close-up of a bitmap graphic

the graphic file communicates to the computer the color value (often a mixture of 256 shades each of red, green, and blue [RGB]) of each pixel. Figure 1-1 shows a close-up of a bitmap graphic; you can see the individual pixels that make up the image. Once it has described each of the 10,000 pixels (100 rows × 100 columns, in our example), the computer can display the graphic. Most web graphics today are bitmap graphics, including both the GIF and JPG formats.

In contrast, vector-based graphic files, which form the core of Fireworks' PNGs, do not analyze the graphic data into individual pixels. Instead, *vector graphics* are described to the computer using mathematical equations. For example, to draw a vector circle, the computer draws a circle with a diameter of x pixels, starting at point x, y from the top left corner of the canvas, with a stroke of 2 pixels in the color black, and a fill of solid blue. Clearly this requires less information to render than a pixel-by-pixel description of the same! Another advantage is also obvious: to make the circle's fill red rather than blue, you need only change one variable, instead of changing the RGB color of thousands of individual pixels. For this reason, you can also scale vector graphics up and down as much as you like without compromising quality or file size—all you are doing is changing the size variables. Figure 1-2 shows a vector-based image (though it was converted to bitmap for publication); notice the smooth, even unnatural, lines.

You might, after this description, wonder why anyone uses bitmaps at all. The reason is simple: it is one thing to describe simple shapes, like circles, fast-food restaurant logos, and the individual letters that make up fonts (which are vector files, by the way). It is quite another to describe a photograph. Different formats have different strengths. Most vector graphics have comparatively few colors,

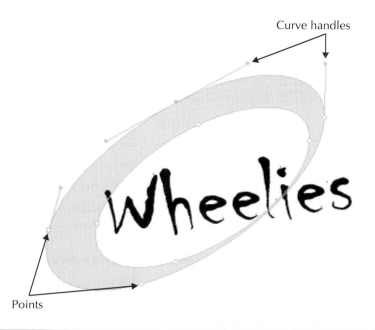

Curve handles

Points

Figure 1-2 A vector graphic is mathematically defined by points connected by curves.

clean edges, and visibly geometric shapes. Bitmaps lend themselves to continuous images, such as photographs and images that are too complex to render with shapes and lines.

Finally, we note significantly that vector graphics can sometimes imitate bitmap graphics: bitmaps created as seamless tiles can be applied as fills to vector graphics in lieu of solid color fills. In this way, a vector shape can take on the appearance of a bitmap graphic and yet retain all of the advantages of a vector graphic. Video games make heavy use of this technique. Fireworks not only allows you to apply bitmap fills to vector graphics, but it also enables you to create several bitmap-like effects—drop shadows, glows, bevels, and even to apply Photoshop filters—by applying textures to vector shapes in the same way that it applies solid color strokes and fills.

What Is Fireworks?

Macromedia built Fireworks from the ground up specifically to address the needs of the web graphic designer. The choice to create a web graphics tool that used vectors, as opposed to bitmaps, was ingenious. Fireworks 1 solved the primary problems of creating graphics for the Web, which included the need for compact file sizes and a tool for designers that empowered them to create and modify common web effects, such as bevels, glows, drop shadows, and textures, with minimal fuss. The reliance on vector drawing tools also enabled the graphics to be exported, adapted, and reused for multiple purposes, including both web and print dissemination. Fireworks has also always been able to import and manipulate bitmaps though its power derives mostly from its robust vector handling capabilities. Macromedia capped the design process with an intuitive yet powerful set of optimization tools that converts the composite vector/bitmap graphics to standard bitmaps (including GIF and JPG), allowing users to balance the twin considerations of quality versus file size.

Later versions dramatically enhanced the ease and power with which users could add interactivity, even as Macromedia has consistently improved both its vector and bitmap handling capabilities. Fireworks 4 further ups the ante with improved Photoshop integration, an improved interface, and a host of other improvements that will speed up your workflow and empower you to be a more creative designer.

Adding Interactivity to Your Designs

Fireworks is clearly a powerful tool for creating graphic images, be they vector, bitmap, or composite. But it is so much more than that. Although most web graphics are themselves bitmaps, most web *pages* are multimedia. When you look at any web page on the Internet, the interface is usually a mix of graphics, photography, and text. And it doesn't stop there. Increasingly, most web pages *do* something; interactivity and dynamic web pages are increasingly common. Specifically, users manipulate elements within graphical interfaces to trigger events—loading data, changing images, accessing a database, and so on. Unlike the group of pixels in a bitmap design, elements in vector graphics—text, shapes, and paths—are all unique, separate objects, even when they are stacked above one another on the same layer . And because they are objects, it is an easy task to isolate them for specific purposes, such as attaching scripts to them. Fireworks makes great-looking static web graphics and enables you to create sleek interfaces loaded with functionality.

Many common behaviors are built into Fireworks and can be added automatically through simple interfaces like the one shown in Figure 1-3. The Set Pop-Up Menu dialog box, new to Fireworks 4, makes deploying dynamic pop-up menus as easy as filling out a short form. Other behaviors that Fireworks can add automatically include the following:

- Image rollovers
- Image swapping
- Status bar messages
- Navigation bars

Extending Fireworks' Interactivity

With the help of other tools (such as Dreamweaver, Flash, and others), and especially if you can program, you can add much more interactivity to your Fireworks interfaces. For example, you can create buttons that control the

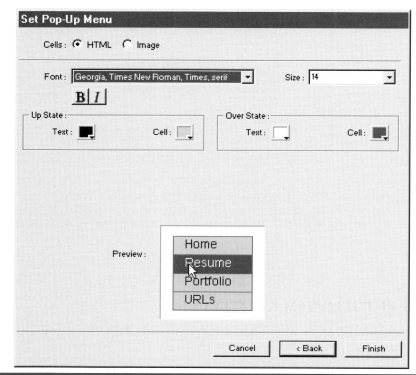

Figure 1-3   The Set Pop-Up Menu dialog box

playback of a Flash movie, using the free JavaScript Integration Kit extension for Dreamweaver. You can use Fireworks rollovers and menus as events that drive ColdFusion or Active Server Pages (ASP). And you can extend Fireworks itself with the Macromedia Exchange, where you can download free extensions that add any number of Fireworks behaviors, from bullet builders to a custom swatch maker!

 FOR MORE INFORMATION! For hundreds of free extensions for several Macromedia products, including Fireworks, go to www.macromedia.com/exchange. Numerous third-party sites contain Fireworks extensions as well. Two of the more notable sites are http://www.massimocorner.com/ and http://dhtmlnirvana.com/ (Fireworks extensions are all located in the "Pretty Lady" section).

Site Design in Fireworks

One of Fireworks' best features for the designer is that it is a very effective tool for developing entire site designs and mock-ups. You can create the look of pages, master pages, and so on, in Fireworks, just as you might create a comp in Quark Express or Adobe InDesign. As you develop the overall look, you can also create the individual graphics that will become elements of that overall look—all in the same program!

You can create a design grid using rulers and guides on a layered canvas that is 600×500 pixels and still have a 100-kilobyte (KB) file (unlike the 20 megabytes [MB] the same file might be in Photoshop), which is easier on your processor and your hard drive. You can then create slides from your comps and have an instant storyboard or presentation. When you have finished the look of the site, you can slice your page into tables and import as-is into Dreamweaver. Not only will your page layout be nearly complete—you will usually end up doing some tweaking in Dreamweaver—but your graphics also will already be optimized, publishable, and in place!

 As you build web pages in Fireworks, it's tempting to build more than one page in the same document as you would in Photoshop. Because Fireworks is geared toward building interactive pages, concentrate on building one web page at a time.

What Is a Fireworks PNG?

Most programs have, in addition to a number of available standard file types, a native file type. Photoshop has the PSD, Word has the DOC, and so on. In each case, the software is able to encode unique features in its native file type, features not available in other programs. While in development, you will typically use the native file type (such as the PSD) and later export a more standard file type (such as a TIF).

Fireworks can be confusing in this regard, because its native file type, the PNG (pronounced "ping"), *is* a standard file type—sort of. Perhaps the best way to think about the Fireworks PNG is as a PNG+. That is, at its base, it is a PNG file, but Fireworks stores additional information in the file that is not readily interpretable by most other programs (the only exceptions are related Macromedia products).

The standard PNG (Portable Network Graphic) is a simple bitmap file type, much like a GIF or a JPG. Indeed, the PNG was initially developed to replace the GIF and JPG file types by combining their best attributes. Like a JPG, the PNG uses 24-bit color (the GIF is limited to 8-bit, or 256 colors). Like a GIF, it uses lossless compression, whereas the JPG uses lossy compression. With ample color and a lossless compression scheme, the PNG results in high-quality graphics files; however, standard PNGs can be a bit larger than both GIF and JPG, depending on the color depth. In addition, PNGs are not widely compatible with browsers, although that is changing as browsers begin to support PNG transparency .

In addition to having the features that were mentioned in the last paragraph, the Fireworks PNG is, like the EPS and WMF graphic file specifications, a *metafile*—a file type that contains both vector and bitmap information. In addition, the Fireworks PNG also stores nongraphic information—such as when you add a behavior to a slice—that is simply not interpretable by virtually any other program. It is as if the other program were to take a picture of your file, rather than opening it. Saving at that point can be disastrous.

If you open a Fireworks PNG in most other programs, the file will be flattened and *rasterized,* that is, converted into a simple bitmap. If you save the file and open it again in Fireworks, you will lose the editability of text, vector graphics, and live effects. Worse, you will lose all behaviors, layers, frames, slices, hotspots, URLs, masks, and so on.

New Features of Fireworks 4

Fireworks 4 has a host of new features, some of which improve productivity in accomplishing specific tasks, while others are more generalized. Here's a list of the more important features along with a description of what we've found most useful about them.

Standardized User Interface

Macromedia has updated and standardized the user interface in recent upgrades of several of its web development products, including Dreamweaver 4 (and Dreamweaver UltraDev 4), Flash 5, and Fireworks 4. Tools, panels, icons, and menu commands are now largely standardized. In addition, all of these products use a similar tabbed panel interface that both appears and functions consistently across the programs that have the new interface.

What's great about the standardized interfaces is that they make it much easier for you to learn and master all the products in the Macromedia family—an increasingly important task since the programs all work so well together.

A convenient feature of the new interface—already familiar to users of Dreamweaver 3—is the Launcher Bar, shown in Figure 1-4. The Launcher Bar is the set of icons in the lower-right corner of the screen that launches frequently used panels, including the Stroke, Mixer, Optimize, and Layers panel sets. This new feature enhances productivity by providing quick access to the most common panels.

 Having too many of these panels open at one time can clutter your screen, especially if you are running at a lower resolution. Now that you can quickly reopen them with a single click (rather than hunting around the Windows menu), you can close the less frequently used panels and get the most out of your screen space.

Figure 1-4   Use The Fireworks Launcher Bar to open the Stroke, Mixer, Optimize, and Layers panel sets.

Enhanced Dreamweaver Integration

With Fireworks 3/Dreamweaver 3, you could launch and edit Fireworks files within Dreamweaver. Fireworks would open the source PNG and then re-export all of the necessary scripts and image files. When you returned to Dreamweaver, the document was already updated. This feature was one of the hallmark features of the two products' integration.

With Fireworks 4, Macromedia has gone a couple steps further. First, they improved the launch and edit window, which allows you to edit Fireworks' files directly in Dreamweaver. Second, whereas in the past, when you opened Fireworks files in Dreamweaver, Fireworks rewrote the Hypertext Markup Language (HTML), it can now leave the HTML alone. This means that you can customize your code as much as you like in Dreamweaver and still edit your Fireworks files at any time without fear.

Improved Batch Processing

Fireworks 4 has a new batch-processing interface shown in Figure 1-5 that makes automating tasks simple, providing control over the tasks, their order, and where to save the resulting files and backups. Figure 1-5 shows step 2 of the new batch-processing interface. As you can see, using Fireworks' robust batch-processing powers is as easy as filling out a form.

Live Animation Controls

Fireworks has made two improvements to its animation controls. First, it now has an animation control interface similar to that of Flash and Director. This interface provides a series of VCR-like controls right in the authoring environment that let you preview the animation and/or move through it one frame at a time.

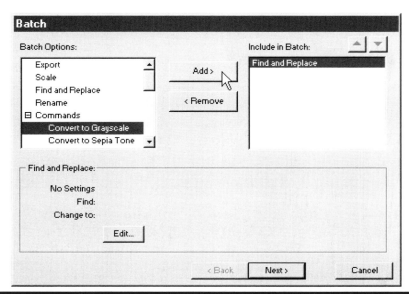

Figure 1-5   The new batch-processing interface

Another powerful innovation is the new Animation Line, seen in Figure 1-6. When you select an animated symbol, each point on the line indicates the relative position of each symbol on each frame of the animation. By adjusting this Animation Line, you can alter the direction and extent of an animation quickly and intuitively, because you can adjust the animation as a whole, rather than skipping back and forth between first and last frames.

Pop-Up Menus

One of the coolest new features of Fireworks 4 is its ability to quickly create hierarchical menus that appear when you roll over a button, as illustrated in Figure 1-7. You can attach a pop-up menu to any slice or hotspot object in Fireworks simply by selecting it and choosing Insert | Pop-Up Menu from the menu. Fireworks then opens a simple two-step dialog box that walks you through the process of building the menu. Better still, this dialog box even provides a live preview as you work, so there is no need to go back and forth to see your design.

Improved Pen Tool

As most designers know, although the Pen tool in most graphics software is quite powerful, it is not the easiest tool to become accustomed to. Even when you do have

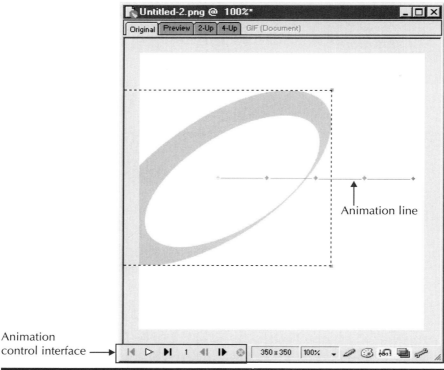

Figure 1-6　Fireworks' new Live Animation feature

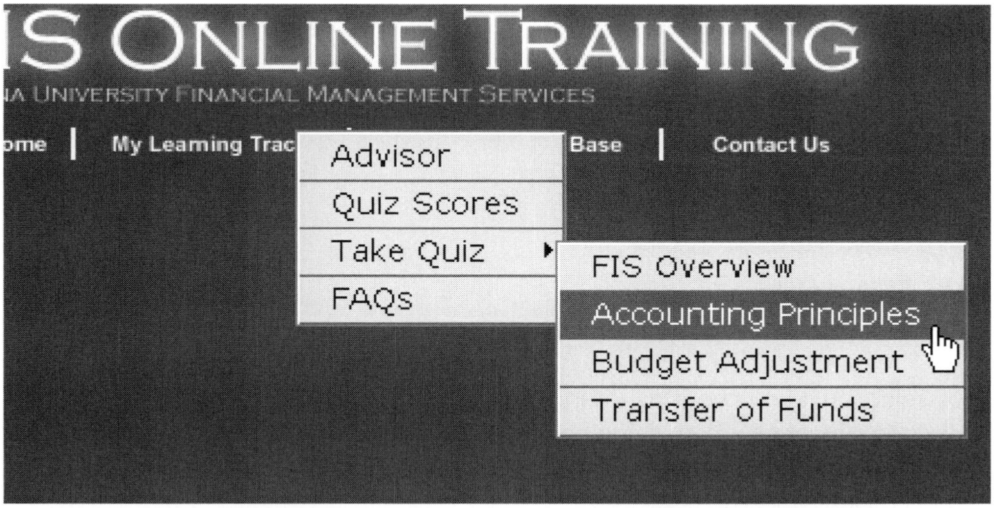

Figure 1-7   A pop-up menu, as seen in a browser

some level of comfort with it, it can sometimes be hard to tell whether you are editing a point, removing it, adding a new one, or simply selecting the whole path. To help you with this, Fireworks 4 now continuously changes its cursor icon while you are working, so you know exactly what you are doing, whether you are plotting a new point or modifying the curve handles on an existing one.

Automatic Scrolling

Working within a graphics program often requires zooming in closely on your work. Often, it happens that a portion of what you want to modify is offscreen. Moving your mouse over to a scroll bar and repositioning takes time and breaks concentration. To minimize this inconvenience, Fireworks 4 has a new automatic scrolling feature. Once you get used to it, you'll wish all of your graphics applications had it. By dragging your cursor beyond the edge of the document window when your document is larger than the window, you cause the screen to scroll with the cursor—no scroll bars to find and no buttons to press.

Selective JPEG Compression

Have you ever tried to compress one of those images in which one item had to be clear, while the remainder of the image was a lower priority? If you made the one item clear by compressing at high quality, the file was too large. Yet if you made the file a reasonable size, the main object's quality was low. With selective JPEG compression, as shown in Figure 1-8, you can compress one part of an image with 90 percent quality, while you can compress the rest of the image, say, the background, at 40 percent quality.

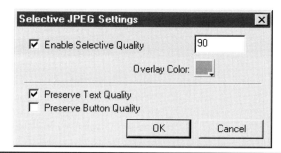

Figure 1-8 The Selective JPEG Compression dialog box

Object Masking

Fireworks has always allowed you to create mask groups whereby the shape of one object determines the visible area of another object. New in Fireworks 4, however, is the ability to *see* your masks in the Layers palette, as shown in Figure 1-9. As you can see in the illustration, Fireworks' object masks look a lot like Photoshop's layer masks in the Layer palette, and function pretty much the same way.

Expanded Import and Export Options

Because it is designed to do so many things at once, Fireworks' Export dialog box has traditionally been somewhat complex. Fireworks 4 streamlines this dialog box, making exporting files simpler and quicker. In it, you can choose, in addition to the various HTML editor options, several other graphics file types.

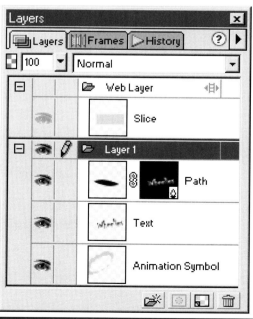

Figure 1-9 In Fireworks 4, object masks appear in the Layers palette as a second thumbnail next to the main image thumbnail.

NOTE The dialog box still has many options. These are now tucked away in an Options dialog box, obtained by clicking the Options button in the Export dialog box. Be sure you select your Save As Type before you click the Options button, since the options change depending on how you are saving the file.

In addition, Fireworks 4 has improved Import and Export features that can import Photoshop PSD files complete with layers, layer masks, and layer names intact. Director integration has also improved, though you will need the Fireworks Import Xtra installed in Director. You can now directly import EPS files into Fireworks; these files are rasterized upon import.

Rectangles with Rounded Corners

One of our favorite new features is the ability to create customized rounded corners on rectangles. This new feature makes creating buttons and tabs that much easier.

How Does Fireworks Compare with Photoshop and ImageReady?

Macromedia is not alone in the world of web development software. Fireworks' most notable competition is, perhaps, Adobe's Photoshop/ImageReady package. Widely recognized as the most robust bitmap image–editing tool, Photoshop has been a favorite among designers for years. When Adobe decided, with version 5.5, to bundle ImageReady with Photoshop, it signaled its intent to make Photoshop as relevant to the web designer as it was (and is) to the print designer. Since ImageReady has animation, interactivity, and optimization tools not unlike those of Fireworks, it is reasonable to ask what Fireworks offers that the Photoshop/ImageReady suite does not—or at least how they differ.

Vector Handling

Perhaps the most fundamental difference between the two programs—when it comes to preparing the web graphics themselves—is that Fireworks is essentially a vector-based program with some bitmap-handling abilities, while Photoshop/ImageReady is the inverse: a bitmap-based program with some vector capabilities. The recently released Photoshop 6 now boasts a number of new vector tools, but at its core, Photoshop remains a bitmap-based program. For this reason, it can't stand up to Fireworks' central claim that everything is editable, all the time. Photoshop has its own pluses, to be sure, but in this sense, it is quite different from Fireworks.

Integration with HTML Editors

Another key difference is that the integration between Fireworks and Dreamweaver is unparalleled. Adobe GoLive, which competes with Dreamweaver, was not

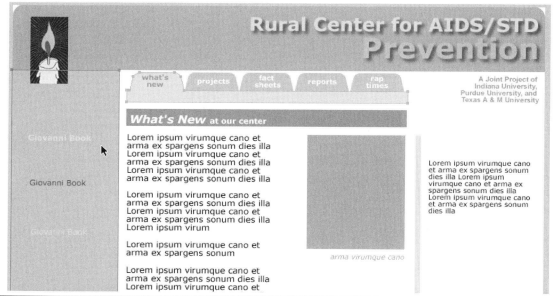

Figure 1-10   Fireworks' lean vector graphics and Dreamweaver integration enable a robust page and site design process not possible in the Adobe suite.

designed in tandem with Photoshop (which preexists it by many years). Macromedia has made a concerted effort to develop Dreamweaver and Fireworks in such a way that they are a complementary suite of programs, even as Dreamweaver has, with UltraDev, evolved into a much more sophisticated tool.

For example, in designing pages for the Habitat for Humanity web site, we started the design in Fireworks and then exported the entire page as a working HTML page that we could edit and refine in Dreamweaver. As shown in Figure 1-10, once in Dreamweaver, it's easy to reopen parts of the page in Fireworks for quick adjustments such as changing a graphic text element.

Between the reliance on vector-based vs. bitmap-based graphics and the tight integration with Dreamweaver, designing entire web pages from the ground up in Fireworks and then moving into Dreamweaver is much easier than designing a page in Photoshop and moving it to GoLive. With the Fireworks/Dreamweaver combination, you can switch back and forth readily between the two programs, updating HTML and graphics until you get the page looking the way you intended.

Integrating Fireworks with Other Programs to Build Web Sites

However great a program is, and Fireworks 4 is indeed great, no software is in itself a comprehensive solution. Web sites are, in the end, multimedia, and graphics and design/layout are only a part of the process. This section is intended to give you a snapshot of how Fireworks 4 might fit into your web design workflow, and how you can use Fireworks in conjunction with other popular design tools—aside from just Dreamweaver. Each heading describes a design task, and below it suggests how you might use Fireworks—alone or in conjunction with other software.

Mock Up a Web Page

Use Fireworks to create a design grid, mock up the elements, and slice the page into an HTML table. Use Dreamweaver to import the Fireworks HTML and to make any necessary adjustments. Use Dreamweaver UltraDev to create a database-driven web site with a sleek Fireworks interface.

Create a Storyboard or Multimedia Presentation of Comps

Use Fireworks to place each design in a separate frame and then use Export As Frames. Alternatively, you can use Fireworks to batch-process a series of page designs into a standard-size image. Use Flash to import incrementally named files as individual keyframes, and create a quick, interactive presentation of your site.

Create Static Graphics

Use Fireworks to design from scratch, or to import design elements from other applications such as Illustrator, Freehand, or Photoshop for final design and optimization. Use Photoshop for cleaning up scans (that is, by adjusting levels and/or curves) and applying pixel-based effects. Though Fireworks has substantially improved its bitmap handling, it is not about to dethrone Photoshop in that area. We recommend that any bitmaps you use in Fireworks, you import in final form, using Fireworks to design further with its native vectors (for example, text) and to optimize. Use Freehand or Illustrator for sophisticated vector artwork that Fireworks was not made to handle. Freehand is a pure vector drawing program and has several drawing tools that Fireworks lacks.

Add Interactivity

Use Fireworks to add a number of common HTML- or JavaScript-based client-side elements, such as buttons, pop-up menus, and so on. Use Dreamweaver to add everything from simple hyperlinks to scripted Flash controls. Use Dreamweaver UltraDev, a middleware solution such as ColdFusion, or Common Gateway Interface (CGI) scripts to create fully customized interactivity. Use Flash and Generator to create robust animated web applications.

Create Animation

Use Fireworks to create animated GIFs and other simple animations. Fireworks boasts a number of animated GIF customization settings, ranging from frame rate to transparency options, as seen in Figure 1-11. Use Flash to import graphics created in Fireworks for more sophisticated animation capabilities. Flash can also import other file types, such as QuickTime, which enables Fireworks-Flash-QuickTime animations.

Optimize Graphics

Use Fireworks to compare different file types and compression schemes to balance file size constraints and image quality. While you can also use Photoshop's Save For The Web feature or ImageReady to optimize graphics for the Web, if you're already working in Fireworks, it makes sense to use Fireworks' optimization tools. In our experience, Fireworks also does a slightly better job of file optimization.

Standardize Graphics

Use Fireworks to change the dimensions, color depth, compression, or filename; to perform a Find and Replace operation within a batch of files; or to create thumbnails.

Figure 1-11 The Fireworks Export Preview dialog box can be used for customizing animated GIFs.

When it comes to automating repetitive tasks, Fireworks should be all you'll ever need. With Find And Replace, Batch Processing, and Scripting (that is, macros), Fireworks has a number of robust automation options.

Coordinate with Print-Based Projects

Use Fireworks to import and export a variety of vector and bitmap file formats from other programs, without any compromise in quality. Use Freehand or Illustrator to use a premier set of drawing tools to create vector artwork for both print and the Web, and then import into Fireworks. Use Photoshop to use the premier image editor to create cutting-edge bitmap images for import into Fireworks—layers and all.

Integrate Scanned Images, Stock Photos, and Other Found Art

Use Fireworks to import and make basic adjustments to scans. Use Photoshop to import scans and prepare them for Fireworks. Photoshop's superior bitmap editing tools—with its histograms, adjustment layers, and its many filters—allow users to improve the visual and artistic quality of bitmaps better than Fireworks. We recommend it over Fireworks for the initial phase of the scan-to-web process. Once the bitmap is clean and ready, import it into Fireworks and work it into your design.

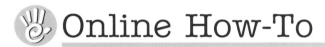 Online How-To

Building a Web Illustration

To introduce you to Fireworks' basic vector and bitmap tools and its integration with other tools like Photoshop, this lesson steps you through the process of creating a web page illustration that includes text, vector shapes, and photographs. During this exercise, you'll also get a taste of using the Fireworks Layers panel, using object masks, and using the Optimize panel to export work ready for the Web.

GO TO THE WEB! For a free, self-paced interactive version of this tutorial, which includes video demonstrations and source files, visit www.expertedge.com.

The Tutorial

We'll begin this tutorial, not surprisingly, by setting up a new file.

1. Launch Fireworks. Choose File | New to create a new file.

2. In the New Document dialog box, set its dimensions to 450×100 pixels, its resolution to 72 dpi (standard for the Web), and its background color to black (hexadecimal #000000).

Before we continue, note that throughout this tutorial, you will use the SHIFT key for two timesaving purposes: (1) Any time you hold down the SHIFT key and drag, your dragging will be constrained. If you are dragging to draw a line, the line will snap to vertical, horizontal, or to a 45-degree angle. If you are drawing a rectangle or an oval, pressing SHIFT will force you to draw a perfect square or circle. If you are scaling an object, holding SHIFT will constrain proportions, so you do not distort the object. If you are moving an object, pressing SHIFT will force you to drag it either horizontally or vertically—whichever is your predominant motion. (2) To select more than one object, hold down the SHIFT key, which functions in Fireworks like holding the CTRL key in Windows, to select multiple files. Note also that most major graphics software (from Macromedia and Adobe) uses SHIFT both as a constraint to dragging and as the means for selection of multiple objects.

Building the Basic Layout

You should now be looking at an empty, black canvas that is wider than it is tall. This graphic is going to contain five bitmap pictures in a photo timeline. We'll begin by creating frames for the pictures, using the Rectangle tool. We'll use the Info and Align panels to size and position the frames with easy precision.

1. Select the Rectangle tool and draw a rectangle on the canvas of any size.

2. With the rectangle selected, use the Info panel to resize it to the following dimensions: W = 50, H = 40. Use the Info panel to both create and lay out objects with pixel-perfect precision.

3. In the Fill panel, use the drop-down list to set the fill to none.

4. In the Stroke panel, use the drop-down list to set it to Pencil. Then set the following attributes: in the Stroke Name drop-down menu, 1 pixel hard; in the color well, white.

5. Still in the Stroke panel, set the stroke's Texture to Grain, and use the slider to adjust the amount of texture to 40%. This should lend a ragged appearance to the line. Who says vector graphics have to look unnaturally smooth?

6. Make four copies of the rectangle so you have five rectangles total. To quickly duplicate, hold down the OPTION/ALT key and click-and-drag. Also hold the SHIFT key to constrain movement horizontally.

7. To make sure the five squares are perfectly spaced, SHIFT-select them all (hold the SHIFT key and click on each one), and then choose Modify | Align | Distribute Widths. This command puts an equal amount of space between each of the rectangles. As with the Info panel, using the Align panel gives you quick control over objects that eyeballing simply can't. When you are finished with this step, your file should appear similar to the one shown here.

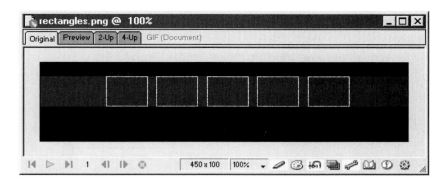

8. Make a background strip that will go behind the rectangles. Draw another rectangle with the Rectangle tool.

9. Using the Info panel, change its dimensions to W = 450, H = 40.

10. In the Fill panel, choose a dark gray color, such as #333333.

11. Set the stroke to None. With the rectangle still selected, send it behind the original five rectangles by choosing Modify | Arrange | Send To Back. All of the rectangles so far are on one layer—the Arrange option allows you to set the stacking order within layers.

12. Open the Layers panel, and you will see the collection of vector objects in Layer 1 that you've assembled so far. All are on Layer 1, though they are listed separately, indicating their within-layer stacking order.

Importing and Masking Bitmap Images

In this procedure, you will import some prebuilt Photoshop files, layers and all. You will use masking to add some effects, and get some practice manipulating bitmaps in general.

1. Import the photos from Photoshop for the photo timeline. Choose File | Import and locate photo1.psd in the media folder included in the online edition of this chapter at www.expertedge.com.

2. When you click Open, your cursor will become a corner icon. Click to place the photo in the document. The picture is much too large for our frames; we'll take care of that in a moment.

3. In the Layers panel, notice that this Photoshop image has a layer mask that is retained in Fireworks. To turn off the layer mask, click the black triangle in the upper-right corner of the Layers panel and choose Disable Mask. Notice the red X that appears on the mask and that you can now see the entire image. You can turn the mask back on by choosing Enable Mask from the Layer panel's pop-up menu, but leave it off for now.

4. Let's choose a portion of the image to fill the frame. In this case, we want to capture the skyline. Scale the image down, so that it is about 112×75 pixels. You can use the Info panel again, or grab one of the corner blue dots on the image, hold the SHIFT key, and drag inward or outward to scale. The SHIFT key constrains proportions, so that your image does not become distorted.

5. Position the resized image over the first rectangle, so that the mountaintop runs through the center, as seen here. To help with positioning, in the Layers panel, drag the first rectangle's layer just over the bitmap layer, so you can see what you are doing.

6. Choose Edit | Cut. This places the bitmap on the Clipboard and enables the next step.

7. With the Pointer tool, select the first rectangle, and then choose Edit | Paste Inside to create a mask group. The portion of the image within the rectangle will be visible, while the rest will be invisible.

8. Repeat steps 1 through 7 to import the remaining photos, resize them, and paste them inside of the remaining rectangles. When you are done, you should have a row of photo icons for our timeline interface:

9. Adjust the coloration of these photo icons so that only one is highlighted/selected, while the others appear dimmed. With the Pointer tool, SHIFT-select four of the five photo icons (the ones you want to dim). In the Layers panel, set their Blending Mode to Luminosity by choosing it from the pull-down menu. The Luminosity option will convert the images to grayscale.

IDEA Fireworks blending modes do not permanently remove color. To return them to their original state, simply set the blending mode back to Normal.

10. Adjust the opacity of the four icons to 35%. This will dim the images.

Adding the Final Touches

The contrast between the selected and unselected icons helps users know where they are and choose where they want to go. Let's enhance this distinction further, improving both usability and aesthetics:

1. To add an extra embellishment to the one that remains highlighted (in Normal blending mode), let's add corner edges that look as though they are holding the photo in place. First, be sure that the settings in the Stroke panel are the same as they were when you drew the rectangles.

2. Select the Pen tool. You might find the following steps easier if you zoom in on the image, to 400% for example.

3. Starting at the upper-right corner of the photo icon, click once to set down the first point.

4. Press and hold the SHIFT key, and click to set down a second point about 10 pixels to the right. Then, still holding the SHIFT key, click to set a third point down 10 pixels. When finished, switch to the Pointer tool and click anywhere to deselect.

5. Move the corner graphic as needed to frame the icon. Repeat these steps to create a corner graphic to frame the remaining corners. Alternatively, you can copy, paste, and rotate your original graphic. The result can be seen here. Magnified like this, the fancy grain stroke set in the Stroke panel doesn't look like much.

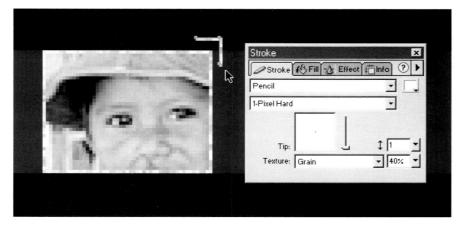

6. Add a text caption for the highlighted icon. Select the Text tool in the toolbar, and click once in the document to start typing.

7. In the Text Editor, type a date followed by a short message of your choice to describe the highlighted photo icon. For the middle image, we typed **10.15.01 The Claros family builds Habitat homes in their community**, with the date in blue (#6699FF) and the sentence in white (#FFFFFF). Click OK.

8. Use the Pointer tool to position the text beneath the pictures.

Optimization and Export

The final step of the development process in Fireworks is optimization and export. Upon export, Fireworks saves a copy of your vector-based metafile as a standard web-friendly bitmap, such as a JPG or a GIF.

1. Open the Optimize panel from the Window menu or Launcher Bar.

2. In the Settings drop-down menu, select GIF WebSnap 128. This limits the illustration to using only 128 colors. Of all the possible colors, it will first choose colors that are best suited to the image, and wherever possible, it will try to use web-safe colors.

3. Click the 2-Up tab on the document window. The image at the left is the original PNG. The image at the right is the 128-color GIF. Beneath each image are file-size statistics. Our original PNG is nearly 93K, while the GIF is a tidy 7K—about 1/13th the size of the original!

4. Before exporting, trim the canvas size to as small as possible to conserve on file size. Choose Modify | Trim Canvas. The canvas automatically shrinks to fit your illustration.

5. Choose File | Export to export this image. In the Export window, choose Images Only from the Save As drop-down.

6. Locate a folder where you want to save the image, and click Save. The final product is shown here.

2 Designing from Scratch

Fireworks is well known for its graphic optimization tools and the ease with which it enables designers to add interactivity to web graphics. But one of Fireworks' most useful features is largely unheralded. Fireworks can be used to design and build entire web pages, from rough sketch to final comp, much like the print designer might use page layout software to design a catalog. But unlike page layout software, Fireworks can also be used to create an instant multimedia presentation of your designs that you can show to your clients.

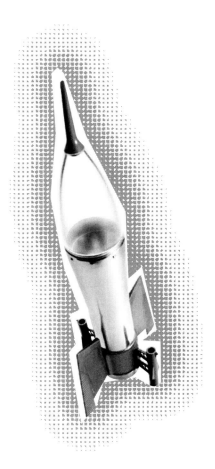

Most people don't realize that they can begin the creative process right in Fireworks and build web pages from concept through to completion. Even today, many designers rely on a more time-consuming approach that often starts in Photoshop and a drawing program (such as Freehand or Illustrator), and then moves into Fireworks or ImageReady for web optimization and export. In fact, Fireworks provides a unique set of graphics tools that enables you to build both great-looking web graphics and entire web page designs quickly and efficiently in a single environment. The tools also minimize, thanks to Fireworks' outstanding integration with Dreamweaver, the reconstructive task of moving the design into a web authoring tool.

Fireworks is an *object-oriented* program; this means that every graphic you create or import is treated as a separate, selectable object. While Fireworks does allow you to organize your graphics into layers, the object-oriented design alters the role of layers, compared with a bitmap editing program like Photoshop. In the most general sense, layers, whether they appear in an image editing program or a vector drawing program, organize content vertically. Objects on layers block objects on layers beneath them.

A second axis of file organization in Fireworks can be thought of as horizontal—elements as they occur over time. Like Director and Flash, Fireworks has a timeline, albeit less robust than those of its multimedia siblings. Fireworks elements are tracked over time using the Frames panel. Although frames elapsing in time are usually represented horizontally (as they are in Flash and ImageReady), the Fireworks Frames panel looks like the Layers panel: frames are represented vertically, top to bottom. In any event, Fireworks frames can be used for a number of different purposes, including the following:

- Animation, usually for animated GIFs
- Rollovers
- Image swapping
- Creating design presentations

In this chapter, you'll explore both the Layer and Frame panels, which you can use to build a series of design sketches for a new web site. After you create these designs, we'll show you how to export them for use in a multimedia presentation for a client.

Building a Whole Web Page in Fireworks

Designing a web page is a bit like furnishing and decorating an empty house. You don't start on one side of the room, completely finish it, and work in a linear manner toward the other. You start by placing the big items like furniture or a favorite painting where you'd like them to go, and finish arranging the rest of the room around them.

Designing a web page is a similar process. In web design, you identify and sketch out the basic layout of the interface—determine the number of columns and the placement of major elements (banner, navigation bar, standard image, copyright information)—before you fire up your pen tablet and start creating finished graphics. Along the way you probably make adjustments to the layout to accommodate a certain element, or to change the emphasis of another.

Fireworks makes it very easy for designers to plan their layout and to start sketching the main elements of the page. In building the home page design for the Habitat for Humanity online module, Lisa started by "wireframing" a basic layout on one layer, as shown in Figure 2-1. Then, in another layer, she built the major interface components using the wireframe layout to guide her in the placement and relative sizing of elements. She also used guides to help her precisely align elements to one another.

IDEA In the bottom layer, build a basic layout, or *wireframe,* with simple shapes. Then build your final graphics in other layers on top, using the wireframe layer to guide positioning and relative sizing.

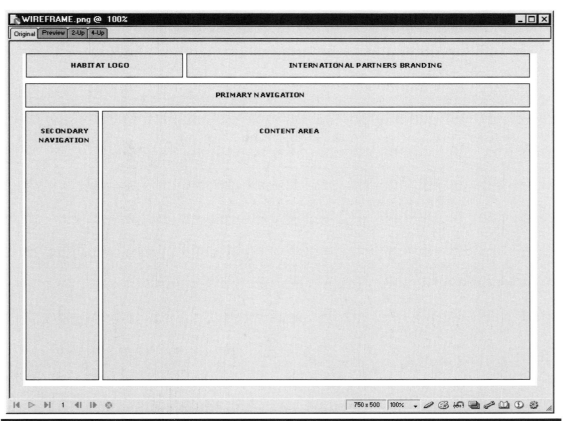

Figure 2-1   Build a rough sketch or "wireframe" for your layout in one layer. Build the actual graphics in a series of new layers.

Fireworks as an All-in-One Comp Tool

Because of Fireworks' robust graphic tools and its ability to export working web pages, it is an ideal environment for the construction of a web page—start to finish. When you begin a new project in Fireworks, we recommend that you design and build an entire web page, rather than just building its constituent parts, like buttons and headers. For example, as shown in Figure 2-2, you should first build the page as you expect it to look in the web browser—complete with navigation, content, and buttons—and even faked HTML elements like input buttons and text fields. You won't use all of the design elements such as the faked HTML elements, but this way, you'll get a better sense of how all of these elements relate to one another while you work.

Creating the Page and Dummy Elements

We like to create a new document that is the dimension you expect your web page to be. For example, most people today have 800×600 pixel monitor displays. Once you factor in a browser's interface buttons and scroll bars, the web viewing space is only about 760×420 pixels, to be conservative. Therefore, when creating a new web page in Fireworks, start a new file that is about these dimensions. Much as you would in a page layout program, create a grid in Fireworks and begin to mock up your page.

Figure 2-2   Build the entire web page in Fireworks. Then slice and export the pieces you need for reassembly in a web authoring tool like Dreamweaver.

CROSS
REFERENCE → See Chapter 4 for more on creating and working with grids in Fireworks.

Initially, you can use different colored rectangles to represent banners, menu bars, and future graphics. Use a paragraph of dummy Latin text ("Lorem ipsum igitur") to mock up different text elements. At this stage you do not want reviewers to focus too much on meaning, rather than design, so you might want to resist using real text even if you have it. Along the way, you can even mock up HTML elements, such as text entry forms and buttons, so you can see how the page will ultimately look in the browser.

Using Screen Shots as Graphic Elements

Including text entry forms in Fireworks comps is as easy as importing screen shots of an existing HTML page that has them. Here's how to bring screen shots into Fireworks:

1. Using Dreamweaver, create a quick form for your mock-up (don't worry about making it actually work with form action scripts). For instance, create buttons and select menus that have the correct text on them like "Enter," "Submit," or "Choose a product." Once you build the page in Dreamweaver, open the page in a web browser. You can use Dreamweaver's File | Preview in Browser (F12) feature to quickly open the page.

2. Adjust the browser window on your screen so that you can see all of the form elements.

3. Windows users, press the PRINT SCREEN key to capture the whole screen. Your computer will place a copy of the image on your Clipboard. Mac users can use the key combination COMMAND-SHIFT-3 to capture a screen. The capture will be saved on your hard drive as Picture 1, Picture 2, and so on.

IDEA Alternatively, Windows users can press ALT-PRINT SCREEN to capture only the active window (in this case, your browser window) and save themselves some cropping time. Mac users can use COMMAND-SHIFT-4, and draw a selection around the area of the screen they want to capture.

4. In Fireworks, choose File | New to open a new file. Notice in the New Document dialog box that the file dimensions are already identical to the size of your screen shot.

5. With the new document window open, choose Edit | Paste, and the document will appear in the window. Mac users must open the screen shot by choosing File | Open.

6. Click the Marquee tool and drag to create a selection area around the text field or other graphic area you desire to move into your comp. The blue and black hash line around the canvas indicates that you have switched into Bitmap mode, as seen in Figure 2-3.

Marquee selection

Figure 2-3   An area of a bitmap selected with the Marquee tool in Bitmap mode

7. Use Copy and Paste from the Edit menu to copy the form element and paste it into your design comp.

IDEA   You can create a small library of common HTML elements in an otherwise blank Fireworks file that you can reuse time and again when you are mocking up designs. These elements might include form fields of different sizes, Submit or Send buttons, and so on. Save these in the Library (Window | Library), and use this blank document as a template when you comp new designs.

Even in the rough state you have now reached, the structure and feel of the design is starting to come together. Keep working in this file, replacing plain rectangles with real graphics as you start to turn your rough sketches into full-blown web designs. Once you build the entire web page, it's easy to export portions of the page as individual web graphics, or even as interactive graphics with rollover behaviors. These pieces can then be reassembled in a web development tool like Dreamweaver—a process that just keeps getting easier.

Basic Vector and Bitmap Building Tools

If you worked through the previous section with Fireworks open, you might have noticed that while you were busy building your designs and placing dummy elements, you were flipping back and forth between two modes. For the most part, you were in the standard Vector mode, but when you started editing the screen captures, you switched into Bitmap mode (called Image Edit mode in previous versions of Fireworks).

Because Fireworks handles both so gracefully, the transition between modes is almost seamless. Indeed, when you merely choose a tool, Fireworks often automatically switches to the appropriate mode. There are some exceptions, though, for tools that can be used natively in both modes. You can also manually change modes by choosing Modify | Edit Bitmap to enter bitmap editing mode, and Modify | Exit Bitmap Mode to return to Vector mode. But you don't want to overlook the differences between the two modes altogether, because each mode has unique tools and capabilities.

CROSS REFERENCE → See Chapter 5 for a detailed discussion on getting the most out of creating art in Vector and Bitmap modes.

Vector Mode

You will spend most of your time in Fireworks in Vector mode. By default, when you open a file or work with any of the graphics tools in the Tools panel, you will be in Vector mode, building vector graphics. When in Vector mode, the following tools create vector paths and shapes: Line, Pen, Rectangle, Rounded Rectangle, Ellipse, Polygon, Pencil, Redraw Path, and even Brush tools.

Normally, vector graphics are used to create smooth curves and shapes—think logos. But Fireworks' vector tools, in combination with an array of Stroke, Fill, and Effect panel options, can be used to mimic the natural media and detail characteristic of bitmap images. Take a look at the illustration in Figure 2-4. Would you believe that this entire illustration is made up of only vector brush strokes? This image was created using the Brush tool in conjunction with the Stroke panel. See Chapter 5 for a more detailed discussion on vector techniques. With the addition of a pressure-sensitive graphics tablet, the possibilities multiply.

Figure 2-4 This painterly looking illustration is made up entirely of vector brush strokes.

In this example, Lisa achieved a natural, painterly effect simply by applying Stroke effects to the brush strokes. And because the strokes are vector, it's easy to select and manipulate the color, shape, and texture of each stroke to change the look of the illustration. Relying on vectors gives you long-term insurance as well: even if the client decides to change the entire color combination—as hard as that must be to imagine—you are only one Find and Replace away from an instant fix.

Bitmap Mode

While there are comparatively fewer advantages to creating graphics or graphic elements in Bitmap mode, there are several reasons why you might need to work in Bitmap mode. Bitmap mode allows you to use the selection tools to select specific portions of an image for editing, much like you do in Photoshop.

NOTE   The selection tools in Fireworks (the Lasso, Magic Wand, and Marquee tools) only work on bitmap graphics. If you try to use a selection tool on a vector object, Fireworks will display a warning message.

Selections, in turn, allow the application of filters and effects (such as Gaussian Blurs) on specific regions of an image rather than on the whole thing. You can also convert selections into masks, which can be used for both graphic effects as well as more practical applications, such as selective JPEG compression.

At this early stage of development, though, you are probably not worried about many of these features. But Bitmap mode still has its uses. As you take your screen grabs of HTML elements, such as forms, you can use Fireworks to edit and manipulate them to suit the needs of your layout.

Creating a Reusable Library of HTML Form Elements

Once you have taken your screen shots, you will probably need to select areas within them and break them out for placement within your design. Figure 2-5 shows a screen grab of an HTML page with a form. This page was chosen because it has several fields of different sizes, which would stock your mock-up library with several good candidates. The first step is to separate the various fields into individual graphics. Then we'll assemble all of the elements in their own PNG file. Finally, we'll resize them and touch them up to make them ready for your comp.

1. Take a screen shot of an HTML form and open it in Fireworks.

2. Double-click the image to activate Bitmap mode. A blue, hatched border indicates that you are in Bitmap mode.

3. Unlike with scanning, the image quality—color balance, lightness, contrast, and so on—of screen shots is usually not a problem. However,

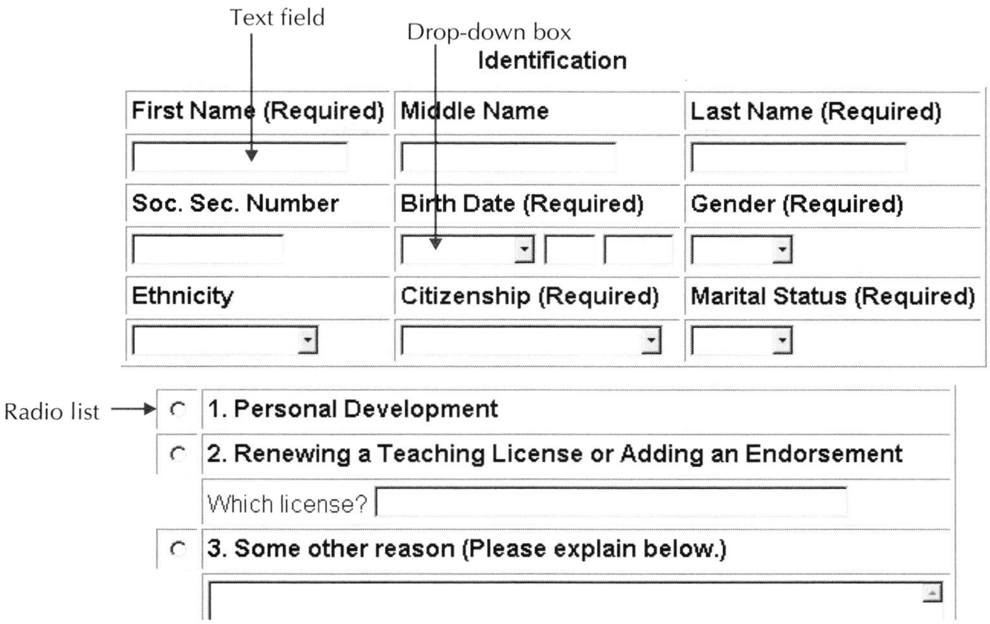

Text field

Drop-down box

Identification

First Name (Required)	Middle Name	Last Name (Required)
Soc. Sec. Number	Birth Date (Required)	Gender (Required)
Ethnicity	Citizenship (Required)	Marital Status (Required)

Radio list ⟶

○ 1. Personal Development

○ 2. Renewing a Teaching License or Adding an Endorsement

Which license?

○ 3. Some other reason (Please explain below.)

Figure 2-5 This screen shot of a simple web form is a good source because it contains several types of elements: text fields of different lengths, drop-down boxes, and a radio list.

Fireworks has several tools that can help you fine-tune these aspects of the image, found in the Xtras | Adjust Color menu. These include controls for Levels, Curves, Hue, Saturation, Brightness, Contrast, Invert, and Auto Levels.

CROSS REFERENCE ⟶ See Chapter 5 for more on using the controls in this menu.

4. Using the Marquee tool, drag a selection around the area you wish to isolate, seen in Figure 2-6. Magnify the image if necessary, and drag the marquee as close to the edges as possible, because if the background of the source image and your comp are different, your elements will have unsightly borders around them.

5. Switch to the Arrow tool and choose Edit | Cut. A hole is left in the original bitmap. Exit bitmap editing mode by choosing Modify | Exit Bitmap Mode from the menu or by clicking on the red *X* at the bottom of your document window. Choose Edit | Paste to paste the form element as a new and separate bitmap object. Because it's a separate object now in Fireworks, you can edit it without affecting the source bitmap file. You can also copy it into your design comp.

6. Sometimes elements culled from screen shots will not be the right size for your design. To resize a bitmap or vector element, you can simply select it and grab one of its blue corner dots. We don't recommend, however, that you scale your form elements. These are HTML elements that the browser always draws at a particular size. Sizing them in your comp will throw off the scale of the rest of your design.

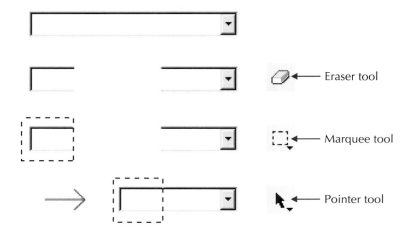

Eraser tool

Marquee tool

Pointer tool

Figure 2-6 Shorten the width of form field screen shots by cutting out the middle and rejoining the sides.

7. Scaling bitmaps larger will always create distortion, because you are enlarging each pixel that makes up the picture. Surprisingly, though, even scaling down bitmaps can create a blurring effect. In both cases, the remedy is to sharpen the element. To do so, with the element selected in either Vector or Bitmap mode, choose Xtras | Sharpen | Unsharp Mask. A dialog box appears that allows you to control the sharpening. Though this tool can be accessed from either Vector or Bitmap mode (it is not grayed out), it is a bitmap operation, meaning that its effects are permanent, and it can only be performed on bitmap graphics (vector graphics are permanently rasterized in the process).

8. When it comes to resizing form fields, you will often need to shorten—or lengthen—their width as opposed to scaling down the entire graphic. To shorten a form element, you can cut out its middle and rejoin the two sides. To cut out the middle, choose the Eraser tool and SHIFT-drag vertical strokes to constrain the erasing to a 90-degree angle, as seen in Figure 2-6.

9. Once you have cut a hole in the middle, select one of the sides with the Marquee tool. Switch to the Pointer tool, hold down the SHIFT key, and move the selection to rejoin the opposite side. The SHIFT key constrains the horizontal movement while you drag, enabling you to align the two sides perfectly.

10. When you have all of your elements on one canvas, switch back to Vector mode. You can click-and-drag each bitmap element as if it were a vector object, arranging them as you please on the canvas. Henceforth, you can also drag-and-drop them into other Fireworks files with ease.

11. Save your PNG as **library_form.png** or something equally descriptive.

This exercise provides you with a library of form elements that you can use and reuse in your future designs. It also gives you a sense of what you can do in Bitmap mode. Even lacking many of Photoshop's features, Fireworks' Bitmap mode is robust enough to handle many common bitmap-editing jobs. What's more, the final product contains individual, bitmap form elements that you can quickly select and move around. In Photoshop, you'd need to first select the bitmap's layer, then move it.

Organizing Content with Layers and Frames

Like many graphics programs, Fireworks uses layers to organize graphics and keep them separate from one another. Fireworks, however, also allows you to build variations of your designs on different frames, such as when you build an animation.

Understanding Layers

Layers work like pieces of transparent acetate that hold different design elements separate from one another, even though they are invisible when you look at the canvas. They are also the first level in the determination of stacking order.

Different kinds of graphics software programs use layers differently. A bitmap image editor, such as Photoshop, uses layers to contain pixels. Where there is a graphic element on the layer, the pixels are colored. Where there is no graphic element, the pixels are transparent, revealing anything beneath them. Elements on Photoshop layers cannot rest above one another; if you place one graphic above another on the same layer, the part that is underneath simply—and permanently—disappears. Photoshop does not generally see elements as objects.

Fireworks layers, however, function more like those in an illustration program such as Illustrator or Freehand. Every stroke you make, every shape you draw, and every bitmap you import is treated as an individual object. For example, one layer can contain three bitmap images—each overlapping one another without becoming merged into one graphic (as would happen in Photoshop). So, although layers in Photoshop are necessary to keep elements separate from one another, Fireworks' layers are not, which means you can use them to structure things logically. For instance, you could use one layer for all the background graphics and one for all the foreground elements.

Take a look at Figure 2-7. In this example, five separate objects are stacked on top of one another in the same layer. The Fireworks Layers panel shown in Figure 2-8 would seem to indicate that each object is a different layer. This is not the case. The layers you see merely indicate the stacking order of the objects, but the objects are all part of "Layer 1." You can customize this view by collapsing and expanding the arrow icon in the Layers panel to open and close the content view of each layer.

Figure 2-7   Five vector and bitmap objects overlap one another in the same layer.

IDEA Holding down the ALT or OPTION key while closing one of the layers will close all of them. Also, Holding the ALT or OPTION key while clicking one of the eyeball (visibility) icons will toggle all of the objects in a layer.

To rearrange the stacking order of the objects in a layer, simply drag their thumbnail representations in the Layers panel to different locations, or select an object in the document and use the Modify | Arrange menu. Because of this object-oriented design, it is possible to build an entire web page on just one layer in Fireworks.

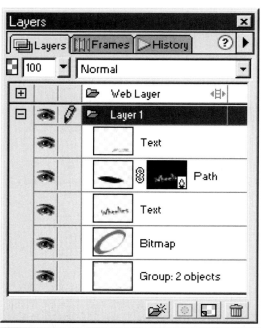

Figure 2-8   "Layer 1" in the Layers panel contains multiple objects.

IDEA To illustrate how Fireworks 4 layers compare with those in Photoshop 6, each layer in Fireworks looks and functions like a "layer set" in Photoshop. *Layer sets* are Photoshop's new way of organizing the multitude of layers common to most Photoshop designs. Layer sets are basically a folder system that allows you to contain a number of layers for organizational purposes.

Understanding Frames

While Fireworks layers allow you to organize your graphics on the page, Fireworks also enables you to organize your design over *time* by using the Frames panel. When you first start a Fireworks document, you are by default working on Layer 1 and Frame 1. As you continue to add layers, you are still working on Frame 1. Frame 1 is where you build the initial state of your web page—the way it should look when people first see your page.

The most common use for frames is building some sort of animation. But you can use frames for more than that. For example, to build a rollover button, you'd add a couple of frames—one for each new state of the button. You'd also use frames to build an animation like the one shown in Figure 2-9.

We can extend this concept of frames to aid us creatively and practically. The purpose of frames is to provide a way for you to represent how your design changes over time. During the early stage of comps and roughs, though, you won't need to build animated GIFs or fancy rollovers. What you want at this point is to generate a lot of design ideas to show the client. For instance, you want to design a home page and a few subpages—pages that link off the home page. You can create several different design sketches, all in the same document, using frames. You save development time, because everything is in one place, and you can create instant consistency by leaving certain elements in place.

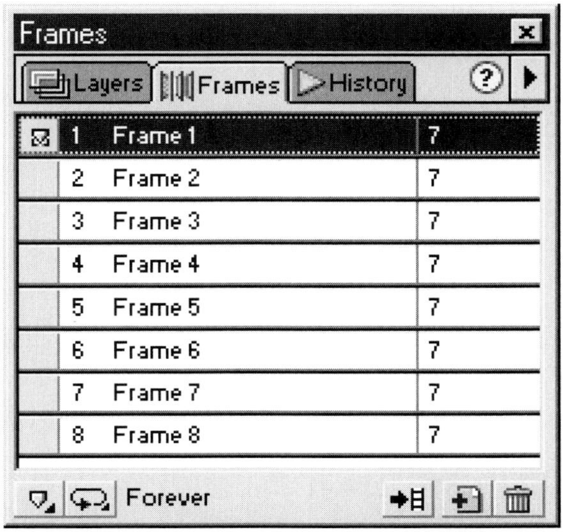

Figure 2-9   Use the Frames panel to build animated GIFs.

Creating a Design Presentation

Let's expand on the idea of using frames to create a design presentation. The first step of designing any new web site is to brainstorm a handful of different *design directions*—design ideas that you can present to the clients so they can choose one they like best for the project. The first step is to "rough" out a handful of different designs, each one giving the clients an idea of one possible direction. In the past, this process involved designing several individual sketches from scratch—each one in a different document. Fireworks provides a more efficient process without losing any of the creative freedom.

Ideally, you should build four or five different design directions for the client to choose from. Each design direction should consist of a home page and a subpage—sometimes with slight variations of each. We like to build the home page on Frame 1, and any variations and subpage options on subsequent frames. Have a different designer do each direction to ensure a variety of design styles. Again, do not add any interactivity to the designs, just keep these preliminary designs as static mock-ups that you can save as GIFs.

IDEA Fireworks 4 allows you to name your frames. This feature comes in handy when using frames to build a design presentation. For instance, you can rename Frame 1 to "home page" and Frame 2 to "subpage A." To name a frame, double-click on its name. When a box appears with a flashing cursor, type a new name.

Once the roughs are complete and contained within a series of frames in one document, you will need to present them. Whereas presentations in the past relied upon print, several options are available now (with different pros and cons). Fireworks is ready for all of them: the print presentation, the PowerPoint-style slide presentation, and a web-based presentation.

CROSS REFERENCE → For hands-on instruction in building a design presentation for the Web, see the "Fireworks in the Real World" sidebar at the end of this chapter.

To quickly export all of your frames as separate GIF images, first open the Optimize panel and choose the GIF format. Because these images are just design comps, don't worry about optimizing their color palette right now; choose an adaptive palette of 256 colors to ensure good quality. Choose File | Export. In the Export dialog box, choose Frames To Files in the Save As Type drop-down list, as shown in Figure 2-10. Choose a folder to save all of the frames in and click Save. In one motion, all of your frames will be saved as individual GIFs! We learned this design tip from David Solhaug of www.sgrafik.com. Thanks, David!

design solution

When exporting design comps for a client, don't worry about image optimization. Choose the highest quality GIF setting: adaptive palette, 256 colors. This setting should work well for displaying each design. In some cases, especially where you are relying on photographs or gradients, an 80 percent quality JPEG might be a better choice. Once the client chooses a design, you can best decide how to slice and optimize the page.

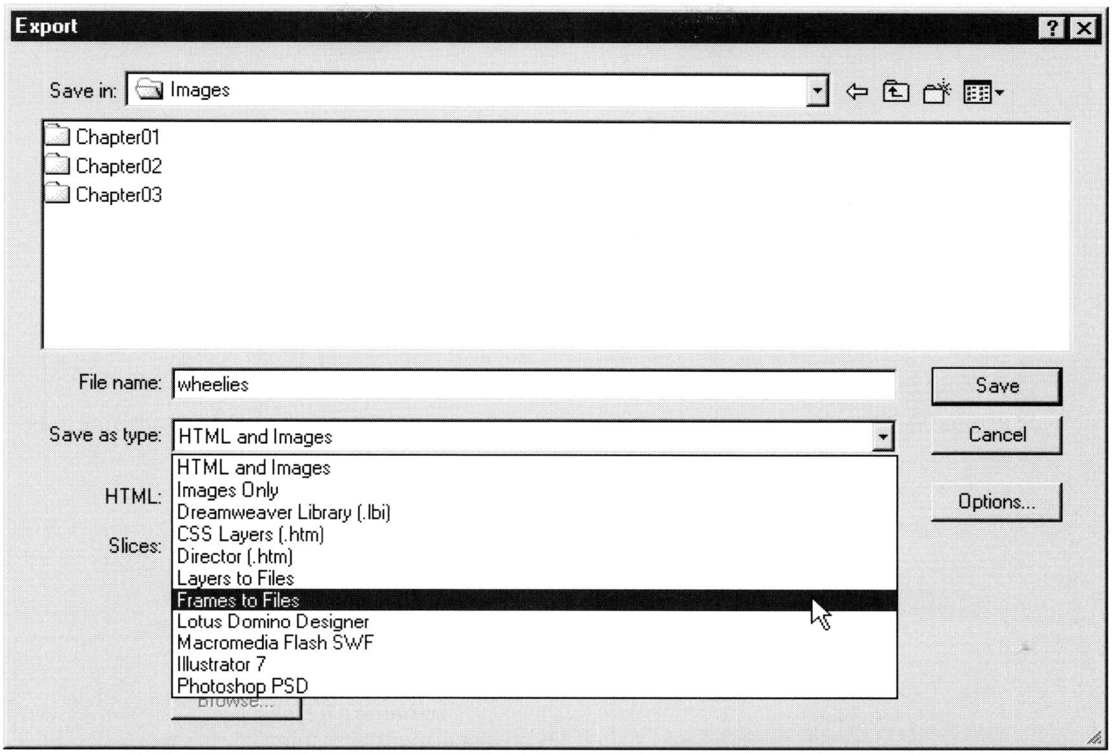

Figure 2-10   Export each frame as a separate GIF using the Frames To Files option in the Export window.

The next step is to organize these static GIF images into an online presentation or click-through. Design the click-through as a branded web site, with the client's logo, your logo, and so on, and publish it at a password-protected or hidden URL that you can share with the client. (A *hidden URL* is a cryptic address that outsiders would never find on their own, and one that no other pages link to.) Make a menu page that links to each design direction. Each direction might have a short description describing the concept behind it. This way, the client can see how the design will look in the browser window and make a better decision.

IDEA Posting your designs online is a great way to work with clients in remote locations. Indeed, the web allows you to work with clients clear around the world! Posting work online is also a great way to let clients review work at their convenience and to discuss it with their coworkers.

In addition, you may want to back up the online presentation with a printed presentation. Print each design direction in color, and mount on sturdy black boards. Be sure to use glossy paper, because the color will be richer. Matte paper, in contrast, soaks up color and gives uneven results that distract from the quality of the design.

Paper-based presentations of web design can be tricky, because the additive color model of computer screens displays the art with a wider gamut of colors than print art (which uses a subtractive color model), even on the finest quality glossy paper. Thus, the colors will not match, and/or the client may be misled by a print-only presentation.

Building Master Design Templates for Speed and Consistency

After a client has chosen (or modified) one of the designs you presented, you can use Fireworks to build master design templates for every design element of a site. Working from largest to smallest, first use Fireworks' vector tools to create the master page layouts for the home and subpages. Use Fireworks on its own or in conjunction with another program, such as Photoshop or Painter, to create the art and interface elements, including standard navigation bars, buttons, and headers.

Your goal at this stage is to create master design templates that the production team can use to produce the art for the entire site. Using a few master templates will ensure design consistently throughout a project. Fireworks provides three ways to automate production as well as ensuring design consistency: styles, libraries, and customized swatches. We'll discuss creating master templates with styles, libraries, and other resources in Chapter 3.

Building a Quick Design Presentation

Because Fireworks is so great at building graphics from the ground up, importing graphics from other programs, and exporting web-enabled interactive pages, it's also an ideal environment to sketch out new designs for a proposed web site. Less known is that it also has a few tricks that can enhance productivity in your workflow.

One such feature is an export option that can be used to allow frames to store all of your design directions for a site in one file. From there, you can export them individually in a series of GIFs that you can use in a multipage web document (one page for each of the designs and one more for a navigation screen that links them).

In the following exercise, you will practice this strategy. After building multiple design directions within different frames of one Fireworks PNG, you will export each frame as its own file. By doing so, you enjoy the double benefit of automating the creation of your design presentation even as you have all your designs in one place during authoring. A design presentation is not the only use for the Export Frames to Files option, but it represents one example of how far a little creativity can go in conjunction with Fireworks' varied export options.

Building a Design Presentation

This section contains an exercise that will show you how to use a less-known feature of Fireworks, the export Frames To Files feature, to create an instant design presentation that shows a client a few different design options for a single page of a web site. You'll create a design presentation of three design ideas for a home page.

The focus of this exercise will be less on your creativity in building the different design options and more on the timesaving technique of placing each design direction in a different frame for easy export.

Setting Up the File

Before you start designing, you need to make some basic, critical decisions. You need to set up your file. Don't just accept the defaults because if you need to change your canvas size or background color down the road, you could have a lot of work to do.

1. Launch Fireworks. Choose File | New to create a new file.

2. In the New Document dialog box, seen in Figure 2-11, set the file's dimensions to 600×400 pixels and its resolution to 72 pixels/inch. Remember, as you create page designs in Fireworks, you want to create not just the banner or individual elements, but the whole page. Thus, the first step is to work with a canvas that is the size of a browser window.

3. Choose white or the color you intend to use as your background on your web page. For this example, we'll use a plain white background.

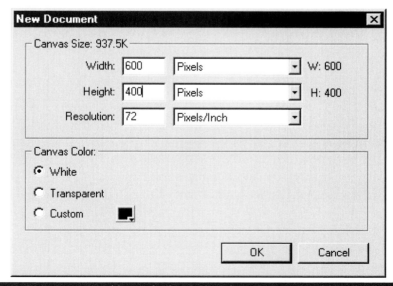

Figure 2-11   Create a new file with the same dimensions and background color of the final web page.

IDEA We don't like to use a transparent background because the checkerboard pattern is distracting, and all objects you create in Fireworks must at some point be rendered against the same color you plan to make your HTML page.

Build Your Design Directions

The purpose of this tutorial is not to teach you creative page design—we'll cover that in spades in the remaining chapters. Our goal here is simply to learn a useful technique.

In the following steps, when you are asked to develop your page designs, you can import some designs you have already built, you can (of course) design entire design directions, or for the sake of this tutorial, you can simply place a colored rectangle and a design number on each page—it's up to you. In a real-world setting, though, you'll want to use vector, bitmap, and type elements to build a flat image of what you envision the page to look like. Again, use screen shots of form elements and pull-down menus and don't worry about interactivity.

IDEA Build HTML elements like pull-down menus and text fields in Dreamweaver, take screen shots, and place these elements in your Fireworks comp.

1. In the first frame, build a web direction. Don't add any interactivity at this stage of the process.

2. In the Frames panel, shown here, click the New Frame icon in the lower-right corner to add a new frame.

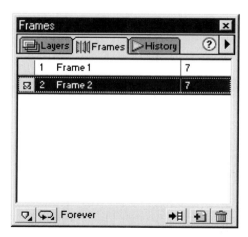

3. Build a second web direction.

4. Add a third frame and a third web direction in it.

Optimize the Document

Now that each of your three designs is in its own frame, the next step is to prepare to export them. Fireworks has, as you know, excellent file optimization tools. While we don't need to get carried away by dividing the file into slices and optimizing each piece, we'll need to choose which format Fireworks should export each frame to.

1. In the Optimize panel, choose GIF Adaptive 256, as shown here. This will set the default settings for the entire document. The reason we're choosing so many colors is to ensure that the designs look good for the client. Once the client chooses a design, we'll optimize it by slicing, and so on. Right now, we'll be exporting the entire page as a static web page mock-up.

2. In the document window, choose 2-Up to preview what the GIF will look like—make sure that your designs are presentable! For designs that make heavy use of photographs or gradients, you might want to choose a flavor of JPG.

Export the Frames as GIFs

Once the client chooses a design, you can strip out the other frames and use Fireworks' tools to make the design interactive. You can also be more particular about optimization at that time. But for now, you need to export each frame as its own image.

1. Choose Export from the menu. Export uses the setting in the Optimize panel.

2. In the Export dialog box, choose Frames To Files from the Save As Type drop-down list, as in Figure 2-12.

3. Select a folder and click Save. This action quickly exports each frame (each design direction) as a static GIF mock-up of the home page.

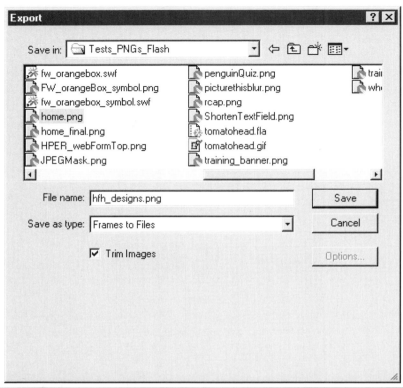

Figure 2-12 Export your document using the Frames To Files option.

Create an HTML Click-Through Site

The last step is to create a simple HTML click-through. Since you are designing for the Web, the Web is the best medium in which to present your designs. All you really need are four simple HTML pages for the three designs and a menu that briefly introduces each one and links to it.

If you use Dreamweaver, the process is fairly straightforward:

1. Create a second Fireworks document that will serve as a menu to access each different design.

2. In this menu file, create three buttons, one for each design direction.

3. Add any links to the buttons, and so on. Use a naming formula that you will remember when you get into Dreamweaver, such as **design_1.html**.

4. In the Optimize panel, choose GIF Adaptive 256 or another appropriate format.

5. Export the illustration. In the Export dialog box, choose HTML And Images from the Save As Type drop-down list. This will create an HTML page that contains the image, links, and JavaScript necessary to make the button rollovers work.

6. Launch Dreamweaver.

7. Create a new page for each design direction, using filenames corresponding to the ones you added to the buttons in Fireworks (in step 3 earlier).

8. In the first of these pages, choose Insert | Image and navigate to the first of the design direction GIFs to insert it.

9. Insert the remaining GIFs into the remaining two pages.

10. Press F12 to test the site.

Fireworks in the Real World

Fireworks in Site Development Workflows

By Nik Schramm

Designing for the web can be a complicated affair involving a whole array of software packages that are not always fully compatible with each other. What's more, content often needs to be changed or repurposed for print output or dynamic delivery, usually at very short notice. The essence of a successful web workflow, therefore, is to preserve artwork in scalable and flexible formats for as long as possible while not losing out on design functionality. For web graphics there is no better solution than Fireworks, because it is equally comfortable with both vector and bitmap formats, keeps all of its effects live and fully editable, and can export to a huge variety of output formats.

Some of our projects here at nae interactive may well begin life outside of Fireworks—in Freehand, Illustrator, or Photoshop, for instance. But all our projects pass through Fireworks at some stage of creative assembly. Content is gathered, placed, preserved, and then exported to Flash (for SWF delivery), Dreamweaver (for HTML delivery), UltraDev (for dynamic web delivery), or FreeHand/Illustrator (for print delivery). In this way artwork created for, say, a Flash web site can be reused for HTML pages or as a set of stationery for printing, with minimal effort and little or no data loss.

Let me illustrate how Fireworks can be put to good use for a wide variety of output situations by using three very different projects, www.industriality.com, www.flash-guru.com, and www.nae.de as examples.

Industriality—From Fireworks to Flash

Industriality is a fully flashed entertainment web site, where both vector graphics and bitmap images abound (see Figure 2-13). It would not be wise to design a site like this in Flash itself, because for all its merits, Flash has no bitmap editing capacity. Consequently, any changing or fine-tuning of a bitmap image would require leaving Flash and re-importing the image. Additionally, exporting artwork from Flash to other vector applications such as FreeHand or Illustrator in the eventuality of print or HTML output is difficult and unreliable. It's much better to use Fireworks with its full vector feature set, live bitmap processing power, and impressive exporting facilities.

Much of the vector artwork for Industriality was created from scratch in Fireworks. External assets, such as the logo and bitmaps, were imported from Illustrator, FreeHand, and Photoshop and processed using Fireworks live effects until the basic

Figure 2-13 Many of the elements of Industriality went through Fireworks before their import into Flash, including the photographs and much of the interface, drawn with Fireworks' vector tools.

layout was finished and exported in SWF format. Because of the tight integration between Fireworks and Flash, the data transfer between the two applications is nigh on seamless. The site was then programmed, animated, and finished in Flash.

Flash-Guru—From Fireworks to Database Front-Ends

Flash-Guru, on the other hand, is a different beast altogether. The site, a major Flash e-learning center, is entirely database driven, using both Flash and HTML front-ends. Additionally, nae interactive designed the entire corporate identity for Flash-Guru, including stationery and logos, so flexibility and the capacity to keep artwork editable for as long as possible were crucial.

One of the first steps of the process was to create a mock-up of the final appearance of the site. Since the site is a Flash-HTML hybrid, it was important to do the mock-up in software that could represent (as a design direction) and export to both formats. Only Fireworks fits that bill. Figure 2-14 shows an early mockup of the Flash-Guru site, as designed in Fireworks.

After the design directions were complete, it was time to start building the site. Once again, all assets for the Flash-Guru site were gathered and assembled in Fireworks and prepared for the various output formats. In this way, the same artwork could then be exported to Flash to create the SWF front-end, as well as to Dreamweaver/UltraDev, where placeholders included in the design of the page were replaced with actual dynamic content from the database for the HTML side of the site. Additionally, the artwork for the stationery was derived from the site design and exported to FreeHand for printing.

Fireworks and Dreamweaver/UltraDev are so well integrated with each other that they feel like two windows of the same application. If you began your page in Dreamweaver/UltraDev with an exported PNG from Fireworks, then nearly everything on your page will remain fully editable throughout. Also, JavaScript code from Fireworks rollovers or pop-up menus is preserved and editable from within Dreamweaver. This means that you can design your page in Fireworks, enjoy the

Figure 2-14   Fireworks is ideal for creating design directions and storyboards for both HTML and Flash projects.

full range of preview mechanisms, and know that you won't have to redo your work once you get to build the actual HTML page. In the hectic and unpredictable reality of web design, that is a tremendous asset.

nae interactive—Using Fireworks for a Power Makeover

A chronic lack of time is a sad side-effect of a busy schedule, so it is no surprise that we had no more than two days in which to conjure up a much-needed rework of nae interactive's very own company page, www.nae.de. The idea was to make a tight and concise HTML site that would explain our activities to prospective clients, simply providing the information required while at the same time conveying our particular brand of graphic style. As it turned out, the site is a very good example of Dreamweaver UltraDev/Fireworks integration and of how Fireworks can get you results quickly and professionally.

To achieve the goal of simplicity and to satisfy the demands of a tight schedule, we based the site on just two pages, one home page and several content pages that share the same graphic content. The second page, which served as the template for the site's pages, contained four separate frames, each with page-appropriate variations (Figure 2-15). We used the Frames To Files export option to make each

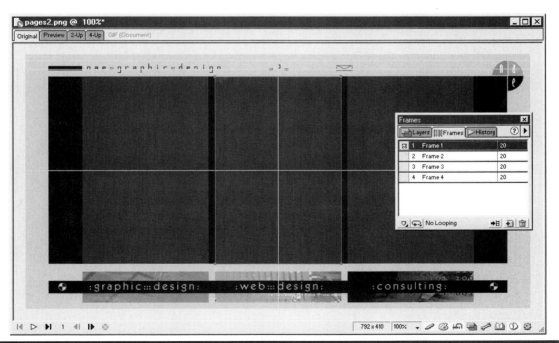

Figure 2-15   Each frame contains the main page architecture and menus. Where eventual content dictated, minor changes were made in the frames.

frame a ready-made template for an HTML page. Additionally, all pages share a common navigation bar. A layout was created in Fireworks for both pages, using bitmap images imported from Photoshop and Fireworks' built-in vector tools. The graphics were then tweaked using Fireworks live effects and masking.

Next, all the pages were sliced in Fireworks to facilitate export and the subsequent reuse of images on multiple HTML pages. Rollovers for the navigation, links for the buttons, and ALT text for the slices were all added right inside Fireworks before optimizing the slices and exporting them for use in Dreamweaver/UltraDev.

The content page was turned into a Dreamweaver/UltraDev template from which the four actual content HTML pages were then derived and filled with the appropriate text. Of course, all the JavaScript rollovers from Fireworks remained intact, so the final site assembly in Dreamweaver/UltraDev took little more than a few hours.

As a final bonus, we developed a new set of company stationery for nae interactive in Freehand/Illustrator using the graphics created in Fireworks during the construction of the site.

3 Collaborative Workflow

Because today's web sites are getting bigger and more complex, gone are the days of the "one-man show" web designer—the designer who did everything from the information architecture and visual design to the HTML and programming. The reality of building web sites today often is to work with a team of designers and developers that range from art directors to production artists and HTML developers and programmers. Even small inhouse web development organizations within universities, nonprofits, and government offices involve a distribution of labor that is different from just a few years ago. The folks at Macromedia recognize this collaborative trend and have made sure that Fireworks accommodates team workflow across its already well-integrated web software suite.

Several of Fireworks' features combine to speed up productivity by automating repetitive tasks while enhancing sitewide consistency. For example, to ensure design consistency throughout a site (for example, use of fonts and the graphic treatment of buttons), Fireworks enables designers to save graphic elements in a *library* that can be shared with coworkers. The elements then become *symbols* that can be used and reused. Going a step further, Fireworks also allows designers to save and retrieve the attributes of their graphic objects as *styles*. These styles can be saved as separate files and kept in project folders.

Fireworks also allows teams to save common processes such as building buttons of an exact size and placement on the canvas, and building standard footer graphics as automated commands that cut down on production time. Fireworks offers three key ways of automating repetitive tasks: a robust *Find and Replace* interface; a *History panel,* which can create macro-like commands; and a *Batch Processing* interface. In addition, advanced users can create their own commands using the Fireworks API.

In this chapter, we'll explore each of these features from the standpoint of the designer who has finalized the main designs and needs to pass on the work to other collaborators. By taking advantage of these features now, you can save substantial production time down the road as you automate the replication of the design and, in so doing, assure its consistency sitewide.

The Team-Oriented Design Process

While the process of creating web sites varies, the major stages of production are similar. Initiating the right features of Fireworks at the right stages of development helps you get the most out of the software and into your designs.

Let's take an example. In graphic design firms, the flow often looks as follows:

1. The workflow starts with the creative director or art director, who builds design directions in Fireworks (see Chapter 2). Next, the client signs off on a direction (perhaps after some modification), and the creative or art director then hands off the design direction to the designer.

2. It becomes the designer's responsibility to figure out the best ways to expand on the design. This includes, among other things, creating design templates for *all* the pages of the site, not just the home and one subpage included in the design direction. Then the designer delegates the graphic production efforts to a team of production artists.

3. Each of the production artists must create final optimized art needed for the site that is consistent with the designs the other production artists are churning out. By the time the art is created, time has elapsed and many hands have touched the product. Consistency becomes a key, since the wrong stroke setting in the right place can create an aesthetic nightmare that makes your client and you appear unprofessional.

In your own situation, the process might not look just like the one described—your staff might be structured differently, especially if you are in a university, nonprofit, or government setting, for instance, or in a small business with its own web team. And even if you *are* still a one-person show, almost everything covered in this chapter will help you improve your productivity; just imagine yourself wearing each of the different hats at a different time in the process! Whatever your workflow, the Fireworks features covered in this chapter marry the concepts of creating consistency and eliminating repetition into one-stop solutions that can and should be implemented *before* the main production begins, rather than simply as Band-Aids once you are well under way.

This chapter, in summary, comes at the stage corresponding to step 2 in the preceding list. Before the art director and designer pass off the production effort to a team, they have the opportunity to make use of several features that can have long-lasting positive effects on the rest of the process. This chapter will help you make the most of that window of opportunity.

Optimizing the Creative Workflow

The first category of features discussed in this chapter consists of those that speed up production by creating reusable elements and element descriptions that will make replication of the initial design a snap. The second category of features, which will be discussed later in this chapter, consists of those that automate significant changes and processes throughout multiple objects and files all at once.

Making templates is a longstanding method of speeding up production and ensuring consistency. Now, when making templates, you can create entire, sophisticated files, or you can build just the elements that compose those files. While building entire template files is optimal when possible, often that approach is too restrictive to be practical. We recommend taking a more modular approach to building templates—building different classes of designs. These classes can include the following:

- A library of prefab graphics, such as buttons, icons, arrows, and bullet graphics
- A collection of styles for both type and graphics
- A library of commonly used URLs

The next section will discuss each of these in turn.

IDEA Create a project folder on your intranet called **Template** that contains a PNG file with a complete symbol and URL library, complete mock-ups of the main page and a subpage (in different frames), and a page of directions on how to use the elements, naming conventions, and so on. In fact this "page of directions" can be an additional layer in Fireworks. You can also store your master styles in that folder as well as a custom color palette. If desired, have an administrator make the contents of that folder Read Only, so nothing is inadvertently overwritten.

Symbol Libraries

One timesaving way to create consistency sitewide is to create libraries. Library creation and management is handled in the Library panel, seen in Figure 3-1. Items are added to a PNG file's library when you convert them to *symbols.* These symbols can then be dragged as instances back onto your canvas for instant replication. What's more, all placed instances of a symbol can be updated instantly, simply by modifying the original symbol upon which they are based.

Fireworks has three different kinds of symbols: *graphic, animation,* and *button.* Flash users may notice the resemblance to graphic, movie clip, and button symbols in Flash. Indeed, two Fireworks symbols—graphic and button—are similar to their Flash counterparts. Table 3-1 describes the symbol types, their definitions, and some tips on how to use them.

In Flash, symbols have a structural necessity; to improve file-size efficiency and to create certain forms of interactivity and special effects, symbols are indispensable. However, symbols have a different role in Fireworks, where they do not significantly improve the file size of exported bitmaps (they will keep the size of your PNG files down). Fireworks symbols are mainly used for organization and consistency and

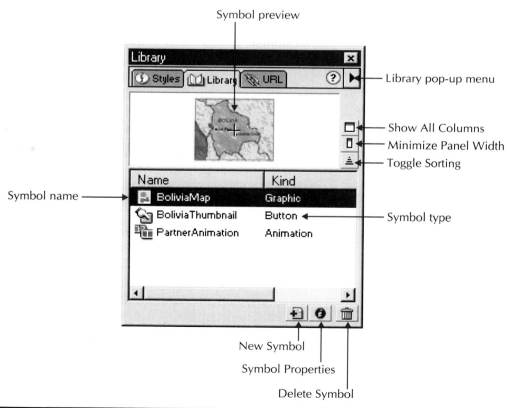

Figure 3-1   The Library panel

Symbol Type	Features	Applications
Graphic	Graphic symbols are static pieces of art; they can comprise groups of objects spread across layers. They, like the other two kinds of symbol, also have web layers, so you can associate them with URLs.	Logos, frequently used static graphics, repeated or reused components of larger illustrations and even animations
Animation	Animation symbols are essentially graphic symbols with frames and several additional attributes, including distance traveled, rotation, direction, opacity, and scale.	Animated GIFs, Flash animations
Button	Button symbols contain five states, which respond to the position and behavior of the mouse: Up, Over, Down, Over While Down, and Active Area.	Buttons, navigation bars, any graphic that triggers an event or responds to the cursor

Table 3-1   Fireworks Symbol Types, Features, and Applications

tweened animation (a *tweened* animation is one that is automatically generated by Fireworks based on a starting and an ending keyframe that you define).

However, Fireworks symbols can also be of benefit in maintaining site consistency. Once you have created your comps, the easiest thing might be to convert your existing artwork into symbols. Converting a piece of existing artwork to a symbol is as easy as selecting the object (or objects—a symbol can be made of a combination of elements, including any combination of lines, shapes, a bitmap, and some text) and choosing Insert | Convert To Symbol or by pressing F8.

You can also create symbols from scratch:

1. Select Insert | New Symbol from the main menu.

2. In the Symbol Properties dialog box, provide a name for the symbol and choose its type.

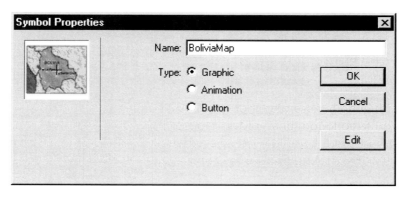

3. Click OK. A blank canvas appears.

4. Place any content—text, vector, or bitmap graphics—on the new canvas. Most options and features available on the main canvas may also be used here, including layers, live effects, grouping, and so on.

To convert an existing piece of art into a symbol:

1. Select the drawing, text, or group that you would like to convert to a symbol. You may also select multiple elements with the SHIFT key; if you do, the symbol will comprise the group of selected elements.

2. Select Insert | Convert Symbol from the main menu.

3. In the Symbol Properties dialog box, provide a name for the symbol and choose its type.

4. Click OK. The selection marquee around the graphic changes to indicate it is now an instance.

As you create symbols, they are put into the library, which resides inside the file in which the symbols were created. Symbol libraries cannot stand on their own—they are a part of the Fireworks PNG metadata.

IDEA People often confuse symbols and instances. *Symbols* reside only in the library. *Instances* are copies of symbols that appear only on the canvas. There is no place that the two can coexist.

However, symbol libraries can be imported and exported in two ways. First, you can import individual symbols from one PNG file to another.

To import symbols from another PNG file's library:

1. Open the destination PNG—the file into which you would like to import the symbols.

2. Choose Window | Library to open the Library panel.

3. Click the triangle in the upper-right corner to open the pop-up menu.

4. Choose Import Symbols.

5. Navigate to the PNG that contains the library you wish to import.

6. Choose which symbols you would like to import, using the Import Symbols dialog box, seen in Figure 3-2. Use the Select All and Deselect buttons in combination with CTRL-click/COMMAND-click to select multiple symbols.

7. Click Import to bring the symbols into the destination file.

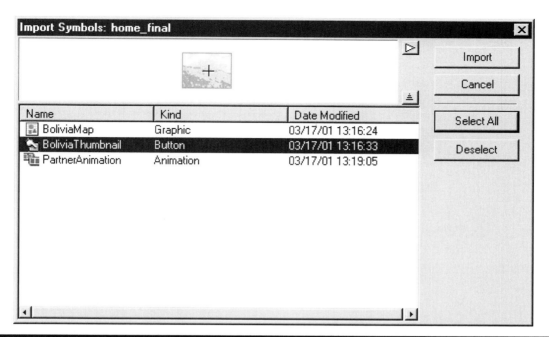

Figure 3-2 The Import Symbols dialog box allows selective import of symbols.

The second way to transfer symbols between files is to export an entire library as a self-standing PNG. Following this method, you first create a comprehensive library of symbols to be used within a project, and then distribute this library as a repository to the production team independent of any built or composite graphic files, such as banners or design directions.

To export a symbol library:

1. Choose Window | Library to open the Library panel.

2. Click the triangle in the upper-right corner to open the pop-up menu.

3. Choose Export Symbols. The Export Symbols dialog box opens, shown in Figure 3-3.

4. Choose which symbols you would like to save. Use CTRL-click/ COMMAND-click to select multiple symbols.

5. Click Export to open the Save As dialog box, and browse to the location in which you would like to save your library (in PNG format).

You can then import the symbols from the master library following the importing instructions shown earlier.

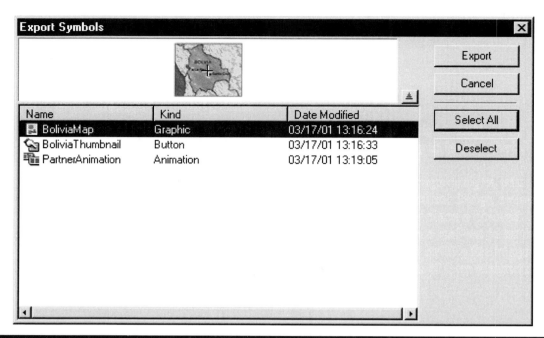

Figure 3-3   The Export Symbols dialog box allows selective exporting of symbols.

IDEA   Just as instances are linked to symbols, imported symbols are linked to their original libraries. This means that if, once in development, a symbol needs to be changed sitewide, simply changing the symbol in the library in the Template folder will change every instance in every PNG throughout the site, so long as you choose Update from the Library panel pop-up menu. Of course, this cuts both ways: a mistake in the source file will ripple throughout the site.

Styles

If you are used to page layout software, or even to your word processor, you probably have some experience with styles. Styles are a way of preserving the format attributes of an object, such as a text block, independent of the object itself. Vector graphics, like fonts (actually, fonts themselves are vector graphics), are rendered via a set of directions, and these directions come with a set of attributes. If you are familiar with HTML, you know that the <table> object comes with attributes like cell spacing, cell padding, width (in pixels or as a percent), border, alignment, and many others. In the case of fonts, attributes include size, points above or below the baseline, and color. Vector graphics likewise have their own set of attributes, and it is these attributes that Fireworks styles allow you to capture.

The attributes that Fireworks tracks, and hence that you are able to embed in styles, include a broad range, as summarized in Table 3-2.

Attribute Name	Examples
Fill Type	Solid, Gradient, Dither, Pattern, Texture, Edge, etc.
Fill Color	Hexadecimal colors from one of the palettes, such as Web Snap, or custom mixed from the Mixer.
Stroke Type	Basic, Pencil, Air Brush, Calligraphy, Texture, Tip, etc.
Stroke Color	Hexadecimal colors from one of the palettes, such as Web Snap, or custom-mixed colors from the Mixer.
Effect	Bevels, Glows, Drop Shadows, Blurs, Color Effects, many Photoshop filters, etc.
Text Font	Verdana, Times, Helvetica, Garamond, etc.
Text Size	In points: 10, 12, 14, etc.
Text Style	Bold, Italic, Underline.

Table 3-2   Attributes That Can Be Stored in Styles

Buttons provide a good occasion to use styles. Most buttons are created out of rectangles with various added attributes, such as stroke color and width, fill color and pattern, and live effects like beveling. Usually if you make one button, you make several more like it, so you can improve your productivity by storing and applying the attributes of the first button to subsequently drawn rectangles.

At the same time, you ensure design consistency, because no one will inadvertently apply a two-point stroke where there should have been only a one-point stroke. As you complete your final comp and prepare to begin production, you have the ideal opportunity to take advantage of styles.

Working with Styles

Styles are managed in the Styles panel, seen in Figure 3-4, which can be accessed via Windows | Styles. Using this panel, you can create, modify, delete, import, and export styles.

Creating styles is largely a matter of creating an object as you would like it to appear and then choosing which attributes to save as a style. The style, then, is no more than a simple grouping of object attributes.

To create styles:

1. Draw an object using the text tool or the vector drawing tool of your choice.

2. Apply the desired styles, including textures and other effects from within the Stroke and Fill panels.

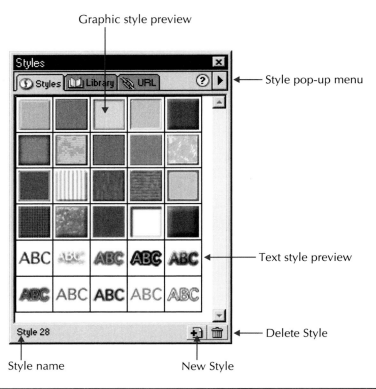

Graphic style preview

Style pop-up menu

Text style preview

Delete Style

Style name

New Style

Figure 3-4   The Styles panel

3. Click the New Style button in the lower-right corner of the Styles panel. The New Style dialog box appears.

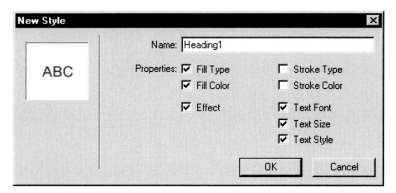

4. Give your file a descriptive name, perhaps referring to the project, so it is easier to identify which styles go with which projects.

5. Choose which of the attributes you wish to save as a part of the style.

6. Click OK.

Once you have created all of the styles you wish to use in your design, applying them is easy.

To apply styles:

1. Using a vector drawing tool or the Text tool, add the new drawing or text object to the canvas.

2. With the Styles panel open, click the desired style, and the object automatically updates.

What's more, even after applying the style, you can modify the object further, without affecting the style. This is a great way to base a new style on an old one. Imagine that you have a navigation bar on the main page, and you need to create a navigation bar for a subpage. The buttons on the new navigation bar will be the same size and shape; really, the only difference will be that the fill color will change. Assuming you already have a style for the main navigation bar button, it is easy to create a new style for buttons on the subpage.

To modify styles:

1. Select the drawing object, such as a plain rectangle, on the canvas to which you would like to add a modified style.

2. Select the original style that you would like to use as the basis for the modified style. The object on the canvas automatically updates.

3. Select the object on the canvas (if necessary) and make the desired adjustments.

4. Click the New Style button in the lower-right corner of the Styles panel. The New Style dialog box appears.

5. Give the new style a name, and choose which attributes to store in the style.

Organizing Styles

Since a key goal of this stage of the design process is to build a set of resources available to the entire production team to enhance productivity and consistency, a logical task is to find a way to organize and store styles. Unfortunately, as you add styles, Fireworks seems to organize styles in the Styles panel according to the date of creation. There is no way to sort them alphabetically, which would have been a real aid to keeping project styles together.

> **IDEA** Since you can name the styles, give them names associated with the project and where they are used, for example, HFH_NavButton.

Although you cannot sort styles within the Styles panel, you can create custom style groups, in which you remove the default styles and create a group of styles used in a given project. One of the convenient aspects of custom style groups is that they are stored outside of Fireworks and individual PNG files—in their own files. This makes organizing and distributing style groups by project an especially convenient way to enhance productivity throughout a project's design cycle, no matter how much the project balloons over time.

NOTE There is a key difference in the creation, storage, and distribution of symbols and libraries on the one hand, and styles on the other. Libraries reside in individual PNG files and have no independence from them. Exporting a library essentially means storing a library (or partial library) in an otherwise empty PNG. If you close the PNG and open a new one, the new library will be empty. In contrast, Styles are stored independently in Fireworks itself and, if you like, in external files. If you export a group of styles, you will create a new STL file, which you can import into Fireworks. Regardless of what file you have open, be it new or old, the styles will persist between files unless you load a different set, restore defaults, or make other adjustments.

To create and distribute custom style sets:

1. Before you begin creating new styles, first open the Styles panel and delete all of the existing styles. To do so, click the first style in the upper-left corner, and then SHIFT-click the last style to select all of the styles. Then choose Delete Styles from the Styles panel pop-up menu to remove them. You can also use CTRL-click/COMMAND-click to select multiple styles to partially delete the current set of styles.

2. Open the client-approved design direction created in Fireworks that will serve as the template for the rest of the site.

3. One by one, use the graphic elements to create each of your graphic and text styles, giving them descriptive names.

IDEA Since you know Fireworks organizes styles according to the order of creation, try to create the styles in a logical order. For example, first create all your text styles, then your button styles, and so on.

When you are finished, your Styles panel should contain a comprehensive group of descriptively named styles that will be used throughout production.

4. Click the triangle in the upper-right corner to open the pop-up menu.

5. Choose Export Styles to save your style set. The Save As dialog box opens.

6. Save the style set in a special master design folder, along with other assets such as custom color palettes and libraries.

NOTE The Style panel's default style set can be restored by choosing Reset Styles from the pop-up menu in the top-right corner of the panel.

Once the set is saved, you or other users can pull in this style set at any time to add to the styles currently loaded in Fireworks or to replace the current set altogether.

To import custom style sets:

1. Decide whether you would like to *add* the style set to the styles already in the Styles panel or whether you would like to *replace* the current set. Importing styles simply adds to the existing set, so if you wish to add, you need do nothing special.

2. To replace the current set, however, you will first need to remove all of the styles in the Styles panel. There is no command to clear all styles, so you will have to select and delete the styles manually.

3. Choose Import Styles from the Styles panel pop-up menu to bring up the Open dialog box, and pull the custom style group into Fireworks.

FOR MORE INFORMATION! You can download more styles from the following URL: http://www.macromedia.com/software/fireworks/download/styles/.

Using the URL Library

The URL panel, which is by default docked with the Styles and Library panels, helps you keep your URLs straight. It is relatively easy to use, with few options, as seen in Figure 3-5.

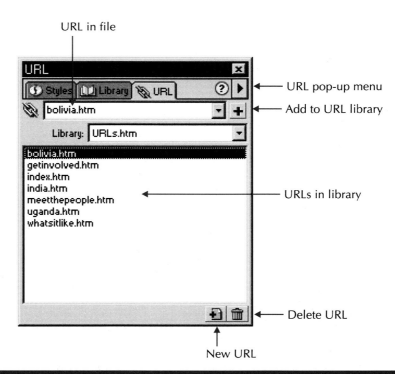

Figure 3-5   The URL panel

The main functionality of the panel can be outlined quickly:

● When you add slices or hotspots, rather than adding the URL to the Object panel, you can simply click a URL in the URL panel.

● When you need to change a URL throughout the file, you can use the URL panel to change the URLs all at once.

● You can export custom URL libraries, which works much like exporting style sets.

To add URLs to the URL library:

1. Add the URL to any slice or hotspot object by using the Object panel.

2. With the object still selected, open the URL panel. The URL is listed in the field at the top of the panel.

3. Click the + symbol to add it to the library. The URL appears in the lower pane.

4. Alternatively, to add a URL without applying it to an object, you can click the New URL icon in the lower-right corner of the panel, which brings up the minimalist New URL dialog box.

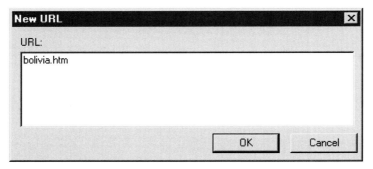

To remove, modify, and export URLs:

1. To remove a URL from the URL panel, select it and click the trash can icon. Note that you cannot select multiple URLs.

2. To edit an existing URL, select it, and choose Edit URL from the URL panel pop-up menu. The Edit URL dialog box opens. Notice the Change All Occurrences In Document check box.

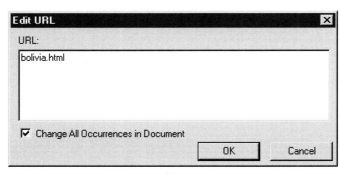

3. To export URLs, choose Export URLs from the pop-up menu. All of the URLs in the library are saved in a single HTML file.

 Another use for the URL panel is for inserting long URLs into pop-up menus. There is a bug in the pop-up menu dialog box that limits the length of URLs to around 48 characters. By adding them to the URL panel first, they are selectable from the drop-down list in the pop-up menu.

You can also directly edit the library loaded in Fireworks at any given moment, if you wish. It is called "URLs.htm" and is located in the Fireworks 4/Configuration/URL Libraries folder.

 The Object panel contains URL information, when hotspots and slices are selected. It also contains a field for the alt tag and Target attribute of the <a> tag. Although whenever you create a URL, it is automatically added to the URL panel, anything you enter into the alt tag and Target fields of the Object panel will *not* be stored in the URL panel. If you apply URLs by selecting hot objects and clicking in the URL panel, you will not copy this information.

Automating Fireworks

The first half of this chapter covered creating an original set of master resources for replicating the original design throughout production. The goal there was to create reusable elements to enhance both speed and consistency during production. Of course, when has it ever happened that the original design ever went completely unmodified throughout production? Whether a client simply wants a single color changed throughout a site, or a reorganization of the site's contents requires substantial new design initiatives, Fireworks has tools that will prevent you from having to start over.

This chapter discusses three powerful tools that enable large-scale changes not just to single graphics, but throughout your entire site. These tools are *Find and Replace, commands,* and *batch processing.* In addition, we'll discuss the *Project Log,* a tool that will help you keep track of and re-export modified files.

Find and Replace

Find and Replace works in Fireworks much like it does in Dreamweaver or a word processor. You specify what you want it to look for, and what you want to replace it with. Then Fireworks does the work for you. A little creativity with the Find and Replace panel can make great strides toward solving tricky problems.

NOTE Find and Replace only works with vector objects in Fireworks' PNG files, such as drawn shapes, text, and live effects. Bitmap graphics will be unaffected. To change one or more colors in a bitmap image, you will need to select the pixels whose color you wish to change, and then use the Paint Bucket to fill the selection with the desired color. Alternatively, you can use a different program, such as Photoshop, to automatically replace colors in bitmap images.

Understanding the Find and Replace Panel

The Find and Replace panel, seen in Figure 3-6, can be accessed via Edit | Find And Replace, Window | Find And Replace, or by pressing CTRL-F/COMMAND-F. At the top of the panel are two drop-down lists that dictate the kind of search. The first allows you to choose where you want to perform the operation. Your Fireworks Find and Replace location search options are summarized in Table 3-3.

The range of choices allows you to pinpoint where you would like to perform the Find and Replace operation, while some of the more expansive options enable you to make sitewide changes instantly.

HAZARD Finding and replacing elements in unopened files usually cannot be undone. This can be especially dangerous if you do not think through the operation beforehand.

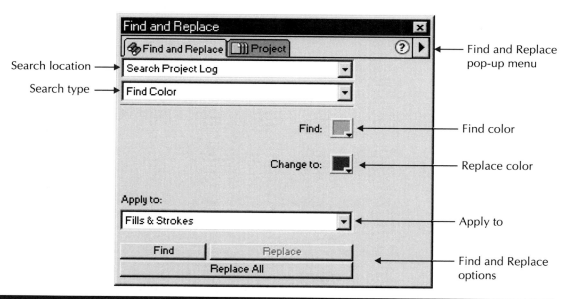

Figure 3-6   The Find Color feature of the Find and Replace panel

Search Location	Searches
Search Selection	Among selected graphic and text objects.
Search Frame	All objects in the selected frame.
Search Document	All objects in the entire document.
Search Project Log	Objects in files placed in the Project Log. (See the "Using the Project Log" section.)
Search Files	A selection of files.

Table 3-3 Search Options in the Find and Replace Panel

Making sitewide changes can be risky, because if you make an error, fixing the problem can be tricky. For instance, imagine you have two types of buttons, distinguished by their fill colors, and you convert the fill color of one type to the same as the other type. Then you realize you need to change them back, and discover that you may not be able to. This is because there may be nothing that distinguishes the formerly two different button types, so there is no way for Fireworks to know which ones to switch back. If this happens, you may have to downgrade from searching multiple files (which is very efficient) to opening each document individually, selecting the buttons you do want changed, and then searching by selection—a time-consuming and error-prone process.

The second drop-down menu in the Find and Replace panel allows you to specify what you would like to change. Table 3-4 summarizes what kinds of Find and Replace options Fireworks can do.

The Find and Replace panel is both powerful and easy to use. But it can be used for more than fixing problems. While you might think of this tool when your client changes a URL in the navigation bar or when some serial error has crept its way throughout a series of files on a project, Find and Replace can also aid the creative process.

IDEA Use Find and Replace when you have created a main site level and you need to create sublevels: let Find and Replace change a color scheme as a quick and dirty way to visualize different possibilities. If you are curious what effect an older style typeface, such as Garamond, might have on a design that currently features a more modernistic typeface, such as Bodoni, Find and Replace can provide a quick answer.

Search Item	Searches For
Find Text	A text string and replaces it with another. There are options for matching case, whole word, and regular expressions.
Find Font	A font and replaces it with another. Additional options allow you to specify font attributes, such as size, and various combinations of bold, italic, and so forth.
Find Color	One color and replaces it with another. You can search individually or collectively on fills, strokes, and effects. This option will be especially welcome to Photoshop users who have to change colors *after* they have applied effects such as glows and drop shadows. Since Fireworks retains all of this information in vector format, even though it anti-aliases text or feathers colors when you apply effects, Fireworks remembers the base color; when you replace it, it automatically adjusts the anti-aliasing, feathering, and so on.
Find URL	URLs much like the Find Text search does, with the same modifiers for matching case, whole word, and so on.
Find Non Web216	Colors outside the so-called web-safe palette of 216 colors that has served as the lowest common denominator for web graphics for years.

Table 3-4   Searchable Elements Using Find and Replace

Using the Project Log

Docked by default with the Find and Replace panel is an easily overlooked tool that can save you a lot of time, especially if you end up with numerous files as a part of a project. While your project may start out as a screen-size design direction spread across multiple frames, as described in Chapter 2, eventually navigation bars, logos, and other elements will likely wind up in their own files. Find and Replace really comes into its own under such circumstances, since you can use it across multiple files.

Things become more complicated when you have already optimized, exported, and deployed some graphics in your HTML editor while you are still developing other graphics. What happens when you need to change your fonts sitewide then? How will you keep all of the files in their various stages straight?

The answer is the Project Log. The Project Log, shown in Figure 3-7, can be brought up by choosing Window | Project Log. The Project Log is used in conjunction with both Find and Replace and batch processing to track changes made to a series of PNG files and helps ensure that modified PNGs are re-exported after automated changes take place.

The panel itself is divided into three columns. In the first column is the name of the file. The second column, which has a film icon above it, signifies the frame in which the last Replace took place. The third column has the time and the date of the change.

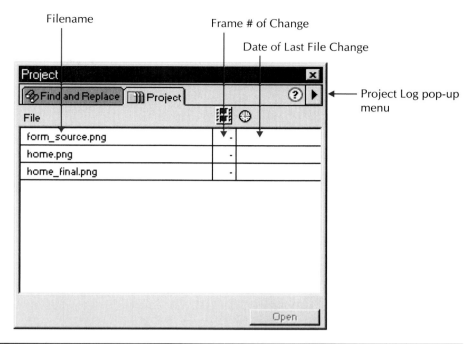

Filename   Frame # of Change

Date of Last File Change

Project Log pop-up
menu

Figure 3-7   The Project Log panel

Using the Project Log involves three steps:

- Adding a set of files to be in the Project Log
- Making any modifications to those files
- Re-exporting the PNGs as GIFs or JPGs, and so on

Adding Files to the Project Log

There are two ways to get files into a given Project Log. First, any time you make
changes to more than one file using Find and Replace, all of the changed files will
be automatically added to the Project File. This is the easiest way to keep track of
which files were actually changed. You might, for example, search all of the PNGs
in a given folder in a Find and Replace operation, and yet only half of the files might
have been changed, with the other half not needing any change. Only those files
that were actually changed will be added to the Project Log, even though all of the
files were searched. This way, you know exactly which files you will need to
re-export.

The second way to get files into a Project Log is to add them manually.
To manually add files to the Project Log:

1. Open the Project Log by choosing Window | Project Log.

2. Click the small triangle in the upper-right corner to open the Project Log
   pop-up menu.

3. Choose Add Files To Log. The standard Open dialog box appears.

4. Choose whichever files you would like to add, using CTRL-click/COMMAND-click to select multiple files.

5. Click Done. The files are added to the Project Log.

Tracking Modifications with the Project Log

Now that your Project Log is constructed, continue to do any further Find and Replace or batch processing operations. The Project Log will be updated as you work. Be sure to make note of which frames of a given file were affected, so that all of your rollovers export as expected. Find and Replace, as with any automated tool, is essentially blind—it makes any changes you ask it to, but it neither exercises judgment nor shows you what it is doing. Taking note of changes according to frame will help decrease the surprise factor and ensure that you export all of the frames of all of the files that you work with.

Updating Optimized Graphics via the Project Log

Once you have completed all of your Find and Replace and Batch Processing operations, your PNGs should all be in order. However, all of the GIFs and JPGs that are currently populating your HTML editor—graphics that you built, optimized, and exported prior to the recent round of changes—are outdated. This is where the Project Log really pays off. Not only does it track which documents and frames had changes, but it also provides a simple way to re-export each of the modified documents. The best part about it is that since Fireworks saves optimization settings as a part of the metadata of every PNG, this re-exporting process is not a one-size-fits-all affair; rather, each file is re-exported using the optimization settings for that file (or even for a given slice of a file).

To re-export modified graphics via the Project Log:

1. Open the Project Log.

2. Select the files you wish to re-export. Use CTRL-click/COMMAND-click to select multiple files.

3. Click the triangle to open the pop-up menu.

4. Choose Export Again. The standard Export dialog box opens.

5. Make any appropriate choices and click Save. Fireworks re-exports all of the graphics according to the optimization settings within each file.

IDEA The Project Log's Export Again feature comes in handy when creating initial design directions in frames for your client. Imagine that you have three different PNG files—each with a number of frames showing design variations. Instead of exporting each PNG file by using the Files To Frames option, you can add all three PNG files to the Project Log, select them, and choose Export Again. Instantly, the frames of all three PNG files are exported!

Saving and Editing the Project Log

One downside to the Project Log is that it seems to have a rather tenuous existence. If you open a new PNG file and perform a new set of operations, the contents will change. There is no option to save the log, either. Generally, you would only need to use a Project Log while in the midst of automated operations anyway. However, if for some reason you wish to save a Project Log, you can.

The Project Log is stored as Project_Log.htm in the Fireworks 4/Configuration folder (the manual has a misprint that indicates it is in the Fireworks 4/Settings folder). Since it is an HTML file, you can open it in your browser to view its contents. To save it, simply navigate to it and rename it. The next time you create a Project Log, Fireworks will automatically regenerate Project_Log.htm.

Commands and Batch Processing with Scriptlets

Fireworks has two other major tool sets that enable automated changes: Commands and Batch Processing. We will hold off a major discussion of these powerful tool sets until Chapter 14. However, we want to call your attention to the fact that both of these, as with Find and Replace, can be useful during this stage of the workflow, when you are preparing a common set of templates and resources for the use of a team.

Commands

As you work in Fireworks, the History panel keeps track of all of your steps. At any time in your workflow, you can simply slide the Undo marker to back up a few steps—sort of like a quick "multiple undo"—as shown in Figure 3-8. The History panel allows you to archive a series of steps as a Command that you can replay over and over, even in subsequent Fireworks sessions or even on another computer or platform.

This feature is ideal for quickly reproducing common steps like assigning a behavior and an optimization setting to a slice object. By assigning a function key to a command, you can quickly replicate numerous steps at the touch of a button. If you share the command with coworkers on the team, everyone working on the project can enjoy your shortcut, and you can be sure that everyone will get the same effect—ensuring consistent production processes across a project.

CROSS REFERENCE → To learn more about creating and distributing commands, see Chapter 14.

NOTE In the History panel, you can save only a sequence of steps that are not separated by a solid line. The line represents a break in the steps, like deselecting a graphic and selecting another, that cannot be duplicated in a saved command.

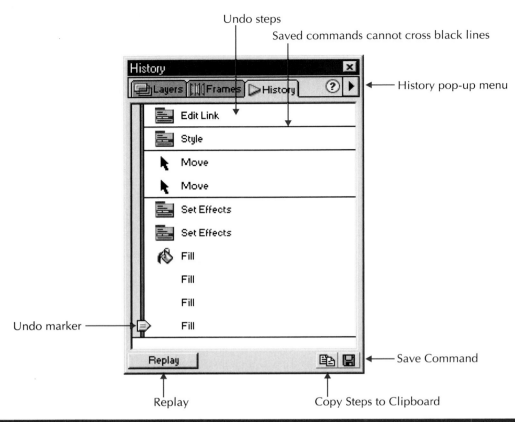

Figure 3-8   The History panel

Batch Processing with Scriptlets

Another means of automating production is the Fireworks Batch Processing interface, which has been revamped for Fireworks 4. The Batch Processing interface, seen in Figure 3-9, allows you to build a script of operations that you would like to perform over a set of files that you designate. These changes can include exporting, scaling, entire Find and Replace operations, file renaming, and a host of others.

Batch processing, like Find and Replace and commands, can serve a creative purpose, as well as serve as a fix-it tool for sweeping errors. It can also be used for any graphic type Fireworks can read; it is not limited to Fireworks PNG graphics.

IDEA   You can use Fireworks' batch processing to standardize a series of already exported bitmap graphics or even to process graphics made in another software package, such as Photoshop.

A key feature of batch processing is that you can save your jobs as *scriptlets*. These scriptlets can then be distributed to your production team, saving time and improving consistency.

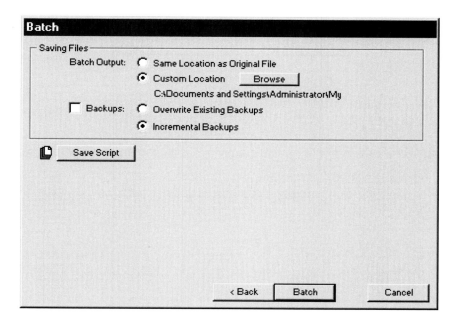

Figure 3-9 The Batch Processing interface

CROSS REFERENCE To learn how to get the most out of batch processing and scriptlets, see Chapter 14.

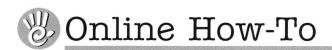 Online How-To

Creating and Distributing a Master Design Repository

One goal of this chapter was to outline some ways that you can use Fireworks tools to create resources that the production team can use and reuse as it produces the site. In this lesson, you will begin with a design direction in a Fireworks PNG and create numerous kinds of template elements. In a template folder, you will place a custom library with symbols, a custom style group, and a URL library.

 GO TO THE WEB! For a free, self-paced interactive version of this tutorial, which includes video demonstrations and source files, visit www.expertedge.com.

Usually when you are creating a master template, you will have at least two files—the main page and the subpages, if not more—which should give you plenty of resources. For the sake of this exercise, we stuck to just one PNG to keep it manageable. In general, your style sets and libraries will be a bit larger than what you will make here.

Preparing for a Master Template

Before you start creating the master template, you should set up your workspace:

1. Create a folder on your intranet or LAN that the whole project team has access to, calling it **HFH_template**. You will put all of the template files in this folder.

2. Make a copy of the master design direction and place it in this folder. For this exercise, you can copy **exercise.png** in this chapter's folder at the book's web site as your master design direction. You will be working from this file, and you do not want to inadvertently change it.

3. If it is not already, open Fireworks and bring up the Styles panel.

4. Remove all of the existing styles by clicking the first and then SHIFT-clicking the last to select them all, and choosing Delete from the Styles pop-up menu.

5. Open the design direction PNG—exercise.png in our case.

Creating a Style Set

In this section, you'll make a custom style set. *Style sets* are stored outside of individual PNGs, residing in the Fireworks application itself and in STL files that you can create yourself.

To create text styles:

1. With home_final.png open, be sure that Frame 1 is active in the Frames panel.

2. Above the first column in the main layout is a date: "9.05.01." That formatting will be reused at the top of every column, so it is a good element from which to create a style. Select that text element.

3. In the Styles panel, click the New Style icon. The New Style dialog box appears.

4. Name the style **Text_Date**. Always give your styles meaningful names.

5. Check Fill Type, so that the current setting in the Fill panel is stored in the style. In this case, the fill type is Solid, Hard, which is what gives the text the aliased appearance (that is, the edges are not softened).

6. Check Fill Color, which will add the particular shade of blue to the style.

7. Uncheck Effect, since there are no effects like shadows applied to this text.

8. Uncheck both Stroke Type and Stroke Color. Fonts are usually not stroked, and the date text is no exception. Oddly, though, Fireworks will *add* whatever the current stroke type and color happen to be to the style, even though the selected text has neither.

9. Check all three of the text attributes: Text Font, Text Size, and Text Style. When you are finished, the New Style dialog box should appear.

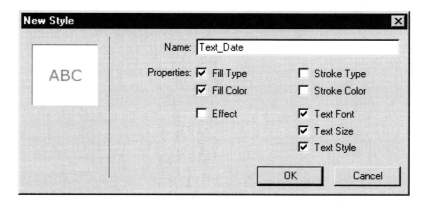

10. Click OK to create the style and add it to the Styles panel.

11. Select the blue headline, "Marta Claros' story."

12. Create a new style from this selection, calling it **Text_Headline** and checking the same boxes you checked with the first style.

13. Create a third style from the body text beneath the blue headline, and call it **Text_Body**.

14. Create a fourth style for the Habitat for Humanity text. When you try to click on the text, the whole block is selected. You might think that this logo is an imported bitmap. In fact, it is a group of text and vector art. To select the text block so you can make a style from it, select the group and choose Modify | Ungroup until you can isolate the text block. Then proceed in the usual way to create a text style.

15. Create styles for other repeated text elements, such as navigation button text, and so on.

IDEA You can only apply styles to entire text blocks; that is, you cannot select a couple words of text in the text editor and selectively create a style from them. Styles are created from objects selected with the Arrow tool. So when developing, it is wise to keep differently formatted text in separate text blocks.

Creating graphic styles is similar to creating text styles:

1. Surrounding each button on the navigation bars is a thin, empty rectangle. Since this element will be reused for every button, it makes a good candidate for a style. Click to select it.

2. With the Styles panel open, click the New Style icon.

3. Name the style **Navbar_Rectangle**, and leave the rest of the check boxes at their defaults.

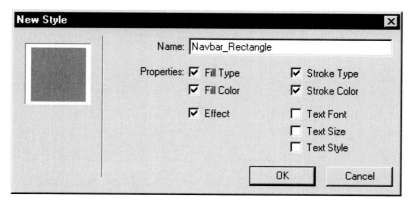

4. Click OK to save the file.

This style can be applied to three kinds of elements in this file. It is used in the rectangles in both the horizontal and vertical navigation bars. In addition, it can be used again for the small boxes that surround the thumbnails. Graphic styles do not store size information, meaning you can use the same style on different graphic elements.

IDEA The application of the same style to the three different types of element not only sped up production, it also brought artistic coherence, since one look appears across diverse elements.

If you need to create several graphics that are the same, you can use styles in combination with the Info panel. Simply size one graphic so that it is the desired size, and then enter its width and height into the remaining elements that need to be the same size. By the time you do all of this, it might be easier just to use Copy and Paste. Nonetheless, it is good to know that the same effect can often be created using very different tools.

Creating a Custom Symbol Library

The library is often used for functional reasons: it is necessary that any animated elements, including button rollovers, be converted to symbols. Using the library for rollovers and animations will be covered in later chapters. For now, another good use for the library is to store graphics that you will use over and over again. In this file, one graphic that will certainly be used throughout the site is the Habitat for Humanity logo in the upper-left corner.

To create a graphic symbol:

1. Select the Habitat for Humanity logo in the upper-left corner. If you ungrouped its components in an earlier step (when creating a text style), be sure you SHIFT-select all the components. You may, but do not need to, regroup the components.

2. Choose Insert | Convert To Symbol. The Symbol Properties dialog box appears.

3. In the Name field, enter **HFH_Logo**.

4. Choose Graphic as the symbol type. This graphic will not be used in a rollover or animation, and Graphic is the type you normally use for static graphics such as this.

5. Click OK. Notice that the selection border changes from the standard blue rectangle to a dashed line with a small arrow in the lower-right corner. This is how Fireworks designates symbol instances. Also, if you look in the library, you'll see the new symbol there, along with a button we included with the file.

6. Repeat this process until your library is stocked with symbols. Also, as you create rollover buttons, these, too, will end up in the library.

For the sake of this exercise, let's move on. Once you have created a library of reusable (and descriptively named) symbols, you want to export it to the Template folder, so the whole team can use it:

1. Open the Library panel, if it isn't already.

2. Click the triangle to open the pop-up menu.

3. Choose Export Symbols. The Export Symbols dialog box appears.

4. As with styles, you can selectively export symbols. Use CTRL-click/COMMAND-click to select multiple symbols, or choose Select All or Deselect to select or deselect the whole group.

5. When you are finished, click Export, and the Save As dialog box appears.

6. Navigate to the Template folder, call it **HFH_Library**, and click Save. Fireworks will create a custom PNG with one instance of each symbol on the otherwise empty canvas.

Other members of the production team can import these symbols into their files as they work on the project.

Creating a Custom URL Library

Fireworks tracks all of a PNG's URLs in the URL panel, which is docked with the Style and Library panels. In the project file, we included a slice. We'll add a URL to that slice, manipulate it in the URL panel, and then export it as a URL library.

To add a URL to a slice:

1. If it is not already on, turn on the Web Layer in the Layers panel, by clicking in the second column so that the eyeball icon appears. As in Figure 3-10, you should see some red guides across the canvas and a green square over one of the thumbnails; collectively, these indicate slicing.

2. Select the green slice region. The arrow in the bottom corner of the thumbnail indicates that it covers a symbol, in this case, a button symbol.

3. Open the Object panel by choosing Window | Object or by pressing ALT-F2. The Object panel, shown next, has different settings depending on the selected object.

Object type (context sensitive)

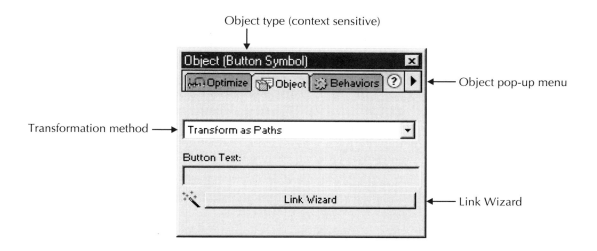

Object pop-up menu

Transformation method

Link Wizard

Slice region

Slice guides

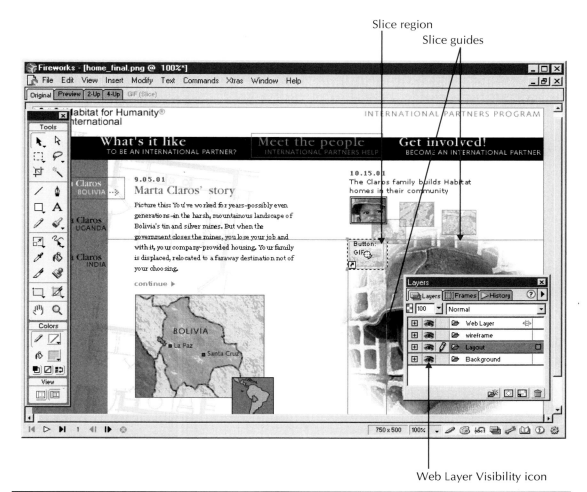

Web Layer Visibility icon

Figure 3-10   With the Web Layer set to visible, the slice region becomes visible as a green box over another object.

4. Leave the first field at its default, Transform As Paths.

5. Click the Link Wizard button to open the Link Wizard. A tabbed interface appears.

6. Click the second tab to open the Link tab, shown in Figure 3-11.

7. Type **bolivia.html** in the first box (with a chain-link icon beside it).

8. In the ALT field, type **Bolivia** and leave the Status Bar Text field blank.

9. Click OK.

To add a URL to the URL library:

1. If it isn't already, open the URL panel.

2. With the slice object still selected, the URL should be listed in the link field at the top.

3. Click the + symbol to add it to the URL library. The link now appears in the bottom pane.

Uh-oh! You called it "bolivia.html," but it turns out that it should have been called "bolivia.htm." No problem.

1. Click the "bolivia.html" link in the lower pane to select it.

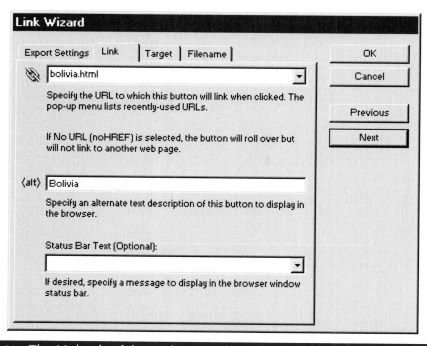

Figure 3-11   The Link tab of the Link Wizard

2. In the pop-up menu, choose Edit URL.

3. Delete that extra "l" from the end.

4. Check the Change All Occurrences In The Document check box.

5. Click OK.

Finally, you'll want to store this URL library in the Template folder created at the beginning of this tutorial.

1. From the URL panel pop-up menu, choose Export URLs.

2. The Save As dialog box appears.

3. Browse to the Template folder and name the file **HFH_URLs**.

4. Click Save to export the URL library.

Part II

Designing Web Graphics

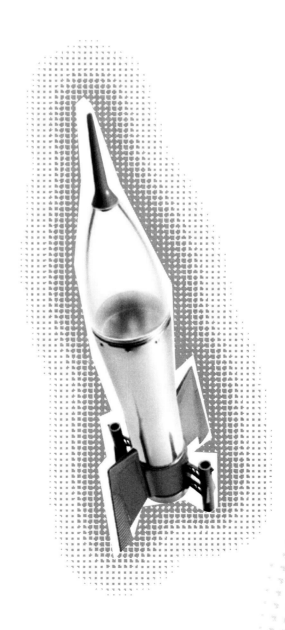

4 Strategies for Building a Complete Web Page

Fireworks is an ideal environment for building and exporting an entire interactive web page complete with navigation, animation, and the HTML to make it all work in a browser. Because of this power, we've seen designers rely completely on Fireworks to build and export each page of a web site—uploading the Fireworks-generated HTML and supporting graphics to a server. The problem with this Fireworks-only approach, however, is that when Fireworks exports a web page, it will consist entirely of graphics—either one big solid graphic, or a collection of sliced-up graphics if you used the Slice tool. The one exception to this rule is if you designate a slice object as "Text" in the Object panel and enter a few lines of text, even HTML, in the small text field. Even still, this limits the page's flexibility because there are not many HTML elements like text and forms.

Indeed, you should use Fireworks to design and build an entire web page, not just pieces of a page like bullets and buttons. But there are ways to maximize your web page's efficiency through strategic page planning and integration with a tool like Dreamweaver. In this chapter, we'll explore such strategies and how you can get your full page designs *out* of Fireworks and into an efficient web page.

To build efficient web pages in Fireworks, start by building the entire design of one page in your Fireworks document; then save it as the master layout. Once you build the entire design, you can then export pieces of it that you can reassemble in Dreamweaver. For example, after building the entire design for the "Meet the people" section of the Habitat site, Lisa cropped the page down to just the navigation portion and saved it as "Nav.png," as in Figure 4-1. The reason for cropping the navigation portion is so that we can export it as a separate HTML page. After exporting the navigation HTML, it's easy to use the Insert Fireworks HTML object in Dreamweaver to integrate the navigation section as a separate piece of the top of each page of the Habitat site.

One Page at a Time

As we discussed in Chapter 2, you can quickly build a series of design options for a new project by using the Frames palette. For example, you could build a sample "Home Page A" in one frame and a sample "Home Page B" in another frame. You could continue to work in the same Fireworks document, adding a new frame for each new design option—even options for subpages that match each home page design. When finished, you have a bunch of designs all conveniently located in the frames of one Fireworks PNG file that you can quickly export as a series of GIFs with the Frames To Files export option.

While this approach of building multiple web pages in one Fireworks document works well in the initial exploratory design phase when the pages are exported as static, noninteractive GIFs, once the client chooses a direction, you must build each major web page in its own Fireworks document. This is because Fireworks' web features are geared toward preparing one web page, not multiple pages. For example, when you use the Slice tool to chop the page into independent regions—either for optimization or interactivity reasons—the slices all go on one Web Layer in the Layers palette and are in positions that relate to the design of your web page (whatever design is in Frame 1). You cannot, for instance, have another Web Layer with a different set of slices that go with a layout on Frame 2.

In addition, Fireworks assumes that designs in the Frames panel are button rollover states, "swap image" rollovers, or animation steps—not design variations for a web page! As such, when you export your Fireworks document as an HTML page, the page's graphics come from Frame 1, while interactive components like swap image rollovers will be drawn from subsequent frames. In addition, unless you build rollover buttons as button symbols, button rollover frames go in the first three or four frames in the Frames panel.

Habitat for Humanity® International

INTERNATIONAL PARTNERS PROGRAM

HOME

What's it like TO BE AN INTERNATIONAL PARTNER?

Meet the people INTERNATIONAL PARTNERS HELP

Get involved! BECOME AN INTERNATIONAL PARTNER

Figure 4-1 After building the page layout, crop important sections and save them as a separate document.

NOTE By contrast to Fireworks, in Photoshop you prepare button rollover states in different layers. For example, one layer contains the normal state, another layer contains the rollover state, and yet another layer contains the click state. When you import a Photoshop document that is prepared like this, you have to do some rearranging to make your buttons work. You must cut-and-paste the rollover state into Frame 2 and cut-and-paste the click state into Frame 3.

Finally, the optimization settings and links you apply to slice objects are also particular to the page's design. For instance, you wouldn't apply a JPEG setting to a slice object covering a text logo. Similarly, you wouldn't attach a link to the home page over a graphic that says "Click here to order." Throughout this chapter, we'll discuss strategies for designing and building one web page in Fireworks and how you can use that page as a master template for building similar pages and for building component pieces.

Modular Page Design

When you are ready to dig in and start building the final source art for a web site, as argued so far in this chapter, the key is to build one web page per Fireworks document. From this master layout, you'll crop and extract the various components you need and reassemble them in a web authoring tool like Dreamweaver.

Not only does reassembling pieces in Dreamweaver give you more flexibility to add other components like Flash movies, text, and interactive forms, but the strategy of cropping and saving constituent parts also allows you to take a modular approach to building the components of a web site. Such a modular approach streamlines your development workflow by allowing you to reuse the same graphics and code on multiple pages throughout the site.

This approach also saves users precious download time, because once they download a page with a bunch of graphics, the graphics are *cached* (saved in memory) by the browser. When a user goes to a new page that has the same graphics, the browser redraws the graphics from memory—a much faster process than downloading the graphics in the first place.

Cropping a Fireworks Document

Once you have built your web layout in a Fireworks document, how do you extract the component parts needed for Dreamweaver? The answer is to crop your master file down to one of the parts by using the Crop tool in the Tools panel:

1. Build a web page layout in a single Fireworks document, and save it as the master layout template. For this exercise, be sure that your layout contains a navigational section like the one shown in Figure 4-1.

2. Select the Crop tool in the Tools panel, and draw a selection around just the navigation portion of the layout, as shown in Figure 4-2. After you draw the selection, you can adjust the corner handles as needed to get the selection just right. Press RETURN or ENTER to crop the document.

3. Choose File | Save As, and give the document a new name, for example, **Navigation.png**.

IDEA Most people don't know that you can actually use the Crop tool to expand the Fireworks canvas size. To do so, draw a selection with the Crop tool around any portion of your document. Then grab the corner handles, and drag them into the gray space beyond the bounds of your document. Press RETURN or ENTER to automatically enlarge your canvas size.

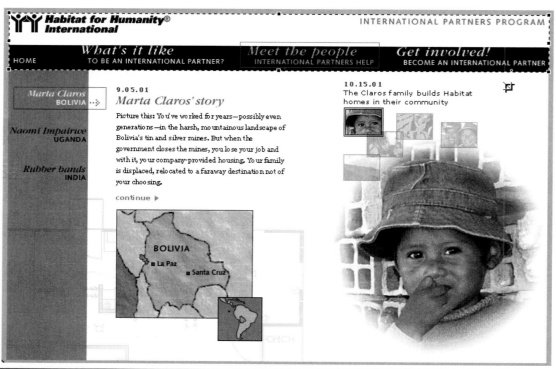

Figure 4-2   Drag the corner handles to adjust crop selection. Press ENTER or RETURN to crop.

Exporting Page Components as HTML

After you have cropped your Fireworks document down to a component area like a navigation bar, the next step is to export it as an HTML element that you can integrate into a Dreamweaver page.

1. To make this exercise a little more interesting, add a few hotspots over the buttons of your navigation bar, as shown here. Select the Hotspot tool at the bottom of the Tools panel and draw an area over each button.

2. To associate a link with each of the hotspots, open the Object panel. With the Pointer tool, select one of the hotspots. Enter a link for the hotspot in the Object panel, for example, **home.htm**.

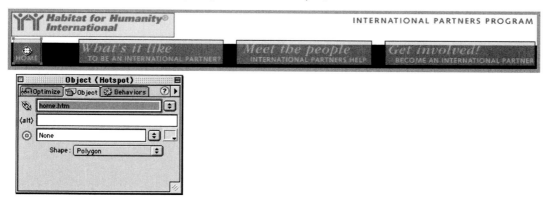

NOTE When entering links in the Object panel, be sure to include the correct path to the page you are linking to. For example, if the linked-to page resides in the same directory, you can simply enter the page's name, for instance, **Page1.htm**. If the page is buried within a folder, you must enter the folder's name followed by a slash and the page's name, for example, **folder/Page1.htm**. If the page resides on another web site, you must enter the full address, for example, **http://www.webpage.com**.

3. In the Optimize panel, choose the GIF setting. Choose as few colors as you can for your particular navigation bar. Usually, 128 colors give fair results for most images.

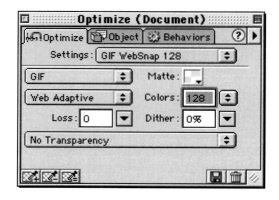

4. Choose File | Export. In the dialog box, choose HTML And Images from the Save As options, as shown in Figure 4-3. Name the file **nav.htm** and save it in a new project folder for this chapter—later in this chapter you'll insert this file into a Dreamweaver page. You may also want to create an Images folder within the project folder and have Fireworks automatically place the graphics for the nav bar inside the Images folder. To do so, check the Put Images In Sub Folder option at the bottom of the Export dialog box. When you check this option, if you have a folder called "Images," Fireworks will place graphics inside it automatically. If not, Fireworks will create an Images folder automatically.

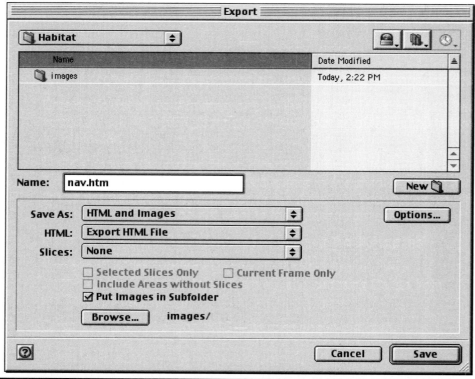

Figure 4-3 Export the design as "HTML and Images."

Though in this exercise you exported a static GIF with a few links, you could just have easily exported a fully sliced, interactive navigation bar complete with rollovers. We'll cover slicing for interactivity in depth in Chapter 11.

Importing Fireworks HTML into Dreamweaver

After you have exported a series of component elements, such as an interactive navigation bar, the final step is to reassemble the pieces in Dreamweaver.

CROSS REFERENCE ➔ The technique of integrating Fireworks HTML elements into Dreamweaver is covered in greater detail in Chapter 12.

1. Launch Dreamweaver and start a new web page. Feel free to make modifications to the page by changing its background color or adding a few text elements.

2. Click on the Insert Fireworks HTML icon on the Objects panel, as shown in Figure 4-4. A dialog box will appear asking you to locate an HTML file. Click the Browse button and locate the nav.htm file you created earlier in this chapter. Click Open to integrate the file into your Dreamweaver page.

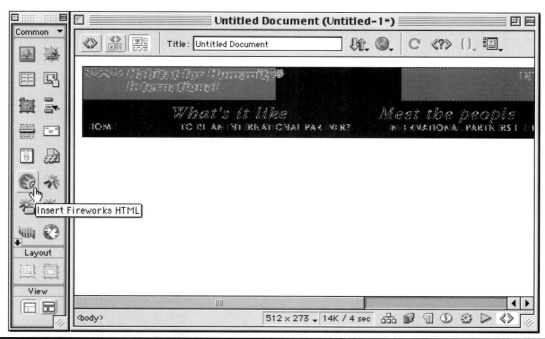

Figure 4-4   The Insert Fireworks HTML icon in the Object panel automatically integrates exported Fireworks HTML files into your Dreamweaver document.

Only Fireworks and Dreamweaver have such automatic integration of HTML pages. If you work with another web authoring tool like GoLive or FrontPage, you'll need to manually copy and paste the Fireworks HTML and JavaScript code into your GoLive or FrontPage web page.

What's interesting to note in this exercise is that by inserting Fireworks HTML into an existing Dreamweaver page, you are not duplicating any HTML tags. Dreamweaver automatically assimilates the Fireworks HTML into the host Dreamweaver page. This means that all of your Fireworks graphics, tables, links, and even JavaScript for rollover buttons are integrated correctly into the Dreamweaver page automatically.

For those of you who do not use Dreamweaver as your primary web authoring tool, you'll have to integrate Fireworks HTML components the old-fashioned way—the ol' copy-and-paste tactic. The danger with this approach is that you must be familiar enough with the way HTML and JavaScript work so that you know where to paste. For instance, if you are integrating a Fireworks element that has rollover buttons, you'll need to copy the rollover JavaScript function separately from the table that contains the graphics and paste it into the Head section of the web page.

Preparing Your Page Layout

Now you've gotten a workflow overview of building a master page in Fireworks and then exporting components of it such as the navigation area for reassembly in Dreamweaver. Next, we want to discuss the details of preparing the master page and its components for optimal output. What size should the page be? How can you use guides to plan your layout for maximum export efficiency? Furthermore, how can you better prepare the individual sections that you will export through slicing? In this part of the chapter, we'll explore such strategies for preparing your web page designs in Fireworks, and how to extract the pieces you'll need to build a final web page.

Sizing Your Web Page

The first consideration you'll make when building a new web page is what size to make the page. This size entirely depends on two things:

- The target monitor resolution for this web site
- Your export strategy for the page

Most people are familiar with the notion of designing a page to fit a certain monitor resolution. For example, if you expect that most users will access the site from 800×600 monitors, you'll start with a Fireworks canvas that is about 760×420 pixels (to account for the browser's interface hogging the screen). With this size set, you can design your master page layout to ensure that all the important elements fall within the viewable space of the page.

This is not to say, however, that you are locked in to these dimensions when you export HTML files. Remember that though you have designed the entire layout in these fixed dimensions, you will export only sections and pieces of the page. Once you export the sections, you can adjust them in Dreamweaver as needed, and even assemble them into a page that expands and contracts to fit the browser window.

In this example, we created a new 600-pixel-wide Fireworks document and designed the banner to look the way we wanted it to look in the final web page. Then we exported just the two graphic pieces and placed them into a percentage-width table in Dreamweaver (covered later in this chapter) that stretches to fit the width of the browser window. With this export approach, the 600-pixel-width of the initial Fireworks document is useful only to ensure that the design's proportions work well on smaller monitors (see Figure 4-5).

Figure 4-5   This page's banner stretches and contracts to fit as users resize their browser window.

Using Grids, Guides, and Rulers

As you design your page, it's difficult to just eyeball the alignment of elements in your layout. Fortunately, Fireworks offers a few tools to help you build a page with pixel-perfect precision: the grid, guides, and rulers.

The Grid

The grid feature in Fireworks displays a hatched square pattern on your canvas according to a pixel size that you specify. For instance, you can decide to make each square a 10-pixel increment. The grid feature is useful for applying consistent spacing between elements or to quickly draw elements to a correct size. To work with the grid, follow these simple steps:

1. Choose View | Grid | Show Grid. This turns on the default grid with distracting black lines spaced 36 pixels apart.

2. To adjust the grid, choose View | Grid | Edit Grid. As shown here, you can change the color from black to a lighter, less distracting tone, and change the pixel size of the grid. We find that setting the grid to 10×10 pixels is most useful. You can also choose the Snap To Grid option, which will make your elements jump to the grid lines—a function that can drive you nuts if you're trying to make something a custom size. When finished, click OK to return to your document.

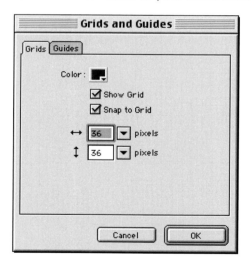

IDEA Once you configure the grid the way you'd like it to appear in all future documents, save the file as **Fireworks Default.png** in the Macromedia\Fireworks\Configuration\Presets folder.

3. To turn off the grid, choose View | Grid | Hide Grid. Remember, however, that even though you cannot see the grid, your elements will still snap to the grid's lines. To disable this, simply uncheck the View | Grid | Snap To Grid option.

Guides

What we find more useful than the grid are the guides. This is because you can use as many or as few guide lines as needed for a particular layout, and you can add and delete them at any time in your workflow. Guides are most useful for demarcating the sections of your layout that you plan to export as separate pieces. For example, if your page has three primary sections—a top navigation banner, a side navigation banner, and a content area in the middle—as illustrated in Figure 4-6, guides can help you isolate these areas.

Guides allow you to design various areas to work together effectively without interfering with each other. For instance, you don't want the graphics of one section overlapping with the graphics of another section, as shown in Figure 4-7. If they do, upon export, the graphic will be chopped in half, and it may be difficult to get the two pieces to match up later when you reassemble the sections in a web authoring tool.

To use guides in Fireworks, follow these steps:

1. To access guides, you first need to turn on the rulers. To do so, choose View | Rulers.

2. To add a horizontal guide, click on the top ruler and drag downward into your document. When you let go, you'll have a guide. To add a vertical guide, the process is the same, only you click-and-drag from the left side's ruler.

3. To delete a guide, reverse the process: click-and-drag a guide from your workspace back to the ruler area, and let go.

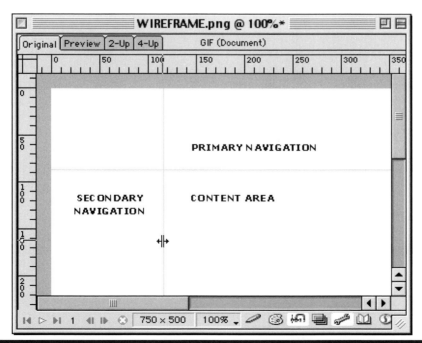

Figure 4-6   Guides can help you demarcate various export sections of your layout.

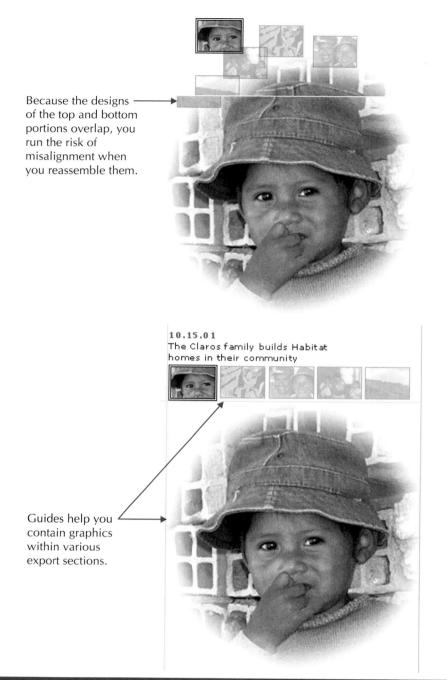

Because the designs of the top and bottom portions overlap, you run the risk of misalignment when you reassemble them.

10.15.01
The Claros family builds Habitat homes in their community

Guides help you contain graphics within various export sections.

Figure 4-7 Use guides to ensure graphics stay within their respective sections. Otherwise, portions of graphics may get cropped upon export.

As with the grid, you have the option of showing and hiding the guides by checking or unchecking the View | Guides | Show/Hide Guides option. You can also edit the color of your guides or turn on the Snap To Guides option all by accessing functions in the View | Guides menu.

Our favorite feature of the guides, however, is that you can double-click on them to enter a precise X or Y value for them. This is extremely useful, for instance, if you want to design a side navigation bar that is exactly 100 pixels wide. You could simply drag out a guide from the left ruler, double-click it, and enter a value of 100. Once the guide is in place, you can turn on the Lock Guides feature in the View | Guides menu so that you do not accidentally move it.

Rulers

The last pixel-precise tool to discuss is the ruler. Apart from their close association with guides (you must turn on the rulers in the View menu in order to gain access to the guides), rulers have one important function on their own: you can set the X and Y coordinates to start anywhere in the document. What does this mean, you ask?

Everything that you place in your Fireworks document is positioned on the page according to its X and Y coordinates. The X coordinate measures how far, in pixels, an image sits from the left edge of the document. The Y coordinate measures how far down, in pixels, the image is from the top edge of the document. The image's upper-left corner is what is measured. So, for example, if your image was placed at X = 0, Y = 0, it would be tucked perfectly up in the upper-left edge of the document.

NOTE Rulers always measure your document in pixels—even if you initially set up your document to be, say, 8×10 inches.

By default, the rulers start the coordinates X = 0, Y = 0 at the uppermost left edge of a document. You can change this starting point, however, to simulate the effect of the default margin a browser leaves around your web page. (Both Netscape and Internet Explorer leave about a 10-pixel margin around your web page unless you specifically adjust margin attributes to zero in the page's HTML code.) To change the ruler's X,Y starting point:

1. Drag a guide down from the top ruler, and drop it in your workspace. Then double-click it to set its position to **10** pixels from the top edge.

2. Drag a guide from the left ruler, and double-click it to set it to **10** pixels from the left edge.

3. To set the new starting point, click-and-drag the corner where the two rulers meet, as shown in Figure 4-8, into the workspace until it snaps to the two guides you've set. Your document's new X,Y coordinates of 0,0 will now start counting 10 pixels down and to the right of the document.

4. To reset the X,Y coordinates to start counting from the actual edge of your document, simply double-click on the corner where the rulers meet.

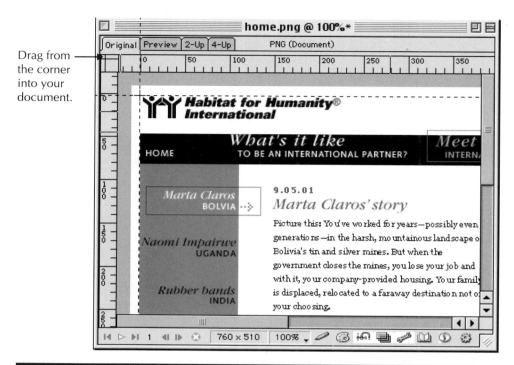

Drag from the corner into your document.

Figure 4-8 Drag the corner where the rulers meet into your document to reset the X,Y coordinate's 0,0 starting point.

Thinking in Pieces

If you build your Fireworks' web-page design anticipating how you will export various regions of it, then the final step of getting your full design out of Fireworks and into a polished, flexible web page will be relatively painless. So far, we've discussed planning a page like the Habitat page in Figure 4-9 with distinct sections. In this case, the page has a top nav section, a side nav section, and a two-column content area, all cordoned off by guides. But what's not defined is *how* we'll export each of these sections.

At this point, we need to start thinking in pieces. Starting with the side navigation bar, it's not enough to export the area as one solid graphic. Sure, we could add hotspot links over the three buttons. But to make the buttons have rollover behavior, we'll need to use the Slice tool to chop the navigation into pieces. The top navigation bar needs a similar treatment, but we also want it to stretch as users resize their browser window. Finally, we want to design the main content area as an empty, two-column table structure that we can easily fill with different text and images. This main content area, if you'll notice in Figure 4-9, also has a background image of a blueprint that overlaps into the side nav area. We'll need to prepare and extract this background element separately.

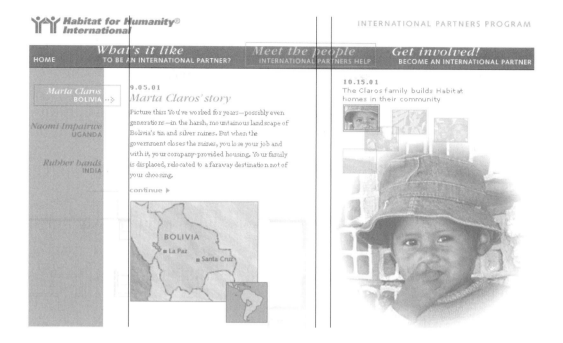

Notice the background blueprint image that covers both the side nav and the content areas.

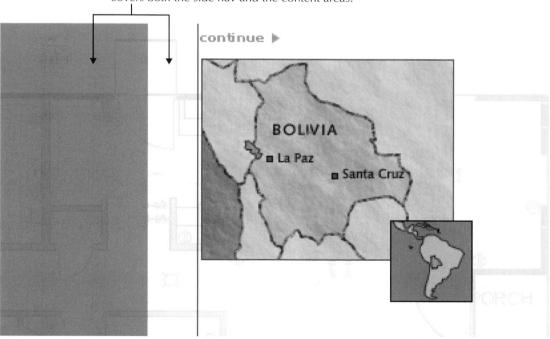

Figure 4-9   This Habitat page shows three major sections.

Slicing a Page

The Slice tool in the Tools panel is used to chop your layout into multiple, independent graphics. There are two reasons why you'd want to do this:

- Better image optimization
- Interactivity such as rollover buttons

In Chapter 2, you exported your whole web-page design as a single GIF image for the purposes of showing the client a design option. When you optimized the page, you chose a GIF setting with an adaptive palette of 256 colors. With such a "one size fits all" setting, the resulting graphic is huge in terms of file size, inefficient, and probably not the best quality. For example, some areas of the page that use photographic elements will appear grainy, while other areas that use two to three colors don't need a palette of 256 colors. By using the Slice tool, you can define independent regions of your layout, as shown in Figure 4-10, and apply a unique optimization setting that is appropriate for each area.

The other reason to use the Slice tool is to chop your layout into independent, interactive pieces like the set of rollover buttons in the Habitat side nav bar. In this case, you draw a slice over each button, as illustrated in Figure 4-11, and then apply a rollover behavior to the slice using the Behaviors palette. Of course, there's more to making a rollover button than simply slicing an area and applying a rollover behavior, but we'll discuss this further in Chapter 11.

Slicing allows us to apply a palette of just two colors to the area above the buttons.

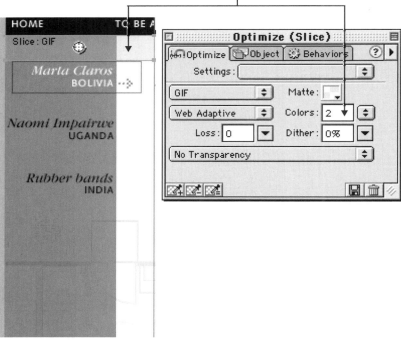

Figure 4-10   Each slice area can have a unique optimization setting.

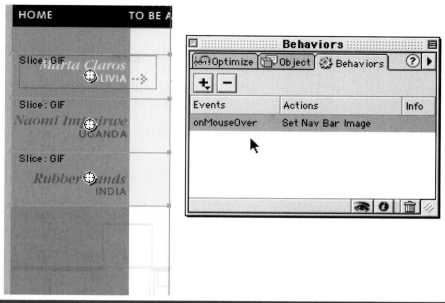

Figure 4-11   Slices are instrumental in building interactive, rollover buttons.

CROSS REFERENCE → Slicing and building interactive buttons is discussed in greater detail in Chapter 11.

We also want to point out that when you use the Slice tool, what you are really doing is chopping the page into a table structure. Each slice you make becomes a table cell when you export your Fireworks document as an HTML page. For this reason, we suggest that you align your slices so there are no weird staggered lines, as illustrated in Figure 4-12. Aligning your slices as in Figure 4-11 will generate a cleaner table structure and reduce the file size. In addition, never overlap your slices, as this will generate unexpected results when you export your page.

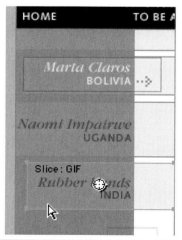

Figure 4-12   Such misaligned slices generate a more complex table and add to the page's file size.

IDEA To avoid overlap and help you align sliced objects, make sure that Snap To Guides is turned on in the View | Guides menu.

Now that the Habitat side navigation bar has been sliced, optimized, and assigned rollover behaviors, it is ready for export as an HTML page that we can integrate into a Dreamweaver page, as demonstrated earlier in this chapter.

Using the Export Area Tool

Our attention now shifts to the top navigation bar of the Habitat site. Like the side nav bar, it, too, needs slicing so that we can apply optimization settings and interactive behaviors. The trick of preparing this section, however, is that we want a top nav that expands and shrinks with the browser window. To accomplish this, we'll use the Export Area tool to export both individual graphics such as the Habitat for Humanity logo, and a set of sliced, interactive buttons. Here's how:

1. Select the Export Area tool. This tool is grouped with the Pointer tool. To access it, click and hold on the Pointer tool to reveal a pop-up set of tools. Select the tool that looks like a camera icon.

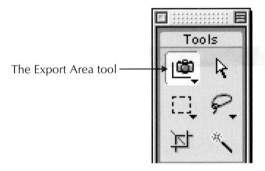

The Export Area tool

2. Draw a selection around a single graphic, such as the Habitat for Humanity logo. You can adjust the size of your export selection by moving the corner handles. To export the selected area, press RETURN or ENTER.

3. The Export Preview window will appear, where you can specify optimization settings for this graphic. Choose the GIF or JPEG format—whatever is appropriate for your particular image—and a number of colors or a quality setting, and click Export.

4. A second dialog box appears, the Export dialog box, where you can choose a Save As option. For a single graphic like the Habitat logo, we chose the Images Only option and clicked Save.

You can use this same technique to export a group of interactive slices such as the rollover buttons of the Habitat top nav bar:

1. With the Export Area tool, drag a selection around the group of slices, as illustrated in Figure 4-13, and press ENTER or RETURN.

2. Again, the Export Preview window appears, where you can set the default optimization settings. Note that if you have already assigned optimization settings to the sliced objects, settings entered here will *not* override them. Settings entered in the Preview window only apply to nonsliced areas included in the selected export area. Click the Export button to continue.

3. In the Export dialog box, this time choose HTML And Images from the Save As options. Name and save the file.

With both the interactive sliced nav bar and the logo exported from Fireworks, you are ready to build a top navigation bar in Dreamweaver that stretches as users resize their browser window.

CROSS REFERENCE → To integrate exported elements exported in Dreamweaver, don't miss this chapter's online lesson.

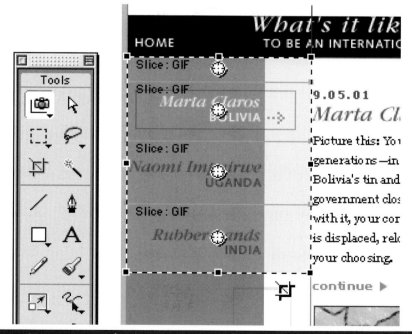

Figure 4-13   You can use the Export Area tool to export a sliced region of your layout.

Working with Background Tiles

Historically, background tiles have been used as the backdrop of an entire web page. They can also, however, be used as the background graphics for individual table cells. This latter method gives you a little more flexibility in your web page design, because each cell could have a different background tile. Either way, what's great about background tiles is that you can place text, graphics, and HTML elements on top of the tile for a layered effect.

The main content area of the Habitat web pages features a flexible two-column table structure that has a faded background image of a blueprint. To achieve this effect, we used the Export Area tool and the guides to export the blueprint image for the left column of the table structure, as shown in Figure 4-14. Because the nature of tiles is to repeat left to right and top to bottom, the key to this tile's success was to make sure we exported an area much longer than needed. Because the table cell's width was going to be fixed, we didn't have to worry about seeing the tile repeat left to right. But since the cell's length would vary with the amount of content, we needed a long tile that wouldn't repeat immediately.

design solution

Lisa Lopuck's personal web site at www.lopuck.com uses background tiles in table cells as the basis of her design, allowing her to gain a rich texture while maintaining text and graphical editability.

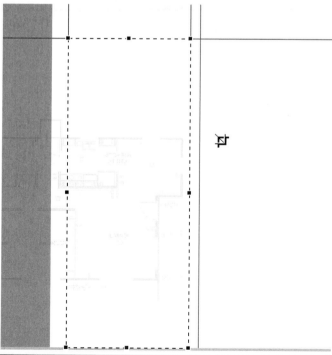

Figure 4-14 The background tile for the content area needed to be long enough that it didn't repeat unless the page was fairly long.

Remember, background tiles can be any size. They don't, for example, need to match the exact dimensions of the table cell where they will be used. If a 100×100 pixel tile goes in a 50×50 pixel table cell, you'll only see the first 50×50 pixels of the tile (starting from its upper-left corner). Whether you are building tiles for an entire web page or for an individual table cell, here are a few strategies to consider:

- **Larger than the page**   If the tile is larger than your web-page design, users won't see it repeat unless they do a lot of scrolling down or to the right. Large tiles like this are useful for complex designs that shouldn't repeat, such as the example in Figure 4-15. The downside to these tiles is that if you don't use a limited color palette, or simple flat-colored areas, the tile can be prohibitively large in file size.

- **A small tile that repeats down and across the page**   The most common tile you see on the Web is the smaller patterned tile that repeats continuously, often without a visible seam. Seamless tiles can be tricky to make; we recommend using Photoshop's Offset filter to help you work the seams out of a pattern.

- **Long, skinny tile that repeats down the page**   Another option is to create a long, skinny tile that repeats across the page in one direction, but the user would have to scroll to see it repeat in the other direction. For example, the rounded band effect of Figure 4-16 is achieved through a thin 5×1,500-pixel graphic.

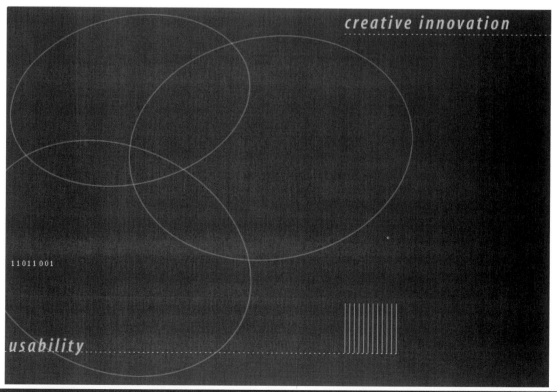

creative innovation

11011001

usability

Figure 4-15   This large tile will not repeat until way off screen.

Figure 4-16   This long, skinny tile repeats down the page to create an interesting band effect.

HAZARD If you use either large or long, thin tiles, make sure you make them big enough that people with large or high resolution monitors do not see the pattern repeat unless they scroll the page.

Simulating Background Tiles in Fireworks

If you plan on using a background tile in your web page, it's a good idea to simulate the tile in Fireworks so that you can get a better idea of how your design elements look when placed on top of the tile. Here's how to preview your tile in Fireworks and use the preview as a backdrop while you design:

1. In Fireworks, build a simple design that you can use as a tiled pattern. For instance, build an illustration of grapes, as shown here. Crop the file down to the size of your tile, and save it as a standard Fireworks PNG file. You can also use other types of files as patterns. Basically, any file type that Fireworks can read (that is, GIF, JPEG, TIF) can be a tile in Fireworks.

2. In your master layout document, make a new layer at the bottom of the stack in the Layers palette. (You may want to turn off the eye icons of the other layers so you don't get confused as you continue with this exercise.)

3. With the Rectangle tool, draw a square shape anywhere on the layer. Use the Info palette to size the rectangle to match the dimensions of your document, and enter an X,Y value of **0,0**.

4. In the Fill palette, choose the Pattern option from the pull-down menu. Your shape will immediately fill with one of the preset patterns that Fireworks offers. To change this, click on the pull-down list of patterns, scroll to the bottom, and select Other from the list. In the dialog box, point to the PNG file illustration you created in step 1 and click OK. You should now see your square shape fill with the pattern, as in Figure 4-17.

HAZARD When designing pages that will use background tiles, it is imperative that you simulate the tile in Fireworks and turn on View | Windows/Mac Gamma to make sure the tile design does not interfere with the legibility of the page. For instance, while the design may appear subtle in the Windows Gamma, it may have too much contrast when viewed in the Mac Gamma.

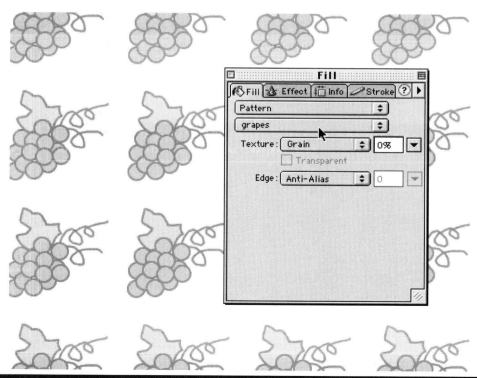

Figure 4-17   You can fill any vector shape with a custom pattern.

Building Better Tables with Fireworks and Dreamweaver

When you export an HTML page from Fireworks, you always end up with a fixed-width table structure. These types of table do not expand and contract as users size their browser window. Instead, the layout remains frozen in the upper-left corner of the browser window, and its dimensions are the same as your original Fireworks PNG file.

By working with Dreamweaver, you can convert these fixed-width Fireworks tables into percentage-width tables. A *percentage-width* table is one that stretches to fill the browser window. For instance, a table that has a 100 percent width will always span 100 percent of the browser's window, stretching to fit as the user resizes the browser.

In this lesson, you'll learn techniques for building better tables by using Fireworks and Dreamweaver together.

GO TO THE WEB! For a free, self-paced interactive version of this tutorial, which includes video demonstrations and source files, visit www.expertedge.com.

Starting in Fireworks

We start by opening the appropriate file:

1. In Fireworks, open the Nav1.png file included in this lesson's media folder. As you can see, this file includes a navigation bar that we have already sliced and optimized. To preview how this nav bar works, click on the Preview tab at the top of the Fireworks document window and roll over the logo and the buttons. Click on the Original tab to return to editing mode.

IDEA When previewing your work in the Preview mode, turn off the Web Layer. This will remove the red slice lines and overlays so you can better see your designs. To turn it off, either click on its eye icon in the Layers panel, or click on the right bottommost icon in the Tool panel.

2. Before exporting any file, you should always check the HTML preferences, because these affect the way your Fireworks tables are created. Choose File | HTML Setup. In the dialog box, leave the General settings as Dreamweaver HTML Style, and click on the Table tab. From the Space With options, choose Nested Tables – No Spacers. From the Contents option, choose None and click OK.

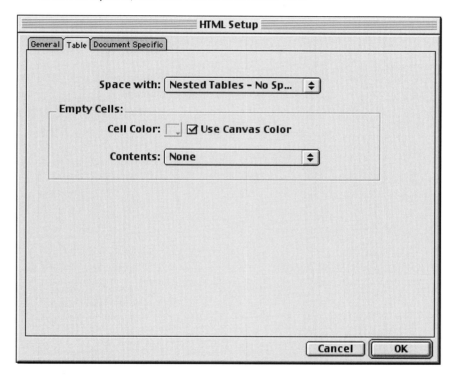

3. To export this nav file, choose File | Export. In the Export window, choose HTML And Images from the Save As options. Leave all other default settings for this option, but check Put Images In Subfolder. Name the file **nav.htm**.

While in the Export window, you can create a new project folder for this lesson. Navigate to a place on your computer where you'd like the new folder—the desktop is always a convenient option—and click the New button. Create a new folder called **Habitat** and within that folder, create another folder called **images**. After creating the folders, move back up a directory level so that you are saving the HTML file into the Habitat folder. Because you have checked the Put Images In Subfolder option, the graphics will automatically be placed inside your images folder, while the nav.htm file will go in the root of the Habitat folder. Now that you've set up your folders, click Save.

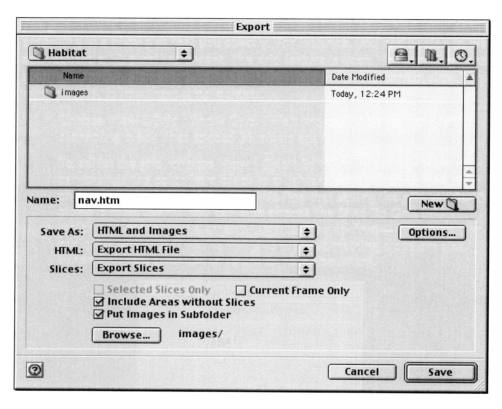

4. Open Dreamweaver and start a new project site by choosing Site | New Site. For Site Name, enter **Habitat**, and then show Dreamweaver where your Habitat project folder is by clicking on the folder icon next to the Local Root Folder text field. In the dialog box that appears, navigate to your Habitat folder and click Choose. Click OK to exit the Site Definition window.

Click the folder icon to browse to
your Habitat project folder.

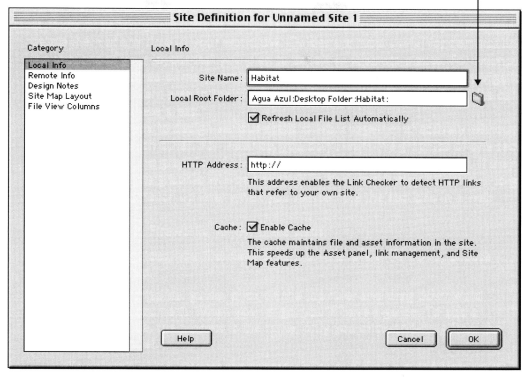

5. The next step is to open the Site window. If it is not already open,
choose Window | Site Files. In the second column of this window, you
should see a listing of files, including the nav.htm file you just exported
from Fireworks. Double-click nav.htm in the Site window to open it.

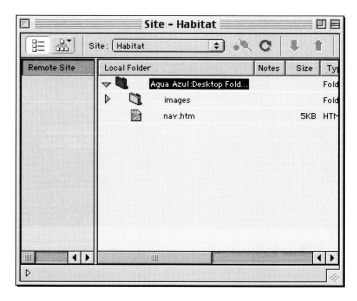

6. As of now, the nav bar consists of two tables nested, or placed, within one main table. To change the main table to become a percentage-based table, you must first select it. The easiest way to select the main table is to click on the `<body>` tag on the lower-left corner of the document window as shown next.

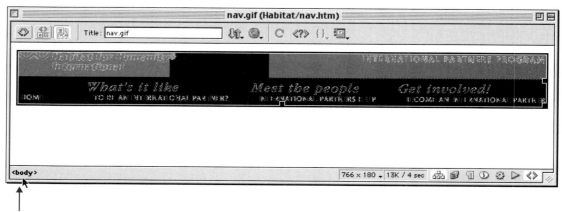

Select the main table with the tag selector.

7. Open the Properties panel by choosing Window | Properties. Here you can manipulate the settings of almost every object in your Dreamweaver layout, including tables. The main table is currently a fixed width of 750 pixels wide. In the pop-up menu, switch from Pixels to %, and enter **100** instead of 750.

Choose % from the pull-down menu and enter 100.

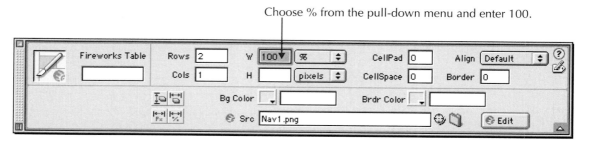

8. Change the width of the two tables within the main table. For this exercise, we'll just change the top table. To select the table, click on the upper-right "International Partners Program" graphic. By selecting this graphic within the top table, you'll see a new set of tags appear in the tag selector at the bottom left of the document window, as shown next. Click on the second `<table>` tag in the list. In the Properties panel, change its width (W) from 750 pixels to **100**%.

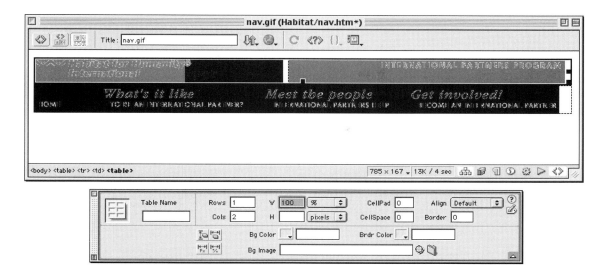

9. To make the "International Partners Program" graphic always be in the upper-right corner of the page as users resize their browser window, we must make its table cell right-justified. To select the cell, Mac users COMMAND-click, Windows users CTRL-click on the "International Partners Program" graphic. In the Properties panel pop-up menu, change the horizontal alignment (Horz) from Default to Right.

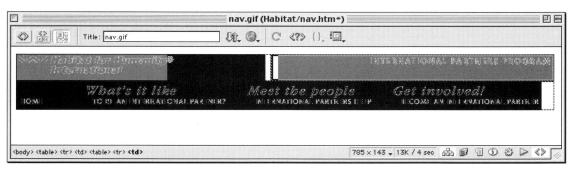

Choose Right from the Horz pull-down menu.

10. Now that this nav bar is a percentage-width table, there's one more detail to include before you test this file in a browser. The graphics in the bottom table are designed on a black strip. As you stretch the web page window wider than 750 pixels, you will see the black strip end. To compensate, we must include a background tile in the main table's

lower cell that matches this black strip. Click on the "Meet the people" graphic in the lower table. In the tag selector, click on the first `<td>` tag in the list; it should be the fourth tag from the left.

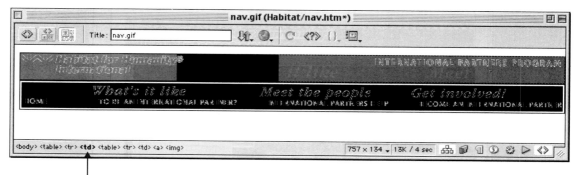

Click on the `<td>` tag.

11. In the Properties panel, click on the folder icon to the right of the Bg text field. In the dialog box that appears, locate nav_tile.gif, contained in this lesson's media folder, and click Open. By placing a matching black strip as the background tile for the lower table cell, you ensure that users will see a continuous design no matter how wide they stretch their browser window.

Click the folder icon to browse to nav_tile.gif.

12. To test your new percentage-width table in a browser, choose File | Preview in Browser | Internet Explorer (or Netscape, whichever one is listed).

5 Building Vector Graphics

Aside from Fireworks' robust interactive capabilities, such as the ability to export working HTML pages with JavaScript, Fireworks features a myriad of powerful tools that allow you to build complex vector illustrations from scratch. In fact, Fireworks' vector tools combined with the depth of color and effect options you have through the Fill, Stroke, Effect, and Object panels are so good that you will rarely need to use programs like Photoshop, Illustrator, or Freehand again to build your web graphics. Everything you need to build professional web graphics is contained neatly within the bounds of the Fireworks interface.

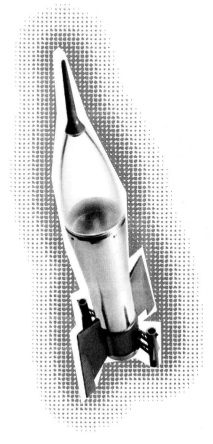

Hard to imagine, you say? Not if you consider that 90 percent of the graphics you see on most web sites are illustrated elements like textured background fields, tabbed buttons, and text—the kind of stuff easily created with Fireworks' vector tools. The remaining 10 percent of a site's graphics is photographic elements like pictures of people, products, and places.

In this chapter, we'll explore the power of Fireworks' vector drawing tools and how you use them in conjunction with the Fill, Stroke, Object, and Effect panels to build complex illustrations that look almost like photographs, such as the one in Figure 5-1. By the end of this chapter, even if you are the staunchest Photoshop, Illustrator, or Freehand fan, you'll consider defecting to Fireworks to use as your primary web graphics tool!

Fireworks' Vector Drawing Capabilities

While Fireworks allows you to create both vector and bitmap graphics from scratch, the program is fundamentally geared toward vector art creation. When you open a new file in Fireworks, the default mode is vector. All of the tools in the Tools panel, like the Rectangle, Pen, and even Brush tool, will produce vector shapes and paths. You must physically change modes in order to draw and edit bitmap graphics.

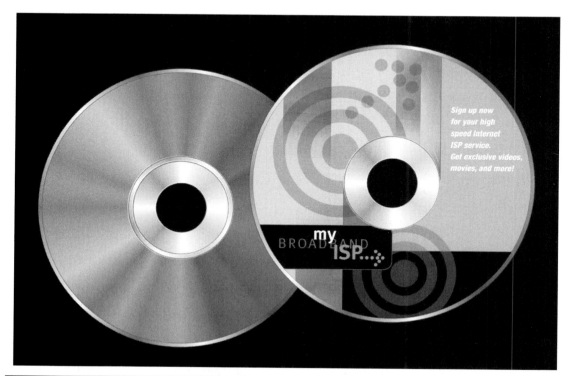

Figure 5-1   This CD illustration and packaging design was entirely built with Fireworks' vector tools.

If you are new to Fireworks but have been building web graphics for some time, it may sound counterintuitive to build your web graphics as vector illustrations. After all, as of this writing, most standard web graphic forms are bitmaps: GIF, JPEG, and PNG. The advantage to building all of your web graphics as vectors, however, is that you retain an unlimited amount of control over your designs *during the creative process.* For example, imagine building a rectangular button of a certain size, as shown here, only for the client to come back and request that the button have rounded corners and different proportions.

If the original button was a vector shape in Fireworks, the change is a simple two-step process accomplished in seconds:

1. In Fireworks, select the Rectangle tool and draw a simple shape in a new document. The size and color of the shape are not important for this exercise. Imagine now that this is the button that the client wants changed to a different size with rounded corners.

2. To change the size of this button, simply select the button with the Pointer tool, and then click-and-drag one of the blue corner handles to resize it.

3. To give the button rounded corners, open the Object panel from the Window menu and enter a number in the Roundness text field, or use the slider interface, as illustrated in Figure 5-2.

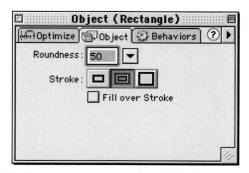

Figure 5-2   The vector button is quickly resized and has new rounded corners.

IDEA As you build your web page layouts in Fireworks, the more you can use vector graphics, the more design flexibility you'll retain for future client changes. Always save your master Fireworks PNG file—with all of its source vector graphics, layers, and frames—so that it's easy to access, make changes, and re-export.

A huge advantage to using vector shapes in your layout is that everything you draw becomes an individual object. With everything separate like this, it's easy to move objects around in your layout to fine-tune the design. You do not, for example, need to switch layers (as in Photoshop) to access and move each object. You simply grab any object in the workspace and move it—no matter what layer it's on. You can also control the stacking order of the objects you create. As you draw objects, they will stack on top of one another in the order you draw them. To move one object to be below or on top of another, your first select it and then choose Modify | Arrange | Send To Back or Front from the menu. You can also use Modify | Arrange | Bring Forward or Send Backward to move an object incrementally in the stacking order. Keep in mind that using the Modify | Arrange menu affects the objects contained in one Fireworks layer. If the object you are trying to arrange exists in a layer on top of another layer, the layer's stacking order supercedes. Elements in upper layers overlap elements in layers lower in the stack.

You can also change the stacking order of objects directly in the Layers panel itself. Each layer has a *turndown arrow* so that you can expand and collapse it to see what's inside. With the layer expanded, you can see the objects within. To reorder an object, simply drag its title to a new location in between two other objects in the layer. To reorder the layers themselves, drag the layer's title above or below another layer.

IDEA Another advantage to building your web graphics as vectors is that you can use the Find and Replace feature to automate changes throughout a file or a series of files.

Grouping Objects to Boost Productivity

The fact that every element is a separate object can sometimes be cumbersome. For example, if you build an illustration of grapes, as shown here, that is made up of multiple vector objects, moving the illustration means selecting each of the objects it contains, or you run the risk of leaving parts behind!

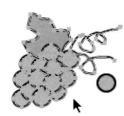

The worst scenario is if you want to change the opacity of an illustration. If you select each of the objects within the illustration and then change the opacity in the Layers palette, each *object* becomes semitransparent, as shown in Figure 5-3—not the illustration as a whole. To solve both of these problems, you must group the elements of an illustration by first selecting all of them and then choosing Modify | Group from the menu. Once grouped, the illustration acts as one object.

Building Vector Graphics

At first glance, the vector creation tools in the Tools panel seem rudimentary— providing only simple shapes like squares, circles, and lines. Creating a complex illustration like the CD image in Figure 5-1, however, requires using the vector tools in the Tools panel—the Pen, Line, Rectangle, Text, Pencil, and Brush tools—in *conjunction* with commands in the menu bar and a handful of panels like the Object and Layer panels. By coordinating these three elements—vector tools, menu commands, and panel options— you have virtually no limit to the complexity of things you can create.

Combining Multiple Shapes

The first key to drawing complex illustrations in Fireworks is understanding how you can combine simple shapes. For example, to create the donut shape of the CD, you draw two circles and use the Modify | Combine | Punch command. This command uses the shape of the smaller topmost circle to punch a hole in the underlying, larger

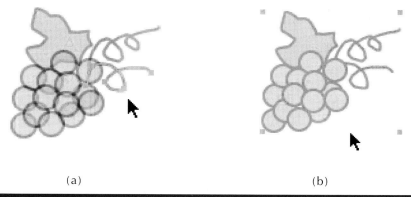

(a)   (b)

Figure 5-3   a) If an illustration is not grouped, changing the opacity affects each object individually. b) A grouped illustration acts as one object.

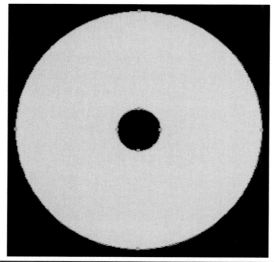

Figure 5-4   Use the Punch command to have one shape punch a hole in another shape.

circle, as shown in Figure 5-4. You should take some time to familiarize yourself with the other commands in the Modify | Combine menu:

- **Union**   This command combines two selected shapes into a new, single shape.
- **Intersect**   To use this command, first overlap two or more shapes. The area where all objects overlap each other will become the new shape after you choose Intersect.
- **Punch**   The Punch command uses one shape to punch a hole in another.
- **Crop**   If you have three overlapping objects, the topmost object becomes the window (crop area) through which you see the underlying objects.

As you become comfortable combining shapes with these commands, you can use these commands on shapes you've already modified. Once you get the shapes looking the way you like, you can use the Modify | Arrange | Send To Back and Front commands to stack the shapes. For example, to build the map shown in Figure 5-5, we used the Pen tool to draw the basic shape of each country and then used the Modify | Combine Punch, Union, and Intersect commands to make all the country and water shapes fit together. We then used the Modify | Arrange menu to ensure they overlapped one another properly. When finished, we grouped the illustration, cut it, and then pasted it inside a square shape, creating a mask group. Masking is covered later in this chapter.

Importing and Exporting Vector Illustrations

In addition to building vector graphics from scratch, you can also import vectors you created in other programs like Illustrator and Freehand. Conversely, you can export the vectors you create in Fireworks to other illustration programs.

This map illustration is composed of numerous odd shapes.

After finishing the map, we grouped it and pasted it inside another shape.

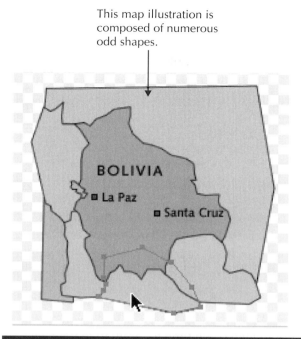

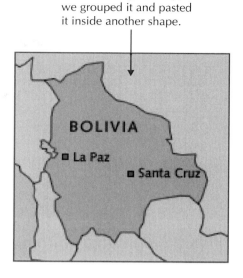

Figure 5-5 Use the Modify | Arrange and Modify | Combine menu commands to build a complex illustration of multiple shapes.

When you import vectors from Illustrator and Freehand, Fireworks retains their vector status. This is great news for building web pages that incorporate a company's existing branding. For example, most companies have their logo in some vector format. After importing a vector logo into Fireworks, you can easily resize it with the Scale tool to fit your layout without losing quality. You can also change the colors of the logo from their PMS or CMYK colors into web-safe equivalents by selecting individual shapes within the logo and applying a new color in the Fill panel. Here's how to import and export vector graphics from Fireworks:

- **Importing vectors** To import a vector from another program, simply choose File | Import from the menu. After locating the file in the dialog box, you'll see another dialog box asking you how you'd like to import the vector. We usually keep the default settings and click OK.

- **Exporting vectors** To export your Fireworks' vector illustration, choose File | Export from the menu. In the Export dialog box, choose "Illustrator 7" from the Save As options. (Ironically, Fireworks only exports to Illustrator, but you can open or import an Illustrator file in Freehand.)

IDEA In the Export window, you can also export your Fireworks document as a Photoshop layered file. To do so, choose Photoshop PSD from the Save As options. All of your Fireworks objects become separate layers. Grouped objects, however, become one layer.

HAZARD When exporting vector graphics from Fireworks, only the basic fill and stroke colors are retained. You cannot, for example, export a vector with a feathered edge, textures, and effects. These attributes will be ignored, and all you'll get is the basic shape.

Precise Sizing and Positioning with the Info Panel

As you draw vector shapes with Fireworks' tools, you'll find that it's not always good enough to just "eyeball it." Often times, you need to create buttons and other design elements that are an exact height and width and are located in a precise X,Y location onscreen. The Info panel offers you such pixel precision. You can use the Info panel to adjust any vector graphic in your Fireworks layout at any time in your workflow. To adjust a vector shape with the Info panel, follow these steps:

1. Select a vector object.

2. Enter new dimensions or a new X,Y location in the Info panel, and then press ENTER or RETURN.

Working with Color, Masks, and Effects

So far, we've discussed the process of using the vector tools in conjunction with menu commands to create complex illustrations. The final dimension, however, is to add color and effects by exploring the Fill, Stroke, Object, Layer, and Effects panels. Fireworks' Fill and Stroke panels offer an array of color effects and textures that can turn lifeless shapes into rich, almost bitmap-like images. The rest of this chapter addresses various techniques using these panels to build an illustration such as the CD design in Figure 5-1.

Applying Color with the Fill Panel

The two fundamental panels you'll use to color your vector graphics are the Fill and Stroke panels. By default, when you draw a vector graphic, it will have a solid color with no texture. To add a texture to the fill, simply choose one from the pop-up menu and choose a percentage, as shown in Figure 5-6. In addition, we've also selected the Transparency check box, so that you can see the black background color coming through. In this example, we are building a portion of the CD's packaging design. Selecting the fill texture is just the first step; we'll continue to apply additional effects.

The shape in Figure 5-6 is currently a simple rectangle. We can, however, use the Fill panel to adjust the image to have a soft, feathered edge instead. To do so, change the Edge option from Anti-Alias to Feather in the pop-up menu, and enter a feather amount, as in Figure 5-7.

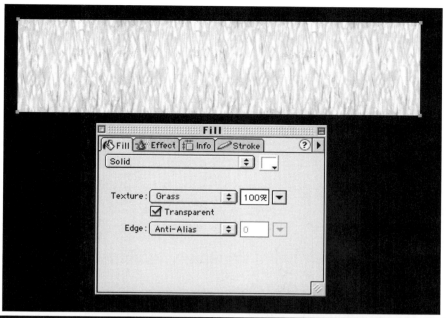

Figure 5-6 A solid yellow fill combined with a transparent "grass" texture applied produces a bitmap-like effect.

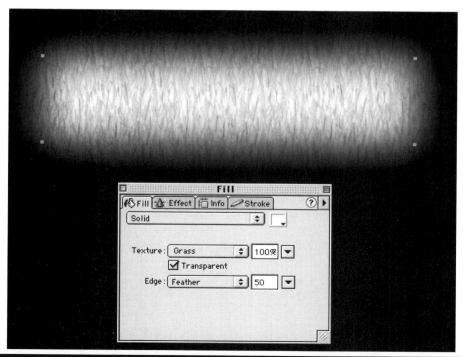

Figure 5-7 The Fill panel allows you to feather the edges of any vector object.

Building Gradients

The Fill panel also allows you to apply a custom gradient to a vector. For example, the CD illustration you've seen throughout this chapter is nothing more than a few vectors stacked on top of one another—each with a slightly different gradient fill. Take a look at the Layers panel in Figure 5-8. As you can see, the "donut" shape, created by using the Modify | Combine menu, is filled with a custom radial gradient. Each CD shape has a different gradient color scheme and has been rotated. By making each shape semitransparent, the composite effect produces an iridescent CD. To get some practice with fills, follow these steps:

1. Create a simple vector shape. For kicks, try creating a donut shape by creating two circles—a smaller one on top of a larger one—and using the Modify | Combine | Punch menu.

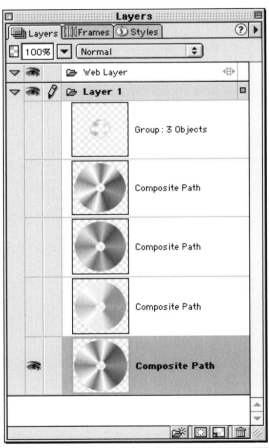

Figure 5-8   The Layers palette reveals multiple "donut" CD shapes filled with different gradients.

2. In the Fill panel, choose Cone from the pop-up menu, as shown here. For the color scheme, choose Pastels. Because this is will be a CD, make sure the texture option is set to **0** percent.

Choose a gradient style and color scheme.

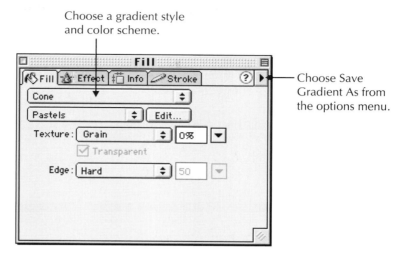

Choose Save Gradient As from the options menu.

3. To edit the colors of the gradient, click the Edit button next to "Pastels." A small window appears, where you can add, change, or remove colors. To add a color, click anywhere on the continuum, as shown here. To change this or any other color in the gradient, click on its color square. To remove a color, drag the color's square off the edge of the window. To accept your changes and close the gradient editor, click anywhere outside the small window.

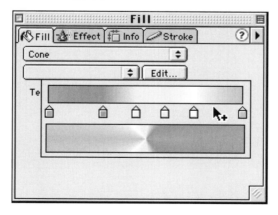

4. Once you've filled a shape with a gradient, you can adjust its direction by playing with the handles that appear on the shape. (To see the handles, either the Pointer or Paint Bucket tool must be selected in the Tools panel.) The circle end of the handle shows you the gradient's starting point. The square represents the ending point. For this exercise, leave the default handles as they are.

5. To save your custom gradient for later use, choose Save Gradient As from the Fill panel's options menu.

Web Dither Fill

Finally, it's also worth mentioning the Web Dither fill option included in the Fill panel. As discussed in Chapter 1, there are only 216 Web-safe colors that do not dither when viewed on various systems with 8-bit monitor displays. Increasingly, the Web-safe color palette is less of an issue, because newer systems are capable of displaying thousands, if not millions, of colors. In any event, there are times, however, when you want to ensure that particular colors—say your company's official colors—do not become altered or look dithered.

More than likely, it's difficult to find a Web-safe color that matches your company's color. This is where the Web Dither option comes in handy. The Web Dither fill is nothing more than a tiny pattern made up of two alternating Web-safe colors, as illustrated in the close-up in Figure 5-9. By visually mixing two colors together, you can simulate a much wider array of colors. To create a Web Dither fill, follow these steps:

1. Import or create a logo. Select the vector shape you want to fill, and then choose Web Dither from the Fill panel.

Figure 5-9   Zoomed in, you can see the pattern of alternating web-safe colors.

2. You'll immediately see a pattern of four colors, as shown here. Click on any of the four color swatches to change their color. Notice, however, that Fireworks only allows you to set two colors—not all four. The closer the two colors are in brightness and hue, the less you'll see the tiny pattern in your image.

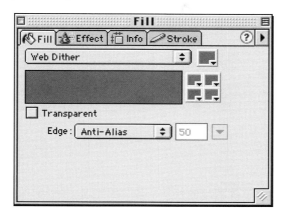

Using the Stroke Panel

Like the Fill panel, the Stroke panel offers an interesting array of bitmap-like effects. On the most basic level, you can apply a Pencil stroke with a soft edge like the one shown in Figure 5-10 around the nav button. If you are going for an interesting texture, however, you can try something like the Unnatural stroke set on Paint Splatter, as shown in Figure 5-11. This is the same vector we built earlier in the chapter—with the feathered, textured fill—now with a wild stroke.

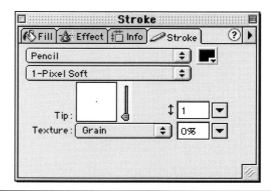

Figure 5-10   The nav buttons in the Habitat site use a simple, 1-pixel Pencil stroke with no fill.

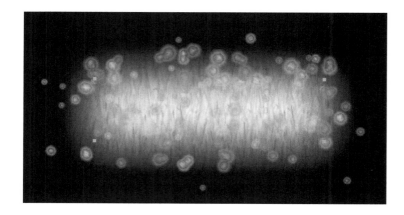

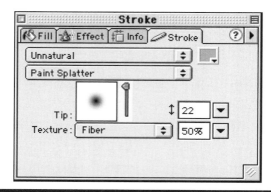

If you want to get really fancy, Fireworks allows you to create custom strokes by modifying the existing ones available in the pop-up menu. For example, to customize and save your own stroke, follow these steps:

1. Draw a shape with the Rectangle tool.

2. In the Stroke panel, choose Unnatural stroke from the top pop-up menu, and choose the Paint Splatter option. Adjust the size of the brush stroke as needed and, if you'd like, add a texture. Remember that to see the texture, you'll need to adjust its percentage.

3. Choose Edit Stroke from the Stroke panel's options menu. In the Edit Stroke window, shown in Figure 5-12, adjust the various settings until you see an effect you like in the lower preview window. Click OK to exit.

4. To save your new stroke, choose Save Stroke As from the Stroke panel's options menu. Name and save the stroke.

Once you apply a stroke to a vector graphic, you have a few choices when it comes to positioning the stroke. While an object (with a stroke) is selected, open the Object panel. There, you'll see a row of three icons, as shown here. By default, the

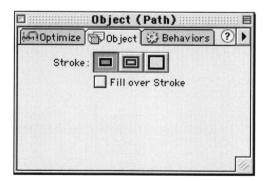

Figure 5-12 Edit an existing stroke in the Edit Stroke window.

central icon is selected. This centers the stroke on the outline of the vector. The left icon insets the stroke within the bounds of the vector's outline, and the right icon places the stroke outside of the vector's outline.

IDEA The Fireworks Brush tool is pressure-sensitive. This means that if you use a tablet, such as the Wacom tablet, instead of a mouse, you can draw strokes that vary in line thickness. The harder you press, the thicker the stroke. This pressure-sensitive effect is most dramatic when you use one of the natural media strokes such as the Crayon in the Stroke panel. Keep in mind, however, that not all strokes are pressure-sensitive (for example, the Pencil stroke).

Applying Masks, Effects, and Filters

Now that you know how to (1) create complex vector shapes by combining multiple shapes together with the Modify menu, and (2) apply bitmap-like colors and textures with the Stroke and Fill panels, there's one final frontier to explore: adding special effects. In this third frontier, we include applying masks, using filters, and applying effects in the Effects panel.

By understanding and utilizing all three of these frontiers, you can use Fireworks to build or draw virtually anything short of photographs. In this last section, we'll further explore the techniques used in the creation of the CD illustration featured throughout this chapter.

Object Masks

The packaging design of the CD illustration in Figure 5-1 is made possible entirely by the use of object masks. An *object mask* is a group of two or more objects where one of the objects acts as the window through which you see the other objects. For those of you familiar with Photoshop, object masks function much like Photoshop's clipping groups.

In the case of the CD illustration, a shape of the CD's interior masks the packaging design elements. If we did not use a mask, the packaging would spill outside the CD's shape. For example, here's a simplified demonstration of how masks were used to create the packaging design in the CD illustration:

1. Create a CD shape by using the Oval tool and the Modify | Combine menu. Don't worry about making the CD look real at this point. Next, create a second shape inset inside the CD that will confine the CD's packaging, as shown here. We'll call this shape the *clipping shape.*

2. With the Rectangle tool, create a simple shape. Use the Fill and Stroke panels to give the shape a highly textured, natural look. Position the shape on top of the clipping shape where you'd like it to appear, as shown here.

3. Choose Edit | Cut. Then select the clipping shape and choose Edit | Paste Inside. As shown here, this action creates a new mask group.

4. Once you've placed an image inside another with the Paste Inside command, you can reposition the pasted element within the mask by clicking and dragging on the central clover-like icon.

In the Layers panel, you'll now notice that the mask object has two thumbnails side by side—one for the image and one for its mask.

The inverse of choosing Paste Inside is Edit | Paste As Mask. In this operation, you cut the shape you want to act as the mask, then select the object and choose Paste As Mask. Another way to create a mask group is to select an object and then click on the Add Mask icon at the bottom of the Layers panel. This action also creates a secondary thumbnail in the Layers panel, but it will be empty. You'll see the braided border in your document that indicates you are in bitmap editing mode. Use the tools in the Tools panel to draw a mask that hides and shows the object. When you are through, you exit mask editing mode the same way you exit bitmap editing mode: by clicking on the red X at the bottom of the document window.

At any time, you can turn off the effects of the mask without deleting it. This is sometimes helpful in order to see the full object that is being masked. To do so, make sure the object is selected, and then choose Disable Mask from the Layers options menu, as shown in Figure 5-13. A red X will appear over the mask thumbnail. To turn the mask back on again, choose Enable Mask from the options menu.

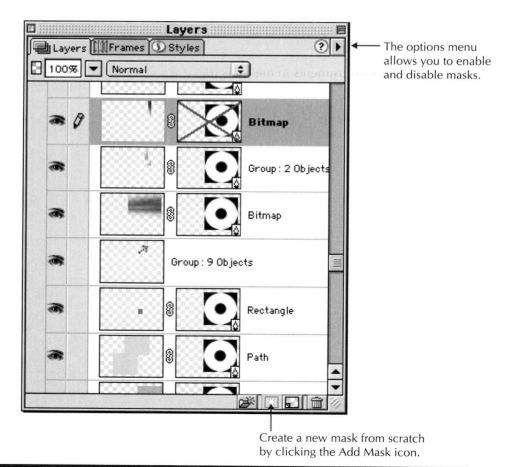

The options menu allows you to enable and disable masks.

Create a new mask from scratch by clicking the Add Mask icon.

Figure 5-13 You can disable masks in the Layers panel without discarding them.

Using the Layers Panel for Transparency and Ink Effects

Many of the effects in the CD's packaging design shown in Figure 5-14 are achieved through the use of transparency and ink effects called *blending modes*. Both ink effects and transparency controls are located in the Layers panel. To use these effects, simply select a bitmap or vector object, enter an opacity amount (or use the slider interface), and select a blending mode from the pull-down menu. To see the effects of your opacity and blending mode settings, however, there must be an object underneath.

The target-like design in Figure 5-14, for example, builds on everything we've discussed so far—using the Modify | Combine menu to create punched shapes and using masks to clip the design inside the CD—and goes a little further to include transparency and blending mode effects. Take a look at the target object selected in the Layers panel in Figure 5-15. At the top of the Layers panel, you'll see that the target object uses the Multiply blending mode and has been set to 39 percent opacity. The Multiply blending mode mixes the colors of the selected object with the underlying colors. In fact, it's a great mode for building realistic shadows.

Filters and Live Effects

To put the finishing touches on both bitmap and vector objects, Fireworks allows you to apply filters and effects through the Xtras menu and the Effect panel. Filters and color adjustments in the Xtras menu work only on bitmap objects. If you try to apply one of these Xtras to a vector object, you'll get a warning notice saying that

Figure 5-14   The target design uses masking, opacity, and blending mode effects.

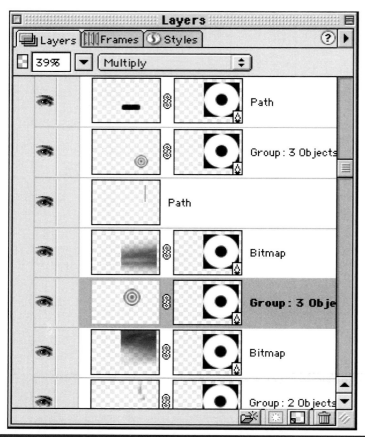

Figure 5-15 Use the functions at the top of the Layers panel to adjust an object's opacity and blending mode.

Fireworks will convert the vector into a bitmap. In addition, when you use the Xtras menu, the effect is permanent. By contrast, effects in the Effect panel are "live" attributes that you can turn on and off at will.

Because of these drawbacks to the Xtras menu, we find that we rarely use it. In addition, when you consider that the Effect panel offers all of the same filters and color adjustments that the Xtras menu has, there's even more reason to stick with the Effect panel.

 Using the Effect panel for color corrections and filters can slow down Fireworks' performance. If you plan on using these effects to correct images or add visual interest, make sure you give at least 50MB of memory to Fireworks.

The effects you'll most commonly use in the Effect panel are the bevel, emboss, and drop shadow effects. These are especially useful for creating interface elements that have visual dimension to them. To apply an effect, first select the object, and then choose an effect from the drop-down menu in the Effect panel. You can apply as many effects to an object as you like. To undo an effect, either uncheck its check box or drag it to the trash.

IDEA The stacking order of effects in the Effect panel is significant. You can achieve remarkably different looks by reordering the effects. To reorder them, simply drag them to different positions in the list.

One of the coolest features in Fireworks is the ability to import Photoshop 5 and other third-party plug-in filters and use them as live effects. (Fireworks does not support Photoshop 6 plug-ins.) Such extensibility gives you a dramatic range of creative options. After you import a set of third-party plug-ins, they will appear in both the Xtras menu and in the Effect panel. Here's how to import Photoshop plug-ins:

1. Choose Edit | Preferences from the menu.

2. In the Preferences window, choose Folders from the top pull-down menu, as shown here. Check the Photoshop Plug-Ins check box, and then click the Browse button to navigate to your plug-ins folder.

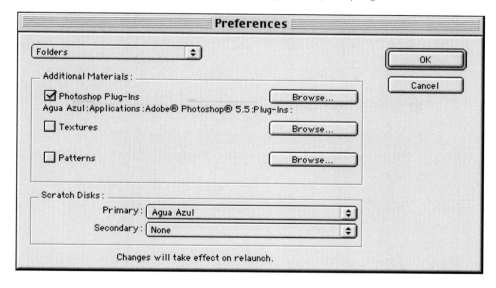

3. After you set the path of the folder, click OK to return to your document. Quit and restart Fireworks. Upon launch, you'll see your Photoshop plug-ins available in both the Xtras menu and the Effect panel.

 Online How-To

Building a CD Illustration

Throughout this chapter, you've seen the power of integrating Fireworks' vector tools with various menu commands and functions in the panels. In this lesson, you'll get a chance to apply all of the techniques discussed here and to re-create the CD illustration for yourself. You'll re-create the iridescent design of a CD by building up a few layers of vector graphics—each with a unique fill and stroke strategy. When you finish this lesson, save your CD so that you can build a packaging design for it in the next lesson.

GO TO THE WEB! For a free, self-paced interactive version of this tutorial, which includes video demonstrations and source files, visit www.expertedge.com.

1. Start a new Fireworks document that is 650×650 pixels, with a black background. Since this will be a web illustration, keep the resolution at 72 dpi. In the Tools panel, select the circle Shape tool and draw a perfect circle (by holding down the SHIFT key) that fills the document. Use the Info panel to resize the circle to exactly 564×564 pixels.

2. Draw another perfect circle, 102×102 pixels, on top of the first circle. To align the two circles so that one is centered inside the other, select them both and choose Modify | Align | Center Vertical from the menu. Follow this by choosing Modify | Align | Center Horizontal. While both circles are still selected, create the basic donut-hole CD shape by choosing Modify | Combine | Punch. This will cause the smaller hole to knock out of the first, leaving you with a single donut-shaped object. Your CD should look like this:

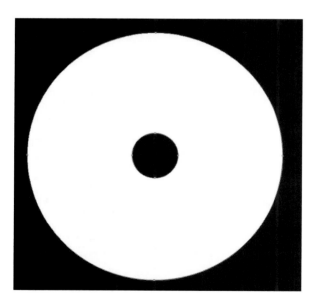

3. Next, change the CD's fill from solid to gradient. In the Fill panel, choose Cone from the pop-up menu. Then choose Silver from the set of color choices in the lower pop-up menu. The illustration should now look a little more like a CD. To brighten the silver effect, click on the Edit

button to adjust the gradient. In the gradient editor window, click on the two interior gray swatches and change their colors to white. Click outside the gradient editor to close the window.

4. This first CD shape you've created thus far will serve as the exterior rim of our final CD illustration. If you look at one of your music CDs, you'll see that every CD has a small translucent edge. You'll now create a second, smaller donut shape that will sit on top of the first shape. Because it will be smaller it will be inset, and you'll be able to see the original shape underneath.

Repeat steps 1–2 to create another perfect circle, this time 548×548 pixels. Create another circle as a "punch" shape; draw it the same size as before: 102×102. Align both circles to be centered to one another, and use the Modify | Combine | Punch command to create the second CD shape.

5. Now that you have two CD shapes, select them both and align them to be centered to one another. Select the topmost, smaller CD shape and in the Fill panel, change its fill from Solid to a Cone gradient. From the pop-up list of colors, choose the Pastels option.

6. Copy the pastel-filled CD shape and paste. The copy should paste directly on top of the original. While the copy is selected, change its gradient from Pastel to Silver in the Fill panel. This time, leave the dingy gray colors in the gradient.

7. Adjust the direction of the top-most Silver gradient by grabbing the square icon on the right end of the gradient line, as shown here, and dragging downward to the 4 o'clock position.

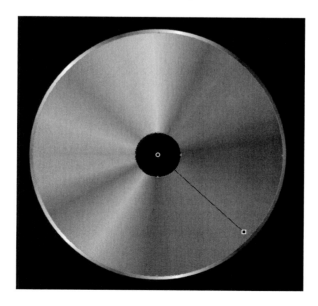

8. Next, in the Layers panel, adjust the shape's opacity to 80 percent and choose the Darken blending mode from the pop-up list. These settings allow the Pastel CD shape underneath to show through.

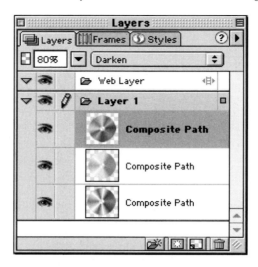

9. Copy the top-most shape and paste. Now, adjust the gradient line by dragging the square end back to the 3 o'clock position. In the Fill panel, adjust the Silver gradient by clicking on the Edit button. Again, change the dingy interior gray swatches to white. In the Stroke panel, choose Pencil and 1-Pixel Soft from the pull-down menus. Choose a dark gray color—almost black.

IDEA Rather than re-applying the Silver gradient and adjusting its colors each time you use it on a shape, you can save your modified gradient as a custom gradient in the Fill panel. Another option is to simply copy the shape with the modified gradient, select a new shape, and choose Edit | Paste Attributes from the menu. This pastes the object's color settings only.

10. Now that the body of the CD is built, the next step is to build the central portion. Create another donut shape for the center. Create a circle that is 209×209 pixels and a "punch" circle that is 102×102 pixels. Align the two circles and choose Modify | Combine | Punch from the menu. In the Fill panel, choose a Cone gradient with the Silver colors. Click the Edit button to lighten the gradient color scheme. Set white as the central and two outside color swatches. Set the two colors in between as light gray. In the Stroke panel, choose a 1-pixel, soft Pencil stroke, white in color.

11. To create a small ring inside the central shape, create another circle that is 206×206 pixels. Set its fill to None, and choose a 1-pixel, soft Pencil stroke, dark gray in color—almost black. Select the circle and the central shape and use the Align function to center them to one another.

12. For the finishing touches, create a smaller edition of the central shape. Make a circle that is 188×188 pixels. Again, make a "punch" shape that is 102×102 and use it to punch out a circle in the middle of the previous shape. Fill this final CD shape with the same lightened Silver gradation that you created for the shape in Step 9. Give this shape a 1-pixel, soft Pencil Stroke, dark gray in color, and center it on the main illustration.

13. Copy this final shape and paste. While the pasted shape is selected, set its fill color to None and change its Stroke color to white. Use the Arrow keys on your keyboard to move the shape one pixel up and one pixel to the left. In the Info panel, resize the shape to 190×190 pixels.

14. Congratulations! You've just created a CD illustration like the one shown here. Choose Edit | Select All and then Modify | Group from the menu to group the illustration into one easy-to-handle unit. You're now ready to build any kind of packaging design you'd like!

Fireworks in the Real World

Illustrating with Fireworks

By Stephen Voisey

Although Fireworks' cachet has always been its optimizations and export simplicity, I'm dismayed that so many web designers leave it at that. Even Macromedia's own showcases fail to pick up on Fireworks' creative potential, preferring to concentrate on its productivity benefits. But Fireworks' ability to translate your creative ideas into web reality is where its true worth begins to shine.

When I picked up Fireworks several years ago, I found it awkward and frustrating at first. Like many web designers, I was not familiar with either Illustrator or Freehand. However, moving from bitmaps to vector-based graphics changed the way I designed, and I soon realized it made things simpler and quicker than ever.

Figure 5-16 shows a recent extranet project for my company. It shows the login page, where users are prompted for a company name and password before

Figure 5-16 The completed login interface features a few different Fireworks illustrations.

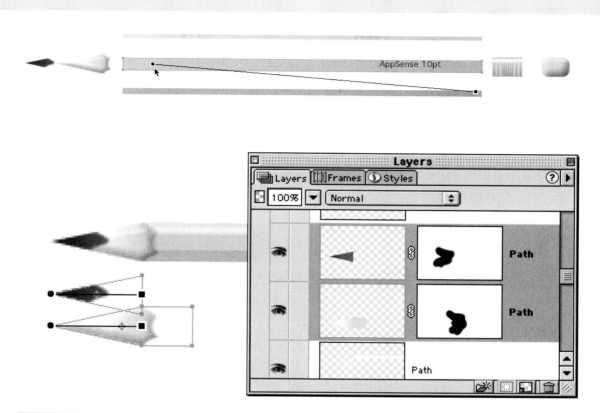

Figure 5-17 The pencil illustration is made up of different vector shapes with unique fill and stroke patterns.

proceeding. Naturally, it all started and ended with Fireworks. The pencil was an easy object to create, primarily because it is nice and straight. Getting the shapes right is the easy part; with vector tools it's simple to draw the various parts and tweak them until you are happy. To build the pencil, I used the Rectangle, Rounded Rectangle, and Polygon tools (see Figure 5-17).

The process of making it look realistic begins by applying gradient fills to the different parts of the pencil. I don't use harsh gradients—just enough color blend to give an initial impression of some lighting. I then add some texture. Subtlety is the key. It's important to not go overboard when applying texture. Often, I replicate the same element to apply another texture, and then adjust the opacity to fade it into the original. Because of Fireworks' live fills, it's easy to play until you find the right texture.

Next, I add little touches with the Line, Bezier, and Brush tools. For example, the notches in the metal that holds the eraser were added in this way. The eraser itself was created with an inner bevel live effect on a rounded rectangle. To create the shine on the pencil, I drew a simple path and used a light airbrush stroke.

To finish the end of the pencil and make the graphite merge seamlessly into the wood, I created two triangles. One sits on top of the other—one has the wood color, and the one on top has the graphite color. I then applied the mask to the graphite triangle and airbrushed out the right edge of the graphite until it looked right. Using masks this way is extremely effective because you can make changes and undo the airbrush until you get it right.

I created the coffee mug in a similar way, although the cup's round shape makes it more of a challenge. And I spent a long time staring inside a real mug of coffee to get the lighting right! I used the Punch and Union tools (in the Modify | Combine menu) extensively to create arcs, circle outlines, and different shapes for pieces like the handle.

Unlike the pencil, however, the cream swirling in the coffee was done in Photoshop. I created the initial circle in Fireworks, pasted it into Photoshop, applied the twirl effect to some white airbrushing, and pasted it back into Fireworks. Don't be afraid to use a combination of tools to achieve the results you require.

I always save the objects as separate files, never part of a whole layout. When you do finally want to integrate them into a layout design, I don't recommend grouping the different elements of an object together. Instead, I convert each object into a bitmap, as this prevents the textures and effects from messing up when you rotate or scale your objects, and makes them easier to handle.

Even 3-D illustrations are achievable, although more complex. The paintbrush and glass of water shown here were created using the same techniques and tools as previously discussed: opacity, masks, and the Punch and Union tools.

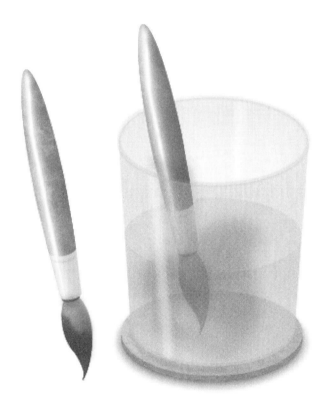

Once you master these techniques, you'll be surprised at how quickly you can build things. The paintbrush and glass of water illustration took only about two hours to build from scratch (which is just as well since it never made it into the final design!). So, to get some practice, why not pick up something off your desk and have a go?

6 Working with Bitmap Graphics

While Fireworks is not as powerful as Photoshop when it comes to editing and creating bitmaps, it has a number of tools to handle the most common tasks like creating soft montages, adjusting color, and using filters to stylize an image. As discussed in Chapter 5, you can create 90 percent of your web graphics with Fireworks' powerful vector tools. In addition, Fireworks readily handles the remaining 10 percent of graphics that are more photographic in nature.

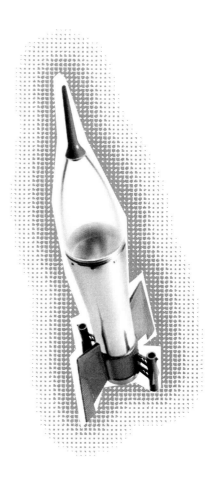

The true magic of Fireworks as a web graphics tool is its ability to handle both vector and bitmap graphics. This combination of both vector and bitmap creation and editing tools in one package makes Fireworks our favorite web graphics tool. In this chapter, we'll take an in-depth look at Fireworks' bitmap creation and editing tools and techniques. Then we'll discuss how you can integrate Fireworks with other graphics software like Photoshop.

Fireworks' Bitmap Drawing and Editing Capabilities

Though Fireworks is heavily skewed toward the creation and manipulation of vector-based web graphics, Fireworks does offer some basic bitmap creation and editing tools. Mostly, you'll work with imported bitmap images such as scans, stock photography, and Photoshop files. You can also, however, create bitmaps from scratch by choosing Insert | Empty Bitmap from the menu. Once you do, you'll see a blue border appear around your document indicating that you're in Bitmap mode. To edit an imported bitmap, simply double-click the image with the Pointer tool to enter Bitmap mode.

In Bitmap mode, all of the tools in the Tools panel will produce or edit *one* bitmap graphic at a time. When you are finished editing the bitmap, you must exit Bitmap mode by clicking on the red X at the bottom of the document window, as shown in Figure 6-1, or by choosing Modify | Exit Bitmap Mode from the menu.

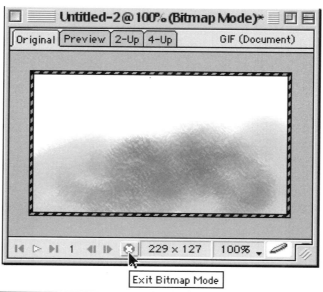

Figure 6-1   Exit bitmap editing mode by clicking the red X at the bottom of your document window.

Once you exit Bitmap mode, the bitmap you created or edited is considered a single object. You can select and move it around in your layout just like any other object and can even use the Modify | Arrange | Send To Back or Front commands in the menu to position it above or below other elements in your layout, just as you do with vector objects.

 When editing an image in Bitmap mode, the order that you draw objects is also their permanent stacking order. You cannot, for example, use the Modify | Arrange | Send To Back or Front commands to rearrange the stacking order of your elements once you've drawn them.

It's important to note that the tools in the Fireworks Tools panel are context sensitive. When you are in Bitmap mode, the Rectangle tool will produce a bitmap—of which you cannot change the size and color once it's drawn. When in the normal, vector mode, the same Rectangle tool will produce a malleable vector shape that you can resize and recolor at will. There are, however, a few tools in the Tools panel that only work on bitmap graphics: the Selection tools. The Selection tools include the Marquee, Lasso, and Magic Wand tools:

The Selection tools——→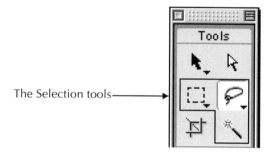

If you try to use one of the Selection tools on a vector object, you will get an error message. The Selection tools exist only for the manipulation of bitmap images. We'll discuss the Selection tools more in depth later in this chapter.

Working with Imported Bitmap Graphics

While you can create a bitmap graphic from scratch in Fireworks, we do not recommend it. This is because anything that you create as a bitmap can just as easily be created as a vector. The only reason you may consider building a bitmap illustration is if you are "painting" an illustration such as the one in Figure 6-2. In this case, if all of the strokes are vectors, you'll end up with hundreds of tiny vector objects that will bloat the source PNG's file size, slowing down Fireworks' performance. This illustration, therefore, is probably better off if you build it as a single bitmap object, as in Figure 6-3. Other than a situation like this painting, we recommend building all of your Fireworks graphics as vectors, and using the bitmap tools mainly for editing imported bitmaps like photographs, scans, or Photoshop layered files.

Figure 6-2   This illustration comprises hundreds of vector strokes.

When you import an existing bitmap image like a stock photo or a scan, Fireworks treats it as a single object. When you import a Photoshop layered file, its layers will become individual bitmap objects stacked on one another in one Fireworks layer.

Figure 6-3   A painting like this is much simpler as a single bitmap illustration.

Once imported, these bitmap objects can be moved, restacked using the Modify | Arrange | Send To Back / Front menu commands, or edited with Fireworks' bitmap tools. Here's how to integrate existing bitmaps into your layout:

1. To open a bitmap graphic, simply choose File | Open and locate the file.

2. To import a bitmap as another object in your layout, choose File | Import. After you locate the file, your cursor will look like a corner icon. Click once to place the file in your layout.

IDEA You can control the scale of graphics you import into Fireworks. After you choose File | Import and locate the file, your cursor will become a corner icon. Instead of clicking once to place the file, click-and-drag a box to dynamically scale the file to your specifications.

It's interesting to note that when you import a Photoshop layered file, Fireworks will retain all text elements as live, editable text. (Note, however, that Fireworks will not import live text from Photoshop 6. The text will become a bitmap.) To edit an imported text element, simply double-click on it to access the Text Editor window. In addition, all Photoshop layer effects like bevel and drop shadow become live effects in the Fireworks Effects panel. This saves a tremendous amount of time when working with a team of designers who all prefer different graphic tools.

After importing a bitmap graphic, or a series of bitmaps as in the case of a Photoshop layered file, you can resize it, crop it, erase parts of it, feather its edges, adjust its color with the traditional Levels and Curves tools (just as in Photoshop), apply filters, and even use an image as a mask. Here's a quick overview of these editing techniques.

Resizing, Rotating, and Distorting Bitmaps

The most common task you'll perform on both bitmap and vector graphics is resizing them to fit your layout. To quickly resize an object, first select it with the Pointer tool. Then click-and-drag one of the corner blue dots—inward to scale down, outward to scale up. Hold down the SHIFT key to constrain proportions. You can also select the object and then click on the Scale tool in the Tools panel. Using the Scale tool gives you access to features such as rotation and skewing, and exact pixel or percentage scaling. To access these added commands, choose them from the Modify | Transform menu.

 Avoid enlarging bitmap graphics. If you scale up a bitmap, effectively what you are doing is stretching the existing pixels. Fireworks has to fill in the gaps with colors it thinks match. The net effect is an image that looks blurred and chunky.

Cropping a Bitmap Object

Another common task is cropping an imported bitmap. Keep in mind that cropping a *bitmap object* in your layout is an entirely different operation than cropping your *whole document* with the Crop tool!

1. To crop an individual bitmap graphic, first double-click it with the Pointer tool. (This action takes you into Bitmap mode and tells Fireworks which bitmap you want to edit.)

2. Select the Marquee tool in the Tools panel, and draw a selection around the area you want to keep.

3. Choose Edit | Crop Selected Bitmap from the menu. Handles will appear around your graphic. Press ENTER or RETURN to crop.

Erasing and Deleting Parts of a Bitmap

After importing a bitmap image, you'll often need to select and delete parts of it or use the Eraser tool to blast away unwanted pixels. For example, a lot of clip art comes on a white background, as shown in Figure 6-4, which must be removed before you can integrate the image into your design properly.

Figure 6-4   The white background on this stock photo image must be removed before we can integrate it into the layout.

To get rid of the white area surrounding the image, use the Magic Wand tool in conjunction with a few panel and menu options:

1. Double-click on the Magic Wand tool in the Tools panel. The Options panel will open in your workspace. In the Tool Options panel, adjust the tolerance level to **32**, and choose Anti-Alias from the pull-down menu.

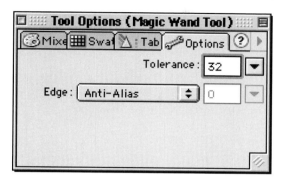

2. Click on the white space surrounding the image to select it.

3. In some cases, you may need to expand the selection by 1 pixel to ensure that you do not include any of the white, anti-aliased pixels around an image. If any of these pixels were left behind with the image, you'd see a thin white halo around the image. To expand the selection, choose Modify | Marquee | Expand and enter a value of **1** pixel. Expanding the selection will grow it so that it creeps slightly into the image.

4. Press BACKSPACE or DELETE to delete the white area surrounding the image.

5. Click on the red X icon at the bottom of the document window to exit bitmap editing mode. You can now place the image in your layout, as shown here.

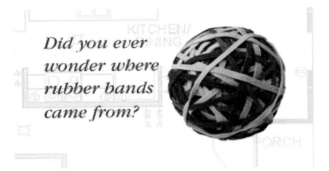

In addition to selecting and deleting parts of an image, you can also use the Eraser tool in the Tools panel to get rid of unwanted pixels. The Eraser tool works just like a brush in that you can control the size and softness of the Eraser's tip. To access the Eraser tool, you must first be in Bitmap mode by double-clicking on a bitmap image. In the Tools panel, the Knife tool changes to become the Eraser tool. As with the Magic Wand tool, to adjust the Eraser's settings, double-click it in the Tools panel to reveal the Options panel. Make your adjustments before you start using the Eraser on an image.

Feathering an Image's Edges

On the Habitat for Humanity web site we have showcased throughout this book, you may have noticed the collection of photographs in the right column of the interface. These photos all have a soft, feathered edge. To achieve this effect, follow these steps:

1. Import an image into your layout. If you are using guides to help you cordon off sections of your layout for export, size your image to fit nicely within the allocated area.

2. With the Marquee tool, draw a selection around the image, as shown in Figure 6-5, being careful to leave at least 15 pixels from the edge of the guides. This selection represents the area of the image you will keep, so make sure you create the selection accordingly. You will feather the selection a radius of 15 pixels, so we want to make sure that the final feathered image fits within the guides.

3. To soften the edges of this photo, you must first feather the selection. Choose Modify | Marquee | Feather, enter a radius of **15** pixels, and click OK.

11.15.00
Rubber bands
Kerala, India

Did you ever wonder where rubber bands come from? Me neither. But this week, I found out.

Nestled in the hills of Kerala in southwest India and, coincidentally, next to a Habitat for Humanity office, is a rubber band factory. As we drove up, I wondered what the heck this place was. It looked like an endless sea of long, plastic tubes in every color of the rainbow. I had seen pictures of this place before, but had no clue what it was.

continue ▶

Did you ever wonder where rubber bands came from?

11.15.00
Insert caption here.

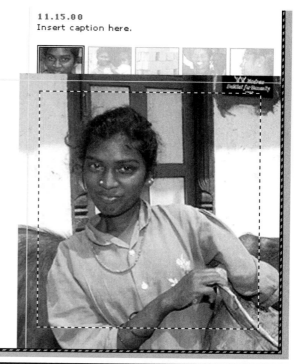

Figure 6-5   Draw a selection around the area you want to keep.

4. Select Modify | Marquee | Select Inverse from the menu. This selects the border area around your image so that you can delete it.

5. At this point, you can either turn the selection into a mask, or you can delete the selected area. Either way, you'll get the same effect. To turn the selection into a mask, click on the Add Mask icon at the bottom of the Layers panel. To delete the selected area, press BACKSPACE or DELETE. Both methods leave a soft, feathered image like in Figure 6-6. The advantage of using a mask, however, is that it gives you greater flexibility. At any time you can modify or remove the mask to restore your original image. Exit bitmap editing mode by clicking on the red X at the bottom of the document window.

Adjusting Color Balance and Colorizing Images

Fireworks has many of the same color adjustment tools as Photoshop. For example, you can adjust an image's Levels, Curves, and Hue/Saturation all through the Xtras | Adjust Color menu. When using the Xtras menu to adjust an image's color, you are applying permanent changes. Fireworks, however, does give you the ability to apply these color adjustments as "live" effects in the Effect panel. By "live," we mean that

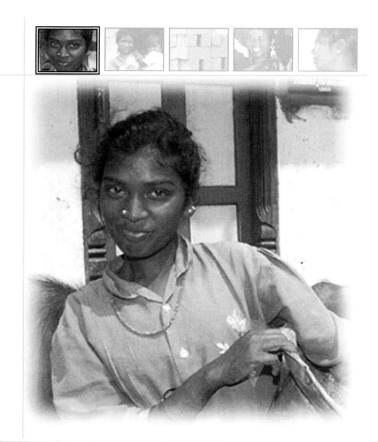

Figure 6-6   The final, feathered image

the effect is treated as an attribute that can be turned on or off at the click of a check box. For example, to colorize an image into a monotone scheme, follow these steps:

1. Select an image with the Pointer tool.

2. In the Effect panel, choose Adjust Color | Hue/Saturation from the pull-down menu.

3. In the dialog box, select the Colorize check box. Then slide the Hue slider to find the right color scheme, as shown here. Click OK.

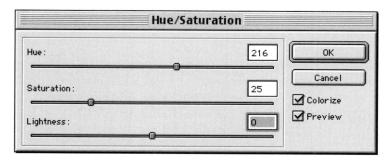

After completing these steps, you'll see the Hue / Saturation effect listed in the Effect panel. You can add as many effects as you want to each bitmap or to a vector object by selecting additional effects from the pull-down menu.

IDEA You can also colorize bitmap and vector objects by choosing a blending mode in the Layers panel. For example, try choosing the Color, Multiply, or Luminosity options in the Blending mode pull-down menu (at the top of the Layers panel).

Applying Filter Effects

Similar to the process of applying color adjustments to an image, you can apply a filter effect to an image by selecting it from the Xtras menu or by choosing it in the Effect panel. The Effect panel is a handy way to adjust images because the effects are nonpermanent. You can add and remove as many effects and filters as you like at the click of the mouse (see Figure 6-7). Interestingly, in addition to the normal Fireworks lineup of filters and effects, you can import and use Photoshop 5 filters in Fireworks—and even apply them as nonpermanent live effects in the Effect panel!

CROSS REFERENCE → See "Filters and Live Effects" in Chapter 5 for a discussion on importing Photoshop plug-ins into Fireworks to use as live effects.

Using a Bitmap Image as a Mask

One of the coolest effects is to use the grayscale values of one image as a mask for another image. By using one image as a mask, you can combine the coloration and texture of one image with the imagery of another. Take a look at the two objects in Figure 6-8. On the left is a vector shape filled with a gradient and a grid texture.

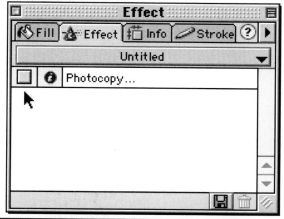

Figure 6-7   To remove a live effect, simply uncheck it in the Effect panel.

Figure 6-8   These two objects—one vector, one bitmap—will be combined in a mask group.

On the right is a bitmap image with a feathered edge. When they are combined in a mask group, the effect is quite interesting, as shown in Figure 6-9. This mask group was created as follows:

1. Place a photograph on top of a textured vector object and choose Edit | Cut.

2. Select the textured vector object, and then choose Edit | Paste As Mask from the menu.

3. Exit bitmap editing mode by clicking on the red X at the bottom of the document window.

Take a look at the Layers panel in Figure 6-9. Notice how the mask group is represented. If you are a Photoshop user, you'll see that the Fireworks mask group is similar to a Photoshop "layer mask." Incidentally, Fireworks honors Photoshop layer masks when you import a Photoshop file and represents them as a mask group in the Layers panel.

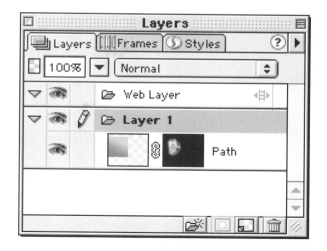

Figure 6-9   Mask groups allow you to create interesting, textured effects.

Working with Selections

So far, we've discussed the basics of bitmap manipulation in Fireworks. The key to fine-tuned bitmap editing, however, is the ability to isolate various regions of the image. For example, if you want to colorize only a portion of a bitmap image, you must be able to select a certain area. Otherwise, the colorized effect will apply to the whole image. To help you achieve such fine-tuned control, Fireworks offers a number of different selection tools: the Marquee, Oval, Lasso, and Magic Wand tools. If you're a Photoshop user, you'll find that they function the same way in Fireworks as they do in Photoshop:

- **Marquee tool**   Use this tool to create rectangular selections. Hold down the SHIFT key to create a perfectly square selection. Hold down the OPTION or ALT key to draw the selection out from the center of where you click.

- **Oval tool**   Access the Oval tool by clicking-and-holding on the Marquee tool. Use this tool to create circular selections. As with the Marquee tool, hold the SHIFT key to create a perfect circle, and hold the OPTION or ALT key to draw the selection from the center out.

- **Lasso tool**   The Lasso tool is a free-form selection tool. Click-and-drag continuously to create a selection. If you find drawing a free-form selection difficult, try holding down the OPTION or ALT keys while you draw. This way, instead of clicking and dragging, you can simply click and set down a series of points. In fact, this "sticky" mode is also available as a tool—click and hold on the Lasso tool in the Tools panel to reveal the Polygon Lasso tool.

● **Magic Wand**   The Magic Wand tool selects a region of color based on the setting you enter in the Options panel. In the Options panel, if you set a low tolerance number, the wand will select a smaller range of colors.

Modifying Selections

Often, the area you want to select for editing is not a perfect oval or square shape, nor is it completely free form. More likely, you must select an odd-shaped area such as a skyline. For example, to select a skyline, you must draw straight and round selections around buildings and draw free-form selections around trees. Fortunately, Fireworks, like other graphics programs, allows you to use the Selection tools together to create complex selections. You can also move your selections around on the screen without affecting the underlying graphic. Here's how:

● **Combining selections**   After you have drawn a selection, you can add to it by holding down the SHIFT key. (When you hold down the SHIFT key, you'll see a + sign appear next to your cursor.) You can either continue using the same selection tool or switch to a different one to add to your current selection.

● **Subtracting from selections**   To shave parts off an existing selection, hold down the OPTION or ALT keys. (When subtracting, you'll see a small minus sign (–) appear next to your cursor.) For example, to draw a crescent moon shaped selection as in Figure 6-10, first draw a circle with the Oval tool, and then hold down the OPTION or ALT key and draw a second circle that cuts into the first circle.

● **Multiplying selections**   To get the intersection of two selections, draw the first selection and then hold down both the OPTION or ALT key and the SHIFT key.

Figure 6-10   To subtract from a selection, hold down the OPTION or ALT keys.

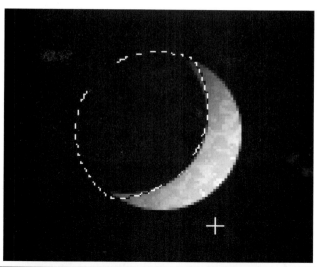

Figure 6-11   To get the intersection of two selections, hold down the OPTION or ALT key and the SHIFT key.

(When you do, you'll see a small X appear next to your cursor.) For example, to select the rest of the moon in Figure 6-11, we first drew a circular selection around the entire moon. Then we held down the OPTION/ALT key and the SHIFT key and drew a circle around the eclipsing shadow.

After drawing a selection, if it is not exactly in the spot you need it, you can move it without affecting the underlying image *if you remain in a Selection tool*. To move a selection, make sure one of the Selection tools is chosen in the Tools panel, as shown in Figure 6-12; then, place your cursor inside the selection and drag it.

To grab the underlying image and move it, you must switch to the Pointer tool. Then, with the Pointer tool, place your cursor inside the selection and drag to move.

Once you build a selection, you can *temporarily* save it by choosing Modify | Marquee | Save Selection. Then you can safely drop the selection and continue working. To restore the selection, choose Modify | Marquee | Restore Selection. This saving device is only a temporary measure. As soon as you close the document, the saved selection will be gone.

 Unfortunately, there's no way to save a selection with a document as there is in Photoshop. Once you close the document and reopen it, the saved selection is gone.

Preserving Transparency

There's one final important Fireworks feature that helps you to edit bitmaps more effectively: the ability to preserve the transparent areas surrounding a bitmap image while you paint. For example, the rubber bands image in Figure 6-13 is a bitmap on a transparent background (we deleted its white background earlier in the chapter).

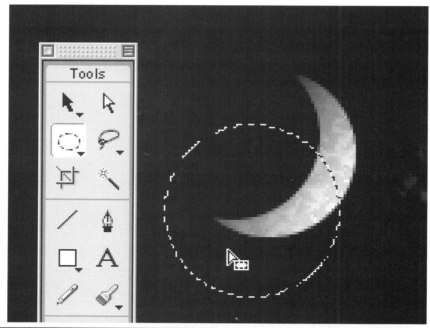

Figure 6-12 To move the selection only, be sure one of the Selection tools is chosen in the Tools panel, and then click-and-drag the selection.

Figure 6-13 The rubber band image is surrounded by transparency.

If we now want to paint effects on the image, we want to make sure our painting does not spill outside the bounds of the image. As shown in Figure 6-14, if we turn on Preserve Transparency in the Tool Options panel, our painting will affect only the image. The Preserve Transparency option in the Tool Options panel appears only when you have selected the Brush or Pencil tools.

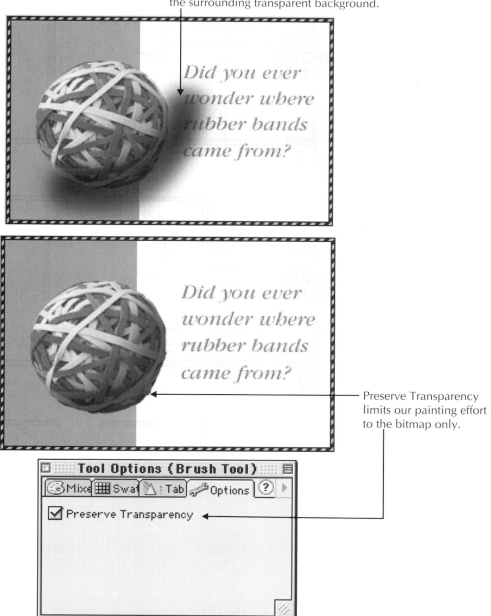

Without Preserve Transparency, our painting spills into the surrounding transparent background.

Preserve Transparency limits our painting effort to the bitmap only.

Figure 6-14　The Preserve Transparency option limits editing to the image only, not the surrounding transparent areas.

Exporting Photoshop Layered Files from Fireworks

Once you are through building your web page layout using a combination of vector and bitmap graphics, you have the option of exporting the design as a layered Photoshop document. For many companies and studios that have standardized on Photoshop for years, this new Fireworks 4 feature is a godsend. We've heard stories of design managers not allowing their designers to work with Fireworks because other designers in the organization were not able to open the resulting files and continue working with them. In the past, if you opened a Fireworks PNG file in Photoshop, it would become a single flattened layer, thereby losing all of its editability. To export a fireworks document as a Photoshop layered file, choose File | Export from the menu. In the Export window, choose Photoshop PSD from the Save As options.

 Online How-To

Creating a Textured Packaging Design

The goal of this lesson is to give you practice with Fireworks' bitmap capabilities while consolidating your vector editing skills to create a CD packaging design that looks like it's printed right on the CD.

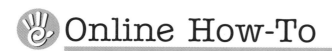

GO TO THE WEB! For a free, self-paced interactive version of this tutorial, which includes video demonstrations and source files, visit www.expertedge.com.

Building upon the previous lesson, where you made a CD illustration with a combination of vector graphics, you'll now continue to create a packaging design by integrating both vector and bitmap images:

1. Open the CD illustration that you created in the last chapter's lesson. Make sure that the illustration is grouped by choosing Edit | Select All and then Modify | Group from the menus. In the Layers panel, lock the CD layer and create a new layer for the packaging design.

2. Before you can start building the package design, you must first create a CD shape that will act as a mask. As you did in the previous lesson, create a donut-like CD shape by combining two circles. Draw the first circle to be 548×548 pixels. Draw the second circle to be 208×208 pixels. Select both circles and align them so they are centered to one another, then choose Modify | Combine | Punch from the menu to create the donut shape. Set the shape's fill and stroke to none. I will refer to this new shape as the "mask" shape.

3. To make the packaging design more interesting, you'll create a multi-colored background in different-shaped regions, as shown here. Start by creating a black rectangle shape and position it over the bottom portion of the CD. Next, create an orange-filled rectangle shape with a dark gray, 1-pixel hard Pencil stroke. This shape should overlap the black shape slightly and extend up to cover the CD's top and right edges. (Note that at this point, the shapes are completely covering the right side of the CD.)

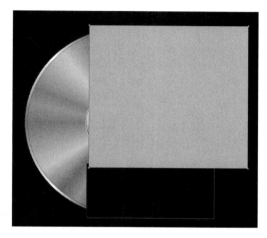

4. Lastly, use the Pen tool to create a yellow-filled shape with the same dark gray Pencil stroke that stairsteps across the CD shape, as shown here. It's helpful to turn off the Eye icons for the previous two shapes so you can see where to draw the yellow shape.

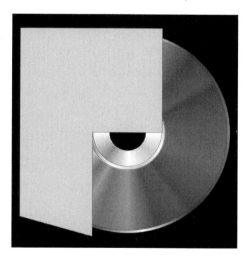

5. Once you've drawn the yellow shape, turn the Eye icons back on for the other two shapes. Select and group all three shapes. Cut the group and then select the mask shape (since the CD layer is locked, it should be the only object you can select). Choose Edit | Paste Inside from the menu.

6. OK, enough work with vectors. The next step is to integrate some interesting bitmap images. Import an industrial-looking photo (for practice purposes, you can download clip art comps from sites such as gettyone.com). Use the Scale tool in the Tools panel to rotate or resize the image as needed, based on where you want it to go. I placed my bitmap in a vertical orientation, on top of the orange shape. Once placed and resized, try using the Marquee tool to feather its edges. Double-click the bitmap to enter bitmap mode and then draw a selection with the Marquee tool around one of its edges. Choose Modify | Marquee | Feather and enter **35** pixels. Press the DELETE key to delete the selected area.

7. The next step is to paste the image inside of our CD mask. To maintain better control over the image, however, I want the image inside its own mask. This way, I can make use of the blending modes in the Layers panel, and I can move the image around inside the mask as needed. To create a copy of the mask shape, choose the Subselect tool (the one to the right of the normal Pointer tool), and click the CD's edge to select the mask. Copy the mask, deselect (Edit | Deselect), and paste. Now, select the bitmap image and cut. Select the mask copy and choose Edit | Paste Inside.

8. With the bitmap in its own mask, you can apply a blending mode like Multiply or Screen to achieve an interesting effect. If you included the bitmap in the prior mask, the blending mode would apply to the whole group. With the bitmap selected, choose a blending mode from the pull-down menu in the Layers panel. In this example, I chose the Screen effect. Also, if you need to move the image around in the mask, click on the central clover-like icon and drag.

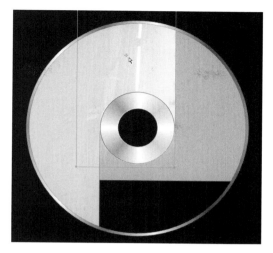

9. Continue to add two–three more bitmap images, repeating steps 7 and 8. Try different blending modes on each image. Remember to create a copy of the mask for each separate bitmap. This will afford you greater control over the placement and blending effect of each image. You may also try adjusting the opacity of the images in the Layers panel.

10. For the finishing touch, create a few vector illustrations such as an arrow made out of circles or a target-like design. Once you build the illustration, group it and, again, paste it inside of its own mask image so you can adjust its opacity, apply blending modes, and move it around independent of the other graphics.

11. Finally, create a logo design for your CD package and add a text tag line component. In this example, I used the Rectangle tool to create a rounded lozenge (using the Object panel to adjust the corner roundness) and the Text tool to add a few words. Voila! You should now have a beautiful CD packaging design.

7 Optimizing Web Graphics

Back in the mid-90s, before the advent of web-centric graphics applications, many designers worked with their old standby, Adobe Photoshop, to create web graphics. At the time, Photoshop still had a print orientation, and while it was a powerful program for creating art, it offered no tools for helping designers walk the fine line between file size and image quality. The effect was often extremely large graphics—exceeding 100K at a time when many people had only 14.4 Kbps modems. Since the emergence of tools like Fireworks and Adobe ImageReady, web graphic optimization has become considerably more powerful. But until broadband becomes a universal reality, graphic optimization will remain a critical component of your design skill set.

Traditionally, file optimization for web graphics has been an issue of finding ways to decrease the file size while preserving as much of the image quality as possible. But this process can be complicated. A first part of file optimization has nothing to do with software: you will need at least passing familiarity with graphics concepts such as color depth and different types of compression. In addition, as the software has evolved, so have the options and capabilities of file optimization.

This chapter is divided into two major sections. The first section is designed to help you understand the concepts and issues related to image optimization. The second section shows you how and where to apply these concepts as you make choices in the Fireworks optimization interface.

Authoring vs. Exported Web Graphics

What happens when you optimize and export a graphic? When you create graphics in Fireworks, your files are saved in a special, proprietary PNG format. This Fireworks PNG format is not the standard PNG format that can be opened in Photoshop or a browser. It is an authoring file that uses vector graphics as its standard. It stores all sorts of special Fireworks authoring information, such as rollover, pop-up menu, layer, style, URL, and even slice optimization settings.

 → See Chapter 1 for a discussion of the Fireworks PNG.

Most likely, the graphics that end up on your web site will be of the GIF or JPG file format. Unlike the Fireworks PNG, both of these are standard, flat bitmaps. They have no layers, interactivity, or object editability. That is, when you optimize and export your Fireworks PNGs, you are creating a new, and fundamentally different, type of graphic.

HAZARD When you export a file, a new file is created. Though it is created from your Fireworks PNG, this file cannot be edited as a Fireworks PNG. When the new file is created, named, and saved (during export), your Fireworks PNG is not saved. Be sure not to simply close Fireworks after you have exported a graphic without first saving the PNG—though Fireworks should warn you if you are trying to close an image without having saved it.

Understanding File Optimization

While Fireworks' visual optimization interface allows you to optimize your files without really understanding what is going on behind the scenes, you can save yourself some trial-and-error time and even design files that will optimize better if you understand some key concepts.

Resolution

As you know, bitmap graphics are made up of rows and columns of pixels. How many rows and columns are in a bitmap depends not on the physical dimensions of the image, but rather on its *resolution.* Resolution is usually measured in dots per inch (dpi). For screen viewing, resolution is often measured in *pixels per inch,* which is the term found in the Fireworks interface. The more pixels per inch, the more information, the better the appearance (with limitations), and the larger the file.

It might seem like optimizing using resolution would be a key part of web graphic optimization. But it is not. Always use 72 pixels per inch as your resolution for web graphics.

Fireworks allows you to set the resolution of an image, and unless you specify otherwise, it will use 72 pixels per inch for all images. However, you may scan or import an image at a higher resolution, in which case, you will want to change the resolution to 72 pixels per inch. Changing an image's resolution is called *resampling.*

To resample an image, follow these steps:

1. With the image open in either standard (vector) mode or Bitmap mode, choose Modify | Image Size. The Image Size dialog box appears, as seen in Figure 7-1.

2. Enter **72** in the Resolution field.

3. Choose Pixels/Inch in the Resolution drop-down list.

4. Click OK.

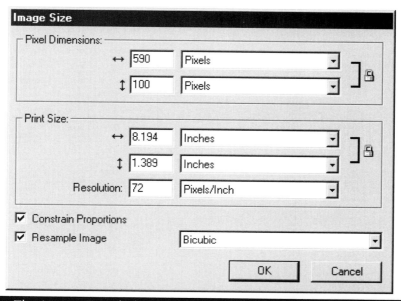

Figure 7-1   The Image Size dialog box

Generally, you only resample images downward. The reason is that resampling upward has no benefit. You are essentially telling the file to use more information to describe the same picture. The picture quality won't be any better; your file size will just be larger.

 Lowering image resolution is a destructive process. Information is thrown out of the file. Once you have resampled a file downward, you cannot bring it back after it has been saved. Back up your files before you resample.

Color Depth, Indexed Color, and Dithering

Resolution affects the raw number of pixels included in a file. A 5×5-inch file at 72 pixels per inch has exactly 129,600 pixels.

Each pixel is capable of having one of millions of colors in a 32-bit color system. Each color is described by the computer as a mix of red, green, and blue. Each of these, in turn, is described as having one out of 256 possible shades for each color (or 8 bits per color). In addition, a fourth channel, used to describe transparency, adds a fourth layer of 256 degrees of transparency. That's a lot of colors! And to describe each pixel—out of thousands—as having one value for each of four 8-bit color channels takes file space.

One way to minimize the amount of space needed to describe a picture is to lower the image's *color depth,* which means to limit the number of colors available to a picture. One method, called *indexed color,* assigns a value to a particular color and limits the file to a certain palette of indexed colors. GIF files, for example, use this method, and Fireworks actually displays and enables manipulation of GIF color palettes, as seen in Figure 7-2. A key limitation of the GIF file format is that it may have no more than 256 colors per file. Each of these colors is assigned an index value. Then each pixel is assigned a single value, rather than a whole descriptive string. The reduced number of colors also makes compression easier.

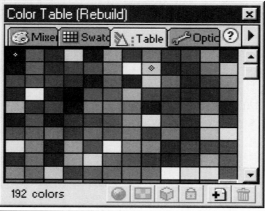

Figure 7-2 The Color Table panel allows you to manipulate a GIF's color palette during export.

The question, when creating a file using a limited number of indexed colors, is which colors to use? If an image initially has millions of colors, and the color depth has to be reduced to 256 colors, how are these colors selected? This process leads to the creation of a *palette,* which is simply the collection of colors used in a given file. When you export a PNG as a GIF, you create a color palette. In Fireworks, you can use one of several standard color palettes (Windows, Macintosh, Web Safe), or let Fireworks create one for you based on the actual colors used in the image (this kind is called an *Adaptive palette*). The smaller the palette, the fewer the colors, the worse the file looks (generally speaking, but not absolutely), and the smaller the file.

So what happens when a region of an image requires a color that is not in the palette? One solution is to simply use the closest color available, which can greatly undermine color fidelity. Another solution is *dithering,* which is when the file alternates two (or more) colors that are in the palette and that are close to the target color. Because the pixels are small, your eye (theoretically) blends the two colors and you see the target color. In reality, the result is often less than desirable—images can look grainy.

Lossy vs. Lossless Compression

Compression refers to an algorithm, or method, that re-encodes files more efficiently to reduce file size. Both ZIP and MP3 are popular compression schemes. Both major web graphic file types, GIF and JPG, use compression schemes. However, their methods of compression are quite different from each other.

The method of compression used in GIF files analyzes the colors in a file. Whenever it finds a group of pixels in a row with the same indexed color value, it compresses the code. How? Rather than describing each pixel's index color one-by-one, the file describes the whole set of pixels as being a certain color value. Over the course of the image, this can happen many times, so the GIF method of compression reduces file size by eliminating one form of redundancy.

The method of compression used in JPG files works differently. It analyzes the colors in an image, looking for groups of related colors. These groups can be in multiple rows, unlike with the GIF, which only looks at one row at a time. Where the JPG method finds a group of closely related colors, it combines them into one color and then encodes them as a group.

A key distinction arises from the two types of compression. The method used by GIF files simply eliminates a certain kind of redundancy. The colors of the pixels, and hence the appearance of the image as a whole, are unchanged. The file size is simply smaller. This kind of compression is called *lossless,* because nothing is lost in the compressing. ZIP is another form of lossless compression.

In contrast, the method used by JPG is *lossy,* because the appearance of some of the pixels, and hence the image itself, is changed. The JPG method can be more or less aggressive, resulting in smaller or larger file sizes, and lower or higher quality. You can see the difference in Figure 7-3. MP3 is another lossy compression method.

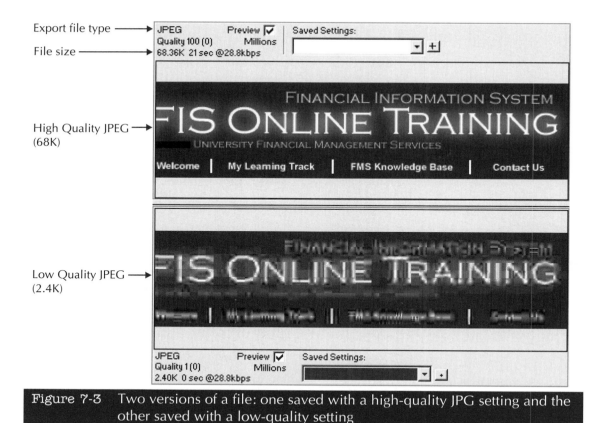

Export file type ⟶ JPEG Preview ☑ Saved Settings:
  Quality 100 (0) Millions
File size ⟶ 68.36K 21 sec @28.8kbps

High Quality JPEG ⟶
(68K)

Low Quality JPEG ⟶
(2.4K)

JPEG Preview ☑ Saved Settings:
Quality 1 (0) Millions
2.40K 0 sec @28.8kbps

Figure 7-3 Two versions of a file: one saved with a high-quality JPG setting and the other saved with a low-quality setting

The Web Safe Palette

The Web Safe palette comprises the 216 colors that the vast majority of web viewers have, whether they are on Windows or Macintosh, old or new machines. Specifically, it represents the overlapping colors that are in 8-bit (color) Windows and Macintosh systems. Each system has its own unique palette colors, and these have been removed from the Web Safe palette to be cross-platform compatible. It is the safest, lowest common denominator palette available. Advocates of web usability recommend sticking to this palette both for images and for HTML elements, such as link color.

The Web Safe palette is easily recognized in code and easy to create when mixing colors, because the numbers of these colors are easily recognized in hexadecimal numbering. Hexadecimal numbering is a method used to create unique IDs for 24-bit color. It uses six digits, two each per color channel (red, green, and blue). Each digit designates one of 16 values, beginning with 0 (digits 10 through 15 are represented using A through F). The two columns of 16, when combined, offer 256 unique possibilities—the number of possible colors per channel in 24-bit color. Colors in the Web Safe palette are always doubles of 0, 3, 6, 9, C, and F. Thus, a #CC3366 is a Web Safe color, while #C396CF is not.

NOTE Colors where all of the digits are the same are monochromatic. #000000 is black, #FFFFFF is white, while #CCCCCC is a light gray, and so on.

Sticking to this palette was essential in an era when many had only 256-color systems. However, it also can be very limiting for designers. As computers continue to improve and most viewers have a considerably larger color palette, the Web Safe palette is becoming less important from the viewpoint of the lowest common denominator. However, as an issue of usability, the Web Safe palette continues to be relevant.

The Appropriate File Type

The Fireworks Optimize panel allows you to choose from 12 different file types, including JPG and two different variants of GIF. The other nine file types, though less used for web graphics, are available and should not be forgotten.

Choosing GIF

As described earlier, GIF files use indexed color and a lossless compression scheme. GIF is well suited to files with crisp (as opposed to soft) edges, few colors, and especially to files with long rows of the same color. Unlike JPG, the GIF format also supports transparency and basic animation. Often, drawings created in vector drawing programs look good as GIFs, because they tend to have a clean and smooth appearance. Graphics with a lot of text also look good as GIFs. Fireworks' vector graphics with added effects such as drop shadows and glows, however, are sometimes an exception to the vector-GIF compatibility, because Fireworks' graphics with live effects often have a textured bitmap-like appearance, making JPG more suitable.

Having explained that GIF used a lossless compression method, we would be remiss not to point out that you *can* enter a loss amount as a GIF setting in the Optimize panel. This will decrease the file size even more than the standard setting, and it will also degrade the quality of the file—just as lossy compression in JPG files does.

Choosing JPG

The JPG file format was created by (and named after) the Joint Photographic Experts Group (JPEG). Not surprisingly, it excels with photographs. JPG does not use indexed color, which means that it has a much wider color gamut than the GIF. It handles smooth transitions with grace. Because of the high number of colors available, JPGs also handle gradients well. On the downside, text or smooth lines can sometimes become blurry and unsightly. When JPG files are compressed too much, unsightly patterns and artifacts may appear. And, of course, those who still have only 8-bit color can't see the full gamut, anyway—their video cards will dither the images. JPG cannot handle animation, and you cannot alter its color index, because it has none. In addition, the JPG format does not support transparency.

Choosing PNG

The PNG file format remains little used on the Web. Notwithstanding that Fireworks commandeers it as its native file type, it was originally designed to combine the best of both the GIF and JPEG formats. It supports transparency, up to 32-bit color (though you can force it down to 8-bits, if desired), and uses a lossless compression method that results in vibrant images. The downside to PNG is that its file sizes tend to run a bit large. In the "Optimizing and Exporting Graphics" section you'll see a Habitat page preview with GIF, JPG, and PNG-32 settings (Figure 7-6). The PNG is considerably larger than the other two. Though it may be hard to tell as printed in your book, it also looks the best, with rich, crisp colors and lines.

We recommend using PNG when you create work in Fireworks that needs to be rasterized and exported to other applications.

 When you export a PNG from Fireworks, the image becomes a flattened, standard bitmap and is no longer editable, even though its icon doesn't change. Be sure to rename it or store it in another folder, so that you do not confuse it with Fireworks PNG authoring files.

Choosing Other File Types

Many people don't realize that Fireworks can optimize and export more than just web graphics. The Optimize panel also has settings for different flavors of TIF and BMP. The TIF file format has long been a stalwart of the print industry. As you might expect, its files tend to be very high quality—and very large. There aren't many options for tweaking the export, but TIF is a viable format for going from Fireworks to a print project.

BMP is a standard graphic file type for Windows users. Its files tend to be both large and high quality. The file type is recognized by all Windows machines.

 Bitmap is the file type used for Windows desktop wallpaper. To create custom wallpaper in Fireworks, create the art and then export it as BMP. Save the file in the Windows system folder (usually "Windows" or "WNNT"), and select it from the Display Settings icon in the Control Panel.

Optimizing and Exporting Graphics

Understanding the first part of this chapter is key to working with the Optimize panel. You use the Optimize panel to select how you would like Fireworks to export your file. In addition to choosing which file type, you can also control which color palette is used, the amount of compression, and other variables. You can then compare previews of each export method in the 2-Up and 4-Up tabs (see Figure 7-4) of the document window—both how they look and their exported file size. With more tweaking, you can be sure that you are exporting the best looking graphic for the lowest file size, which means it will require the least download time.

Figure 7-4 The Preview tabs are found on the top of the document window.

The workflow for optimizing a straightforward PNG file is as follows:

● Create the art.

● Use the Optimize panel in conjunction with the Preview tabs of the document window to find the optimal file configuration.

● Export the graphic.

Coordinating the Optimize Panel with the Preview Tab

The Optimize panel, seen in Figure 7-5, is docked with the Object and Behaviors panels by default and can also be launched by choosing Window | Optimize or via the Launcher Bar. Whatever settings you use for a file (including slice settings) are actually stored in the file as the default export option for that file. If you use the Project Log to update files, it will use the settings stored in the Optimize panel of each PNG.

The Optimize panel is usually used in conjunction with the Preview tabs on the document window. This way, you can see the effects each setting will have on image quality and file size.

To optimize a simple graphic, do the following:

1. Click the 4-Up tab in the document window. When you do, four preview windows open, as seen in Figure 7-6.

Figure 7-5   The Optimize panel

Original PNG file size

Original preview

Export file size

Export file type

Export file type options

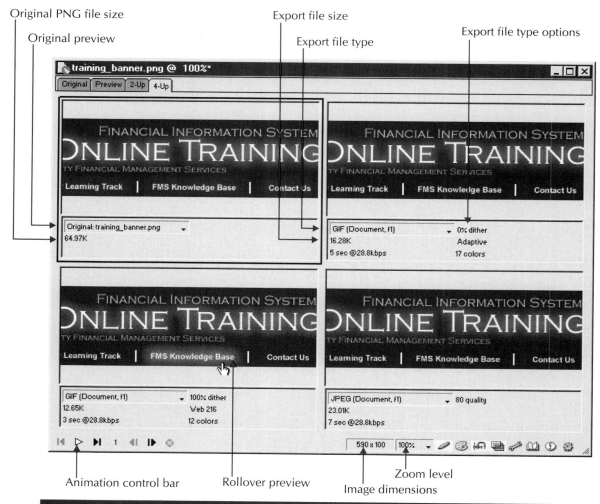

Animation control bar

Rollover preview

Image dimensions

Zoom level

Figure 7-6   Fireworks 4-Up preview, with the original and three optimization settings

2. Initially, the pane in the top-left corner shows the Fireworks PNG file in the authoring environment. Leave this one alone, so you have the original to which you can compare all of the export possibilities.

NOTE If you wish to make all four windows preview windows (which we do not generally recommend), simply select the first window, and click the box just below the image, where you see "Original:" followed by the filename. Choose Export Preview to make this pane behave like the other three.

3. Click the preview window in the top-right corner. Notice the black border around it, which indicates that it is selected.

4. Choose a setting from the Optimize panel. Initially, you may wish to use one of the presets, such as GIF Adaptive 256, in the Settings drop-down list.

5. Click the preview window in the bottom-left corner to select it.

6. Choose a different setting from the Optimize panel. You might want to choose JPEG – Better Quality so you can get a quick sense for how a high-quality GIF compares with a high-quality JPG.

7. Compare each of the two optimized previews with the original to determine which maintains the highest fidelity.

8. Compare the file size projection of each file to see which is more reasonable.

9. Click to select the fourth preview window.

10. Choose (or custom create) an optimization setting based on what you learned from the first two.

11. Proceed by changing the optimization settings for each preview until you have created the optimal setting.

12. With the desired preview still selected, click the Original tab in the document window to return to the document and save the appropriate settings in the Optimize panel. Unless you make further changes, these settings will remain with the file as long as it exists.

HAZARD Before you click the Original tab to leave the optimization environment and return to the main canvas, be sure that the desired preview window is selected. If the wrong one is selected, Fireworks will use and store the wrong settings.

Using the Optimize Panel

Now that you understand the outlines of the optimization process, let's take a closer look at what you can do with the Optimize panel.

The Settings Drop-Down List

The first option, the Settings drop-down list, contains a handful of common optimization profiles. By default, you will have the options seen in Table 7-1.

Over-relying on these presets is unwise. The variations in both image quality and final file size are significant enough to justify exploration on your own.

IDEA Use the presets to get a general idea of which setting produces the best results, and then use that as the basis for creating custom settings.

The Optimize panel is at its best when you begin creating custom settings. You usually begin with whichever active preset is in the Settings drop-down list, so be sure to select the one that is the closest to the desired custom setting.

The Export File Format Drop-Down List

The first, and most important, choice is which file format. For web graphics, you will most likely be using a flavor of GIF or JPG. You make this selection in the Export File Format drop-down list, seen in Figure 7-7. Depending on which of these you select, the rest of the Optimize panel will change, since different file types have different options. When creating custom settings, be sure to select the file type first.

File types were discussed in detail in the "Choosing an Appropriate File Type" section earlier.

Setting	Use For
GIF Web 216	Graphics that must conform to the Web Safe palette, even at the expense of image quality
GIF WebSnap 256	Graphics with 256 or more colors, where there is a preference to use colors from the Web Safe palette where convenient
GIF WebSnap 128	Graphics with fewer than 256 colors and where file size is important
GIF Adaptive 256	Graphics with 256 or more colors, where image quality matters more than file size or Web Safe compatibility
JPEG Better Quality	Soft-edged or photographic images with more than 256 colors, where image quality is more important than file size
JPEG Smaller File	Soft-edged or photographic images, where small file size is the priority

Table 7-1   Summary of the Fireworks Optimization Presets

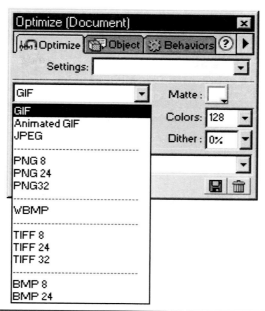

Figure 7-7   The Export File Format drop-down list

IDEA   When you are creating custom settings, at first try both GIF and JPG file types, so you can get a sense of the scope of export effects. Then, as you narrow down your choices, you can create three previews of the same file type with three different variations, such as three different JPG quality settings.

The Indexed Palette Drop-Down List: GIF and PNG-8 Only

If you choose GIF or PNG-8 as your file type, the Indexed Palette drop-down list appears. Fireworks will often have to lower the color depth of your file to export to this format, and this drop-down list gives you control over how that happens. Which palette you choose depends on several variables, including file size, color fidelity, and degree of conformity with the Web Safe palette. Each palette is discussed in Table 7-2.

Palette Name	Description
Adaptive	Adaptive palettes are intended to produce the results closest to the original. They result in the highest-fidelity images. However, they do not even attempt to work with the Web Safe palette, and so may render very poorly on older systems and/or create issues of usability.

Table 7-2   Available Palettes During the Optimize and Export Process

Palette Name	Description
WebSnap Adaptive	WebSnap Adaptive is a technology that Macromedia developed as a compromise between a purely Adaptive palette and forcing everything to the Web Safe palette. Those colors that are already similar to colors in the Web Safe palette are converted to that palette, while those colors that would be significantly altered are left alone.
Web 216	Web 216 is the Web Safe palette. Using this palette will make your picture *web safe,* meaning that what you see is what almost all of your users will see. Be sure to compare it carefully with the original file, however, because converting to this palette can substantially change the appearance of your file.
Exact	Exact uses only the colors that are already in the image. It only works if there are 256 or fewer colors. If there are more, Fireworks automatically switches to an Adaptive palette.
Macintosh	This palette represents the 256 colors used by the Macintosh operating system. Of these colors, 216 are in the Web Safe palette, while 40 are unique to the Macintosh operating system. This has all of the disadvantages of the Web 216 palette, without its advantage of being nearly universal. We do not recommend it.
Windows	Like the Macintosh palette, this is the 256-color palette of the Windows operating system. As with the Macintosh palette, we don't generally recommend that you use it, for the same reasons.
Gray	This palette converts the image to 256 shades of gray—that is, to grayscale.
Black and White	This palette has exactly two colors: black and white. Any color lighter than the median becomes white. Any color darker than the median becomes black. Having just two colors has its advantages in terms of file size, but there is an enormous cost in image quality. Use it only for special effects.
Uniform	The Macromedia documentation describes Uniform as "a mathematical palette based on RGB pixel values." In our experience, it lowers the overall number of colors in a document, often at the expense of quality.
Custom	This option allows you to import a saved color table (ACT) file. This topic is covered in the next chapter.

Table 7-2 Available Palettes During the Optimize and Export Process *(continued)*

Other GIF and PNG-8 Settings

There are a handful of other settings available if you choose GIF or PNG-8:

- **Loss** (GIF only)   This applies additional lossy compression to the file. It further decreases file size and degrades image quality. If you choose to use it, the recommended setting is between 5 and 15.

- **Matte**   This applies a background canvas color. The default setting is None.

  > **IDEA** If you are using a transparent background and wish to remove halos around anti-aliased text and images, set the matte color to the color in the background of the destination HTML document.

- **Colors**   This forces the palette below the number you set. By default, the number is 256, the maximum, unless you choose Web 216. However, for additional file size savings, you might force an image that has 77 colors down to 64 colors as one way to save on file size.

- **Dither**   Measured as a percent, dithering is a method used to approximate colors in the original that are not in the final palette. Dithering can enhance color fidelity to the original; however, it can also greatly increase file size, as it undermines the GIF compression algorithm.

  > **IDEA** Consider using dithering when you have selected a Web Safe palette, but avoid it (as a rule) when you are using an Adaptive palette.

- **Transparency type**   Choose Alpha Transparency if your canvas is set to transparent (Modify | Canvas Color). Choose Index Transparency when you are manually setting transparency colors for web graphics for which you do not have source Fireworks PNG files.

Transparency Eyedropper Tools
At the bottom of the panel are three eyedroppers, which you can use to select colors and set their transparency. They are fairly intuitive.

- Use the eyedropper with a + sign, Add Color To Transparency, to select a color and make it transparent.

- The eyedropper with a – sign, Remove Color From Transparency, removes the transparency from a color, so that it appears as itself.

- The eyedropper with an equal sign (=), Set Transparent Index Color, sets the selected color to be the transparent color, and any other color currently set to transparent will return to its original color.

There are two places you can use the eyedropper. You can simply click any color in the preview to select it. The problem with this is that individual pixels may be too small to select accurately. You can also open the Color Table panel (Window | Color

Table). This panel contains all of the colors in the selected preview (assuming it has an 8-bit or smaller palette). Use the eyedroppers to select individual swatches in this table. The only disadvantage to using the table is that it may be hard to match a color in the preview with its corresponding swatch. Fortunately, transparent pixels are shown in the preview panel, so a little trial and error is usually sufficient.

You can also find the transparency options (including the eyedropper tools), the swatches in the Color Table, and previews in the Export Preview dialog box. See Chapter 8 for more about editing color palettes using the Export Wizard.

JPG Settings

As a rule, JPG files are easier to optimize than GIF files, because there are considerably fewer settings. The main reason is that JPG files do not lower the color depth of source files the way GIF files often do.

- **Matte**   As with GIF, this setting changes the image's exported background color.

- **Quality**   This is the most important setting in JPG optimization, because it dramatically affects both the image quality and file size. The default is 80, which is a fairly high quality. You can often go down to 60 before the compression starts to become highly apparent. A setting of 40 is about as low as you are likely to go. You will find considerable file-size savings at these lower levels. You will definitely want to have the 2-Up or 4-Up Preview tab open when you determine the Quality setting.

- **Selective Quality**   Use this option for Selective JPG (covered in the next chapter).

- **Smoothing**   Smoothing blurs the hard edges in JPG images, enabling more efficient compression. Along with file-size savings there will often be dramatic degradation of text and other elements that rely on hard edges. However, images such as photographs often benefit from smoothing.

Creating and Saving Your Own Presets

In the lower-right corner, there is a Save icon. Use this to save your carefully constructed custom settings for later work with similar needs. When you click the Save icon, you will be prompted to enter a name:

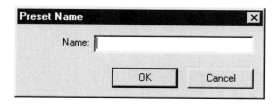

After entering a descriptive name, click OK. The new setting will be saved in Fireworks and available in other files. The new preset will be located in the Settings drop-down list. Note that at least one setting, Matte color, is not saved with the rest of the settings.

Deleting custom presets is also easy. Choose the setting and click the Delete (trash can) icon in the lower-right corner of the Optimize panel.

The Optimize Panel Pop-Up Menu

Like most Fireworks panels, the Optimize panel has a pop-up menu:

This menu adds a handful of other options:

- **Save and Delete Settings**   This is the same functionality as the Save and Delete icons in the lower corner of the panel.

- **Optimize to Size**   This allows you to enter a desired size, and Fireworks tries to create settings that accommodate it.

- **Open the Export Wizard**   This has more optimization settings (covered in the next chapter).

- **Remove Unused Colors**   This helps you minimize the size of your color palettes.

- **Interlaced (GIFs) and Progressive (JPEG)**   These enable the viewer to see low-resolution versions of the images while they are downloading. These settings do not significantly affect file size, though progressive JPGs can be slightly smaller, while interlaced GIFs can be slightly larger.

- **Sharpen JPEG Edges**   This improves the crispness of JPG files, often at the expense of file size.

The Optimize panel puts a surprising number of powerful optimization features at your fingertips. In spite of how much Macromedia managed to pack into this panel, it is not the whole story. The File menu contains an Export Wizard that ultimately gives you much more control over file optimization. The Export Wizard is covered in the next chapter.

Also covered in the next chapter are several more advanced strategies, from gaining total control over your palettes, to using image slicing and optimization. Using image slices is a powerful way to resolve the problems created when some image elements, such as photographs, are well suited for JPG export, while other elements, such as text, are better suited for GIF format. Rather than compromising one or the other, you'll learn how to use slicing to get the best of both worlds.

Working with Macintosh/Windows Gamma Settings

Macintosh and Windows by default have different gamma settings in their displays. In practical terms, Macintosh systems tend to display brighter than Windows systems. This can have a dramatic effect on your web graphics, since they will be viewed on both systems. Often, graphics made on a Macintosh may appear dark and dull in Windows, while graphics created in Windows may appear faded, bleached, or washed out on a Mac.

Solving this problem is not easy, but even identifying it can be very difficult for those with access to only one platform. A nifty feature in Fireworks, however, simulates how your graphic would appear in the other operating system. Simply choose View | Macintosh Gamma in Windows, or View | Windows Gamma on a Mac to toggle the simulation on and off.

You can switch back and forth while authoring, but we also recommend it when exporting, especially if you are reducing color depth or modifying the file's palette. Your tweaks may look fabulous in Windows, even as they appear strange on a Mac.

 Online How-To

Exporting a Banner

Throughout this book, we have recommended that you design entire web pages in Fireworks, even parts that will later be reconstructed in standard HTML. At some point, though, you will begin to slice up your document and export individual assets that you can drop into HTML code. The next chapter covers the art of slicing and selective exporting. This tutorial walks you through the basic process of optimizing a graphic.

 GO TO THE WEB! For a free, self-paced interactive version of this tutorial, which includes video demonstrations and source files, visit www.expertedge.com.

Among the most common tasks will be exporting a banner. In this tutorial, you will optimize the banner for a Habitat for Humanity page. You will explore different settings, including file types, palettes, color depth, and other settings, so you can see some of the concepts discussed throughout this chapter in action.

Prepare Your Workspace for Optimization

Before you optimize, you'll need to set up your workspace:

1. Open the file exercise.png from the Chapter 7 folder at the book's web site.

2. Click the 4-Up tab to bring up the preview windows.

3. Be sure that the window in the top-left corner (pane 1) is set to Original and not Export Preview. You'll want to see the original for purposes of comparison.

4. Click the Optimize icon in the Launcher Bar to activate the Optimize panel, if it isn't already open.

Optimize the Image: General Directions

Optimization is often a trial-and-error process. That means that you often don't know in advance whether a file will work better as a GIF (and if so, with which settings) or as a JPG. As you get more experienced exporting files, you'll get better at predicting. But in the end, there is almost always some tinkering.

Given this state of affairs, you'll want to approach optimization tactically. If you tinker with dithering for ten minutes and then change the file type, you'll waste ten minutes of work. The strategy, then, is to go from general to specific. Your first task is to get the big picture: what will the best file type be for this image?

1. Click the Zoom tool, and click on the orange text in the image. If the orange text is not visible, use the Hand tool and scroll the image until it is. Your four panes at this point should appear are they do in Figure 7-8.

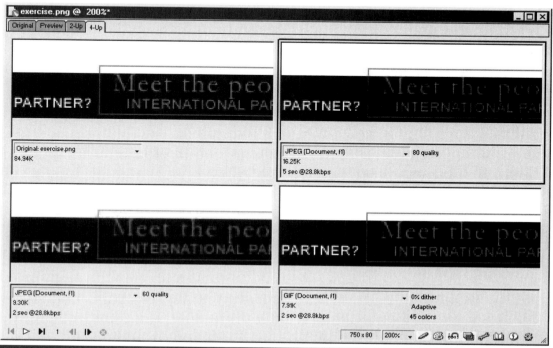

Figure 7-8   Zoom in on an area with different colors and types of elements.

We recommend that you zoom in once, so that you view the image at 200 percent. This makes the subtle differences between previews more visible. We chose the orange text, because it is the area where color is most likely to be affected by changes in color depth and lossy compression.

> **NOTE** All four panes change views when you zoom or scroll in any one of them, ensuring that you are always comparing apples to apples.

1. In the top-right pane (pane 2), choose JPEG – Better Quality from the Settings drop-down list.

2. In the lower-left pane (pane 3), choose JPEG – Smaller File from the Settings drop-down list.

3. In the lower-right (pane 4), choose GIF Adaptive 256 from the Settings drop-down list.

4. Inspect the four panes, comparing color, clarity, and file size (which is specified below each preview).

Here's what we found:

- The JPEG – Better Quality had pretty good fidelity to the original. Its colors—especially the orange—were slightly worse than in the original, but acceptable. Its file size, however, was a whopping 16K.

- The JPEG – Smaller File had a more acceptable file size at just over 9K. But the image looks awful. The orange has degraded considerably, becoming dull and lifeless. The text is also blurrier than before.

- The GIF Adaptive 256 retained the same crispness as the original, the orange text is bright and lively, and the resulting file size was the smallest of the pack at less than 8K!

We have the big picture for this file: it makes a much better GIF than JPG. Earlier in the chapter, we mentioned that GIFs do well with text, crisp transitions, and solid colors. You have before you some good evidence to support that claim. Had this been a photograph, most likely the GIF would have looked worse and been a larger file than the JPG.

Optimize the Image: Fine-Tuning

You know that the final output of this file will be in the GIF format. The question is, which flavor of GIF? Generally, when dealing with GIF files, you have to decide how important sticking to the Web Safe palette is, as well as how important it is to get the smallest possible file.

The first part of tweaking will be to convert the two panes currently set to JPG to different forms of GIF:

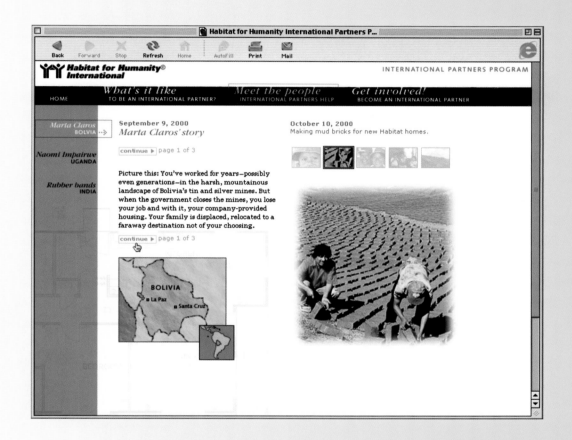

The Habitat for Humanity International Partners Program web site layout was built entirely using Fireworks, Flash, and Dreamweaver together. This book shows you how each portion of the site was built. Some of the elements are shown here.

The web site opens with an elegant Flash animation that sets an inspiring tone for the rest of the site.

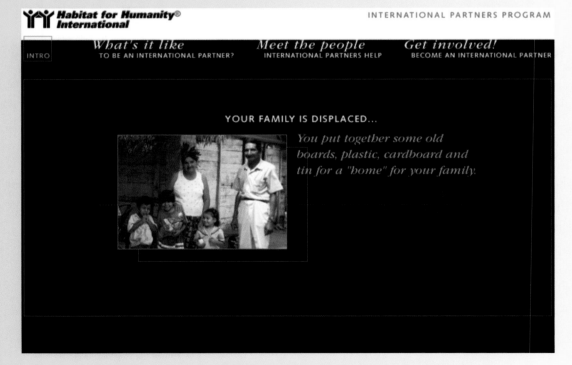

Habitat for Humanity® International

INTERNATIONAL PARTNERS PROGRAM

INTRO

What's it like
TO BE AN INTERNATIONAL PARTNER?

Meet the people
INTERNATIONAL PARTNERS HELP

Get involved!
BECOME AN INTERNATIONAL PARTNER

This is just one
OF THOUSANDS OF STORIES
Around the World

Habitat for Humanity® International

INTERNATIONAL PARTNERS PROGRAM

INTRO

What's it like
TO BE AN INTERNATIONAL PARTNER?

Meet the people
INTERNATIONAL PARTNERS HELP

Get involved!
BECOME AN INTERNATIONAL PARTNER

YOU CAN HELP
Make a difference

The primary and secondary navigation bars feature rollover buttons. See Chapters 4 and 11 for more details on building interactive rollover buttons with Fireworks.

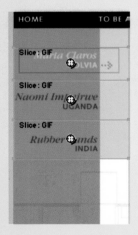

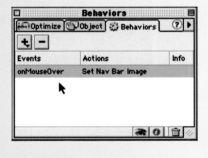

Imported bitmap elements were processed in Fireworks to remove their white backgrounds.

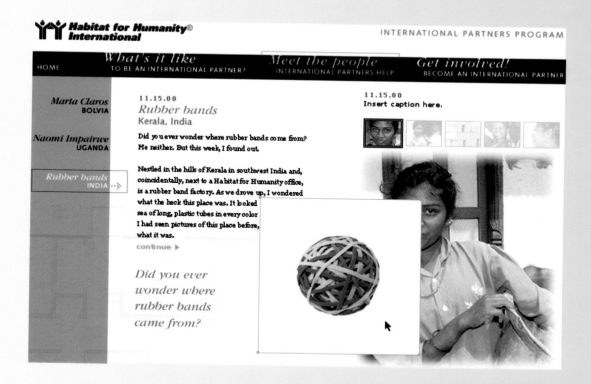

We used the Preserve Transparency option in the Tool Options panel to add shading within the bounds of the image. See Chapter 6 for more bitmap editing techniques.

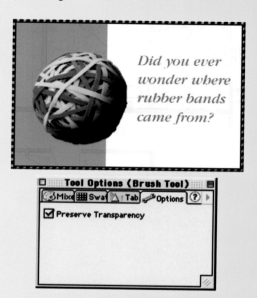

To help promote the Habitat for Humanity International Partners Program web site, we created a simple 9-frame GIF animation. Notice that each frame has different time delays set in the right column of the Frames panel. See Chapter 9 for more information on creating animation with Fireworks.

Frames panel

Frame 1

Frame 2

Frame 3

Frame 4

YOU CAN
Make a difference

Frame 5

YOU CAN
Make a difference

Frame 6

SEE WHAT IT'S LIKE TO BE AN
International Partner

Frame 7

SEE WHAT IT'S LIKE TO BE AN
International Partner

Frame 8

SEE WHAT IT'S LIKE TO BE AN
International Partner

Frame 9

Many designers don't realize the extent of Fireworks' illustration capabilities. This CD and packaging design were created entirely with Fireworks' vector and bitmap tools.

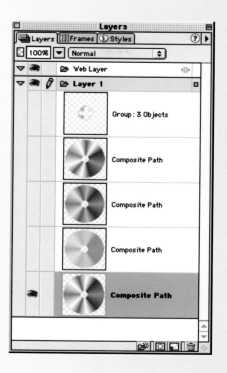

The Layers panel reveals a number of objects stacked on top of one another to create the CD's rich, iridescent effect.

This shape is just one of five objects stacked on top of one another to create the final CD illustration. Each shape has a slightly different gradient fill, rotation, and opacity setting.

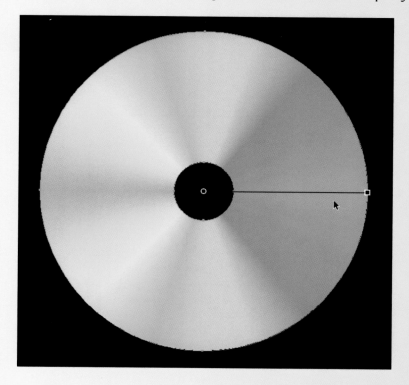

The CD's packaging uses bitmap and vector graphics together, all controlled by masks. See Chapter 5 for more details.

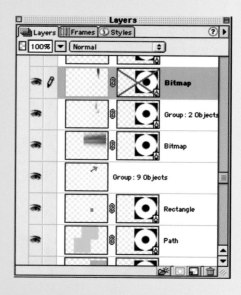

One of Fireworks' underappreciated capabilities is its diverse export options. We created a DHTML puzzle by taking advantage of one of these options. First, we drew a grid of slice regions on top of an image. When the grid was complete, rather than exporting to standard HTML, which would have reassembled the slices in a table, we exported the slices to CSS Layers.

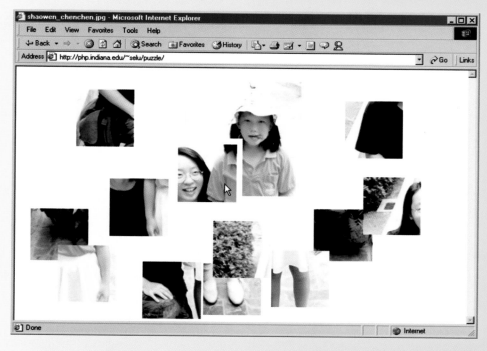

From there, we opened the resulting HTML file in Dreamweaver and applied a Drag Layer behavior (with a drop target) to each of the pieces. We then scrambled the pieces on screen, added some directions in a JavaScript pop-up alert, and voila! We have a quick and easy interactive DHTML puzzle. See Chapter 13 for more on integrating Dreamweaver and Fireworks.

Stephen Voisey built the new AppSense Technologies web site using Fireworks, Dreamweaver, and UltraDev.

Stephen Voisey created this illustrated web page entirely with Fireworks' vector tools. See the "Fireworks in the Real World" section in Chapter 5 for Stephen's illustration tips.

Adam Bell makes extensive use of pop-up menus in the crazy-looking Hot Sauce Zone web site. See Chapter 11 to learn how to make pop-up menus in Fireworks.

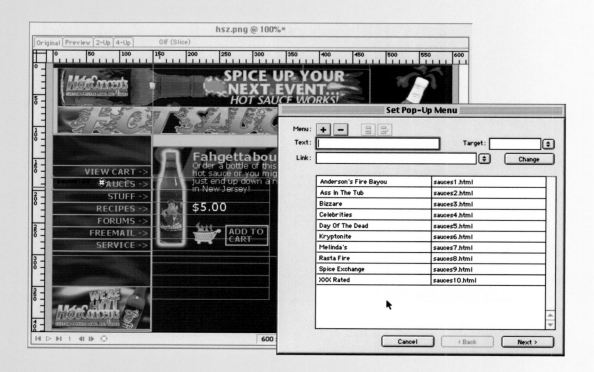

This final display shows one of the finished pop-up menus.

Nik Schramm redesigned his corporate web site in just two days using Fireworks, Dreamweaver, and UltraDev together. Using Fireworks' diverse vector-to-bitmap export options, he also created supporting postcards and business cards.

Stephen Voisey created these beautiful illustrations with "Twist and Fade," a custom JavaScript command he wrote to manipulate basic shapes. See Chapter 14 to learn how to write this and other custom scripts.

1. Click anywhere in pane 2 to select it, and choose GIF Web 216 from the Settings drop-down list.

2. Click in pane 3, and choose GIF WebSnap 128 from the Settings drop-down list. All three of your preview panes should now be different kinds of GIF.

An inspection of the three formats reveals that the Web 216 has a smaller file size than the other two, which are both almost identical in size. The explanation can probably be found in the number of colors: the previews in panes 3 and 4 have 44–45 colors each, while the Web 216 version has only 25. But the fewer colors come at a price. If you look closely at the orange text in the Web 216 version, you will see dithering in effect; the alternation of pixel colors makes the orange text look grainy.

Let's get rid of the Web 216, but try reducing the color depth of an Adaptive palette to try to get the file size down without undermining image quality.

1. Click pane 2 (the one currently set at Web 216), and select Adaptive from the Indexed Palette drop-down list.

2. In the Colors drop-down list, choose 16. The Optimize panel should look like the one shown here. We know that the image only needs 45 colors or so, maximum, but forcing it down using an Adaptive palette might improve file size without adversely affecting image quality.

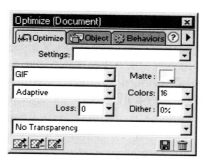

3. Use the Zoom and Hand tools to check out different parts of the images with different levels of zoom.

   The image in pane 2 is the smallest at 6K. Different zoom levels reveal that the images are very similar in quality. Let's keep tweaking.

4. Set panes 3 and 4 so they are also Adaptive, with 16 colors.

5. Select pane 3, and drag the Loss slider in the Optimize panel to **15**. This introduces some lossy compression, and generally anything over a setting of 15 will produce unattractive results.

6. Compare panes 2 and 3.

The image in pane 3 doesn't look any worse than the one in pane 2—that's the good news. Oddly enough, though, the file size actually increased!

Another option in the Optimize panel is Dither. You use dithering to approximate colors that are not in the palette. Dithering typically increases file size. Since the images already have acceptable fidelity to the original (the adaptive palette helps ensure that), we have little advantage in experimenting here with dithering.

It appears, then, that the image currently in pane 2 is the best one for exporting.

7. Click pane 2 to select it.

8. Click the Original tab to return to the main document.

9. Save your file by choosing File | Save. The optimization information in panel 2 will be stored in this file, and whenever you open it, it will remember this setting, even if you open and optimize other files in the meantime.

10. Export the file using these settings by choosing File | Export.

8 Optimization: Beyond the Basics

After exploring the Optimize panel in the last chapter, you might be surprised to know that Fireworks also has a powerful optimization interface separate from the Optimize panel. This is the Export Preview dialog box, which contains several tabs, enabling you to do diverse tasks such as managing animation, palette customization, and image scaling/cropping, while viewing up to four simultaneous live previews. In addition, Fireworks ships with an Export Wizard that will help those new to file optimization make good export choices. Among Firework's most powerful features, though, is the ability to optimize your image…by the slice! Toss in Selective JPEG Compression, and you have a tremendous set of tools that enables you to optimize not only images, but also parts of images.

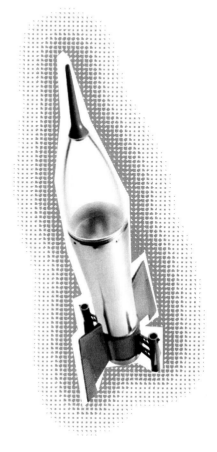

189

n spite of the power of all of the optimization tools discussed in Chapter 7, you may find yourself faced with a problem that you cannot solve with the Optimize panel alone. Consider the following situations:

- You want to stick to the Web Safe palette—except for one color that is a part of your client's company logo.
- Some parts of your graphic only look good when you export to GIF, while others only look good when you export to JPG.
- You need to keep your file size under a certain number of kilobytes, and yet doing so compromises a key area of your image.
- You can't get acceptable results using a GIF adaptive palette and want to edit or create your own export palette.
- You have mocked up entire pages in Fireworks and now want to optimize and export only certainly portions of the file.

Fireworks provides tools that will enable you to resolve each of these problems. Many of these situations involve a complex whole that has no one-size-fits-all solution. A graphic with both photographic images and text, for instance, may not export acceptably as a whole, requiring you to break it into parts. A color palette may look fine overall, but it may shift a key color. When you are ready to get into the nuts and bolts of your file, Fireworks is there with the advanced customization tools you need.

The purpose of this chapter is to introduce you to the advanced tools of the Fireworks optimization and export interface, including editing color palettes, using masks for selective JPEG compression, and slicing graphics for optimization and not just functionality.

Using the Export Wizard

The Export Wizard (File | Export Wizard) is not Fireworks' deepest feature, and unless you are fairly new to optimization, you might avoid it altogether. Its purpose is to ask you a few questions and then give you some suggested optimization strategies. When it is finished, the Export Preview dialog box (discussed in the next section) appears. The wizard places a couple sample optimization settings, based on your input, into the preview panes of the Export Preview dialog box.

It is a serviceable tool for those still unsure of themselves during the optimization process. It can also be used as a first step in optimizing, since it creates export configurations that suffice as a good starting point, based on your responses. However, no wizard is a replacement for human eye and judgment, which is why it connects directly to the Export Preview upon completion.

On the first screen of the wizard, seen in Figure 8-1, you usually choose to select an export format. You can also specify a target file size, an option that is also available in the Optimize panel pop-up menu.

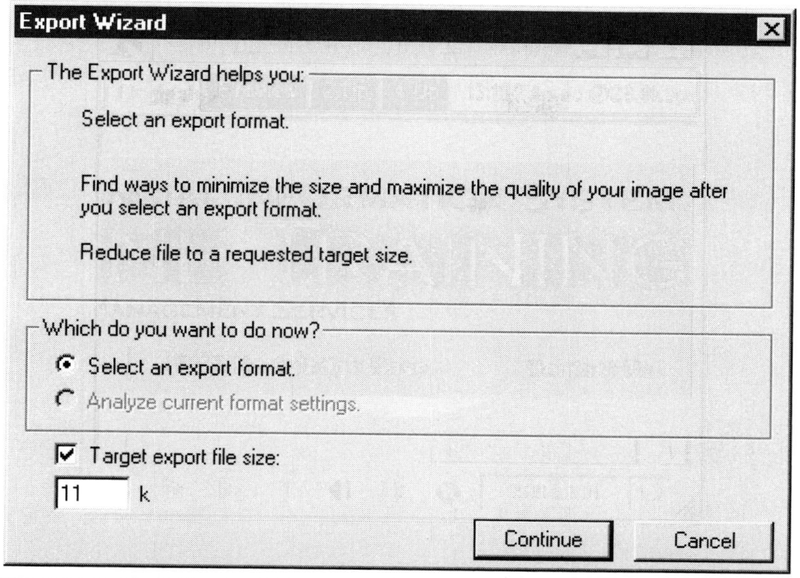

Figure 8-1 The first page of the Export Wizard

If your document has frames, you will be asked whether you want to export the document as an Animated GIF, a JavaScript Rollover, or a Single Image File (which, during testing, created JavaScript rollovers, anyway, even when TIF was selected as the file format!). Depending on how you instructed Fireworks to deal with frames, or if you had no frames, the wizard will ask what the destination for the exported file will be. Once you choose, you will be given a final analysis. However, although there are four export destination choices, Fireworks only seems to offer two possible wizard results, as seen in Table 8-1.

Option	Recommended File Type; Wizard Result
The Web	GIF or JPG; you will see one of each when you get to the Export Preview dialog box
An Image-Editing Application	TIF; you will see a TIF in the Export Preview dialog box
A Desktop Publishing Application	TIF; you will see a TIF in the Export Preview dialog box
Dreamweaver	GIF or JPG; you will see one of each when you get to the Export Preview dialog box

Table 8-1 Choices and Consequences in the Export Wizard

When the Wizard is through, it opens up a two-pane Export Preview with two configurations that are consistent with your specifications, unless TIF was the export file type, in which case there will only be one pane.

In summary, the Export Wizard does not provide terribly useful information. However, it might fit into your workflow in the following situations:

- New users who don't know where to begin with optimization
- As a convenient all-in-one tool when you need to optimize according to size and you want to take advantage of the Export Preview

Since it outputs into the Export Preview dialog box, however, it provides a segue into one of our favorite Fireworks features.

Using the Export Preview

Back in Fireworks 1, there was no Optimize panel. At that time, when you were ready to optimize your graphics, you opened what is now, with some changes, called the Export Preview dialog box (see Figure 8-2). The changes aside, the Export Preview dialog box's origins as an all-in-one optimization interface are clear. It is the most comprehensive optimization interface in Fireworks, though the majority of its tools are now replicated in other areas—the Optimize panel, the Color Table panel, the Frames panel, and so on.

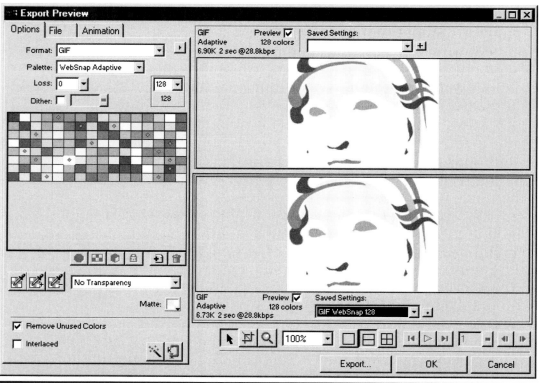

Figure 8-2 The Export Preview dialog box

To access the Export Preview, choose File | Export Preview. Alternatively, you can use the Export Area tool, draw a marquee around an area, and press ENTER or RETURN to get the Export Preview window. As discussed earlier, it also appears automatically after the Export Wizard.

Limitations of the Export Preview

In spite of the Export Preview's many strengths, it has a couple disadvantages. First, the Export Preview is intended to export whole areas—either the entire canvas or areas selected with the Export Area tool. You cannot use it to optimize individual objects, in particular, slices. You can only set the export default for the entire image. To customize individual slices (discussed next), you will need to use the Optimize panel.

A second disadvantage is that its preview panes tend to be smaller than the equivalent 2-Up and 4-Up tabs in the document window. Still, for any full images beyond simple optimizations, we skip the Optimize panel and come straight to the Export Preview dialog box to set the Export default for the entire document. Afterwards, you can modify individual slices, as appropriate.

IDEA You can enlarge the whole Export Preview dialog box—and the preview windows with it—by dragging edges of the dialog box. This works best in monitors with high resolutions (for example, 1024×768 and up).

Understanding the Export Preview Interface

The Export Preview dialog box is divided into two sections. On the left is a three-tabbed pane with a comprehensive set of options for each setting. Each of these tabs and its options will be discussed momentarily. On the right is the main window, many of whose options probably look familiar. Use the main window for its preview interface and major settings, while you use the three-tabbed pane on the left side for further customization.

Working with the Main Window

On the right side of the dialog box (see Figure 8-3) are up to four preview panes, some tools for working with them, and the main command buttons of the dialog box.

At the top are the same basic optimization settings and features that are in the Optimize panel. These include information about the previewed image—its file type, estimated export size, palette type (if necessary), quality (if necessary), and so forth. You can also access the optimize presets.

The preview panes work much like the 2-Up and 4-Up tabs in the document window. But there is a difference: by default, the Export dialog box does not reserve a space for the original, meaning that all you see are previews. As discussed earlier, since the interface takes up extra room, your preview panes are typically smaller in

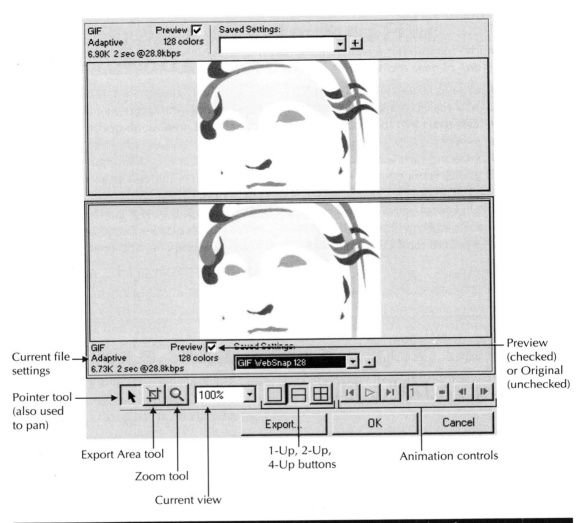

Figure 8-3   The right side of the Export Preview dialog box and its features

Labels on figure:
- Current file settings
- Pointer tool (also used to pan)
- Export Area tool
- Zoom tool
- Current view
- 1-Up, 2-Up, 4-Up buttons
- Animation controls
- Preview (checked) or Original (unchecked)

this dialog box. Perhaps for that reason, Macromedia set the default so that you do not see the preview. The advantage of saving room aside, the disadvantage of using this setting is, of course, that without the original, you lose your basis for comparison.

IDEA   To see the original at any time, uncheck the Preview check box in any of the preview panes. The original PNG will appear.

Beneath the preview panes are a series of familiar buttons. You will find the Pointer tool; the Export Area tool (which looks like the Crop tool in this interface); the Zoom tool; 1-Up, 2-Up, and 4-Up preview buttons; and an animation control bar.

Near the bottom-right corner are the main commands of the dialog box. Two of the buttons are self-explanatory, while the third may be somewhat confusing.

- **Export**   Export applies the chosen optimization settings as the export default and actually brings up the Export dialog box.
- **Cancel**   Cancel simply returns you to the main document, without applying or saving any of your work in the Export Preview dialog box.
- **OK**   The OK button could also be called "Save," since when you click it, it saves the settings as the export default for that document, but it does not bring up the Export dialog box. Assuming you do not make any further optimization changes to the document as a whole, the settings in the Export Preview will be used upon all subsequent exports, including those done externally via the Project Log.

Working with the Tabbed Panes

Notice the three tabs above the left pane. Taken together, these are like the Optimize panel on steroids. You have more options and more room to work with them. While many of the advanced options are available in other places, the Export Preview dialog box is the only place where you can manipulate the palettes of exported areas of several frames of an animation in one location.

Working with the Options Tab

The Options tab, seen in Figure 8-4, offers context-sensitive options by file format. Many of these settings are familiar from the Optimize panel. If you choose JPEG as your export file type, you will see settings for Quality, Smoothing, and so on.

If you choose an 8-bit color format, such as GIF, PNG-8, or TIF-8, you will see, in addition to the standard tools, a complete color palette along with the palette manipulation tools of the Color Table panel. This interface allows you to manipulate the color palette and see the effects of your work in a live preview at the same time. The color palette tools (seen in Figure 8-5) allow you to accomplish the following tasks: edit a given color, set a color to be transparent, snap the color to the nearest web safe color, and lock a color so that it cannot be edited.

Customizing Color Palettes

Perhaps the greatest advantage in limiting the color depth of your image is that when producing indexed color, you can more easily manage the size of your exported file. However, reducing the color depth and using indexed color enables you to gain control over individual colors in your files, with some impressive results.

You may not often need to get to the level of detail that you are editing individual colors, but you can. Editing individual colors, which in this case simply means changing a given swatch's color, can be useful when you are trying to balance two competing needs, such as sticking to the Web Safe palette while preserving a key color in a company logo.

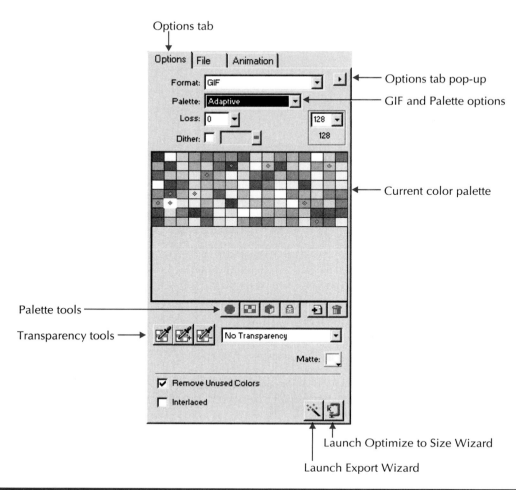

Figure 8-4 The Options tab of the Export Preview dialog box with GIF format selected

You might have noticed small symbols inside individual colors within the color palette. Each of these provides some information about the color, as explained in Figure 8-6. As you modify individual swatches, these symbols will help you and your colleagues understand changes. In addition, as you roll over swatches,

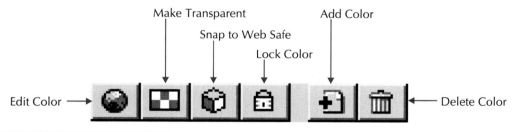

Figure 8-5 Color palette manipulation tools

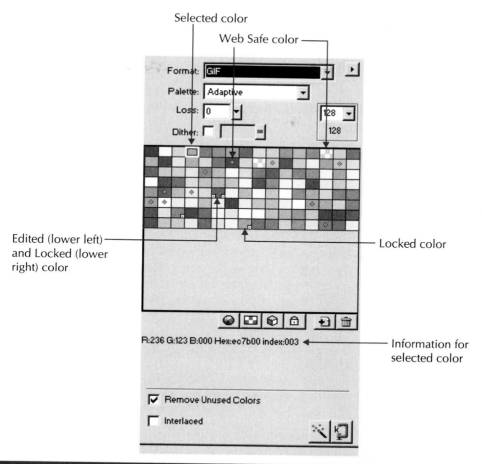

Selected color

Web Safe color

Edited (lower left) and Locked (lower right) color

Locked color

R:236 G:123 B:000 Hex:ec7b00 index:003

Information for selected color

Figure 8-6   The color palette in the Export Preview dialog box

information is displayed about each color, including RGB color values, hexadecimal values, and the index number assigned to this particular swatch.

NOTE These tools and symbols are also all available in the Color Table panel.

One final note before you begin modifying your palettes: the changes you make are all nondestructive. That is, if you change a color's value to make it more red, or if you choose to make it transparent, you are not permanently stuck with the decision. Save the file, make other changes, bring it into Dreamweaver—you can still come back and undo any of the edits you make to the color palette.

 The one exception to the ability to undo or restore colors to their original state is the Add Color tool, which replaces an existing color with a new color.

Editing Colors
To edit a swatch in the color palette, do the following:

1. Click to select the color.

2. Click the Edit Color button. The Color dialog box appears (see Figure 8-7).

3. Choose, mix, or enter RGB values to create a color.

4. Click OK to return to the Export Preview. The swatch color updates, the swatch also now displays the edited symbol in its corner, and the new color also appears in the preview pane at right. If you select the color again, you will notice that the Edit Color button will be toggled to the On position.

Working with Transparency in GIFs
Applying transparency to swatches works much the same way as editing colors:

1. Click to select the color in the palette.

2. Click the Transparent button. This adds this color to the transparent colors index, and the swatch now displays a gray and white checker pattern, which Fireworks uses to indicate transparency. Another way to apply transparency to a given color is to click the Add Color To Transparency eyedropper tool (the one with a + sign in the transparency section beneath the color palette), and click the desired color. This looks and works just like it did in the Optimize panel, covered in Chapter 7.

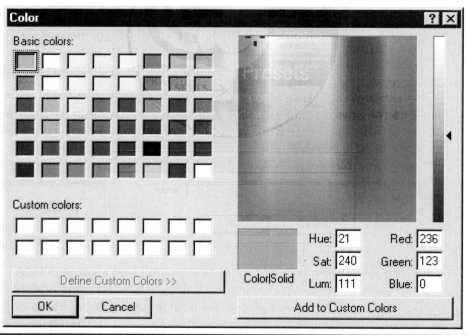

Figure 8-7   The Color dialog box

You may also remove a color from the index of transparent colors:

1. Click to select the transparent color in the palette. Notice that the Transparent button will appear to be toggled to the On position.

2. Click the Transparent button once to toggle it to off. The original color reappears. Alternatively, you can click the Remove Color From Transparency eyedropper tool (the one with a – sign beside it) and choose a color.

If you wish to make a given swatch the only transparent color—meaning that all other colors set to transparent will be restored to their original values—you can do that, too:

1. Click the Set Transparency Color eyedropper tool (the one with neither a + nor – sign beside it).

2. Click the desired color in the palette. It becomes transparent and the preview is updated as well.

Snapping to Web Safe Color
Macromedia's WebSnap Adaptive palette is an impressive innovation. However, it bases its judgment on whether to snap a color to Web Safe based on the color's proximity to a color in the Web Safe palette. It cannot take into account a color's relative importance, compared with other colors, and so it cannot force less important colors to snap or more important colors to remain. But you can.

To snap a color to the Web Safe palette, simply follow these steps:

1. Click to select the color in the palette.

2. Click the Snap To Web Safe (cube) tool. The color updates in the palette as well as in the preview. An icon appears in the center of the swatch to indicate that it is a Web Safe color, and an icon appears in the lower-left corner of the swatch to indicate that it has been edited.

Locking Colors
An alternative scenario is that in creating a palette, a key color shifted, such as the primary color of your client's logo. You know that whatever edits and optimizations you may make, that color simply *has* to appear in the proper shade. You can accomplish this by choosing and locking the color:

1. Click to select the color that you wish to lock.

2. If the color is not yet the proper color, edit it so that it is the desired shade.

3. Click the Lock Color tool. The color is locked, an icon appears in the lower-right corner of the swatch indicating as much, and if you select the swatch, you will see that the Lock Color tool is toggled to the On position.

The Options Tab Pop-Up Not only can you apply a number of diverse palette optimization strategies, but you also can apply multiple strategies to each swatch. The small symbols that appear in the swatches provide some cue, as do the toggle states of the various tools. To help you manage all of this, the Options tab has its own pop-up menu, seen in Figure 8-8.

NOTE This pop-up menu is available only if you choose an 8-bit color format.

Many of the options are redundant—mainly providing you easy access to commonly used tools. However, there are a handful of options that we have not yet discussed, outlined in Table 8-2.

By default the swatches are unsorted, but be aware that if you choose one of the sorting options, such as Sort By Luminance, you cannot return to the original sorting, even if you select Unsorted again.

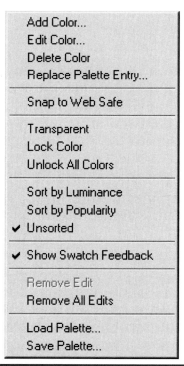

Figure 8-8   The Options tab pop-up menu

Option	Description
Add Color	Adds a color to the palette; functions the same as the Add Color tool beside the Remove Color (trash icon) tool
Replace Palette Entry	Replaces the selected color with the color of your choice
Unlock All Colors	Enables editability of all colors
Sort by Luminance	Sorts colors from lightest to darkest
Sort by Popularity	Sorts colors according to how often they appear in the exported image
Unsorted	The default; colors are not sorted
Show Swatch Feedback	The default; displays the icons that indicate locking, editing, and transparency status
Remove Edit	Removes editing to selected swatch; functions the same as toggling the Edit Color tool to the Off position for a selected color
Remove All Edits	Reverts all colors to their original colors; does not affect colors with applied transparency, but does revert edited colors that have also been locked (it leaves the locking intact)
Load Palette	Allows you to load a color palette (ACT) file
Save Palette	Saves the current palette as an ACT file

Table 8-2   Selected Features of the Options Tab Pop-Up

Other Settings of the Options Tab

A great amount of space has been devoted to color palette optimization strategies in the previous section, but for those image types that don't use indexed color, such as JPEG, most of these options are not applicable. The Options tab for files using the JPEG format is considerably simpler, as seen in Figure 8-9. Even the pop-up menu is gone.

The settings are the same as those in the Optimize panel, covered in Chapter 7, except, oddly enough, the selective JPEG option is unavailable.

If you choose a 24-bit or higher TIF or BMP, there are no options beyond the Matte color.

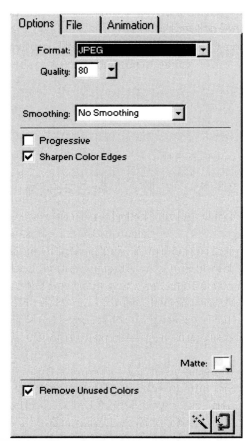

Figure 8-9   The Options tab with a JPEG file type selected

Working with the File Tab

When you create files, you set their physical dimensions in the New dialog box, and you can modify these anytime using Modify | Image Size. If, for some reason, you wish to scale an image up or down upon export, you can use the Scale settings of the File tab in the Export Preview dialog box, seen in Figure 8-10.

 One of the advantages of vector graphics is that they can be scaled up or down, and they will always appear at their optimal resolution. Bitmap graphics, however, when scaled up show pixellation the more you scale up. If your image has bitmaps, this dialog box is not the optimal method for scaling up. Rather, you should enlarge your canvas size in the authoring environment, return to your bitmap editor, and enlarge and re-export your bitmap at its target final size.

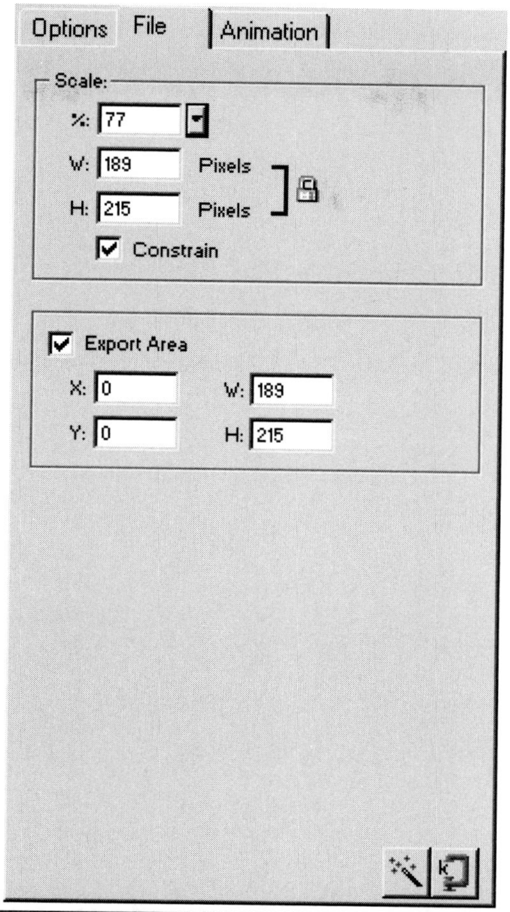

Figure 8-10   The File tab of the Export Preview dialog box

A common use for scaling would be if you used Fireworks to create a logo, and you need to export it in different sizes for different uses—a version for a banner on the Web (GIF), one version for a splash page on the Web (GIF), and several different sizes to be used for paper marketing (TIF)—letterhead, envelopes, business cards, and so forth.

Scaling Images upon Export

To scale an image, follow these steps:

1. Determine whether you want to constrain proportions, and check the Constrain check box accordingly. Not checking this box will usually lead to distortion, so we generally recommend selecting this box.

2. If you know the final target dimensions, enter pixel values in the W(idth) and H(eight) text fields. If you want to scale by percent, you can use the slider or simply type in a number in the % field.

3. Choose OK to simply save the settings, or choose Export to save the settings and initiate the Export dialog box.

IDEA Another way to scale images for multiple uses is to use Fireworks batch processing. See Chapter 14 for more on batch processing.

Exporting Areas of (Cropping) Images upon Export

Just as you can select individual objects in vector mode, or areas of pixels in Bitmap mode, when exporting regions, you can do it by the object (slice) or region. We'll cover exporting slices later in this chapter. Exporting areas does preserve behaviors and slice information.

IDEA Use this tool when you have mocked up an entire HTML page design in Fireworks, but wish to export a banner with rollovers as an independent entity.

To export a region of an image, follow these steps:

1. Check the Export Area check box in the File tab of the Export Preview dialog box.

2. To enter numerically the export region, enter the top (Y) and side (X) coordinates to indicate the top-left corner of the crop region. The coordinates 0,0 will include the top-left corner of the document. Then enter the size of the crop region itself in pixels, W(idth) and H(eight).

3. To enter this information visually, choose the Export Area (Crop) tool in the main window at right, and drag the edges until you have isolated the desired region, shown in Figure 8-11.

4. To start over, uncheck the Export Area check box and then select it again.

IDEA Activate only one preview and use the Zoom tool or View settings to make cropping easier.

Working with the Animation Tab

The Animation tab of the Export Preview dialog box (shown in Figure 8-12) contains most of the same options available in the Frame panel. You can set the frame delay, loop amount, and disposal method, right in the export interface, seeing a live preview of your animation as you work.

CROSS REFERENCE → See Chapter 9 for details about these and other animation settings.

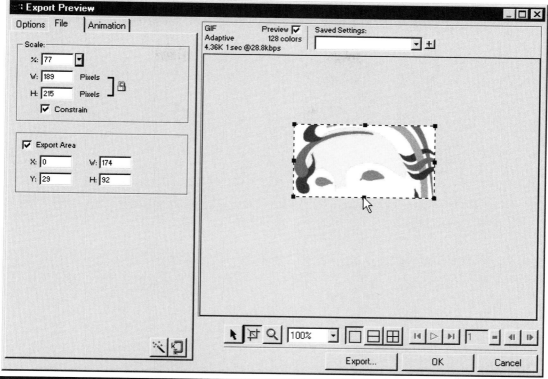

Figure 8-11 Exporting an area visually in the Export Preview

Slicing Graphics for Optimization

In Chapter 4, we discussed two reasons why you would slice a file in Fireworks:

- To optimize complex graphics more efficiently
- To add interactivity, such as buttons, rollovers, image swaps

CROSS REFERENCE → Slicing for interactivity is discussed in Chapter 11.

One of the limitations of the Export Preview is that you can only set the export default for the entire image—it is a one-size-fits-all approach. Unfortunately, whole graphics often have different areas that would do well with different forms of optimization. An area with a bitmap image or a faux-bitmap Live Effect might look better and download faster as a JPG, while another area of the same image with a lot of solid color might look better and download faster as a GIF.

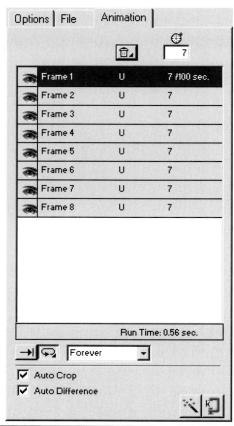

Figure 8-12   The Animation tab of the Export Preview dialog box

Export Default vs. Slice Optimization

Fireworks makes a key distinction between two levels of optimization. First, there is a default optimization setting for the PNG as a whole. This is referred to as the *export default,* and it is what you set when you work in the Export Preview or work in the Optimize panel with no slices selected.

The second level of optimization is for individual slices. Slice optimization settings override those of the export default, using a principle of inheritance similar to object-oriented programming.

> NOTE   In addition to storing optimization settings, slice objects can also store URLs, `<alt>` tags, target information, and behaviors.

Both sets of optimization setting (export default and slice) are stored in a Fireworks PNG's metadata, meaning that all optimization settings persist, even after you close the file.

Optimizing—By the Slice

If you know how to optimize in general, then optimizing individual slices is easy:

1. With the Web Layer active, click with the Pointer tool to select a slice.

2. Choose the 2-Up or 4-Up tab in the document window.

3. If necessary, use the Hand tool to pan to make the selected slice visible. Notice that the whole image is partially shaded, except the slice region, as seen in Figure 8-13. Areas covered by the shading will not be affected by the optimization settings entered as long as the slice is selected. In addition, below the preview, the name of the slice, rather than the file, appears.

4. Apply the desired optimization settings to the slice.

 When you optimize by the slice, all of the frames in that slice will have the same optimization setting. In such cases (buttons, rollovers, and so on), make sure you check the preview of each frame, so that you do not optimize for only one state!

Selected slice (original)   Shaded area (not affected)

Active area (being optimized)

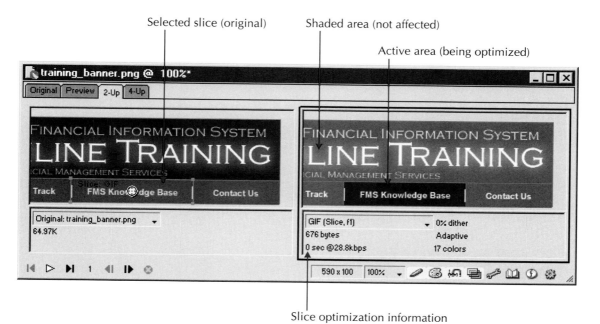

Slice optimization information

Figure 8-13 When optimizing slices, all other regions of the image are partially shaded.

Exporting Individual Slices

In addition to optimizing by the slice, Fireworks also allows you to export individual slices. This comes in handy when you need to make a minor change to a single button in a nav bar that has already been integrated in your HTML editor. It also provides a work-around for the limitation that different optimization settings cannot be applied to different frames of the same slice.

To export an individual slice, do the following:

1. Choose and optimize the slice as described earlier, using the Optimize panel and the preview panes.

2. Choose File | Export. The Export dialog box appears. Use the settings shown in Figure 8-14 to export an individual slice.

3. Choose Images Only as the Save As Type.

4. Choose Export Slices in the Slices drop-down list.

5. Check the Selected Slices Only check box.

6. Uncheck the Include Areas Without Slices check box.

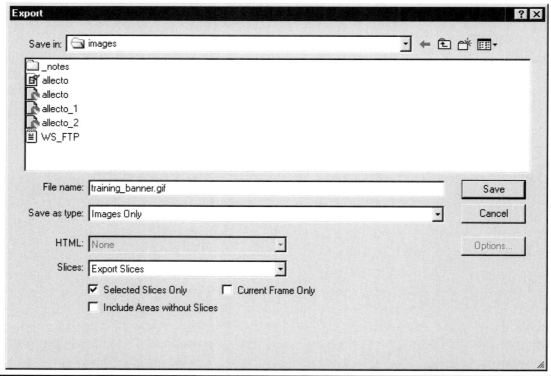

Figure 8-14   Settings used in the Export dialog box to export an individual slice

7. See the next section in this chapter to determine whether you should check the Current Frame Only check box.

8. Click Save.

The Same-Slice/Different-Frame Work-Around

You may find that you need to save one frame of a slice with one optimization setting, while another frame will have a different setting. This might happen, for instance, if one frame has a black and white bitmap (which lends itself to GIF), while the rollover frame has the same bitmap in full color (which lends itself to JPG).

Take these steps to export the frames with different optimization settings:

1. Follow the preceding steps to optimize the first frame.

2. Choose File | Export to bring up the Export dialog box.

3. In the Export dialog box, be sure to select Current Frame Only and click Save.

4. Return to the Preview and optimize the second frame.

5. Bring up the Export dialog box again, and with Current Frame Only still checked, click Save to export the second frame.

6. Repeat as necessary until all frames are exported.

 Although you have exported each frame with its own optimization settings, Fireworks only remembers the last one. Thus, if you export the slice again, either manually (with Current Frame Only unchecked) or through an automated process such as the Project Log, all of the slices will be exported using the same settings as a group.

Using Selective JPEG Compression

Fireworks 4 ships with a new feature that solves—or goes a ways toward resolving—an old problem. As you know, you can export JPEG images using more or less compression, with more or less loss of image quality. The problem occurs when you have an image that contains some areas (such as the foreground) that are important, while other areas (such as the background) are not. The JPEG compression scheme typically applies equally across the entire image.

Enter Selective JPEG Compression, a feature that allows you to select areas of the image and compress them with a different quality than the rest of the image. In most cases you will probably set the mask area's quality to be higher than that of the rest of the image, but there is no reason you could not make it lower, if, say, it was easier to mask the less important area than the more important area.

Creating and Optimizing Masks
for JPEG Compression

Basically, you use masking to set off the different areas and then optimize each in the Optimize panel.

1. Choose one of the Marquee tools in the Tools panel, and draw a selection around the area you wish to apply special settings to. Fireworks automatically switches to Bitmap mode whenever you use the Marquee tool.

2. With the marquee active, choose Modify | Selective JPEG | Save Selection As JPEG Mask. The marquee region turns pink (by default) to show where the Selective JPEG region is, though that pink overlay will not appear, of course, in the exported file.

3. Switch to the 2-Up or 4-Up preview mode in the document window, and in the Optimize panel, choose JPEG as the file type.

4. Apply appropriate settings for all areas *outside* of the masked area. If your primary image is within the JPEG mask, then you should select a relatively low setting here, such as 60.

5. Click the Edit Selective Quality Options in the Optimize panel to open the Selective JPEG Settings dialog box:

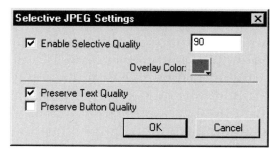

6. Choose appropriate settings for the region *within* the mask region. If the area within the mask region is the most important, you might choose a high setting such as 90.

7. Select the Preserve Text Quality and Preserve Button Quality options to ensure that these compress cleanly; however, your file size will likely increase as a result.

8. Click OK to apply the settings and return to the preview.

Techniques for Selecting the Right Area

Your chances of an effective Selective JPEG Compression are slim if your JPEG masks are simple rectangles. It is a rare photographic element that just happens to be perfectly rectangular. Remember that to make a Selective JPEG mask, you can use any of the bitmap selection tools—with some limitations. We'd like to credit our friend Brian Baker for some key insights in this section.

Creating Soft-Edged Selective Compression Masks with the Polygon Lasso Tool

One common way to select the right part of an image for selective compression is to use the Polygon Lasso tool, which is grouped with the regular Lasso tool in the Tools panel.

1. If the Polygon Lasso tool is not visible, click and hold the Lasso tool until a small pop-up panel appears that contains the Polygon Lasso tool.

2. Click the desired tool to activate it.

3. Click around the edges of the area you wish to select, creating a closed shape around the desired region of an image. When you are done, a polygonal selection area appears.

4. Convert the selection to a JPEG mask and optimize as earlier.

It is reasonable to infer that anything you can do with the bitmap selection tools can also be used to create a JPEG mask. However, this is not the case. Fireworks bitmap selection tools enable 256 degrees of selection. Features like feathering take advantage of this. If you create a JPEG mask using a feathered selection, Fireworks will dutifully display a feathered, pink mask. Unfortunately, Selective JPEG Compression does not support 256 levels; it is either on or off. So even though your Selective JPEG Compression mask appears feathered in the authoring environment, exported images will simply be at one compression setting (outside the mask, including the feather area) or the other (inside the mask, excluding the feathering).

 If your two selection areas (masked and unmasked) are compressed at widely different levels, say 90% and 30% quality, there could be a sharp, unnatural line dividing the two areas. Be careful to mask the right area, and be sure to look for such a line in all exported JPGs that use this feature.

Creating Selective Compression Masks with the Magic Wand Tool

Another way to create effective Selective JPEG Compression masks is to use the Magic Wand tool. This technique is a little more quick and dirty, but for the right kind of image, it works like a charm. Use it when the object that you wish to demarcate is primarily a different color than the rest of the image. The child in Figure 8-15 has a blue hat, and if for some reason you wanted to isolate your compression

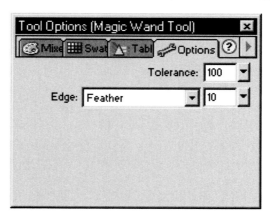

Figure 8-15 The blue hat contains almost all of the blue pixels in this image, making it ripe for Magic Wand selection.

on the hat only (say, you were doing an ad for the hat), the Magic Wand tool would give you a quick way to add a mask just to the hat.

1. Choose the Magic Wand tool in the Tools panel.

2. In the Tool Options panel, shown here, drag the Tolerance slider to a fairly high number, such as 100. Tolerance determines how close in value a color has to be to the actual pixel clicked with the tool. A higher number picks up more colors, while a low number picks up fewer colors. You may need to do some trial and error before you select the right region.

3. Convert the selection to a Selective JPEG Compression mask and optimize as described earlier.

NOTE Because Selective JPEG Compression works in Bitmap mode, you can use it not just for your Fireworks PNG authoring files, but for any bitmap images. That means you can use it to improve existing JPG images, by further compressing unimportant regions, while leaving the main area at the highest quality setting so that you do not degrade it more.

Creating Complex Selective Masks

To create complex Selective JPEG Compression masks, you follow the same steps you would use to create complex marquee areas in Bitmap mode.

1. Choose the Lasso Tool to draw a marquee area.

2. With the marquee area still active, press and hold the SHIFT key and draw another area. If the two areas intersect, Fireworks will join them into a single marquee area. If they do not overlap, you will end up with two selection regions.

3. With the new marquee area still active, press and hold the ALT key, and draw another selection area with the Lasso tool that intersects with a portion of the original marquee. Fireworks cuts the new area out of the original area, so that the original area is smaller than it was before.

4. In this way, even those who can't draw with a mouse can draw a selection area, and from it create a Selective JPEG Compression mask, with precision.

Exporting a Transparent GIF

One of the oldest tricks of HTML layout is using a transparent GIF to position text and other objects. The `<img>` tag in HTML has both width and height attributes, allowing you to stretch graphics to fit a desired size. By placing a transparent graphic into a document, you can effectively take up space and force another object to lay out around the graphic.

NOTE Common names for transparent GIFs are shim.gif, transparent.gif, and spacer.gif. When Fireworks generates them to create spacing for tables, it calls them spacer.gif.

Creating a Transparent GIF in Fireworks

Fireworks makes creating transparent GIFs quite easy.

1. Choose File | New to open the New Document dialog box.

2. Enter **1** pixel for both the Width and Height. You will resize the graphic in the HTML document itself.

3. Leave the Resolution at 72 pixels per inch.

4. Choose Transparent as the Canvas Color. The dialog box should appear as shown here.

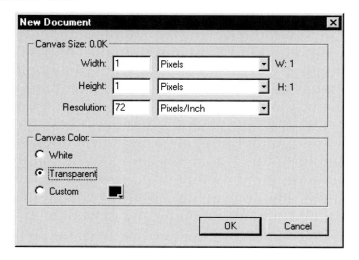

5. Click OK. The document opens with a very small graphic in it.

6. Choose File | Export Preview to open the Export Preview dialog box.

7. Choose GIF as the file format; JPG does not support transparency.

8. Choose Exact as the palette type.

9. Oddly enough, a two-color palette appears, shown here. One color is white, while the other is transparent.

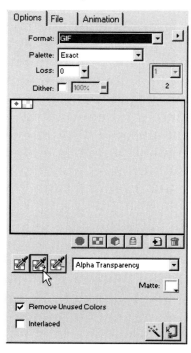

10. Click the Add Color To Transparency (+ eyedropper) tool.

11. Click the white color swatch to make it transparent. Both colors are now transparent.

12. Click Export.

Setting Up HTML to Use a Transparent GIF

Transparent GIFs are used to create pixel-precise positioning effects in HTML. You can use the indent paragraphs with much greater precision than the `<blockquote>` tag. Use them to add space between several images in a row. Use them to position nested tables. Anytime you need absolute control over the positioning of any HTML object, you can use a transparent GIF. The best part is that you can use and reuse the same, tiny GIF throughout your site.

Stretching it to all sorts of dimensions isn't a problem—it's transparent!

Example: Indenting and Positioning a Text Paragraph

In the following simple example, one paragraph of text is positioned to the right of the others, and the space between two paragraphs is also controlled, using a transparent GIF.

```
<TABLE>
  <TR>
    <TD>
      <P>This line is left-aligned.</P>
      <P><IMG SRC="images/transparent.gif" WIDTH="22" ¬
          HEIGHT="55" ALIGN="TOP">This line is indented
          22 pixels and the next line is at least 55 pixels
          lower than the top of this one.</P
      <P>Proof is in the pudding. This line really is spaced
          further apart from the first two lines.</P>
    </TD>
  <TR>
</TABLE>
```

Figure 8-16 shows an HTML page with this table in it.

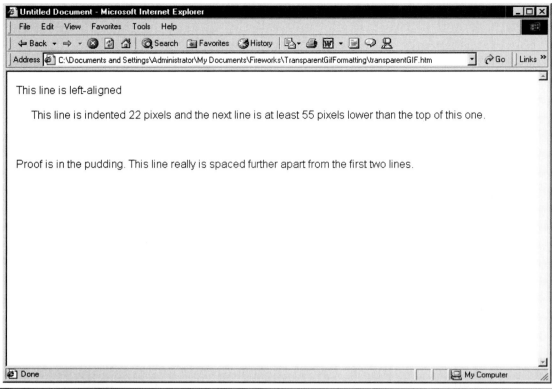

Figure 8-16 The HTML code as rendered in a browser

9 Animating with Fireworks

In addition to its powerful web graphics capabilities, Fireworks is also an excellent animation tool—great for creating animated GIF portions of your web layout, animated banners, or for exporting a Flash SWF file. With Fireworks, you can build animation either in a traditional frame-by-frame method, or you can use Fireworks' "tween" feature to build animations automatically based on parameters that you define. Fireworks 4 also offers a new "live animation" feature that allows you to quickly turn any selected graphic into an instant animation. After using any of these techniques to create an animation, Fireworks allows you to export either the entire document or a portion of it as an animated GIF or Flash SWF file, optimized and ready for the Web.

217

I n this chapter, we'll start by introducing you to basic frame-by-frame animation techniques using the Frames panel. Once you've mastered the basics, you'll learn how to use symbols and instances, the new live animation effects feature, and Fireworks' tweening abilities to create more efficient animations ready for web export.

Frame-by-Frame Animation

The most straightforward means of animating in Fireworks is to build each frame one at a time. With this method, called *frame-by-frame animation,* you simply change the location, color, size, or shape of an image or images on each successive frame until you achieve the desired effect. For example, the abstracted text animation in Figure 9-1 shows slightly blurred words flashing around a central message. Only one layer was used to create this five-frame animation. On each frame, the text elements of Layer 1 have been altered, blurred, or deleted.

IDEA   You can open existing animated GIF files in Fireworks. Fireworks will place each frame sequentially in the Frames panel.

Using the Frames Panel

The key to creating an animation as shown in Figure 9-1 is using the versatile Frames panel. In Chapter 1, we discussed using the Frames panel to build different design directions for a client. As you'll see in this chapter, however, the more common use of the Frames panel is to build animation steps. The Frames panel offers an array of features that help to streamline the animation process. For example, the "onion skinning" feature allows you to view multiple frames at once, so you can better assess the relative locations of images on each frame. You can also set the timing and loop values of your animation. Once you've built an animation in a series of frames, you can even preview the animation right in the document workspace before exporting.

design solution

When building designs and animations in Fireworks, you are often working with multiple source images like scans and photos. To keep all of your source documents neatly in one file, try opening them all as an animation in one document. Choose File | Open. In the Open dialog box, SHIFT-select multiple files and then check the Open As Animation option. This places each image in a different frame. Then name each of the frames to remind you of their contents. (See "Naming Frames" in this chapter.)

Adding, Subtracting, and Reordering Frames

When you start a new Fireworks document, there is one layer in the Layers panel and one

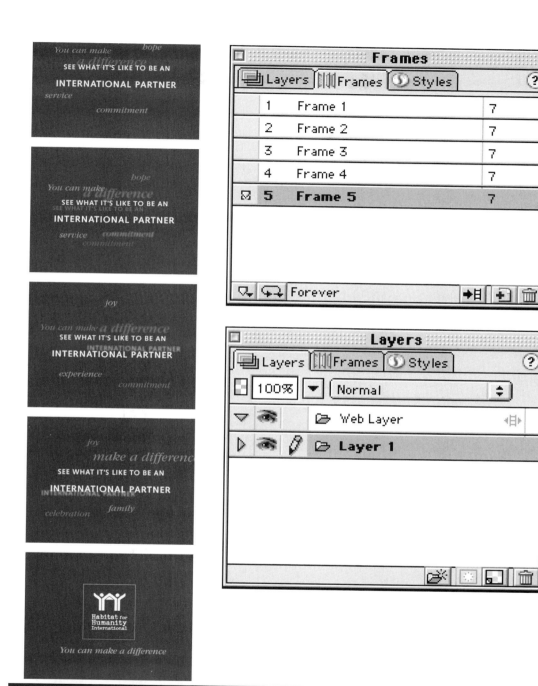

Figure 9-1 By changing the size, location, and content of elements on each successive frame, you create a frame-by-frame animation.

frame in the Frames panel. To build an animation, therefore, you'll need to add more frames. As you progress with the design of your animation, you'll find that you'll also need to reorder the sequence of frames or to delete frames to optimize the design.

Here are quick steps to building a simple frame-by-frame animation like the one in Figure 9-1:

1. In Fireworks, create a new document that is 400×400 pixels with a black background.

2. Create a few text elements that are different sizes, colors, and fonts. Pick one text message that will remain constant, and place it in the middle of your layout. Sprinkle the remaining text elements around the central message. Remember that you are just building Frame 1 of your animation in this step. You don't have to include all of the text elements that will ultimately appear in this animation. For example, you can have just two text elements on Frame 1 and three or four elements on Frame 2.

3. To create visual interest, select each surrounding text element and either fade it out by adjusting its opacity in the Layers panel, or apply an effect to it in the Effect panel.

4. In the Frames panel, choose Duplicate Frame from the Options menu, as shown in Figure 9-2. In the Duplicate Frame window, enter **4** as the Number (of frames) and click OK. This action results in a total of five frames, because you are adding four after Frame 1.

5. Click on Frame 2 in the Frames panel. One by one, select each of the surrounding text elements and make changes to them. You can adjust the opacity, color, or font of the words by double-clicking them. You can even delete some text elements or add more. When finished, click on Frame 3 and repeat the process. Continue adjusting the text elements in the remaining frames.

Choose Duplicate Frame
from the Options menu.

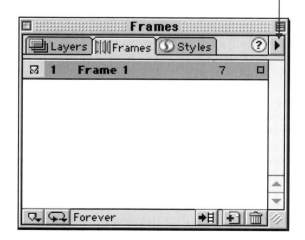 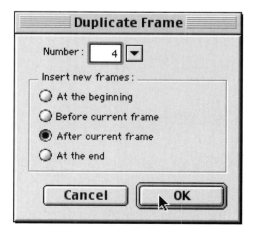

Figure 9-2   To add more frames, choose either Add Frames or Duplicate Frame from the Options menu.

6. To see how your animation is shaping up, click on each frame in the Frames panel successively. (See "Previewing Your Animation," later in this chapter, for other means of previewing your work.) Try reordering the frame sequence by clicking and dragging a frame in between two others. To delete one of your frames, select it and then click on the Trash icon at the bottom of the Frames panel.

 When building Animated GIFs, use as few frames as possible. This will help keep the file size down and lessen the download time. Remember that each frame becomes a separate GIF image, so fewer frames and a smaller document size will help achieve better optimization results.

Naming Frames

As you build more complex animations, you'll find it necessary to name your frames to better keep track of them. For example, if you are building a ten-frame animated banner with different messages on each frame, it's helpful to name the frames according to the message. This way, when glancing at the Frames panel, you can quickly identify each frame to move it to a new position in the sequence or to delete it.

To name a frame, simply double-click on its name, "Frame 1," in the Frames panel. Enter a new name and click anywhere outside the text field to exit. To adjust the frame's delay, and specify whether the frame is included in the final animation output (discussed later in this chapter), double-click the number *to the right* of the frame's name and enter the appropriate settings in the pop-up Frame Properties window. Click anywhere outside the window to close it.

 Naming frames is helpful not only when building animation, but also, as discussed in Chapter 1, when using frames to build different design directions. You could name each frame according to the design style and type of page it contains, like "geometric home" or "illustrated home."

Onion Skinning

While you build an animation over a series of frames, it's critical to see the placement of elements in the other frames. If you can see the contents of other frames, then you can more accurately position elements in the selected frame. For example, to build an animation of the moon moving smoothly across the night sky as in Figure 9-3, each step must be evenly spaced.

To help you see all steps of the moon at once, turn on Fireworks' onion skinning by choosing Show All Frames in the pull-down menu at the bottom of the Frames panel. In the pull-down menu, you'll notice that there are a few other options for onion skinning, like Show Next Frame and Before And After. We find that it's best to start with Show All Frames because you can manually adjust the range of frames later in the Frames panel itself.

Once onion skinning is on, you'll see a line extending in the left column of the Frames panel. This line represents the range of frames included in the onion skin

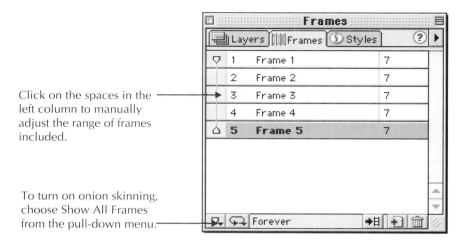

Click on the spaces in the left column to manually adjust the range of frames included.

To turn on onion skinning, choose Show All Frames from the pull-down menu.

Figure 9-3   Turning on onion skinning allows you to see the contents of multiple frames at once.

view. To adjust the range of frames, click in the spaces next to each frame. To turn onion skinning off, either click once on the onion skin line next to the selected frame, or choose No Onion Skinning from the pull-down menu at the bottom of the Frames panel.

Multiframe Editing

While onion skinning is turned on, it's possible to select and edit objects in your design that reside on nonselected frames. For example, though Frame 3 is selected in

Figure 9-4, you could pick up and move the moons in Frames 1, 2, and 3. (Notice the blue dots in the right column of the Frames panel. These represent selected items.)

This Multi-Frame Editing feature is both a timesaver and an annoyance. On the one hand, multiframe editing makes it quick and easy for you to adjust all of the frames of an animation, for example, to make sure they are evenly spaced. On the other hand, we've found that multiframe editing can make it difficult to select a particular object, say, the object on Frame 3. For animations that have tightly spaced animation steps, we've found it easier to keep multiframe editing turned off. To turn multiframe editing off, uncheck it in the pull-down menu at the bottom of the Frames panel.

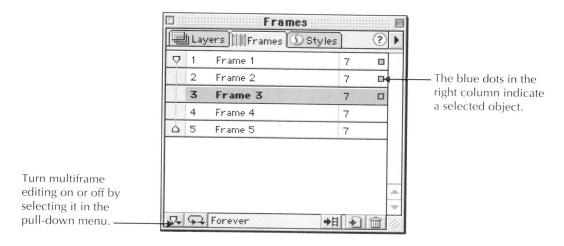

The blue dots in the right column indicate a selected object.

Turn multiframe editing on or off by selecting it in the pull-down menu.

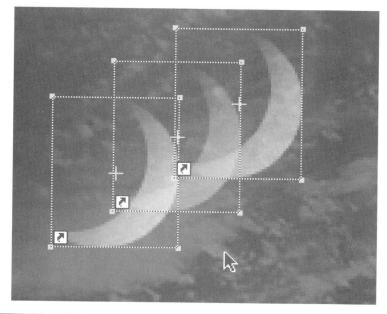

Figure 9-4   While onion skinning is on, you can select and edit objects on multiple frames.

NOTE Turning off multiframe editing does not automatically deselect everything you have already selected. To deselect, you must manually choose Edit | Deselect from the menu.

Setting Frame Rates and Looping

Two important elements in building effective animation are the abilities to control the duration of each frame before it advances to the next frame and to control the number of times the animation repeats, or *loops.* For example, a lot of animated banner ads on the Web use a small number of frames in order to keep the file size down. To make the animation *feel* longer, however, designers will place delays on certain frames with key messages. In addition, the designers often make the animation loop indefinitely. For example, take a look at the Frames panel for the Habitat for Humanity banner animation in Figure 9-5. Notice that we named the frames according to the message they contain. Also, notice the different numbers in the rightmost column, such as "7" and "400." These numbers, measured in hundredths of a second, represent the amount of delay on the frame: that is, 400 equals a four-second delay, and 100 equals a one-second delay.

NOTE Fireworks 4 does not support interframe transitions such as the wipes and dissolves you can set up in programs like PowerPoint.

To set the delay of a given frame, simply double-click on the number in its right column. To set the delay of multiple frames at once, first hold down the SHIFT key

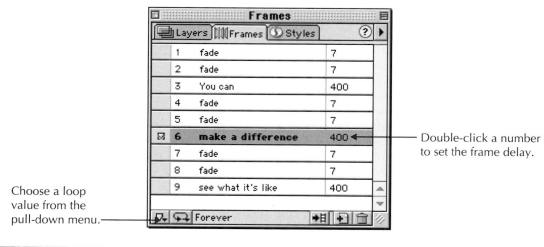

Choose a loop value from the pull-down menu.

Double-click a number to set the frame delay.

Figure 9-5   You can pace your animation by setting interframe delays.

and select a few frames. Then double-click one frame's delay number to set the delay for all of them.

After adjusting the frame delays of your animation, the next decision is whether to loop the animation so that it plays over and over. If you don't want the animation to loop, choose No Looping from the pull-down menu at the bottom of the Frames panel. If you do want it to loop, you have a few choices. You can either set it to loop a specific number of times by choosing one of the preset numbers in the looping pull-down menu, or you can choose Forever, which makes the animation loop indefinitely.

Previewing Your Animation

Rather than clicking on each of your frames in the Frames panel to manually preview the effect of your animation, Fireworks has Play and Stop controls, shown in Figure 9-6, that allow you to preview your animation right in the document window. For a more realistic effect, Fireworks also allows you to launch a web browser and to preview your animation the way it will look and play once exported.

To preview your work in the document or in a web browser, follow these steps:

1. Build a simple animation that consists of five to ten frames. Set different frame delays for each frame. Make some frames have short durations by entering a low number like 7 (hundredths of a second), and make others hold for 4 to 5 seconds by entering a number like 400 or 500.

2. Use the video-like Play and Stop controls in the lower-left corner of the document window to set your animation in motion. Notice that Fireworks does its best to approximate the delays you have set for each frame. (If a frame takes a while to render because it has complex graphics, the performance may be slower than the actual frame delay value.)

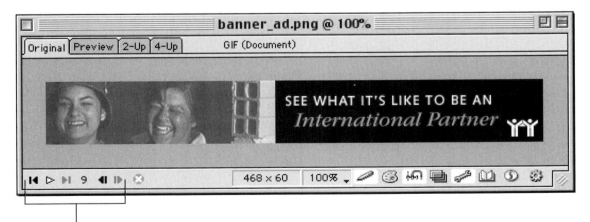

Rewind, Play/Stop, Fast Forward, Step Back, Step Forward buttons.

Figure 9-6 Use the video-like controls to preview an animation in the document window.

3. To preview your work in a web browser, choose File | Preview In Browser | Preview In (Internet Explorer or Netscape). If you don't see a browser listed, choose File | Preview In Browser | Set Primary Browser, and follow the ensuing steps to locate your browser.

Setting Background Imagery

As you build an animation, you may find that some images, like a background scene, should appear on every frame. Rather than copying and pasting the image every time you create a new frame, or worse, having to reposition the same image on each frame if you decide to move it, you can set up a "shared" layer in the Layers panel. Once you have a shared layer, anything that you place in the shared layer will appear automatically on every frame you create. If you delete an element from a shared layer, it will be deleted from all frames. Similarly, if you move an item on a shared layer, its position is updated throughout each frame of your animation.

To convert a layer to become a shared layer, follow these steps:

1. Create a new Fireworks file, and in the Layers panel, add a new layer. Double-click on the bottom layer to access a mini window, as shown next. Name the layer **Background**, and check the Share Layer option. Click anywhere outside the window to close it.

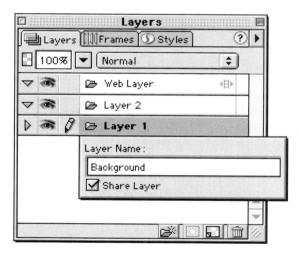

2. Place an image in the shared "Background" layer that will serve as a background for your animation.

3. In the normal (nonshared) top layer, place an element that you want to animate.

4. In the Frames panel, choose Add Frames from the Options menu, as indicated in the following illustration, and add four frames. To see the effects of the shared layer, click on each of the frames. You should see only your background element in Frames 2–5. The object you want to animate should appear only in Frame 1.

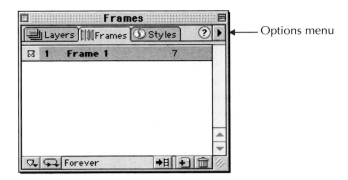

Options menu

If you have a multiframe animation already built, take caution when you turn a layer into a shared layer—you may end up deleting your work. For example, remember that you can have different objects in different frames that all use the same layer. If you're on Frame 3 when you turn the layer into a shared layer, the contents of Frame 3 will replace everything on the remaining frames that use that layer.

5. Click on Frame 1 and select the object in the nonshared layer to animate. To quickly copy this image to each of the other frames, choose Copy To Frames from the Options menu. In the dialog box, choose All Frames and click OK. Then click on each frame successively, and reposition the copied object to animate it. Notice that if you click on each frame to preview the animation effect, your object jumps around the screen according to how you've repositioned it.

6. Select and move the background object in the shared layer. Now, click on each frame in the Frames panel, and notice how the object's new position is the same in each frame. Ah, the beauty of shared layers.

If you use a shared layer, you must have one normal layer in order to build an animation. Remember, anytime you move an element in a shared layer, it moves in each frame. The only way to build movement, therefore, is to change elements in normal, nonshared layers.

Symbols and Instances

So far in this chapter, we've addressed techniques for building a basic animation whereby you change the size, location, and other attributes of an object in each frame—one at a time. This frame-by-frame approach is labor intensive and is less accurate, because it's difficult to "eyeball" the amount of change needed in each step to create a smooth look. Instead of manually animating each step, you can ask Fireworks to automatically generate a number of steps for you. Such automatic animation, called *tweening,* works by calculating the difference between a starting and an ending point that you define. You can, for example, create a 30-frame animation simply by setting up a starting and an ending graphic. To take advantage of tweening, however, you cannot use just any graphics. You must be working with symbols and instances.

For those of you familiar with Flash, the concept of symbols and instances should be familiar. A *symbol* is a vector or bitmap object that lives in the Fireworks Library panel. Generally, the concept behind symbols is that they are ordinary graphics set aside in a special library to facilitate using them over and over again. For example, rather than working with a number of copies of the same graphic, you can keep the original as a symbol in the Library panel, and use *instances,* or copies, of it in your layout. In this context, using symbols in the Library panel is also a great way for a web team to use a standardized set of graphics such as a company logo, tag line, and buttons.

NOTE   Unlike Flash, Fireworks does not realize any file savings from using symbol instances. The purpose of symbols and instances in Fireworks is to facilitate reuse of the same graphic and to create tweened animation.

You can turn any selected bitmap or vector object—or group of vector and bitmap objects—into a symbol. To do so, choose Insert | Convert To Symbol from the menu. You can also build a new symbol from scratch by choosing Insert | New Symbol. Once an object or group of objects is a symbol, it appears in the Library panel. Now that you have a symbol, you can start building tweened animations.

Tweening Instances

Tweening, for those of you new to animation, is the ability to set a starting and an ending point and have Fireworks automatically generate a number of animation steps in between (hence the name "tween"). To use the Fireworks tween feature, you must first prepare two instances of the *same* symbol. You cannot, for example, build a morph animation of one symbol instance turning into another symbol instance. One instance of a symbol will become the starting point on Frame 1, and the second instance of the same symbol becomes the ending point. Here's a brief overview of the tweening process:

1. Create a graphic object that you wish to animate. To keep it simple, you can create either a text element or a graphic shape like a circle.

2. Select the object and choose Insert | Convert To Symbol. In the window that appears, give the new symbol a name and be sure to choose Graphic as the Type, as shown next. Click OK to exit.

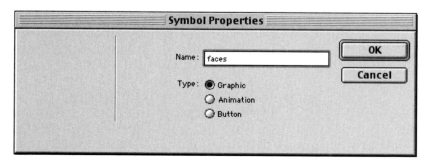

3. The image in your workspace is now an *instance* of a master symbol housed in the Library panel. If you notice, the instance looks a little different when selected. Instead of having a blue outline around it, it now has a dotted outline with an arrow icon in the lower-left corner, as shown next. This difference is how you can recognize normal objects from symbol instances in your layout.

4. To animate the instance, you need two copies of it. To quickly create a copy, hold down the OPTION or ALT key while you select and drag the instance. Position the copy off to the right.

5. The original instance will be the starting point of the animation. Therefore, select it and change its size, opacity, location, and so on, to the way you want it to appear at the start of the animation. Select the second instance and make changes that reflect how you want the animation to end up. For example, in the following illustration, the first instance is nearly invisible, off to the left, and is much smaller than the second instance. The second instance is at full opacity, full size, and is placed off to the right of the first instance.

6. SHIFT-select both instances and choose Modify | Symbol | Tween Instances from the menu. In the window that appears, enter **8** steps and check the Distribute To Frames option. If you do not check Distribute To Frames, all eight animation steps will end up on Frame 1. The Distribute To Frames option places each step on a successive frame.

NOTE   Once an image is turned into a symbol, you can undo the operation at any time and make the graphic a normal object. To do so, select the instance of the symbol in your document, and choose Modify | Symbol | Break Apart from the menu.

The Symbol Library

All symbols that you create are stored in the Fireworks Library panel accessed from the Window menu. The Library, as shown in Figure 9-7, shows a list of all graphic, button, and animated symbols you've built to date for the *active document*. (Note that "animated" symbols are different from the tweened animation built with "graphic" symbols. See "Live Animation Effects" in this chapter for information on animated symbols.)

Unfortunately, the Library does not keep a running tab of all symbols you've ever built. The symbols are specific to the current document. You can, however, export some or all of a document's symbols as a set that other people can import. Or, you can simply save the document as normal. When you do, all of its symbols are saved with it. Once you export a set of symbols or simply save a Fireworks document that has symbols, importing the symbols into another document is easy, and the process is the same:

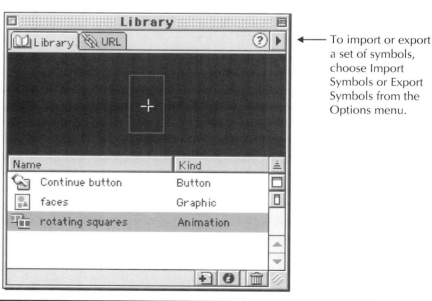

To import or export a set of symbols, choose Import Symbols or Export Symbols from the Options menu.

Figure 9-7   The Fireworks Library panel shows a list of symbols for the active document only.

1. Create a new Fireworks document, and create a few new graphic symbols. Use the Shape, Pen, or Text tools to create a few objects. If you like, you can group some of the objects together into a more complex illustration. Select the object or group, and choose Insert | Convert To Symbol from the menu. In the Symbol Properties window, give the new symbol a name, and make sure it is a graphic symbol. Repeat this process until you have at least three separate graphic symbols.

2. Save the document to your desktop (or other place where you can easily find it again). Name the file **Symbols_1**.

3. Working with this same Symbols_1 file, you'll now export a subset of the symbols from the Library. In the Library panel, choose Export Symbols from the Options menu (see Figure 9-7).

4. The Export Symbols window allows you to select a few or all of a document's symbols for export. To select all of them, click the Select All button. To select just a few, hold down the COMMAND (Mac) or CTRL key and click the ones you want, as shown in Figure 9-8. When ready, click the Export button and name the file **Symbols_2**. Notice that this new Symbols_2 file is a PNG file just like an ordinary Fireworks document.

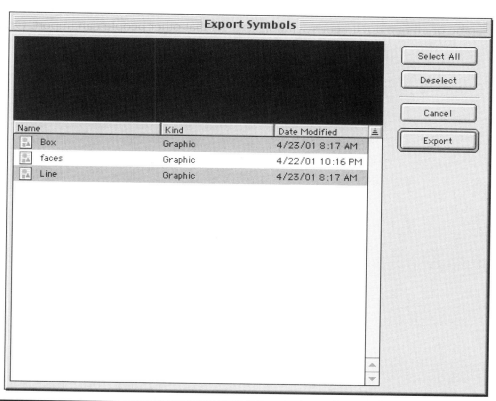

Figure 9-8 You can select a subset of symbols to export from a document.

5. To import the symbols from Symbols_1.png or the subset of symbols in Symbols_2, first create a new file. In the Library panel, choose Import Symbols from the Options menu and locate Symbols_1.png. In the Import Symbols window, you'll see the list of symbols contained within Symbols_1. Again, either click the Select All button, or hold down the COMMAND or CTRL key to select the symbols you want, and click Import. The process is the same for importing the subset of symbols contained in Symbols_2.png.

In addition to allowing you to create automatic animation with the tween feature, symbols and instances also make it possible to share consistent files across a team of people. For example, you can create one document that is a collection of frequently used graphics, logos, buttons, animations, and so on, that are all converted into symbols. Once you save the document, the symbols are saved with it. Other people can then import some or all of the symbols of this document into the Library panel of their document.

Of course, people could also just open a PNG file that has all of the standardized graphics, but that means that they will have two open document windows to juggle. By importing the graphics as symbols into their Library panel, people can make better use of their workspace.

Live Animation Effects

When you create a tweened animation of two "graphic" symbol instances, you cannot save the animation as something other people can use in their layouts. For example, if you build an animated logo that must be included in banners, pages, and all other web media, you'd either have to re-create the animation each time, or constantly modify the one PNG file that has the animation. To solve this problem, and to make the process of tweened animation that much easier, Fireworks 4 introduced "live" animation effects. Now, you can select any static object and turn it into an animated symbol. When you do, a control window lets you apply animation effects such as changing the size, movement, number of frames, opacity, and rotation of an object, just like you'd apply a drop shadow in the Effect panel.

We find that the biggest benefit of using animated symbols instead of tweened graphic symbols, however, is that you can move them around and place them anywhere in your layout simply by selecting and dragging them. In contrast, if you try to move a tweened animation, you must move the contents of each frame one at a time—basically doing frame-by-frame animation.

There are three ways to create an animated symbol:

● Select an object or group of objects, and choose Modify | Animate | Animate Selection. The Animation window will appear where you can apply settings.

● Select an object or group, and choose Insert | Convert To Symbol from the menu. In the Symbol Properties window, name the symbol and choose the Animation option. Click OK. The Animation window will appear.

● And finally, without having an object already built or selected, choose Insert | New Symbol from the menu. In the Symbol Properties window, name the symbol, choose the Animation option, and click OK. A new window appears where you can use the standard tools in the Tools panel to create an object or illustration to animate. When finished building the image, close the window to return to your document. At this point, you'll have an "animated" symbol without any animation settings. To apply settings, choose Modify | Animate | Settings from the menu.

The Animation Settings Window

Once you create an animated symbol, use the Animate window to adjust its settings (see Figure 9-9). This window appears automatically if you converted an object into an animated symbol or if you chose Modify | Animate | Animate Selection, but you can access the window at any time (that is, to adjust an animated symbol in the future) by choosing Modify | Animate | Settings. There are six things you can adjust:

● **Frames**   Enter the number of frames, or steps, the animation will have.

● **Movement**   Use this slider to enter the number of pixels that the animation will travel from the starting to the ending point. If the animation should stay in place (for instance, if you are rotating an object in place), enter **0** for movement.

● **Direction**   If you have specified movement, then you must specify a direction for the movement. Use the directional interface to choose an angle of departure.

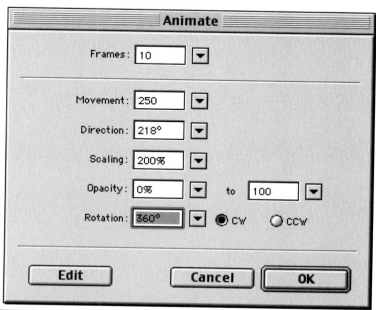

Figure 9-9   The Animate window allows you to animate six attributes of an animated symbol.

- **Scaling**   The scaling option applies to the *ending* point. For example, if you want the object to enlarge as it animates, choose a percentage greater than 100%. To shrink the object, choose a percentage less than 100%.

- **Opacity**   The opacity option allows you to adjust both the starting and the ending point. For example, in Figure 9-9, we are animating an object from 0% to 100% opacity.

- **Rotation**   Use this control to spin an object a number of degrees either clockwise (CW) or counter clockwise (CCW).

Use the Animate window to enter the settings for the animated symbol, and click OK to exit back to your document. If you have specified a number of frames that exceeds the current number of frames in your document, Fireworks will display a message asking if it's OK to add the number of frames needed.

Adjusting an Animated Symbol in the Workspace

After you use the Animate window to build an animated symbol, you can dynamically adjust your animation directly in the workspace. We find this especially helpful since you cannot see the effects of your settings while in the Animate window. To test your new animated symbol, use the Play and Stop controls at the bottom of the document window. Keep in mind, however, that Fireworks' animation preview is not 100 percent accurate in terms of timing between frames. For a more accurate preview, choose File | Preview In Browser.

As Figure 9-10 shows, an animated symbol looks very different from other symbols. The blue directional line shows the path of movement. The green dot at one end of the directional line represents the starting point, while the red dot at the other end represents the ending point. The smaller dots along the directional path indicate the steps on different frames in between.

To change the direction of movement as well as the distance covered, simply grab either ending point on the directional line and drag. To quickly see each step along the way, click on one of the smaller blue dots along the directional line. Continue to preview the animation, and adjust the movement and direction until you get the desired effect. To make more fundamental changes, such as rotation and scaling, access the Animation window again by choosing Modify | Animate | Settings from the menu. You can also access this window by right-clicking (Windows users) or by CTRL-clicking (Mac users) on the symbol and choosing Animate | Settings from the contextual pull-down menu.

To edit the actual graphic of the symbol, double-click within the dotted outline surrounding the main image. This accesses a mini, pop-up document window where you can use the tools in the Tools Panel to adjust the image. Close the window after editing to return to your main document.

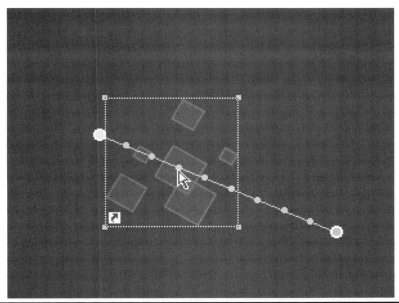

Figure 9-10   An animated symbol shows a directional path with the starting and ending points as well as the steps in between.

IDEA   At any time, you can turn a symbol back into an ordinary object by selecting it and then choosing Modify | Symbol | Break Apart from the menu.

Exporting Animation

Now that you're an animation expert, we want to discuss how you integrate animation into your layout along with all the other graphics and navigation, and how you prepare it for export. As you've seen throughout this book, you can use Fireworks to lay out and prepare a complete web page, and then export pieces of it as needed for reassembly in a web authoring tool like Dreamweaver. If you are working on a file that contains just the animation, you can simply export the whole document as either an animated GIF or as a Flash SWF file. If, however, you've built the animation as part of a master web page layout, you can export just the animated areas by using the Export Area tool or a slice object.

Exporting a Document as an Animation

If you are building an animation in its own document—apart from the main web page layout—be sure that you choose the dimensions of the file carefully. Usually, an animation is a portion of a complete web page. For example, you may include an animation instead of a static image to illustrate a column of text. Figure out the dimensions you need first, the background color or tile requirements, and then create a new file in Fireworks and build your animation.

To export the document as an animated GIF, open the Optimize panel and select the Animated GIF format from the pull-down menu. In addition, choose the number of colors you want the animation to use and whether to use transparency. Then choose File | Export from the menu, and choose Images Only (or Images And HTML if you want an accompanying HTML file) from the Save As pull-down menu.

CROSS REFERENCE → For more information on using the Optimize panel to optimize images, see Chapters 7 and 8.

To export a Flash SWF file, choose File | Export and select Macromedia Flash SWF from the Save As pull-down menu. We do, however, caution you about using the SWF export feature. Each frame of your Fireworks animation will become a keyframe in Flash. For this reason, we do not recommend building a 30- (or so) frame animation in Fireworks as a way of building a final Flash animation. If you do, the 30 frames will become 30 keyframes, resulting in a bloated SWF file that could otherwise benefit from Flash's more advanced tweening features.

The best way to approach Fireworks/Flash integration is to prepare source graphics in a few frames and export these as a SWF file. Fireworks' drawing and bitmap tools are much more powerful than Flash's for building graphics from scratch. You can then import the SWF file with the source graphics into Flash, and turn the source graphics into Flash symbols for animation.

Exporting a Region of a Document as an Animation

Often it's helpful to design an animation in the context of your final web layout. Doing so gives you a better sense of size, placement, and movement of the animation as it relates to the rest of the page design. Using this approach, design your web page layout in Frame 1. Frame 1 is always the "this is what the users see when they first load the page" frame. Then pick an area that will be animated and, starting on Frame 1, use a number of frames to build the animation. You can use a frame-by-frame technique, tween two symbol instances, or build an animation symbol. Be sure to use guides to contain the animation within a specific area of your layout. After building an animation, you can export it apart from the rest of the page in two ways: by using the Export Area tool, or by using the Slice tool. The catch, however, is that using these two methods limits you to exporting an Animated GIF. You cannot export a region of your document as an SWF file.

Using the Export Area Tool

In the same way that you can use the Export Area tool to export a region of your document as a static GIF or JPEG image, you can also use it to export an area as an Animated GIF.

1. Build an animation in a portion of your web page layout. Then select the Export Area tool, and draw a selection around the animation. If you used guides to control the containment of your animation, the Export Area tool will snap to them.

2. Press RETURN or ENTER to access the Export Preview window. In the first Options tab, select Animated GIF, choose a number of colors, and set any transparency options, as shown in Figure 9-11.

3. While still in the Export Preview window, click on the Animation tab. The Export Preview window allows you to select which frames to include in the animation. By default, all frames are included. To exclude a frame, click on its Eye icon. You can also set the frame delay of individual frames just as you do in the Frames panel. Finally, you can set the loop value of an animation. Before exporting, it's interesting to note that you can also control the scaling. Because we've already built the animation to size, leave the animation at 100% and click Export.

Using the Slice Tool

Another way to export an area of your document is to draw a slice object over it. To export a sliced region of your document, follow these steps:

1. Build an animation in a region of your document. Again, use guides to confine your work to a particular area.

2. Select the Slice tool in the Tools Panel, and draw a slice over the animated region.

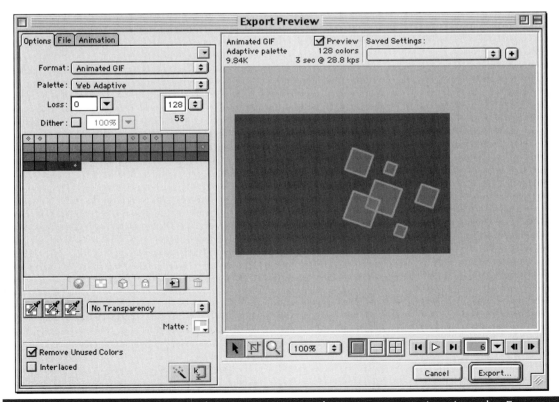

Figure 9-11 When you use the Export Area tool to export an animation, the Export Preview window allows you to adjust settings.

3. While the slice is selected, open the Optimize panel and choose Animated GIF from the pull-down menu. Then press CTRL (Mac) or right-click (Windows) on the slice, and choose Export Selected Slice from the contextual pop-up menu. In the Export window, the settings should be correctly configured to export the slice as an Animated GIF. Name and save the file.

Excluding Specific Frames from Export

By default, when you export an animation, all of the frames in the Frames panel will be included. As you've seen, however, the Export Preview window allows you to click on the Eye icon of certain frames to exclude them. You can also exclude frames directly in the Frames panel. The ability to exclude frames from export is useful, for instance, if you build two or more animations in the same region of your document. For example, if you want to build three different animations that will alternate playing in the same lower corner of your layout, you can build all three at once to save time and then export them separately. The first animation could use Frames 1–5; the second animation, Frames 6–10; and the third, Frames 11–15. To exclude certain frames from export, follow these steps:

1. Start a new Fireworks document and build a five-frame animation either by using the tween feature with graphic instances, or by creating an animation symbol. Fireworks will automatically create the four additional frames needed to build the five-frame animation.

2. Add a new frame, Frame 6, and begin a new animation. Make this new animation also extend over five frames. Again, Fireworks will add the needed frames so that your Frames panel contains ten frames.

3. To keep track, double-click on each frame and rename it according to the animation sequence it contains. For example, we named the first five frames "boxes" and the remaining frames "circles."

4. As shown in Figure 9-12, SHIFT-select the first five animation frames. Then double-click on the delay number in the right column to access the Frame Properties window. In the window, uncheck Include When Exporting. Click anywhere outside the window to close it. The Frames panel should now have a series of red Xs in the right column, as shown in Figure 9-13.

5. In the Optimize panel, choose Animated GIF and a number of colors. To export, choose File | Export from the menu. Your final exported animation should consist only of Frames 6–10.

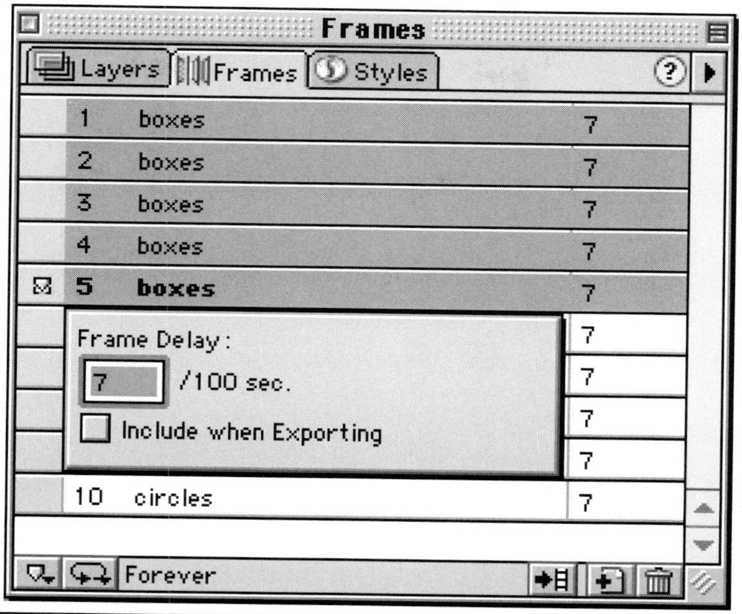

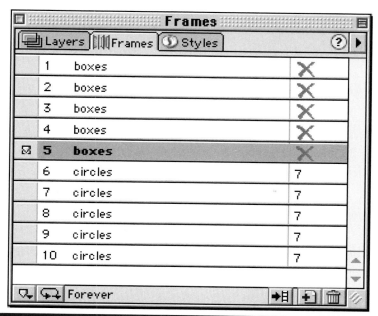

Figure 9-12 To exclude multiple frames at once, SHIFT-select them and then double-click on the Frame Delay number to access the Frame Properties window.

Figure 9-13 The red *X* in the right column indicates that the frame will be excluded from export.

Online How-To

Building an Animated Ad Banner

In this lesson, you'll learn how to combine Fireworks 4's new live animation feature along with traditional animation techniques using the tween feature to create an Animated GIF ad banner for the web.

GO TO THE WEB! For a free, self-paced interactive version of this tutorial, which includes video demonstrations and source files, visit www.expertedge.com.

In Fireworks, open the file Animation.png included in this chapter's online media kit. In this lesson, you'll animate the colored circles so that they spin and fade across the screen to the left behind the Isotope logo. Notice in the Layers panel that the layer named "Background" is a shared layer (there is a film strip icon on the layer). We've placed the gray circles and square boxes in the shared layer so that as you add animation frames for the colored graphic, the graphics will appear on each frame. The Isotope logo, however, is not on a shared layer and so will only appear on Frame 1 of the animation (which we'll address later in this lesson).

1. Select the colored circles graphic and choose Modify | Animate | Animate Selection from the menu. The Animate window will appear.

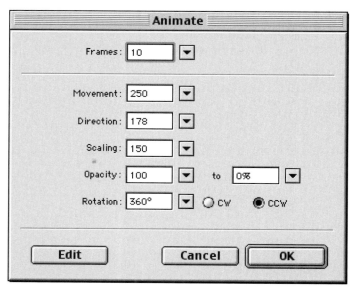

2. Set the following parameters and click OK:
   - Frames = 10
   - Movement = 250
   - Direction = 178°

- Scaling = 150%
- Opacity = from 100% to 0%
- Rotation = 360° CCW

Once you click OK, Fireworks will ask you if it can add the necessary extra frames to accommodate the animation, click OK. You've just created a new animation symbol.

3. Press the Play button in the lower-left corner of the document window to preview the animation. You'll notice how the animation whizzes along while the gray circles and boxes stay put. The Isotope logo, however, flashes on and off because it only exists on Frame 1. Press the Stop button.

4. In the Frames panel, click on Frame 7. Click on the animation to select it. You'll notice that the animated symbol has a line through it marked by blue dots. These blue dots represent the different frames of the animation. In fact, you can click on any of the blue dots to quickly jump to that frame. The end points of the line are also important: the green one represents the starting frame of the animation and the red dot represents the ending frame. You can click and drag the starting or ending dot anywhere on the screen to reposition the animation, stretch it across the screen, or change the direction of movement.

5. In the Frames panel, click on Frame 7, then select, copy, and paste the animation symbol. When Fireworks asks if it should add more frames, click OK. Select and move the new animation symbol over to the left side of the canvas. Now, grab the red ending frame dot (which should be off to the left, perhaps off the canvas), as shown here, and move it over to the right, on top of the Isotope logo.

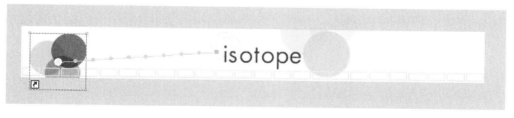

6. To change the number of frames, the opacity, scaling, rotation, etc. of any animation symbol, first select it in the document and then open the Object panel. In the Object panel, you can adjust the animation and immediately see the effects in your workspace. Adjust the two symbols until you have an animation effect you like (use the Play and Stop buttons to preview).

7. In the Frames panel, select Frame 1. Select the Isotope logo and choose Insert | Convert to Symbol from the menu. In the dialog, name the symbol **logo** and make it a Graphic symbol. You'll now animate a drop shadow moving from right to left behind the logo. To animate a graphic symbol, you must first have two copies, or "instances," of it. The two copies represent the beginning and ending points of an animation.

As of now, you have one *instance* of the symbol (when you convert a graphic to a symbol, the symbol lives in the Library and your graphic onscreen becomes an instance of the symbol). Before copying and pasting this instance, in the Effects panel, choose Shadow and Glow | Drop Shadow from the pull-down menu. Adjust the drop shadow so that it is cast 25 pixels off to the right (as shown next).

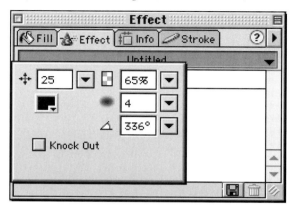

8. Copy and paste the instance. The copied instance will paste directly on top of the first instance and will be selected. In the Effects panel, click on the "i" icon to adjust the drop shadow parameters of the copied instance. Change the angle of shadow so that it is cast 25 pixels off to the left.

9. Select both instances and choose Modify | Symbol | Tween Instances from the menu. Enter 14 steps, check the Distribute To Frames option, and click OK. The reason you entered 14 steps is because you have 16 frames in the Frames panel. In between Frame 1 and 16 you need 14 steps. The Distribute To Frames option spreads all 16 steps of the animation over 16 frames. If you did not choose this option, all 16 steps would end up on the same frame!

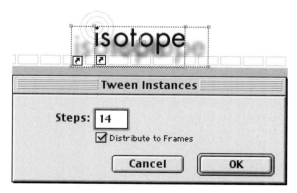

Use the Play and Stop buttons to preview your work. To export this animation as an Animated GIF, select the Animated GIF setting in the Optimize panel. Then, choose File | Export from the menu.

10 Flash Integration

If Macromedia has but one "killer app," it surely is Flash. With over 90 percent of installed web users already having the plug-in, it is ubiquitous. Versions of it are already being developed for PDAs, game consoles such as the Sega Dreamcast and Sony Playstation 2, and other devices. As a vector-based animation and interactive format, Flash can be used for everything from broadcast quality cartoons to interactive front-ends for database-driven web sites. Coming from another vector graphics medium, Fireworks content would seem ideal for Flash, and in some ways it is. But the way from Fireworks to Flash (and back again) is somewhere between a smooth and a rocky road.

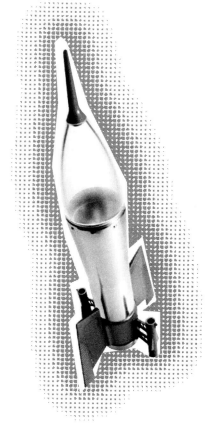

Fireworks and Flash are not as closely integrated as designers might hope, for reasons that we will get into shortly. After the initial discouragement, however, it turns out that there are a number of ways to move content—even interactive content—between the apps. The key to maximizing your productivity between the two is to understand where they do and do not understand each other.

The first part of this chapter will provide some background information on the Fireworks-Flash problem as a setup to the rest of the chapter, which will provide a series of practical solutions for their integration.

What Is Flash?

Macromedia Flash in its first incarnation was neither from Macromedia nor called Flash. When the world first saw the application that would become Flash, it was called FutureSplash, and it was intended to create vector-based animation. One of its earliest uses was to create a more file-efficient and aesthetically effective alternative to the Animated GIF.

By August 2000, when Flash 5 was released, the program had emerged as a robust authoring environment in its own right. Now including a robust object-oriented scripting language (ActionScript), with the ability to pass variables to web sites, Flash is fully able to act as a front-end for today's complex, data-driven, tailored-to-each-user web sites. It can communicate with JavaScript, CGI scripts, middleware solutions (ASP, ColdFusion, PHP, and so on), as well as with Macromedia Generator. Its animation capabilities have grown from simple tweening (also used by Fireworks) to fully scripted animation, better enabling the creation of games.

In spite of all these powerful features, there are a few issues that web developers have to deal with when working with Flash. Above all, there is the plug-in problem. To view Flash content, users must have installed the free Flash player plug-in. The good news is that Macromedia says that 90 percent of users have the Flash player. The bad news is that 10 percent is a lot of customers to be leaving out. In addition, of those 90 percent only a subset has an up-to-date Flash player. Those who still have the Flash 3 player, for example, are counted in the 90 percent who have Flash, but they will be unable to view many Flash movies done in Flash today.

Another drawback to Flash is the flip side of the media-rich coin. While Flash is more powerful and robust than HTML as a content delivery medium, its file sizes can be larger than comparable HTML sites (of course, this is not always the case). Macromedia has made an effort to keep file sizes down—both the size of its player (a 200–300KB download, depending on your browser) and of its movies. One consequence is that it does not fully support certain kinds of media. Unfortunately for Fireworks designers, certain Fireworks effects are not supported in Flash for this reason.

Know Your Plug-In: Shockwave, Flash, and SVG

People are often confused by different available plug-ins and multimedia formats, making it difficult to design with these formats in mind. Table 10-1 defines the three of them and briefly discusses their implications for Fireworks designers.

Format Name	Size and Location of Download	Description	Implications for Fireworks Designers
Shockwave	3,400K www.macromedia.com/downloads	The most robust widespread multimedia format, Shockwave files are produced in Director. This is a great format for CD-ROM–based and high-bandwidth movies, and with care, low-bandwidth movies as well.	You can design almost anything you want, and Director can pull it in using the new Fireworks Xtra. However, its file sizes can add up quickly.
Flash	219K www.macromedia.com/downloads	The most ubiquitous multimedia format available, after HTML, though it is not quite as fully featured as Shockwave.	To move content from Fireworks to Flash, you will need to plan ahead and develop your content more carefully. Just about everything can make it into Flash one way or another.
Scaleable Vector Graphics (SVG)	3,000K www.adobe.com/svg/viewer/install/main.html	SVG is a nonproprietary alternative to Flash, currently a "candidate" before the W3 Consortium. It is not yet widely supported, but appears to have a future. See www.w3.org/Graphics/SVG/Overview.htm8.	At this early stage, it is difficult to tell exactly how to develop for this medium. Given its promotion by Adobe (presumably as an alternative to Flash), we wonder to what extent Macromedia will support it.

Table 10-1 Comparison Between Flash and Alternatives

At this point, Fireworks can be easily integrated only with Director/Shockwave and Flash. Using the new Fireworks Xtra for Director makes Fireworks integration even easier. As far as Fireworks and Flash, they integrate very well in those areas where they think alike. For those Fireworks features that Flash doesn't support, you will have to use a (usually simple) work-around.

If you must output to SVG at this point, the best workflow would probably be to go through an Adobe product, such as Illustrator or LiveMotion, both of which can output to SVG. Needless to say, integration between Fireworks and either of these two products will not be great.

Fireworks and Flash

By now you understand the key principle behind Fireworks-Flash integration. You are probably wondering what kinds of things do not go well into Flash. Generally they fall into two categories: certain Fireworks advanced vector features and any features specific to HTML documents.

Advanced Vector Effects

Fireworks' main claim to fame is that everything is editable, all the time. It makes sense that you can edit the size of a square in Fireworks, since it is a simple vector object. But some of Fireworks editable effects are pretty impressive. For example, pretty much everything from the Effect panel—drop shadows, bevels, blurs, glows, and even Photoshop plug-ins—can be applied as vector graphics, which are editable later.

Unfortunately, such effects cannot be transplanted to Flash as-is. If you draw a rectangle, add a bevel, and type a label to make a button, Flash will not be able to read the bevel. The simple work-around for this (discussed next) is to convert the button to a bitmap and pull it into Flash that way.

HTML Output

The other category of Fireworks features that Flash cannot handle are those related to HTML output. They include slices, JavaScript, behaviors, and so on. That means that you cannot create a simple rollover in Fireworks and expect it to work in Flash. What makes it work in Fireworks is a JavaScript that you attach to the target HTML file. But Flash does not generally work with JavaScript. (You can create interactivity between the two to pass data and for some control over Flash movies from the HTML page, but it is not nearly the same relationship that JavaScript has with HTML.)

Slices also don't work in Flash. Remember that Fireworks exports all slices, no matter what their use, in HTML tables. The HTML tables reconstruct the slices back to seamless images, so that the viewer doesn't even know that the image is sliced. Since Flash does not use HTML, slice objects (and their URLs, ALT descriptions, and optimization settings) are all lost.

 → Variations of Fireworks HTML output, including an extended discussion of using slices, can be found in Chapter 12.

From Fireworks to Flash

We normally think of Fireworks-Flash integration the same way we think of Fireworks-Dreamweaver integration: first build your designs and assets in Fireworks, and then move over the relevant portions to the authoring application. Both Dreamweaver and Flash are *final platforms*—that is, they often make use of files created in other applications, and what they output in turn is the final version seen by the viewer. However, there are some uses for inverting the process, going from Flash to Fireworks. We will discuss those later in the chapter.

Moving Basic Assets to Flash

When going from Fireworks to HTML, you can often do a single export and get everything in one swoop; Fireworks exports images usually as GIFs or JPGs according to your optimization settings. When going from Fireworks to Flash, however, you will have to use different methods, depending on the nature of the asset.

Simple Bitmap to Simple Bitmap

If you have a bitmap in your Fireworks PNG file (that is, the image is a bitmap prior to export), such as a scan of a photograph, you may want to do all of your optimization in Fireworks. Flash does optimize images, but it usually does so in a one-size-fits-all way. There are ways to work around this in Flash, but why should you? You've got Fireworks—the best software on the market for optimizing images.

1. Optimize the bitmap in Fireworks just as you would for export to an HTML editor.

2. Choose File | Export, choosing Images Only in the Save As Type drop-down list. You won't need any HTML where you're going.

3. Open Flash, and choose File | Import to bring the bitmap into Flash. The bitmap is placed on the stage, and it also appears in the Flash file's Library, seen in Figure 10-1.

4. Double-click the Bitmap (tree) icon in the Library to open the Bitmap Properties dialog box, seen in Figure 10-2.

5. Be sure that the Use Imported JPG Data (if it is a JPG file) or Use Document Default Quality (all other file types) check box is selected. Upon export, Flash by default adds JPG compression to bitmap images. When it does, your image gets double-compressed, once painstakingly by you, and once mechanically by Flash. This does not generally yield desirable results. Choosing this option prevents the second round of compression.

When we pull a bitmap into Flash, we usually do two things. First, we immediately convert it to a graphic or movie clip symbol, which will enable us to use the bitmap as an object (in tweens, for example). Second, using the Transform

Figure 10-1 All imported assets end up in the Flash Library.

panel, we change the size (you can also use alpha) of all placed instances to 99% or 101% (Figure 10-3), which takes care of a frustrating bug that makes bitmaps appear to bounce or shift during tweens and at other times.

Vector Graphics Without Effects

Fireworks and Flash are both vector-based programs, and the best-case scenario is to move your vector graphics into Flash as such. That way, your vector graphics will be both fully editable and low bandwidth throughout the Flash workflow. Provided that your vector graphics have no bitmap effects, such as glows, drop shadows, and so on, you can use the Clipboard, rather than exporting and importing.

1. Create your vector graphics in Fireworks.

2. Choose Edit | Copy As Vectors. If you choose plain old Edit | Copy, Fireworks will place a rasterized version of your vectors in Flash, you lose the benefit of working with vectors, and pay the price of higher file size.

3. Choose Edit | Paste in Flash.

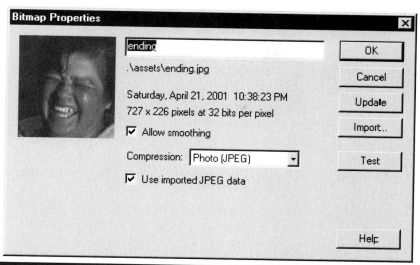

Figure 10-2 The Bitmap Properties dialog box in Flash

If you selected more than one vector graphic object in Fireworks, the objects will come through grouped. However, you can choose Modify | Ungroup in Flash to separate them.

One further note: When you copy and paste vector objects into Flash, they are not added to the Library. That means that while you are benefiting from the fact that these are compact vector graphics, they are still contributing to file size. If there is a possibility that you will reuse any of these graphics elsewhere in the movie, you should convert them to symbols as soon as you paste them in.

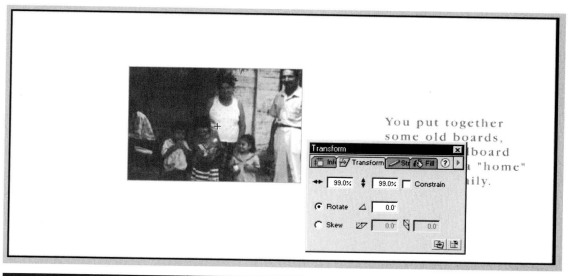

Figure 10-3 Transforming the dimensions of bitmaps in Flash by 1 percent can prevent some annoying bugs.

Vector Graphics with Effects

When you create vector graphics with bitmap-like effects (such as those found in the Effect panel) and you want to move them into Flash, you are faced with a dilemma. You can either keep the effects, (but lose the editability) and convert the graphic to a bitmap, or you can maintain its editability by using Copy As Vectors, but have Flash discard the effects.

To maintain the editability, simply follow the preceding directions—select the desired graphic, choose Copy As Vectors, and paste the graphic into Flash. The dirty work of removing the effects is done for you. Figure 10-4 shows some text with a blur effect added in Fireworks compared with its Flash counterpart, using Copy As Vectors.

If you wish to preserve the appearance, you will need to convert the Fireworks vectors into bitmaps. Going with this option is a signal of defeat, but sometimes it is necessary. Essentially, you are converting a Fireworks vector graphic into a bitmap object and bringing it into Flash, another vector-based program, meaning that you lose its editability.

1. Create your graphic in Fireworks.

2. Add any effects.

3. Select the desired graphic object(s).

4. Choose Edit | Copy.

5. In Flash, choose Edit | Paste. The results are shown in Figure 10-5.

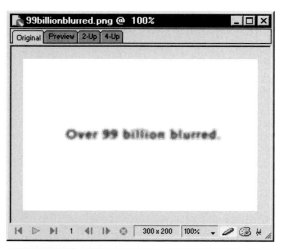

Figure 10-4 Text with added effects in Fireworks (left) compared with the same text after being moved into Flash via Copy As Vectors (right)

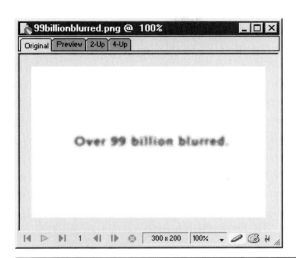
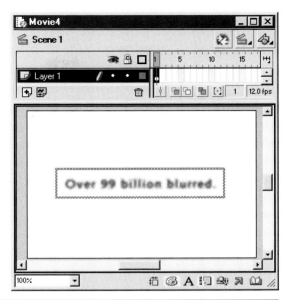

Figure 10-5   Text with added effects in Fireworks (left) compared with the same text after being moved into Flash via Copy; the gray hatching indicates that the object is a bitmap.

Moving Advanced Assets to Flash

So much for simple graphic objects. The truth is, you want to use Fireworks' more robust features to make assets for your Flash movies as well. Both programs allow you to create animations. Both allow you to create interactivity, with rollovers, and so on. Both support alpha transparency, enabling you to create and share some special effects. The question is, how do you get these assets from Fireworks into Flash?

Fireworks Animation vs. Flash Animation

In most programs that deal with the fourth dimension, the passing of time is represented through the use of *frames.* Fireworks and Flash are no exceptions. However, there are a couple of differences between Flash and Fireworks animation.

First, there is the appearance of the frames. Flash uses a timeline, which conveys considerable information about the contents on the timeline. Fireworks lacks a timeline and uses a Frames panel. While there is some information in the Frames panel, it is not as informative as a Flash timeline. The truth is, Fireworks animations are fairly simple. When you create an animation in Fireworks, a copy of the object is placed in each successive frame with enough displacement to cause the illusion of movement over time.

Flash, in contrast, has several different kinds of animation. In Flash you can create an animation whereby you move an object one frame at a time. This is called *frame-by-frame animation.* In this sense, it works just like Fireworks' animation. But Flash also uses *tweens,* which is when you specify a beginning and ending point (and optionally a path of travel) and Flash interpolates the remaining frames. Tweening is superior to frame-by-frame animation because it is easier for the developer (since Flash does all the work), but also because it creates smaller file sizes. Flash uses only one symbol, placing an instance of it in each successive frame—but the user need download this symbol only once, whereas in frame-by-frame animation, the user must download the same object repeatedly.

Figure 10-6 shows a Flash timeline. In the lower layer, you will see a frame-by-frame animation. Note that every frame is a keyframe (symbolized by the black circle in the frame). In the upper layer, there is a tween. Note that the intervening frames have only an arrow, used to signify a tween. The point is that if you create an animation in Fireworks and export it as a Flash SWF, Fireworks will create a frame-by-frame animation—even if you use Fireworks symbols. In most cases, it is simply more advantageous to create animations directly in Flash than in Fireworks—if your final destination is Flash.

There is yet another key difference between Fireworks and Flash frames. Fireworks uses only one timeline. That means that if you create an animation and a rollover, Frame 2 of the rollover will also be Frame 2 of the animation, making it difficult to separate elements. Flash can have thousands of independent timelines in a single movie.

If for some reason you do want to export a Fireworks animation to Flash, here's how:

1. Create the animation in Fireworks.

2. Choose File | Export to open the Export dialog box.

3. In the Save As Type drop-down list, choose Macromedia Flash SWF.

4. Click the Options button to choose appropriate options, based on your animation (see Figure 10-7).

5. Click OK to return to the Export dialog box and then choose Save.

6. Open a new Flash movie.

7. Choose File | Import and navigate to the SWF file you just saved. You will need to import the SWF, rather than just open it, if you wish to edit it. Simply opening it brings it up in the Flash player, rather than in the authoring environment.

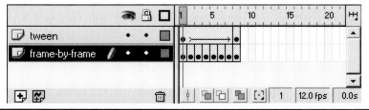

Figure 10-6   A Flash timeline showing the difference between frame-by-frame animation (lower layer) and a tween (upper layer)

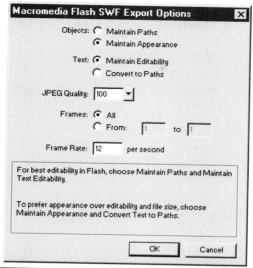

Figure 10-7 The Macromedia Flash SWF Export Options dialog box in Fireworks

Buttons: From Fireworks into Flash

Moving buttons from Fireworks to Flash is not exactly an intuitive process, but there is a way to pull your buttons into Flash so that they appear just as they do in Fireworks.

 This section assumes you are moving a Fireworks *button symbol* into Flash. Do not confuse Fireworks button symbols with traditional Fireworks rollovers. The following instructions will not work for rollovers.

Here's how to do it:

1. Choose Insert | New Button and create a button in the button editor (see Figure 10-8). Note that the canvas in the button editor is the same size as the main canvas. If you are building assets one at a time, you will want to make the main canvas the exact size as your button, so that Fireworks doesn't export unneeded border area. Alternatively, you can also crop off the border in the Export Preview dialog box.

2. Create all of the states that you want to appear in Flash. Do not add an Over While Down state, since Flash doesn't support them. Also, do not bother adding URLs—they will not export with the SWF.

3. While still in the button editor, choose File | Export or File | Export Preview to prepare to export the file. Do not export from the main canvas, or you will only get the button's Up state.

4. Once you are in the Export dialog box, choose Macromedia Flash SWF from the Save As Type drop-down list.

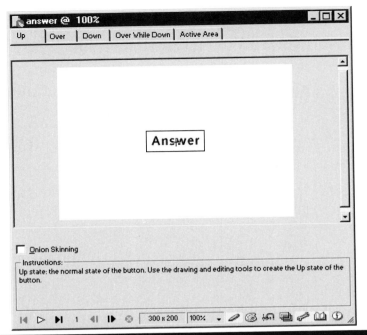

Figure 10-8   The Fireworks button editor

5. Click the Options button that appears to open the verbosely named Macromedia Flash SWF Export Options dialog box.

6. Choose Maintain Appearance in the Objects list if you used any effects. This will convert the Fireworks objects to bitmaps. If you used only simple vectors (which kind of defeats the purpose of building the button in Fireworks), you can choose Maintain Paths.

7. Choose Maintain Editability for any text, though we usually add text in Flash.

8. Click OK to leave this dialog box, and then click Save to export the SWF.

9. In Flash, open the target file.

10. Choose File | Import and navigate to and import the SWF. The three button states (assuming you used three) will appear automatically as separate keyframes of the main timeline. Three new bitmaps, called Bitmap 1, Bitmap 2, and so on, will appear in the Flash Library.

 You might be inclined to import the button SWF right into a Flash button symbol (we were). The images come in just fine and even appear on the right frames. Drag an instance of the button onto the stage, add ActionScript to the button, and all looks well. Test the movie, though, and the button doesn't work. Not only does the ActionScript not function, but Flash also doesn't even recognize when your cursor passes over the button.

11. Choose Insert | New Symbol in Flash to open the Symbol Properties dialog box.

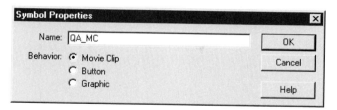

12. Give your button a name, and choose Button as its Behavior.

13. Click OK. An empty screen appears, and you are in Symbol Editing mode. Notice that the timeline for the button symbol has only four frames, one each for the different states (Up, Over, and so on).

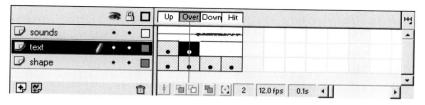

14. In the Up frame, drag in a copy of Bitmap1 from the Library.

15. Use the Align panel (COMMAND-K or CTRL-K) to align the image to the center of the stage.

16. Successively, drag the remaining bitmaps into the appropriate frames, and use the Align panel to center them. If all of your states are the same size and in the same position, you do not need to add a hit area. If they are not positioned in the same place (for example, the Down state moves down and to the right a few pixels), or if the states are not all the same shape, make sure your hit area covers all of the needed space.

17. Choose Edit | Movie to exit Image Editing mode and return to the main movie.

18. Drag an instance of the button onto the stage. Use ActionScript to add the necessary functionality to the button. The following code listing shows the code for a script that will open an HTML page in a new window, once the movie is embedded in a web page.

```
on (release) {
    getURL ("http://www.allecto.net", "_blank");
}
```

Sharing Files with Alpha Transparency

One overlooked compatibility between Fireworks and Flash is that since they both support the standard PNG file format, both can make use of PNG capabilities. As a 32-bit color file format, PNG supports alpha transparency.

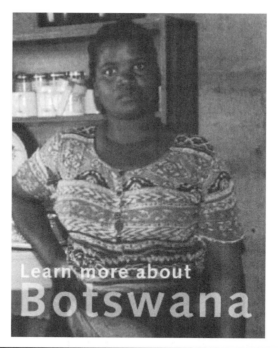

Figure 10-9   The text blocks both use alpha transparency.

Alpha transparency should not be confused with indexed transparency. *Indexed transparency,* often used in GIFs, allows you to make certain pixel color values become transparent. But these pixels are either on or off—there is nothing in between. *Alpha transparency,* in contrast, enables you to make objects partially transparent, as in Figure 10-9. It supports 256 "shades" of transparency, providing a range from near-opaque to barely visible.

If you create an image that makes use of alpha transparency in Fireworks, simply export it as a PNG-32. When you import it into Flash, the transparency information will still be there.

From Flash to Fireworks: Creating Animated GIFs

Way back at the beginning of the chapter, we characterized Flash as a destination program into which you will often pull content from all sorts of sources—bitmap, vector, video, sound, and word processor programs. Fireworks can be, as we have shown in this chapter, one such inputting program. Now we are reversing the flow, but why?

Flash has a few features that can make it a viable source for authoring content that you would want to pull into Fireworks. First, perhaps above all, Flash has unique drawing tools. Animators around the world are falling in love with Flash because its drawing tools have features that are not implemented elsewhere. One of the neatest features is that you can apply shape recognition as you draw with a Wacom or other graphics tablet. This includes *live smoothing,* which takes out the bumps as you draw, as well as *straightening,* which makes drawing rectangles with the Pencil tool a cinch.

Flash also shines as an animation tool. It has both Shape tweens, which allows you to morph graphics, and Motion tweens. You can use ActionScript to animate. Flash allows you to create motion paths that guide your animations along twisting and curling paths, rather than in a straight line, as in Fireworks. Add to that rotation along paths, easing (acceleration and deceleration of animated objects), and independent layer animation, and you have quite a few animation options in Flash not available in Fireworks.

The other feature that makes it viable as a place to create content destined for Fireworks is that Flash offers an impressive variety of export options, including an option that enables you to export to the Animated GIF format. That means that you can create a cartoon in Flash, making use of its superior animation tools, and then you can import it into Fireworks and optimize it or add other effects.

1. Create your animation in Flash. Pay special attention to your frame rate, but don't worry too much about frame delay, and so on—you can tweak all of that in Fireworks.

2. Choose File | Publish Settings. The Publish Settings dialog box opens.

3. In the Formats tab of the Publish Settings dialog box (shown here), uncheck everything (including Flash) and then check GIF Image. Notice that the GIF tab appears after the Formats tab.

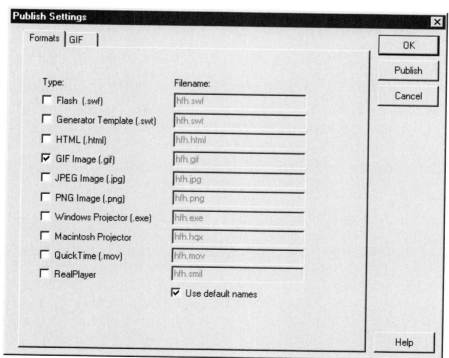

4. Optional step: if you wish for Flash to generate an HTML document to hold the Animated GIF, also check the HTML box.

5. Click the GIF tab.

6. In most cases, you can use the options chosen as shown here, which are all defaults except for the Playback type, which needs to be set to Animated.

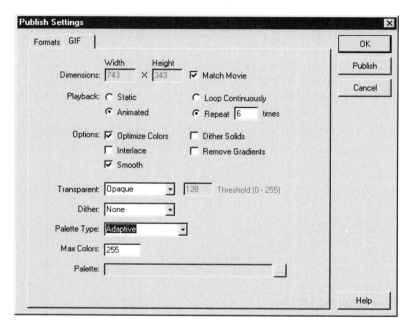

7. Choose an appropriate color palette. The default is Web 216, but if you are going into Fireworks anyway, you might as well choose GIF Adaptive.

8. Click the Publish button. Flash generates the animated GIF and any other files selected in the Formats tab (such as HTML).

9. Open (generally, you do not want to import) the Animated GIF into Fireworks. Notice that the requisite additional frames have been added to the Fireworks file.

10. Edit the animated GIF as you would a native Fireworks animation; set the frame delay, optimization settings, and so on.

Online How-To

Replicating Fireworks Disjoint Rollovers in Flash

Disjoint rollovers are like short animations driven by events (such as mouse overs), rather than by the simple passage of time, like standard animations. When the user's mouse rolls over a *trigger,* such as a button, a swap image occurs in a different slice. Both Fireworks and Flash can do disjoint rollovers, which is the good news. The bad news is that you cannot simply import Fireworks disjoint rollovers into Flash.

Why would you need to? Oftentimes, when you make a high-impact site that requires Flash, clients will also want a non-Flash version of the site for those who do not have or do not use the Flash plug-in. In such cases, you can often replicate many interactive and animated elements in both formats.

In this tutorial, you will learn how to replicate a Fireworks disjoint rollover in Flash. You will first assemble a small quiz in Fireworks (Figure 10-10), using the disjoint rollover behavior, and then you will transfer its pieces into Flash and reconstruct it. One of the goals of this tutorial is to acquaint you with the ways that each program handles interactivity. As you will see, they are quite different. And though Fireworks is the less powerful of the two, when it comes to interactivity, it is also generally easier to create interactive elements in Fireworks, since no scripting is required on your end.

The Flash ActionScript that you will learn in this tutorial may be intimidating to nonprogrammers, but we will explain everything, and you will come away with a pretty good idea of what makes it tick.

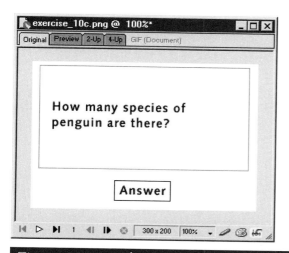 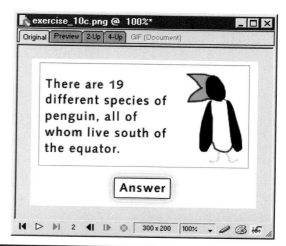

Figure 10-10   The two frames of the quiz, as seen in Fireworks

GO TO THE WEB! For a free, self-paced interactive version of this tutorial, which includes video demonstrations and source files, visit www.expertedge.com.

Creating the Source Quiz in Fireworks

The quiz you will assemble has been partially constructed for you in the exercise_10.png file available in this chapter's folder on the Web.

1. Open the file exercise_10.png from this chapter's folder.

2. Explore the file for a moment. On the first frame, you will see a text question, bounded by a box. On the second frame, you will see the same box in the same place, but the text has changed and there is a penguin drawing. The Library has all of the symbols you will need for this file.

3. In the first frame, drag a copy of the Answer button symbol onto the stage.

4. Be sure that the Web Layer Visibility (eyeball) icon is on. A slice appears around the button.

5. Position the button at the bottom center, so that the bottom of the slice region snaps to the bottom of the canvas, as in Figure 10-11. Using the Info panel, we positioned this button at the following coordinates: X = 81, Y = 131.

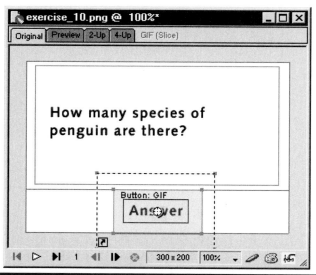

Figure 10-11   Place the button along the bottom center of the canvas.

You can test the image so far by choosing the Preview tab at the top of the document window. The button lights up on rollover, but that's about it. The next step is to add the disjoint rollover, as shown here:

CROSS REFERENCE → To learn how to make disjoint rollovers, see Chapter 10.

1. In the first frame, click the rectangle to select it. Choose Insert | Slice to add a slice object over it.

2. Click to select the button. In the center of the button is a target symbol.

3. Drag this target symbol over the new slice you just created over the question box.

4. A swirly line appears, connecting the button to the top-left corner of the slice you just created (Figure 10-12).

5. A small swap image dialog box appears. Just accept the default, Frame 2, by selecting OK.

6. Choose the Preview tab to test the image. When you roll over the Answer button, the area enclosed in the gray box should change to show the answer and the penguin.

You should, by this point, have a rough idea of how this will work when exported. Fireworks will slice the image, rebuild it into a table, and add the necessary JavaScript to swap the question/answer images when the user rolls over the button. Satisfied? Let's take this over to Flash.

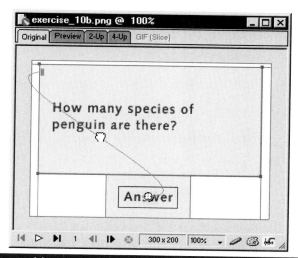

Figure 10-12 A curved line connects the rollover trigger and rollover target.

Transferring the Assets to Flash Objects

In Flash, the behind-the-scenes functioning of this file will be quite different. Rather than being a sliced-up image with a couple of different frames, each of your objects will be completely independent of one another. The rectangle containing the question and answer will be in a movie clip object (instance). A separate button will activate this movie clip instance (via a script that we will have to write) and will make it advance to the frame with the answer and penguin. Nothing is sliced, and the scripts are attached to relevant objects, rather than to the HTML page.

1. Open Flash 5 and create a new movie. Set the background color to white and the movie dimensions to 300×200 pixels, using the Movie Properties dialog box (Modify | Movie).

2. With the first frame on the timeline selected, open the Actions panel (Window | Actions).

3. Click the + symbol in the upper-left corner. In the Basic Actions group, choose Stop. A one-line script appears in the pane on the right side of the Actions panel. When you click elsewhere, you will also see that an *a* appears in the timeline, indicating the presence of the stop( ) action.

4. Follow the instructions in the "Buttons: From Fireworks into Flash" section earlier to get the Answer button in the Fireworks PNG into a Flash button symbol. When you are done, your Flash canvas should be empty, and the Answer button symbol should be in the Library.

NOTE   We noticed that the alignment of the button elements (surrounding rectangle and the word "Answer") was a bit off when imported. If necessary, use the Align panel to align all objects to the center of the canvas.

5. Drag an instance of the Answer button onto the stage, positioning it near the bottom, as before. You do not need to add any scripts to the button just yet.

6. Choose Insert | Create New Symbol. The Symbol Properties dialog box appears.

7. Type **QA_MC** as the name, and leave the default behavior set to Movie Clip. You now enter Symbol Editing mode—notice that the button disappears and that your canvas is empty. Just above the timeline, in the top-left corner, is a new tab (shown here) with your symbol's name and the blue movie clip symbol logo. This tab indicates that you are in Symbol Editing mode. You can always click the Scene 1 tab to return to the main movie. But stay in the movie clip for now.

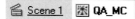

Setting Up the Movie Clip's Timeline

Let's set up the movie clip's timeline. Notice that Flash movie clips offer all of the functionality of the main stage—they have their own timelines, stages, and so on.

1. In the lower-left corner of the timeline, click the white page icon to insert a new layer.

2. Double-click the new layer's name (probably "Layer 2") and call it **actions**.

3. Add a `stop( )` action to the first frame of the actions layer.

4. Add a third layer above actions and name it **labels**.

5. With the first frame of the labels layer selected, type **question** in the Label field of the Frame panel (Window | Panels | Frame). Be sure to press ENTER or to TAB out of the field to make the label "stick." A red flag should appear in the timeline, indicating the presence of a frame label. The label itself will also appear, but only if there are enough frames in the timeline—at this point there are probably not.

6. Click to select Frame 10 of the labels layer of the timeline.

7. Press F6 to insert a new keyframe in Frame 10. You should now be able to see the "question" label in the labels layer of the timeline.

8. With Frame 10 in the labels layer still selected, add a frame label called **answer**.

9. Click Frame 20 of the labels layer, and press F5 to add regular frames out that far.

10. Click Frame 20 of the actions layer, and press F5 to add frames all the way out to Frame 20.

11. Click Frame 10 of the first layer, still called "Layer 1," unless you've renamed it. Press F6 to insert a keyframe in Frame 10.

12. Click Frame 20 of Layer 1, and press F5 to add static frames out to that point. Your completed movie clip timeline should look like the one in Figure 10-13.

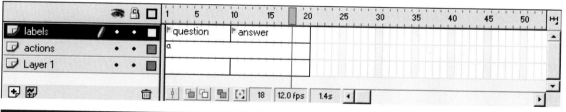

Figure 10-13 The completed movie clip timeline contains room for both question and answer.

Importing the Fireworks Assets

The Fireworks pieces are made and the Flash movie has been set up for the elements. It's time to bring them over.

1. Switch back to Fireworks.

2. In Frame 1, with the Pointer tool, click to select the question text, and then SHIFT-click to add the gray rectangle to the selection.

3. Choose Edit | Copy As Vectors.

4. Returning to Flash, with your QA_MC movie clip still open in Symbol Editing mode, select the first frame of Layer 1.

5. Choose Edit | Paste.

6. With the pasted objects still selected (they will come through in a group), use the Align panel to align them to the center of the movie clip's canvas.

7. Go back to Fireworks, Frame 2, and copy (as vectors) the gray box, the answer text, and the penguin drawing.

8. In Flash again, still in the movie clip symbol, select the (presently empty) keyframe in Frame 10 of Layer 1.

9. Choose Edit | Paste. Again, use the align panel to center the pasted group on the canvas.

10. Your movie clip object is now complete. Whew!

Final Placement

Everything is inside of Flash. The next step is to put things in the right places.

1. Choose Edit | Movie to return to the main movie. Your button sure looks lonely on that canvas!

2. From the Flash Library (Window | Library), drag an instance of the QA_MC movie clip onto the stage.

3. Position it so that it is roughly in the same position as in the Fireworks image. We used the following coordinates, which you can set with the Info panel (Window | Panels | Info): X = 10, Y = 9.

4. This would be a good time to save your file!

Replicating the Functionality in Flash

Here is where things get a little tricky. We can't just drag-and-drop a behavior from the button to the movie clip. We'll have to add a short script to the button to make things work.

There is a key concept to grasp here. Flash is an object-oriented program. It sees now only two objects on the stage, even though you know there are drawings, text, and so forth. The trick is that we have to get these two objects to be able to talk to each other. Specifically, we need the button to be able to talk to the movie clip. And a great way to get someone's attention is to call him or her by name.

1. In Frame 1 of the main timeline/main stage, click to select the movie clip.

2. Open the Instance panel (Window | Panels | Instance), and in the name field, type **QA**. This gives the movie clip instance a name so that the Answer button can send it commands.

3. Click the button and open the Actions panel. Be sure that it says "Object Actions" in the title bar and not "Frame Actions." If it does say "Frame Actions," with it still open, click again on the button until it says "Object Actions."

4. Click the + symbol, and from the Basic Actions book, add a Go To action. A script appears that looks as follows:

```
on (release) {
    gotoAndPlay (1);
}
```

5. Assuming you are in Normal mode (choose Normal Mode from the pop-up menu in the Object Actions panel), click the first line of code. The lower part of the Actions panel changes to show a series of check boxes for different kinds of events (Figure 10-14). The Release check box is selected already, because Flash assumes that you want the action to be triggered when the user clicks the button. In our quiz, though, the event was actually triggered by rolling over the button.

6. Clear the Release check box, and select the Roll Over check box. Notice that the script is updated on the right.

7. Click the second line of the script, and the Actions panel again changes. In the lower half, you will see options for Scene, Type, and Frame. Unfortunately, this is not quite what we want. Flash here is assuming that we want to apply the Go To command to the main timeline. In fact, we want it to apply to the movie clip object (the one we named "QA" earlier). These options give us no way to address QA, so we'll have to bypass them.

8. In the Actions panel pop-up menu located in the upper-right corner of the panel, choose Expert Mode. This converts the Actions panel essentially to a text editor and allows us to type code directly.

9. Replace the line that says

```
gotoAndPlay (1);
```

with the following text (be sure to enter this exactly):

```
QA.gotoAndStop ("answer");
```

The final code should appear as follows:

```
on (rollOver) {
        QA.gotoAndStop("answer");
```

Let's pause and explain that second line of code (the one that is indented and begins with QA). The line enables the button to tell the movie clip ("QA") to go to and stop at the frame labeled "answer." Remember the "question" and "answer" labels you entered when you were setting up the movie clip? This bit of script is advancing the movie clip playhead to the "answer" label, which conveniently is where the answer content can be found! The quotes around the label name tell Flash to look for a *literal*—that is, an actual piece of text with these letters—as opposed to an *expression,* such as a number or variable.

NOTE   If you are a Flash 4 user, this line replaces the Tell Target action.

If you were to test this movie now, what you would find is that when you roll over the answer button, the answer does show up. But when you move your cursor

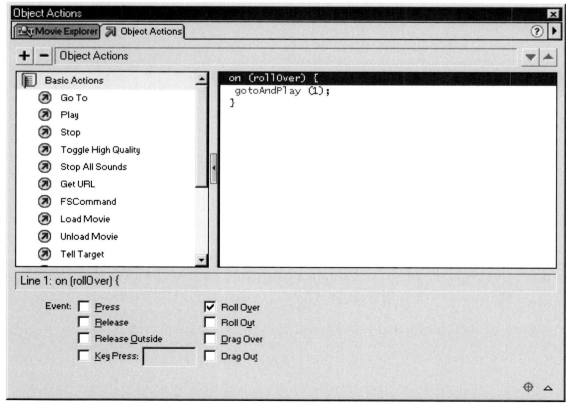

Figure 10-14   Flash button event handlers

away from the Answer button, the answer still shows and there is no way to get back to the question! Let's add some more script.

1. With the button selected and the Object Actions panel open (you should be able to see your script), make sure you are in Expert mode. (Use the pop-up menu to toggle back and forth between Normal and Expert modes.) One nice thing about Expert mode is that it allows you to copy-and-paste code.

2. Copy all three lines of code. (Don't forget the curly bracket in the third line!)

3. Press COMMAND-C/CTRL-C to copy the selected text.

4. Move your cursor so that it is after the final curly bracket, and press RETURN or ENTER to move to the fourth line.

5. Press COMMAND-V/CTRL-V to paste the first three lines of code. You should now have six lines of code—two sets of three lines that are the same. We will modify the second set to enable the user to get back to the question.

6. Use the Object Actions pop-up menu to return to Normal mode.

7. Click line 5 (which is the second `QA.gotoAndStop ("answer");` line). Notice that a box appears beneath, labeled "Expression." Inside is the full text of the line of code.

8. Where you see the word "answer" in quotes and parentheses, replace it with **"question"**. Now the script will advance the playhead of the movie clip back to the question. The only problem is, our event is wrong! As it stands, the Go To action will be triggered when the user rolls over the button, but we want the initial image to be restored when the user rolls away from the button.

9. Click the fourth line of the script (the second `on (rollOver) {` line). The event check boxes appear at the bottom of the Actions panel.

10. Clear Roll Over and select Roll Out. Your final script should appear as follows:

```
on (rollOver) {
    QA.gotoAndStop("answer");
}
on (rollOut) {
    QA.gotoAndStop("question");
}
```

You have now completed the movie. This would be another good time to save it. When you have done so, Press COMMAND-RETURN/CTRL-ENTER to export the movie as an SWF.

Troubleshooting the Flash Movie

If the movie does not work as expected, here are a couple of things to look for:

- Be sure your script is exactly like the one shown earlier—including the periods, quotes, and semicolons.
- In your movie clip, be sure that your frame labels are spelled correctly, marked with a red flag, and that they are in the same frame number as the content they are associated with.
- Be sure that there is a stop( ) action in the first frame of the movie clip.
- Verify that you entered an instance name for your movie clip (this is not the same as the symbol name in the Library). The instance name should appear in the Instance panel when the instance is selected. Also be sure that the ActionScript on the button actually points to this instance name—spelling counts!

Conclusion

Clearly, Fireworks and Flash handle this quiz interaction quite differently. Flash is a bit harder for the developer, since there are no one-step behaviors that do all the dirty work. But if you look at the Fireworks-generated JavaScript code, you will see it is actually quite a bit more involved than the simple script that we wrote! The other difference is that the exported assets that Fireworks creates are simply bitmap graphics, HTML tables, and JavaScript. Fireworks has to output to a standard format, a format (HTML) that has serious limitations. The result is a fundamentally different creature from the vector objects you were working with in the authoring environment.

Flash, on the other hand, is a plug-in built from the ground up to deliver animation and interactivity. Although it is a bit harder at the beginning, it can create far more powerful applications that behave much more predictably than many HTML projects do, once you test them with different browsers on different platforms. Still, for all of their differences, both programs enable nonprogrammers to build interactive applications, be they slick nav bars or learning applications. Not bad!

Finally, it is worth mentioning that the Flash version of our quiz did not actually need to be done using a movie clip. We could have put the quiz content right on the main timeline and let the button navigate that. On a small project like this, it doesn't matter much. But when you start building more serious Flash projects, such a Flash architecture can be crippling. It is better to get in the habit of thinking like Flash does and to start using object-oriented graphics and scripting. A great way to do that is to isolate pieces of content in movie clips—you have already seen how well a button can communicate with a movie clip instance. So can frame actions, other movie clips, and even content from a database that is sent through ColdFusion or ASP!

III Part

Building and Exporting Interactive Web Pages

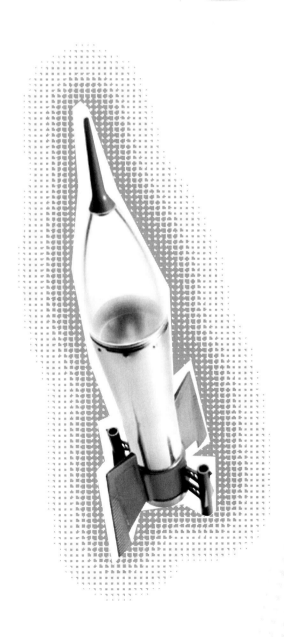

11 Building Interactive Pages

Fireworks is probably best known for its extensive abilities to turn static web page designs into fully functional, JavaScript-enabled, HTML pages ready for the Web or for further massaging in a web development tool like Dreamweaver. With Fireworks, you can create *image maps* (a set of invisible links on an image), buttons that change their color and shape as the user rolls over and clicks them, that trigger an image or animation to appear somewhere on the web page, and that even build pop-up menus that hide and show a set of links. Best of all, you can do all of these things without typing a single line of code.

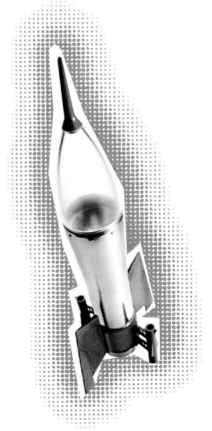

Such extensive interactive capabilities housed in an easy-to-use graphical interface have significantly democratized the process of building great looking, media-rich web pages. In this chapter, you'll learn how to add interactive behaviors like rollover navigation bars and pop-up menus to your web page designs by using the Hotspot and Slice tools in conjunction with the Frames, Object, and Behaviors panels. In addition, we'll discuss ways to ensure link consistency across a team of designers and developers by importing and managing links in the URL Manager.

Fireworks Web Objects

Before you can add any kind of interactivity to your Fireworks document, you must first create either a hotspot or a slice object. These two "web objects," as Fireworks refers to them, form the basis of all interactivity, from simple links to complex, hierarchical pop-up menus. A *hotspot* is a shape that defines an interactive region to which you can apply a link or a rollover behavior (see Figure 11-1). Similarly, a *slice* defines an interactive region, but with additional properties.

Not only does a slice allow you to apply interactive behaviors like links and rollovers, but it also allows you to apply optimization settings specific to that region. For example, you can draw a slice over a photographic element of your layout and apply a JPEG setting while the rest of your layout uses a GIF setting. How does this work? A slice, as shown in Figure 11-2, literally cuts the layout into pieces. Technically, a slice becomes a table cell once you export the document. Because each slice becomes a separate graphic piece, you have the option to save each piece with different optimization settings or to apply different interactive behaviors to them.

The Hotspot tools. Click and hold to reveal a set of different hotspot shapes.

A hotspot in the document appears as a semitransparent blue overlay. You can change the color of hotspots in the Object panel.

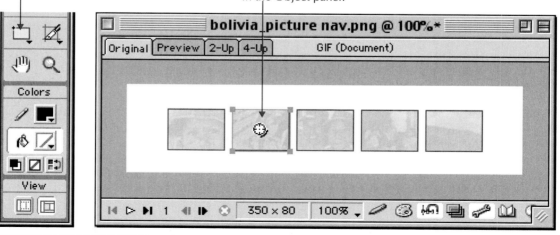

Figure 11-1   Create interactive regions in your document with the Hotspot tool.

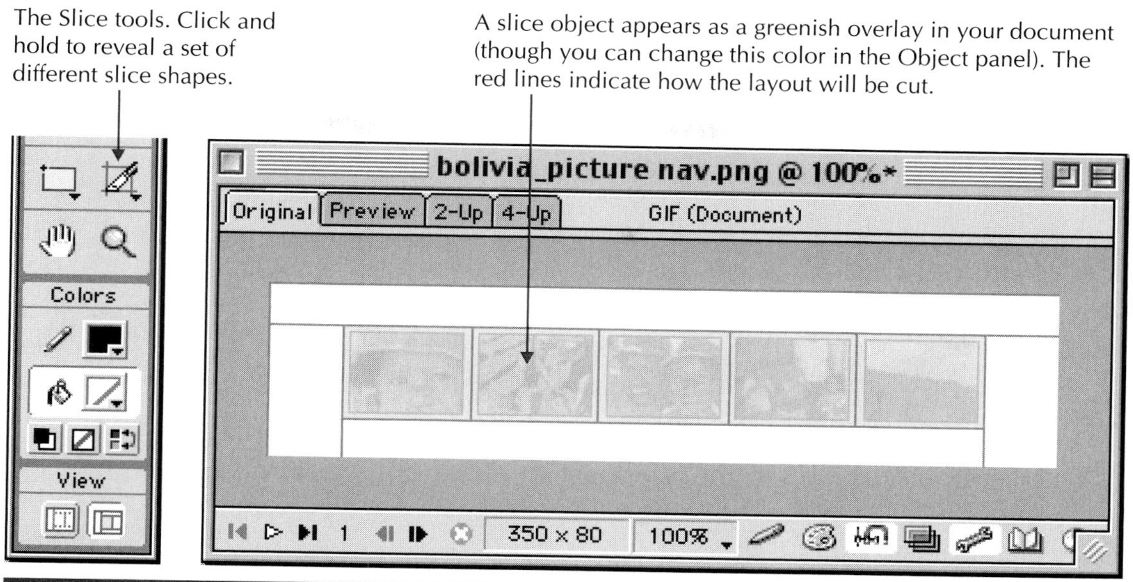

The Slice tools. Click and hold to reveal a set of different slice shapes.

A slice object appears as a greenish overlay in your document (though you can change this color in the Object panel). The red lines indicate how the layout will be cut.

bolivia_picture nav.png @ 100%*

Original | Preview | 2-Up | 4-Up   GIF (Document)

350 × 80   100%

Figure 11-2   The Slice tool chops your layout into a table structure. Each slice object defines a table cell.

The Web Layer

Once you draw a hotspot or a slice object with the Hotspot and Slice tools in the Tools panel, it appears in the Web Layer of the Layers panel. Hotspots and slices are the only objects that can go in the Web Layer. You cannot, for example, add shapes, paths, or text objects to the Web Layer. You may have also noticed that the Web Layer, shown in Figure 11-3, is always the topmost layer in the Layers panel. Unlike other layers in the Layers panel, the Web Layer cannot be dragged to another position in the stacking order—it is always the topmost layer.

Slicing Your Document

Because slices are used for two different purposes—individually optimizing areas of your layout and adding interactive behaviors—you must plan ahead how you want to slice your layout. Many designers new to Fireworks will draw slices haphazardly in the middle of their documents without regard to the fact that they are actually creating a table structure. Each slice you create becomes a table cell. As the red lines coming off the slice object in Figure 11-2 indicate, whenever you draw one slice, Fireworks automatically determines how the rest of the layout will be chopped. You may see, for example, a red line slicing right through your company's logo! While Fireworks' HTML does a good job of reassembling the layout when viewed in a browser, the two halves of the logo may be saved with different color schemes, and you may see a noticeable difference. When slicing, you should always anticipate how the one slice object affects the rest of the design.

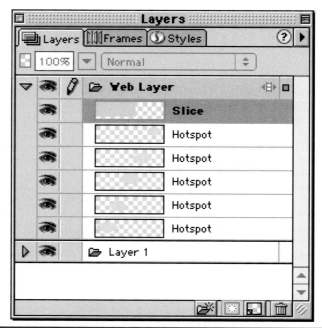

Figure 11-3 The Web Layer contains only slices and hotspots.

Also, always try to create the simplest table structure possible. For example, get in the habit of always butting two slices right next to one another, as in Figure 11-4. Avoid leaving any gaps between slices, as in Figure 11-5, because this creates a third slice for the gap—adding more complexity to the design and HTML table than is necessary, and increasing the download time. Also, take care not to stagger slices. Staggering also creates additional slices to cover the gaps and adds to the complexity and download time.

IDEA To ensure that your slices butt up next to one another as you draw them, avoiding overlap and creating a cleaner table structure, make sure that Snap To Guides is turned on in the View | Guides menu.

To create a slice, select the Slice tool in the Tools panel, and draw a rectangular shape covering the area you want to carve out for either optimization or interactive purposes. For example, if you are building an interactive button, draw the slice to cover just the button area. It's important to not overlap slice objects. Overlapping two slices also results in a third slice (for the intersection) and adds unnecessarily to the file's complexity and size.

NOTE There are two different Slice tools in the Tools panel to choose from: the normal rectangular Slice tool that you'll use most often and the Polygon Slice tool. (Click and hold on the Slice tool to reveal the Polygon Slice tool.) The Polygon Slice tool is used for specific situations where you have overlapping rollover buttons.

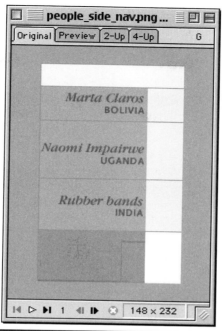

Figure 11-4 To reduce file size and complexity, always butt slices next to one another.

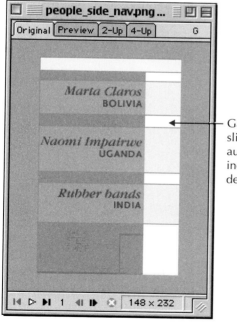

Gaps left between slices will be automatically sliced, increasing the design's complexity.

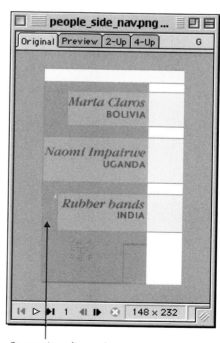

Staggering slices also creates gaps that Fireworks will slice automatically.

Figure 11-5 Gaps left between slices or staggered slices unnecessarily add to the HTML file's complexity and increase download time.

Creating Hotspots

Unlike slices, hotspots do not chop your layout into a table structure of individual graphic pieces. Instead, hotspots allow you to define multiple interactive regions of either a single graphic or sliced graphic. For example, as Figure 11-6 indicates, it's possible to slice an area, like the top banner of your design, and then add one or more hotspots on top of the slice. In this scenario, the slice serves to chop the banner into a separate graphic, while the hotspot allows you to define a linked area.

 If you use hotspots on top of a slice object, the slice's link (if you've assigned one in the Object panel) will not work. The hotspots will override the slice's link.

Hotspots are invisible once you export the design. Their only purpose is to define an area that people can roll over or click to trigger an interaction. For those of you familiar with HTML, hotspots create an image map for a particular graphic when you export it from Fireworks.

There are three different hotspot tools to choose from: a Rectangular tool, an Oval tool, and a Freeform Polygon tool. To access them, simply click and hold on the Hotspot tool to reveal them. Each tool allows you to define shapes best suited to your design. You can also turn any object in your design into a hotspot (without

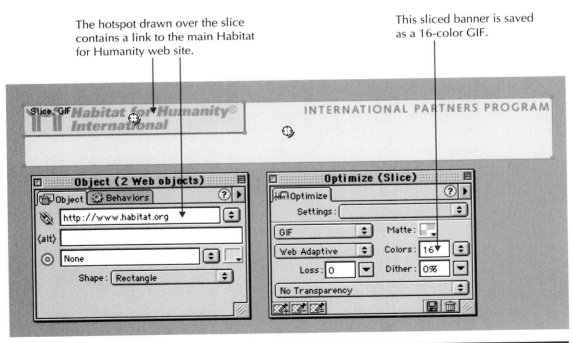

Figure 11-6   You can use slices and hotspots together.

losing the object). This technique is a great shortcut for instantly building odd-shaped hotspots. To build custom-shaped hotspots, follow these steps:

1. Create a new Fireworks document, and use the Oval tool to build a series of overlapping ovals that will become buttons. Feel free to use the Text tool to add labels to each button.

2. Hold the SHIFT key down and select each of the ovals. Choose Insert | Hotspot from the menu. Because you have selected multiple objects, click the Multiple button in the alert window. This action creates a handful of individual hotspots—one for each oval shape you selected— rather than one big hotspot. It's important to remember that you are only using the *shape* of your designs to define the hotspots. You do not lose your original designs by creating hotspots out of them. Figure 11-7 shows the final result.

Changing the Stacking Order of Hotspots

In this exercise, you created a collection of overlapping hotspots. Unlike overlapping slices, overlapping hotspots do not add to the complexity or file size of your final HTML file. Because each hotspot will have a unique link, what happens when a user clicks on the area where two hotspots overlap? The rule is that the topmost hotspot's behavior or link overrides the underlying hotspot. It's important, therefore, to control the stacking order of your hotspots. Just as you can reorder objects in normal layers, you can reorder hotspots by using the Modify | Arrange | Bring To Front / Send To Back, or Bring Forward / Send Backward menu commands. You could also reorder hotspots by dragging them above or below one another in the Layers panel.

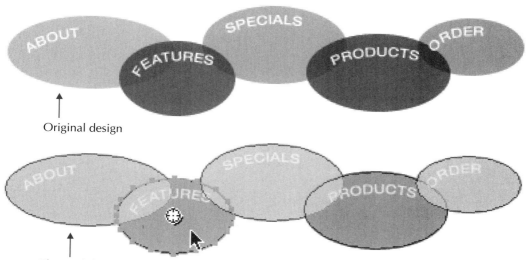

Original design

The oval shapes can define hotspots. Notice that the original design is retained underneath.

Figure 11-7 You can turn any object's shape into a hotspot.

Adding and Managing Links

Once you've created a number of hotspots and slices for each interactive region in your design, the next step is to assign links to them. To add links to hotspots and slices, you can use either the Object panel or the URL panel found in the Window menu. Both panels allow you to add a link to a selected hotspot or slice simply by typing it into the text field. The difference between the two panels is that the Object panel allows you to fine-tune each link, while the URL panel is more of a storage device that keeps a library of frequently used links.

Adding Links in the Object Panel

In addition to allowing you to add links to selected web objects, the Object panel allows you to fine-tune each link. For example, if your web page uses frames, the Object panel allows you to enter a target frame for the link. The Object panel also allows you to enter an `<alt>` tag (a text message that appears before the graphic fully loads into the browser). If you are working with a slice object, the Object panel allows you to name the slice. (Remember that each sliced area becomes a separate graphic, so it's important to be able to name each slice to keep track of them.)

> NOTE The Object panel also enables you to turn a slice object into a text-only region instead of a graphic. If you select the Text option for Type, you can enter HTML code right into the Object panel. If you choose the Text option, however, you can only preview the HTML effects in a browser, not in Fireworks' Preview mode.

As you use the Object panel to assign links to selected hotspots and slices, it keeps a running tab of all the links you create. This list of links is helpful if you are working on multiple documents in one Fireworks session. You can, for example, create a link in one document and then quickly apply it to another slice or hotspot in a different document without having to retype it. Each time you enter a link in the Object panel, it is temporarily stored in a pull-down menu next to the link field, as shown in Figure 11-8. When you select a slice or hotspot, you can either type the link in the text field or choose one of the already-typed links from the pull-down menu. This temporary storage feature is a great timesaver when working on multiple documents of a project that all use the same links. Once you quit Fireworks, however, the Object panel does not store your list of links for future sessions.

> NOTE The links you enter in the Object panel should follow relative and absolute addressing standards. For example, if you are linking to a page that exists in the same folder, you can simply enter the page's name, for example, "page1.htm." If the page is buried inside a folder, enter the folder name followed by the page name, such as "folder/page1.htm." If you are linking to a web address, enter the full path name, like "http://www.company.com."

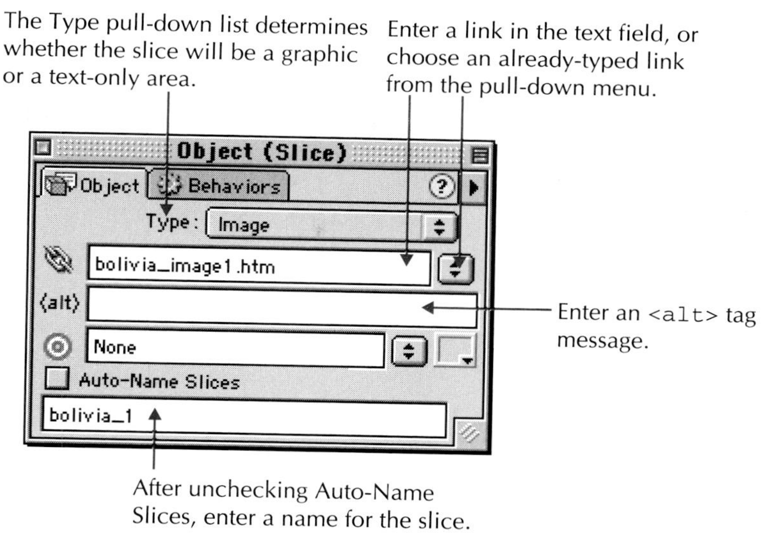

The Type pull-down list determines whether the slice will be a graphic or a text-only area.

Enter a link in the text field, or choose an already-typed link from the pull-down menu.

Enter an <alt> tag message.

After unchecking Auto-Name Slices, enter a name for the slice.

Figure 11-8 Use the Object panel to add a link to a selected hotspot or slice.

Using the URL Manager

While the Object panel keeps a temporary list of all the links you used in one Fireworks session, the URL Manager allows you to create permanent link libraries called *URL libraries*. URL libraries are a great way to store a handful of frequently used links that you, and an entire production team, can use throughout a project. Use link libraries not only to save typing time, but also to ensure link consistency across multiple files.

To create a new URL library and then export it so that other members of a production team can use it, follow these steps:

1. Launch Fireworks and open the URL panel from the Window menu. Select New URL Library from the Options pull-down menu, as shown in Figure 11-9, and give the library a new name.

2. Type a link into the text field at the top of the URL panel, and then click the + symbol to add it to the library list.

3. If the next link you plan to enter is similar, you can use the link you just entered as a starting point. Click on the link in the list that you just entered. It should appear in the text field above. Make the required changes to the link, and then click the + symbol to add it to the list.

4. To export your list of links, choose Export URLs from the Options pull-down menu. Name the file and save. What you are exporting is actually a standard HTML file with a set of text links—try opening it in a browser to take a look.

5. You can then e-mail the exported HTML file of links to other production team members. They can, in turn, import the file into their URL panel by choosing Import URLs from the Options pull-down menu.

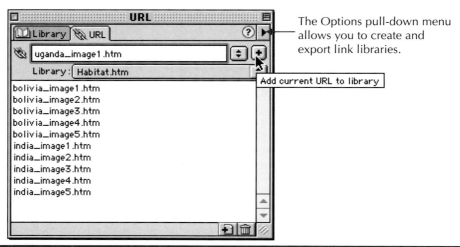

The Options pull-down menu allows you to create and export link libraries.

Add current URL to library

Figure 11-9   Use the URL panel to manage sets of links.

IDEA You can import any HTML file into the URL panel. The URL panel will read each of the links contained within the file and place them in the list.

Once you've created or imported a set of links in the URL panel, applying links to selected hotspots and slices is easy. Simply select the web object, and click on one of the links in the URL panel's list. To fine-tune the link, open the Object panel and make the necessary adjustments, like targeting a frame or entering an <alt> tag.

Adding JavaScript Behaviors

In addition to assigning a link to a hotspot or slice, you can also assign a JavaScript behavior. To add a JavaScript behavior such as a *rollover,* a graphic that changes appearance when the mouse "rolls over" or clicks it, you'll need to coordinate three elements of your document:

- **Frames**   Most of the behaviors in the Behaviors panel require that you prepare a series of frames. For example, the rollover behavior (where an image changes its appearance when the mouse rolls over it) requires graphics on at least two frames—Frame 1 for the initial state of the graphic and Frame 2 for the rollover state.

- **Slices**   If you are creating a series of rollover graphics in the same document, you'll need to create a series of slices. Each sliced area operates independently of the other. For example, when the user rolls over one slice, it is the only one that changes. The other sliced areas remain in their initial states.

- **Behaviors panel**   To set slices and hotspots in motion, and to animate a series of frames, you need to choose a behavior from the Behaviors panel. As a shortcut, you can click on the Center icon of a slice or hotspot and choose a behavior from the drop-down list that appears.

Preparing Frames for Rollover Buttons

Because slicing chops your layout into individual pieces, you have the ability to apply different interactive behaviors to each piece. For example, in the same way that you can apply different optimization settings to each sliced graphic, you can also apply different behaviors to each slice that act independently of one another. This independence is the key to creating rollover buttons—buttons that animate or change appearance when the user rolls over or clicks them. For example, when the user rolls over a button, it should be the only button that highlights. The rest of the buttons should remain unchanged, as in Figure 11-10.

To build a rollover button like the one in Figure 11-10, slicing is just the beginning. You also need to prepare a series of frames that represent at least two *states* of the button. The Up state (the way the button looks before a user touches it) always goes on Frame 1. The Over state (the way the button looks when a user rolls over it with the mouse) always goes on Frame 2. The Down state (the way the button looks when the user clicks it) always goes on Frame 3.

When you apply a rollover behavior to a slice in the Behaviors panel, the slice knows to use the contents of the various frames for the different button states. Effectively, the slice takes a core sample of your document—drilling downward through each of the frames and using the graphics on each as different button states. Here's how to prepare frames for an interactive navigation bar:

1. Start a new Fireworks document, and use the Shape and Text tools to build three buttons for a navigation bar.

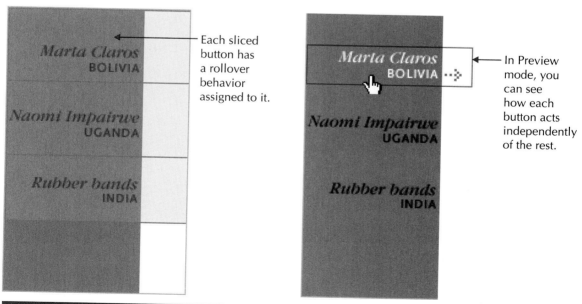

Each sliced button has a rollover behavior assigned to it.

In Preview mode, you can see how each button acts independently of the rest.

Figure 11-10   Slicing allows you to create a series of buttons that act independently of each other.

2. In the Frames panel, choose Duplicate Frame from the Options pull-down menu. In the dialog box that appears, enter **2** to create two copies of Frame 1. Click OK.

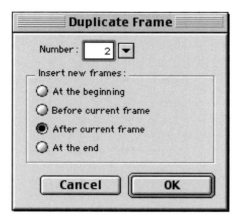

3. Click on Frame 2 in the Frames panel. Select the three button shapes, and change their fill color to reflect how you want the buttons to appear when the mouse rolls over them.

4. Click on Frame 3 in the Frames panel. Again, select the three button shapes, but this time change their fill to reflect how you want the buttons to appear when the user clicks them.

5. Select the Slice tool in the Tools panel. Draw three slice objects—each covering a different button. Remember to butt the slices up next to one another so that they share the same cut mark, leaving no gaps in between them. This will create a simpler HTML table structure.

Now that you've prepared a series of frames and drawn a slice over each interactive area, you are ready to apply rollover behaviors using the Behaviors panel. If you've finished this exercise, save it and use it for the next lesson.

Assigning Behaviors

The Behaviors panel allows you to add JavaScript actions to your hotspots and slices without writing a single line of code. To apply a behavior to a hotspot or slice, select it and then choose a behavior like Simple Rollover from the "+" pull-down menu in the Behaviors panel. There are five behaviors you can choose from:

- Simple Rollover
- Swap Image
- Set Nav Bar Image
- Set Pop-Up Menu
- Set Text of Status Bar

Simple Rollover

The simple rollover behavior uses just two frames—the contents of Frame 1 for the initial state and the contents of Frame 2 for the rollover state. When you apply this behavior to a hotspot or slice, no Down state will appear when the user clicks the region. To use this behavior, follow these steps:

1. Prepare two frames and draw slices as you did in the previous lesson. Draw the initial button states on Frame 1 and the rollover states on Frame 2, as shown in Figure 11-11.

2. Select each slice (you can hold down the SHIFT key to select multiple slices), and choose Simple Rollover from the + menu in the Behaviors panel.

3. Preview your work by clicking the Preview tab at the top of your document. When finished previewing, click the Original tab to return to editing mode.

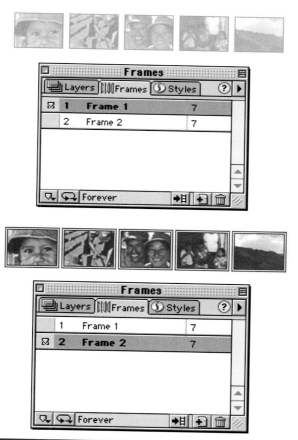

Figure 11-11   Draw the initial button states on Frame 1 and the rollover states on Frame 2.

Using Rollovers with Polygon Slices In a situation where your button elements overlap, as in Figure 11-12, using rectangular slices for each button presents problems when you apply a rollover behavior. Because the sliced area includes parts of an adjoining button, you'll see part of that button highlight, too. To get around this, you can use the Polygon slice tool in the Tools panel to carefully trace the shape of each button. Fireworks will ultimately create a rectangular slice around the button, but will use the polygon shape to define a "window" for the rollover. We've found that this tool, however, gives mixed results and that the window does not always work as defined. The stacking order of the slices seems to affect which window works—the topmost slice wins.

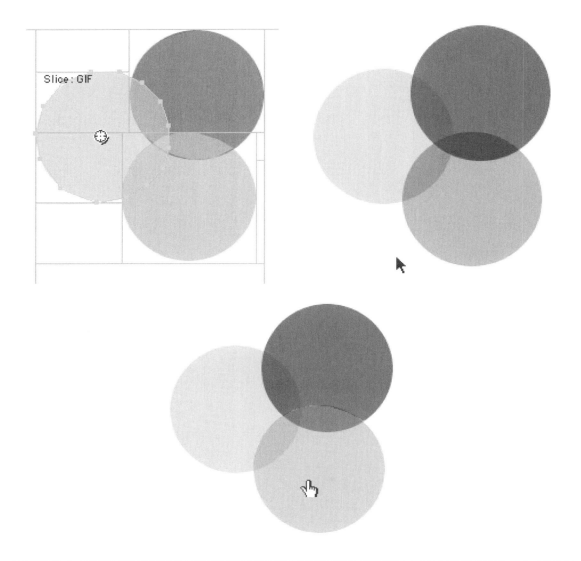

Figure 11-12   The Polygon slice tool allows you to control the window through which the rollover appears.

The better option with a scenario like this is to draw one slice over the whole area. Then draw three Polygon hotspots—one over each button. Assign the Swap Image behavior to each hotspot—swapping in a different frame for each button's rollover. See the "Swap Image" section, next, for more details.

Swap Image

A variation on the Simple Rollover is the Swap Image behavior. This behavior allows you to cause the rollover to appear in a *different* slice. Or, if you like, you can also cause the Swap Image behavior to occur in the same slice. Using a Swap Image behavior gives you more interactive control than a Simple Rollover because you can choose any frame you like as the source of the rollover.

For example, when the user rolls over one slice, an image appears elsewhere on the page. The Swap Image behavior is great for making custom messages appear when a user rolls over a button. Take a look at the navigation bar in Figure 11-13. In this example, there are five buttons—each with a Simple Rollover behavior. In addition to the Simple Rollover, each button also has a Swap Image behavior that makes a custom message appear in the lower slice area describing the button.

IDEA Each slice or hotspot can have multiple behaviors. You can, for example, assign a Simple Rollover, a Swap Image, and a Pop-Up Menu behavior to a single slice or hotspot.

To use the Swap Image behavior, you must have at least one slice in your document. The slice acts as a window where the swap image can appear. The next ingredient is the frame. When you set up a Swap Image behavior, not only do you target a slice where the slice is to occur, but you must also tell Fireworks which frame holds the image you'd like to swap in. To build a Swap Image behavior, follow these steps:

1. Design a navigation bar like the one in Figure 11-13 that has a row of three buttons above a message area. On Frame 1, build the Up states of the buttons (the way they should look when the user first sees them) and leave the message area blank. A message will only appear in the lower space when the user rolls over one of the buttons.

Figure 11-13 A Swap Image behavior triggers a graphic to appear in a different slice.

2. In the Frames panel, duplicate the frame to create Frame 2. On Frame 2, alter the buttons to reflect the rollover state. Also, in the message area below, enter a text message that should appear when the user rolls over the first button.

3. Duplicate Frame 2 to create two additional frames—Frames 3 and 4. On Frame 3, double-click the text message and change it to become the rollover message for the second button. On Frame 4, change the message to become the rollover message for the third button.

4. Draw a slice over each of the three buttons and a fourth slice covering the message area below.

5. SHIFT-select the three button slices and, in the Behaviors panel, choose Simple Rollover from the + menu. Deselect the slices and select just the first button slice. Grab the Center icon (the central circle on the slice), and drag it to the lower message slice, as illustrated in Figure 11-14. This action adds the Swap Image behavior automatically and connects the two slices. In the window that appears, select the frame that contains the appropriate swap image for the button slice and click OK. Repeat these steps to set up the Swap Image behavior for the remaining two buttons: select the button's slice, drag the Center icon to the message slice, choose the appropriate frame, and click OK.

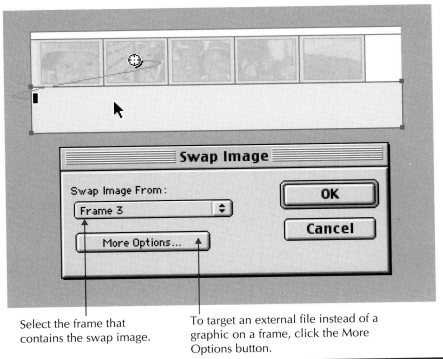

Select the frame that contains the swap image.

To target an external file instead of a graphic on a frame, click the More Options button.

Figure 11-14 Click-and-drag the Center icon of a slice to another slice to set up a Swap Image behavior.

You can also add a Swap Image behavior to a slice directly in the Behaviors panel. Adding the behavior this way opens the Swap Image window, shown in Figure 11-15, where you can choose the target slice by clicking it in the mini map of your slices. This window also allows you to use an external file—even an Animated GIF—as the swapped image instead of a graphic on a particular frame.

 If you use an external file as the swapped image, however, make sure that it has the same dimensions as the target slice where it will appear. Otherwise, Fireworks will resize it to fit.

Once you are finished adding the Swap Image behaviors to each of the three buttons, preview your handiwork by clicking on the Preview tab at the top of the document window. Try rolling the mouse over each of the three buttons, and watch how a unique message appears for each button.

Set Nav Bar Image

The Set Nav Bar Image behavior is like Simple Rollover, but includes a Down state (the state users see when they click) and an optional Over While Down state—the state users see when they roll over a button that's already selected (in its Down state). This behavior also allows you to coordinate a set of buttons so that they can

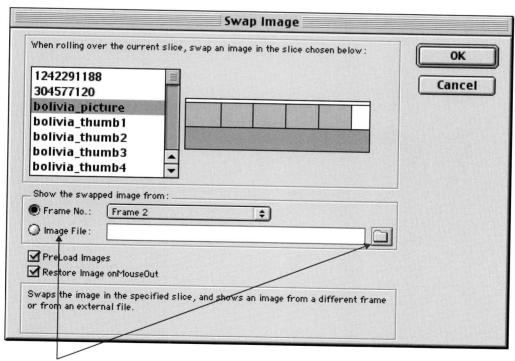

Choose Image File and click the folder icon to point to an external file as the source of the swapped image.

Figure 11-15 The Swap Image window

act together as one navigation bar. For example, if you apply the Set Nav Bar Image to a set of four buttons, only one of them appears highlighted at any one time—the rest will reset to their initial states.

NOTE All the indented behaviors under Set Nav Bar Image in the Behaviors panel are included automatically when you choose the top-level Set Nav Bar Image behavior. They are indented so that you can see what behaviors are included and, if you wish, select them separately.

You can also select one of the buttons to be highlighted when users first load the page. For example, if you have created a navigation bar that takes users to four different sections of a web site, you can highlight the button that represents the current page. To use the Set Nav Bar Image behavior, follow these steps:

1. Design a set of four buttons, and build their Up, Over, and Down states on Frames 1–3.

2. Draw a slice over each of the buttons. SHIFT-select each of the slices, and in the Behaviors panel, choose Set Nav Bar Image from the + pull-down menu.

3. Deselect the slices and then select just the slice for the button that should be highlighted when the user first loads the page. In the Behaviors panel, double-click on the Set Nav Bar Image behavior listed in the window. In the window that appears, shown in Figure 11-16, check the Show Down Image Upon Load option and click OK.

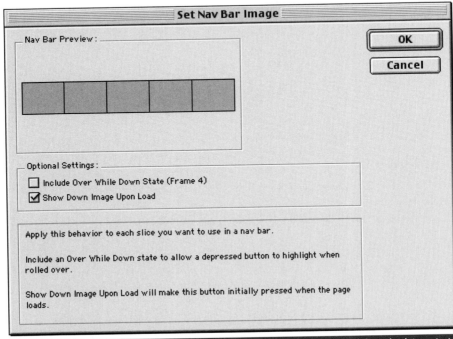

Figure 11-16 Adjust the Set Nav Bar Image behavior by double-clicking it in the Behaviors panel.

Creating Pop-Up Menus

A pop-up menu is a list of links that appears only when the user rolls over a hotspot or sliced region. Notice how the pop-up window appears a little off to the side of the main button that triggered it, as shown here. Technically, the pop-up window appears in a layer floating above the rest of your web page layout, so it will temporarily cover up any design underneath. As soon as the user rolls off the pop-up, it will disappear. Pop-up menus are a great way to collapse a lot of functionality into a small space. For example, one "Catalog" button could reveal a handful of links to every page within the Catalog section.

 A pop-up window will not work if it appears on top of any kind of active media, such as a Flash movie.

Fireworks provides you with a wizard-like interface that steps you through the process of building a pop-up menu. Here's how to make one:

1. Select a slice or hotspot in your layout, and either choose Insert | Pop-Up Menu from the menu, or select Set Pop-Up Menu from the + menu in the Behaviors panel.

2. In the window that appears, enter in the Text field the words or phrase that the user will see in the pop-up list. In the Link field, enter the actual link for the phrase. To add the text and link to the list, click the + symbol, as shown in Figure 11-17.

3. To indent a link below another, creating a hierarchy, first add the text and link set, as in step 2. Then select the link in the list, and click the Create Menu button. In Figure 11-17, Bolivia, India, and Uganda are indented under "Where will I go?" You could keep going and indent other links to appear under Bolivia, India, or Uganda. To undo an indentation, click the Promote Menu button. When finished adding links and building the hierarchical structure of the links, click the Next button at the bottom of the window.

4. In the next window, you can control the appearance of the pop-up window. You can create either an HTML or an Image-based window, and select the font and coloration of the menu. When finished, click the Finish button.

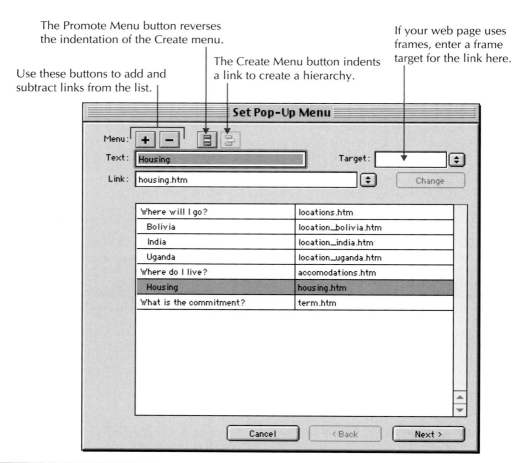

The Promote Menu button reverses the indentation of the Create menu.

The Create Menu button indents a link to create a hierarchy.

Use these buttons to add and subtract links from the list.

If your web page uses frames, enter a frame target for the link here.

Figure 11-17 The first step of building a pop-up menu is adding links and setting their hierarchical structure.

5. You'll now return to your document and see blue outlines representing the placement of the pop-up menu. You can click-and-drag the pop-up menu and position it where you'd like it to appear when the user "mouses over" the button.

Once you've created a pop-up menu, you can edit it at any time by double-clicking it in the Behaviors panel list. This accesses the wizard-like interface where you can make changes. To preview your new pop-up list, you cannot use the Preview tab in the document. You must choose File | Preview In Browser from the menu.

Troubleshooting Pop-Up Menus One bug we've noticed with pop-up windows, however, is that Internet Explorer 5 on the Mac places the pop-up menu relative to where the JavaScript code appears in the HTML—not necessarily where you positioned it in the document window. To fix this problem, you must open the exported Fireworks HTML page in a text editor and move the line that reads

```
<Script Language=JavaScript1.5>fwLoadMenus();</Script>
```

and place it immediately below the `<body>` tag.

Setting Status Bar Messages

The fifth behavior in the Behaviors panel allows you to display a custom message in the lower-left corner of the browser window when the mouse rolls over a hotspot or slice area. To add this behavior, select the hotspot or slice, and choose Set Text Of Status Bar from the + menu in the Behaviors panel. A small window appears, where you can add a custom message. We find that these kinds of custom messages are most useful as quasi "tool tips" that help clarify buttons or provide more information about what users will see when they click. The tip, however, is subtle since it's so detached from the user's main area of focus.

Changing the Mouse Event

In addition to selecting one of the five behaviors, you can also modify the *mouse event* (what the users must do with their mouse to trigger the behavior). For example, the default mouse event for behaviors like Simple Rollover and Set Nav Bar Image is a *mouse over,* meaning that the events trigger when the user rolls the mouse over the slice or hotspot area. In fact, for these two behaviors, you have no choice in the matter. But for other behaviors, like Swap Image, Set Pop-Up Menu, and Set Text of Status Bar, you could change the mouse event to onClick (where the user would have to click to see the action) or to MouseOut (where the action is triggered as soon as the mouse leaves the area). Some of these mouse events make more sense than others for a given behavior. For example, the Set Text Of Status Bar behavior may work well with the MouseOut option because the message would be placed in the status bar as soon as the mouse leaves the hotspot or slice. Because of this MouseOut effect, the message will remain in the browser window.

Creating Button Symbols

Now that you've seen how to coordinate frames, slices, and hotspots with the Object and Behaviors panels to add interactivity to your document, it's only fair to introduce you to a much simpler method of adding interactivity—creating button symbols. We save these for the end of this chapter only because you must understand the fundamental structure of Fireworks interactivity before you can appreciate how button symbols work and how best to use them in your design.

A *button symbol* is an individual rollover button—with an optional click and Over While Down state—that you can drag around and place anywhere in your document. A button symbol is a sliced object, so it *will* slice the rest of your document. What's interesting to note, however, is that button symbols are easy to pick up and drag around—automatically updating the slicing of your document. Compare this with the process of designing buttons in a fixed location in your layout and drawing slices over them. To move a button drawn this way, you'd have to move the contents of each frame individually as well as the slice.

To build a button symbol, follow these steps:

1. **Choose Insert | New Button from the menu.** The button editor window appears where you can build the various states of your button. Use the tools in the Tools panel to build the initial state of the button just as you would in the normal document window.

2. **After building the Up state, click on the Over tab to build the rollover state.** Rather than re-creating the graphics of the Up state, click on the Copy Up Graphic button, as shown in Figure 11-18. Then modify the graphic to reflect the rollover state. Continue building the Down and Over While Down states in this manner.

3. **To add a link to the button, click on the Active Area tab.** By default, the slice object will cover the contents of your graphics, but you can adjust as needed. Remember, however, that the slice defines not only the active area, but also the window through which you'll see the rollover and down states. If you shrink the slice area, therefore, you may clip the rollover and down state graphics. Click the Link Wizard button to add a link to the sliced area. A secondary window appears with many of the features found in the Optimize and Object panels.

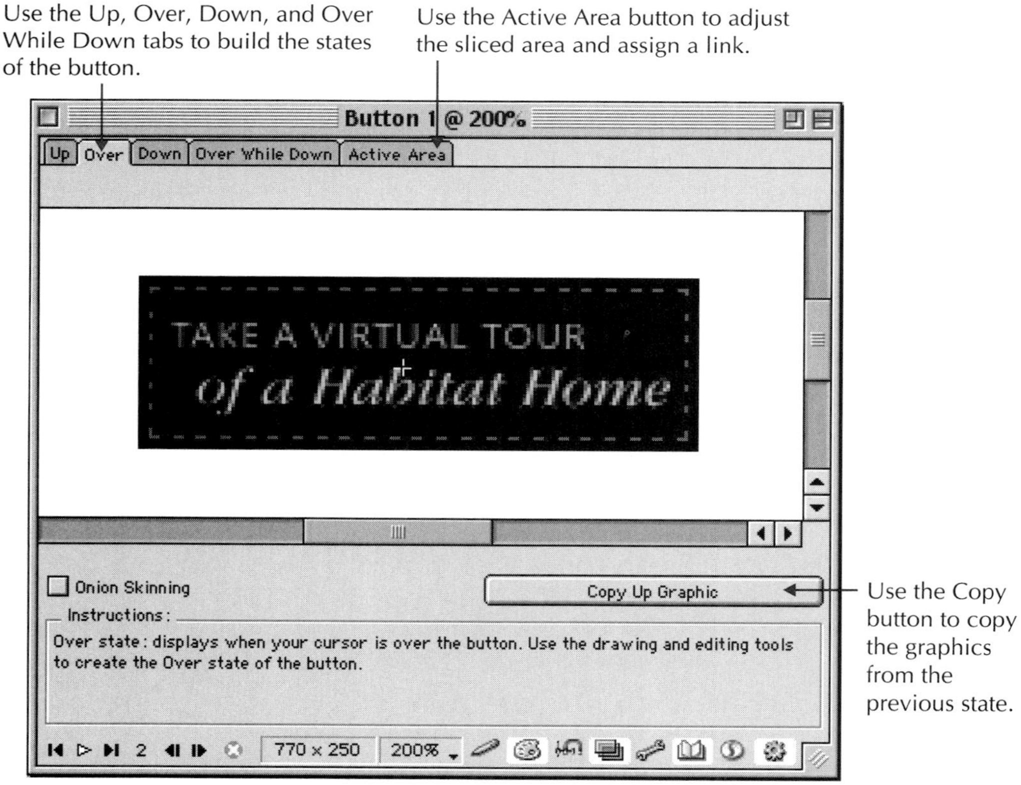

Use the Up, Over, Down, and Over While Down tabs to build the states of the button.

Use the Active Area button to adjust the sliced area and assign a link.

Use the Copy button to copy the graphics from the previous state.

Figure 11-18   The button symbol editor window allows you to build a linked, multistate button.

4. Click through each of the tabs on the Link Wizard to assign the appropriate optimization and link setting to the button and then click OK. Close the button editor window. In your document, you'll now see your new button. Click-and-drag to place the button anywhere you'd like in your layout.

Like a graphic or animation symbol, your new button symbol lives in the Library panel. An *instance* of the button appears in your document. To build a row of buttons based on your button, simply drag another instance from the Library panel into your document. You can also duplicate the instance already in your document. To do so, hold down the ALT or OPTION key and click-and-drag.

Now that you have a few copies of the button symbol, we're sure you're wondering why you'd want three copies of the same button! As shown in Figure 11-19, the Object panel allows you to quickly customize each button—changing its link and even the content of its text label. Select one of the button instances and, in the Object panel, enter new text for the button. To change its link, click on the Link Wizard. An alert will appear asking whether you want to change just the selected, or "current," button or all of them.

NOTE Button symbols do not rely on frames like traditionally created buttons—they are completely self-contained. In fact, if you look in the Frames panel, you'll see just the default Frame 1 (unless, of course, you've already created a handful of frames, in which case, you will see your button states on each successive frame).

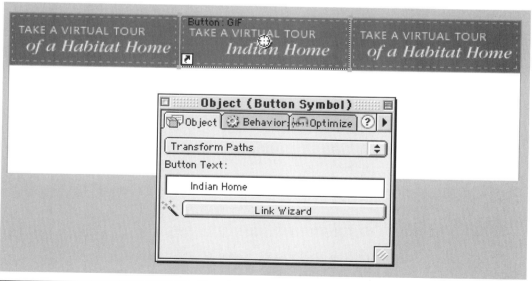

Figure 11-19 The Object panel allows you to quickly customize instances of the same button symbol.

You can also convert buttons that you built the old-fashioned way—with frames and slices—into button symbols:

1. Choose Show All Frames from the pull-down menu at the bottom of the Frames panel.

2. SHIFT-select all the elements of the button across all frames. (If you have multiple buttons in your design, selecting the elements of just one button can be tricky. We suggest you click-and-drag with the Pointer tool to capture the area around the button as a way of quickly selecting everything within a given area.)

3. Choose Insert | Convert To Symbol from the menu. In the window that appears, select the Button symbol option, name the button, and click OK.

Fireworks in the Real World

Building Custom Pop-Up Menus

By Adam Bell

Having designed web sites for five years, I've learned not to incorporate the newest trends in web design just because you can. In most cases, doing so will alienate a majority of your potential audience because they are unable to view your content.

Enter Pop-Up Menus

I've been intrigued by pop-up menus for a long time, and I even tried a simple one about three years ago. I created one for my local Macintosh User Group's site (http://www.nomug.org/)—where I knew most of the members actually had the latest browsers. For the rest of my clients, however, I avoided using pop-ups, because it would mean creating two versions of the same site: one version with the pop-up menus that worked on 4.0 browsers and one version for the 3.0 browser audience.

By now, the majority of web surfers are using 4.0 browsers on their machines. The 3.0 era is pretty much dead. So now, we designers can create those dynamic HTML effects we've always wanted to create, and pop-up menus certainly are at the top of the list. The cool thing about pop-ups is that they increase the usability of the site. Every page offers more one-click options to both the main sections *and* the subsections of your site. With pop-up menus, your audience immediately knows the location of every section in your site without having to sift through a site map or scroll through a long menu to find what they want.

Unfortunately, creating pop-ups hasn't exactly been easy. Using tools like Dreamweaver and GoLive has still made the creation of pop-ups a tedious prospect at best. You would have to create your graphics in Fireworks, bring them into Dreamweaver, and then create the menus (and hopefully get the alignment right). No fun there, right? This is where Fireworks 4 comes in. One of the most exciting new features of Fireworks 4 is the easy creation of pop-up menus. Using the Insert | Pop-Up Menu command opens a wizard-like interface that drastically speeds up the creation process from a couple of hours to a couple of minutes.

Creating the Pop-Up Menu for Hot Sauce Zone

Here's how I built a pop-up for a client's site, called the Hot Sauce Zone (http://www.hotsaucezone.com/), which offers more than 100 different types of sauces and spices in a variety of different brands and categories (see Figure 11-20).

295

Figure 11-20 When the user rolls over one of the buttons on the left, a pop-up menu appears with additional choices.

In addition to listing hundreds of products, this site offers a large recipe area that is also divided into subsections—one for each recipe category (Appetizers, Meat, Poultry, Vegan, and so on). In the past, the only way people would know about these subsections was to click on the main section's link and then view a list of subsections. The new pop-up menu command in Fireworks allows me to set up links to all of these areas on every page of the web site.

To build a pop-up, first design your page (without the pop-ups) and decide exactly where the buttons and pop-ups should go. After I designed the page, I created slices over each main section button. I then selected one of the slices, let's say SAUCES, and chose Insert | Pop-Up Menu.

At this point, the Set Pop-Up Menu dialog box appeared, where I built a list of subsections and entered links for each (see Figure 11-21). I entered the name of each subarea in the Text field followed by the actual URL (absolute or relative) in the Link field. I didn't use framesets, so I skipped the Target pull-down menu. In addition, my list of subsections will not have any nested sections within them. If there had been, I would have needed to use the Create Menu button to indent a section under another section.

After I finished entering all of my subsections and their links, I clicked the Next button at the bottom of the window to advance to the next step. In the next step I chose colors and fonts for the pop-up. Fireworks 4 pop-up menus use HTML-based text created from a CSS style sheet. Therefore, you're limited to basic typefaces to choose from. In this case, I selected Verdana, Arial, Helvetica, sans-serif from the Font pull-down menu, and a point size of 14. Rather than making the cells HTML only, I decided these cells should be image based. I selected the Image option and then chose an orange cell color and a yellow text color.

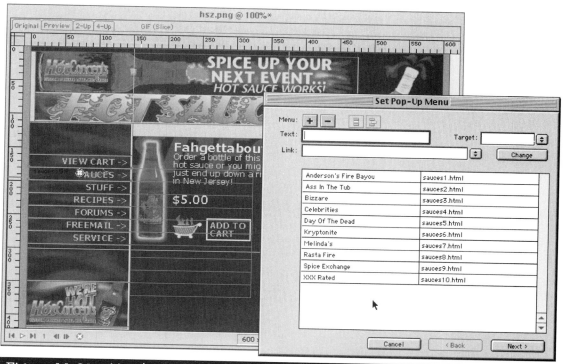

Figure 11-21   Use the Set Pop-Up Menu window to build a list of menu items and links.

The cell color could really be anything I wanted since I wouldn't be using it for my final pop-ups. With the new pop-up completed, I clicked the Finish button to return to the document. In the document, a blue outline—indicating the location of the pop-up menu—now appeared next to my slice object. To reposition the placement of my pop-up, I simply clicked-and-dragged the blue outline. Before continuing to build pop-ups for my remaining slices, I previewed the effect in a browser by choosing File | Preview In Browser.

Editing the Code to Enhance the Menus

Once I had a complete interface with pop-up menus in place, I still wasn't happy with the final look. To make changes, I accepted the ultimate dare for any designer…I opened up the code and started hacking! To make changes to your pop-up, open the HTML file exported from Fireworks into BBEdit, HomeSite, or any text editor.

In the JavaScript code, look for the names of the graphic files used in the pop-up's table cells. In my case, the code I was looking for was

```
fw_menu_0.bgImageUp="main/fwmenu6_176x19_up.gif";
fw_menu_0.bgImageOver="main/fwmenu6_176x19_over.gif";
```

When Fireworks saves GIF files for the pop-up's cells, it includes the file's height and width in the file's name. In this case, I knew that the graphic was 176 pixels wide and 19 pixels high. Back in Fireworks, I could open both the Up state image (fwmenu6_176x19_up.gif) and the Over state image (fwmenu6_176x19_over.gif) and edit away. I added a flame-like texture to each graphic and then re-exported them using the same names—replacing the old graphics. When finished editing the pop-up graphics, I tested the page in both Explorer and Netscape on both Mac and PC just to make sure everything worked.

The next thing I could tweak in the code was the actual placement of the pop-up menu. In Fireworks, I positioned the menu by dragging the blue outline, but I could also open the code and adjust the placement by hand. Open the HTML file in a text editor and look for the following code:

```
onMouseOver="window.FW_showMenu(window.fw_menu_0,149,199)
```

In this case, 0 means that this line of code pertains to the first pop-up menu. Its location is X = 149, and Y = 199. I could adjust these last two numbers until the menu was right where it should be.

Finally, once I was satisfied with the layout, I opened the HTML page in Dreamweaver and added any additional information into the content area. I also like to set my page margins to zero by choosing Modify | Page Properties from the menu. In the Page Properties window, set all four margin options to zero and click

OK. Lastly, I checked the page one more time in browsers before uploading it. Once it was online, I called the client and let them oooh and aaah over my mastery!

Of course, it's not really necessary to make changes like this to the code in order to create working pop-up menus. If you're happy with the range of design options in Fireworks' Set Pop-Up window, you can simply export the pop-up and use it as-is. Building custom-designed pop-ups, however, by coordinating Fireworks and an HTML editor significantly extends your creative freedom. Though it may take a little extra time, it certainly beats doing it the old-fashioned way in the pre-Fireworks 4 era!

12 From Fireworks to HTML and Beyond

To export your sliced images, image maps, button rollovers, pop-up menus, and so on, you need to let Fireworks generate an HTML document that contains all of the necessary tables (HTML) and scripts (JavaScript). The tricky part is that Fireworks is not an HTML editor, so in most cases, you will have to import Fireworks' HTML into your HTML editor. Whether you use a GUI-based HTML editor, such as Dreamweaver, FrontPage, or GoLive, or whether you do it all by hand in a code editor, such as Allaire HomeSite or BBEdit, you need to make the right choices to make the Fireworks-to–HTML editor process as smooth as possible. Fortunately, the developers at Macromedia took this into account and provided numerous tools that will take (some of) the stress out of going from Fireworks to HTML and beyond.

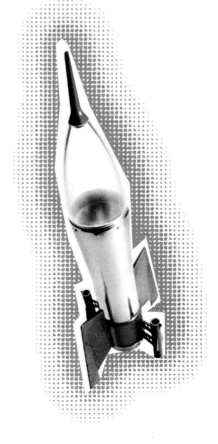

Creating interactive behaviors, image maps, and the like is surprisingly easy in Fireworks: you choose a slice or hotspot, and use one of the simple wizards in the Behaviors panel. You test in Preview mode and can't believe how fast you were able to make that navigation bar. But it's getting that nav bar into your HTML editor—and making edits to it once it's there—that can be confusing.

Let's stick with the nav bar example for a moment. If you are bringing your nav bar into an existing page, you don't need a document title and much of the header information. Nor do you need <body> tags. All of this is already in your HTML document. If those are in your Fireworks HTML as well, then you have some redundancy. You will not want to copy these Fireworks HTML elements into your HTML editor. And that means that you have to selectively copy and paste.

What's worse is that you can't even paste the appropriate portions of code into one place. Some of the JavaScript goes into the header, while other parts go with the regular HTML in the body. If JavaScript looks like Classical Greek to you (and you are not a Hellenist), not knowing what and where to cut, and what and where to paste, can spell trouble.

This chapter will discuss each of the different HTML export options, help you read Fireworks HTML (we'll assume you already know some HTML), explore the HTML export options, and show you how to find the best way to get it into your HTML editor. In addition, we'll show you some strategies for converting entire Fireworks page designs into a workable HTML template.

Understanding Fireworks HTML

You might not immediately think of Fireworks, a graphics application, as an HTML authoring format. You might even fear that Fireworks might produce HTML very badly, like other non–web authoring formats. But fear not: Fireworks will not generate thousands of lines of gratuitous code like some applications. It typically writes fairly minimal, straightforward code, just like you would want it to. The only strictly unnecessary code it adds to the file consists of comments intended to help you use it.

Deconstructing Fireworks HTML

Let's take a look at some basic Fireworks HTML. Figure 12-1 shows some Fireworks HTML code inside of Allaire HomeSite, a code-based HTML editor. The various elements are numbered and explained in the following list. HomeSite, like the code editor in Dreamweaver 4, color-codes different code elements to enhance readability. The HTML document contains only two slices, with no interactivity. It was exported using the Generic HTML setting. Since there is no interactivity, you will not see any JavaScript in the file.

1. The <!— prefix in HTML is used to set off *comments,* which are textual notes added to aid human readers; browsers ignore comments. In this comment, Fireworks provides overview directions for using its HTML. Note that it provides directions for JavaScript even though there is none in this file.

2. Here is where the HTML file begins, as far as the browser is concerned. All HTML documents open with <head> sections. These tags are almost invariably placed automatically in all documents in HTML editors, so in most cases, you will not need to copy these tags from Fireworks.

3. This comment communicates which Fireworks HTML export format was used—in this case, Generic.

4. The </head> tag indicates the end of the header section and the beginning of the body section.

```
<!--To put this html into an existing HTML document, you must copy the JavaScript and-->
<!--paste it in a specific location within the destination HTML document. You must then copy-->      (1)
<!--and paste the table in a different location.-->


<html>   (2)
<head>
<title>export_slice.gif</title>
<meta http-equiv="Content-Type" content="text/html;">
<meta name="description" content="FW4 Generic HTML">
<!--Fireworks 4.0 Generic target.    Created Sun Apr 08 15:30:44 GMT+0800 (Taipei Standard Time) 2001--   (3)

</head>   (4)
<body bgcolor="#ffffff" onload="" topmargin="0" leftmargin="0" marginheight="0" marginwidth="0">
<!--The following section is an image or HTML table which reassembles the sliced image in a browser.-->
<!--Copy the table section including the opening and closing table tags, and paste the data where-->   (5)
<!--you want the reassembled image to appear in the destination document. -->

<!------------------------ BEGIN COPYING THE HTML ------------------------->
<table border="0" cellpadding="0" cellspacing="0" width="200">   (6)
<!-- fwtable fwsrc="Untitled" fwbase="export_slice.gif" fwstyle="Generic" fwdocid = "742308039" fwneste
  <tr><!-- row 1 -->
   <td><img name="export_slice_r1_c1" src="export_slice_r1_c1.gif" width="200" height="96" border="0"><   (7)
  </tr>
  <tr><!-- row 2 -->
   <td><img name="export_slice_r2_c1" src="export_slice_r2_c1.gif" width="200" height="104" border="0">
  </tr>

<!--    This HTML was automatically created with Macromedia Fireworks 4.0    -->   (8)
<!--    http://www.macromedia.com   -->

</table>
<!------------------------ STOP COPYING THE HTML HERE ------------------------->   (9)

</body>   (10)
</html>
```

Figure 12-1 A simple slice in Fireworks HTML, as seen in HomeSite

5. A series of comments indicates where you should begin copying, to move the Fireworks content into your HTML editor.

IDEA Since comments are ignored, you do not need to copy them—begin copying just after the comments so you do not include them.

6. The first, and in this case, only, HTML element that you have to copy from this file is the table. All slices created in Fireworks, whether they contain interactive elements or not, are reconstructed using HTML tables.

7. Fireworks automatically names each slice upon export. You have some control over this process. Its default setting, used here, is *filename_rx_cx*, where *r* and *c* represent rows and columns, and *x* represents the column/row number. A quick look at the two slices will reveal that this particular file had two slice regions in one column and two rows.

8. Here Macromedia uses a comment for a little PR work. No harm would be done if you neglected to copy this into your HTML document. Just don't leave out that `</table>` tag conveniently placed after it.

9. This comment tells you where to stop copying. Again, you do not need to copy the comment itself.

10. These are the closing tags of the document. They most likely do not need to be copied into your HTML editor.

Exporting Fireworks HTML

The simple preceding explication probably gave you at least some idea of moving Fireworks Generic HTML into an HTML editor, but let's not get ahead of ourselves. Before you start copying and pasting Fireworks HTML, you have a host of settings to make before you even let Fireworks create the HTML file.

Fireworks HTML Export Options

Fireworks generally does not generate any HTML unless you export a PNG with slices, hotspots, and/or behaviors. (For an exception, see Note.)

NOTE You can force Fireworks to write code even for a simple graphic with no hotspots, slices, or behaviors, simply by choosing HTML And Images as the Save As Type in the Export dialog box. With simple graphics, however, Fireworks will default to Images Only, and there is generally no real need for Fireworks to generate any code in these circumstances. But the option is there.

Fireworks doesn't generate any HTML at all, until you export. Options for HTML appear logically enough in the Export dialog box. Simply click the Options button beside the HTML drop-down list menu. You can also access HTML options by choosing File | HTML Setup.

The General Tab

When you open the HTML Setup dialog box, you will first see the General tab (Figure 12-2). Using this tab, you can set several parameters of the resulting HTML.

You can select which of four styles you wish to use: Dreamweaver, FrontPage, Generic, or GoLive. Unless you are using one of the three applications named specifically, you will want to use Generic. The code for each of the three is fairly similar, the exception being GoLive, which has a considerable JavaScript attached, even for files composed of a single graphic with no behaviors, slices, or hotspots.

In all cases, Fireworks will generate a fully functional, autonomous HTML page, complete with a document header, and so forth. For this reason, you could literally use Fireworks as a one-step web authoring tool. We do not recommend it, however, since Fireworks does not give you code-level control over the HTML. And, unless you are careful, it places graphics in every cell of every table, making for much larger downloads than necessary. Fireworks HTML also makes it difficult to link pages to one another and to edit pages. However, in certain situations, including times when you need a quick mock-up (such as a design presentation—see Chapter 2), Fireworks HTML can suffice.

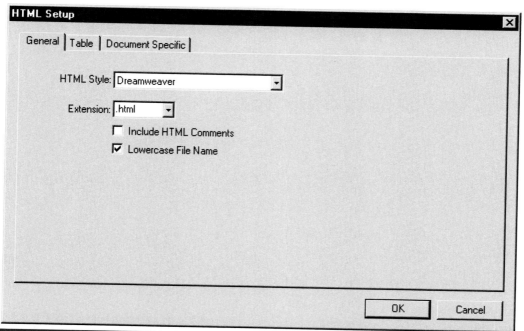

Figure 12-2 Choose an HTML style with the General tab of the HTML Setup dialog box.

In addition to the HTML style, you can choose default extensions here. Note that besides .htm and .html, you can also specify popular extensions for middleware solutions, like ColdFusion. Extensions include .asp, .cfm, .php, .jsp, and .shtml.

IDEA If your Fireworks code will be used in conjunction with a dynamic web page technology, such as Microsoft Active Server Pages, Allaire ColdFusion, or PHP, be sure to give your Fireworks HTML the proper extension.

The Include HTML Comments check box determines whether Fireworks inserts comments. Comments are used to show where to copy and paste to move the code into your HTML editor. If you know HTML fairly well, we suggest that you uncheck this, to cut down on unnecessary lines of code.

The Lowercase File Name check box forces all filenames to lowercase. Since most servers are case sensitive, upper- and lowercase mix-ups are a common cause of broken links. We recommend that you use a consistent method of capitalization in your filenames, the easiest perhaps being to force everything to lowercase.

The Table Tab

The Table tab, seen in Figure 12-3, provides several useful options for the exporting of tables. Fireworks generates tables whenever slices are used. A key concept to understand is the meaning of spacers. *Spacers* are simply transparent GIFs used for formatting (see Chapter 8). Table 12-2 summarizes each of the Space With choices and provides suggestions for when to use them.

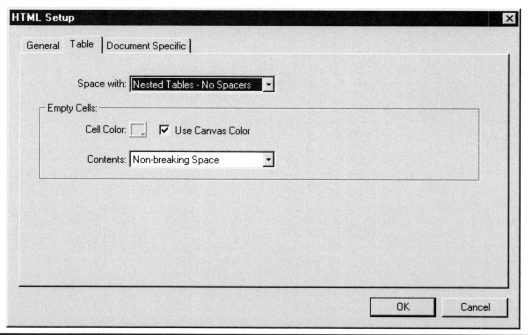

Figure 12-3 The Table tab

Option	Explanation	Suggested Use
Nested Tables – No Spacers	Slices are enclosed within their own tables, creating tables within tables. This results in fairly accurate layout replication and rather complicated code.	Projects where rendered HTML appearance is more important than optimized code. You can also use this setting to move page elements (rather than whole pages) into target HTML files. (See "Strategies for Exporting Complex Elements" later.)
Single Table – No Spacers	Slices are organized within a single HTML table. HTML code is minimal, though often somewhat unreliable graphically.	Projects where the code must be optimized. Advanced HTML coders who are going to run over every line of code anyway can use this setting to get a rough-and-ready page layout to work from. This setting is good for moving entire page designs into HTML.
1-pixel Transparent Spacer	Fireworks inserts transparent GIFs to ensure reliable layout replication. The code is not generally as crazy as with nested tables.	A good middle ground for most users who will tweak the Fireworks HTML but not necessarily overhaul it.

Table 12-1   Fireworks HTML Table Options

 Using the 1-pixel spacer method (the Fireworks default) has been known to cause problems with Netscape 6 when a DTD (Document Type Definition) is used.

In addition to the overall table settings, there are a number of options for handling empty cells. For their background color, you can either check Use Canvas Color, which will set the background color attribute of empty cells to the canvas color, or you can uncheck that option and pick a color yourself from the color well.

The last setting determines what is placed in empty cells. Browsers have a hard time rendering empty table cells. In general, you should never see <td></td> in an HTML document. In the case of empty cells, Fireworks allows you to determine what should go in between the tags.

- **None**   This setting leaves the tags empty. We generally do not recommend this option.
- **Spacer Image**   Again, a transparent GIF is inserted as a placeholder.

- **Non-breaking Space**   Fireworks inserts the text equivalent of a spacer image: the ASCII code for an empty space, which is . This is a good choice for power users who like maximum control over code.

The Document Specific Tab

The third tab of the HTML Setup dialog box, seen in Figure 12-4, allows you to customize how Fireworks names individual slices. We have found that the default settings work fairly well and are fairly easily interpreted in code. However, if you wish to tinker with the naming scheme, you have a buffet of options available.

Other options on this tab allow you to enter an Alternate Image Description (the text of the alt attribute of the <img> tag). We recommend that you set alternate descriptions for each slice by selecting the slice and entering a description in the Alt field of the Object panel, but if you wish for your entire table to have the same alternate description, you can enter it here.

> **IDEA** Alternate descriptions enhance your site's usability. For users who have turned off image display to speed up downloading, alternate descriptions provide some information about what they are missing. More importantly, for visually impaired users, alternate descriptions may be the only way they can experience your images.

If you have created a nav bar and your HTML document does not use frames, be sure to check the Multiple Nav Bar HTML Pages check box. Fireworks will generate

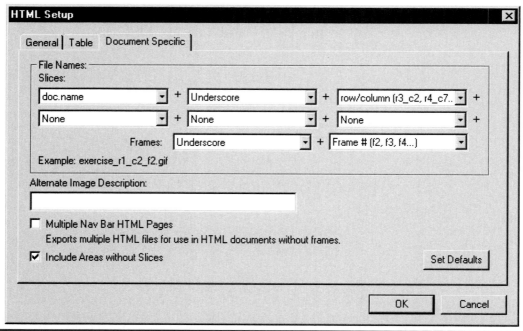

Figure 12-4   Use the Document Specific tab to customize slice names.

separate pages for each nav bar item, which is important when a button in its Down state indicates which page the user is on.

Check the Include Areas Without Slices check box to ensure that your entire document is exported.

If you find yourself changing the settings in this dialog box over and over, and always to the same settings, you should click the Set Defaults button, which will save the current settings as the defaults henceforth.

Importing Fireworks HTML into GUI-Based HTML Editors

Once you have created your Fireworks code, you'll need to get it into your HTML editor. But even though there are many GUI-based HTML editors, and Fireworks itself is GUI-based, moving Fireworks HTML into target HTML documents usually requires messing with the code. The only exception is Dreamweaver, which provides a GUI interface for pulling Fireworks HTML into Dreamweaver documents. This approach has its limitations, though.

You probably already know this if you bought this book, but even though GUI editors make it so that you don't have to know how to code, in reality, you actually do need to know how to code if you are doing anything beyond columns of text.

Dreamweaver

Fireworks/Dreamweaver integration is surely one of the most impressive integrations of two different kinds of software that has ever existed. In fact, this integration is so powerful, and so complex, that we cannot do it justice in a small section such as this.

 See Chapter 13 for coverage of Fireworks/Dreamweaver integration and how you can use it to improve your workflow.

We'll at least show you how to import Fireworks HTML into Dreamweaver:

1. Upon export, choose HTML And Images in the Save As Type drop-down list.

2. Be sure that Dreamweaver is the selected HTML Style in the HTML Setup dialog box.

3. Export the file.

4. Open Dreamweaver and the desired HTML file within Dreamweaver.

5. Place the cursor where you would like to insert the Fireworks HTML. If you are moving an entire page design, you will probably place the cursor at the top of an empty page. If you are moving only an element, such as a banner, you will probably place the cursor inside a table cell.

6. Click the Insert Fireworks HTML button on the Dreamweaver toolbar. The Insert Fireworks HTML dialog box appears.

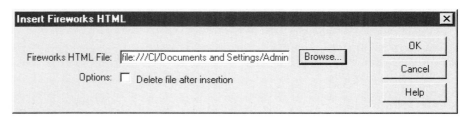

7. Click the Browse button to navigate to the Fireworks HTML file.

NOTE In the Insert Fireworks HTML dialog box, you are searching for an HTML file—not a graphic file, such as a PNG or a GIF. Dreamweaver will pull in all the appropriate graphic assets with the HTML file. If all you want to do is pull in a simple graphic (such as an optimized JPG), use the Insert Image tool, rather than the Insert Fireworks HTML tool.

We'll delve into Fireworks/Dreamweaver integration more in the next chapter.

GoLive 5 and FrontPage 2000

Lacking, for obvious reasons, Insert Fireworks HTML buttons, GoLive and FrontPage have no reliable GUI-based way of inserting Fireworks HTML code. However, both programs have built-in HTML editors. Here's the basic process:

1. Create the Fireworks file, choosing optimization settings, and so forth.

2. Choose File | Export to bring up the Export dialog box.

3. Choose HTML And Images from the Save As Type drop-down list.

4. Choose Export Slices from the Slice drop-down list.

5. Click the Options button to open the HTML Setup dialog box.

6. Choose FrontPage or GoLive as the HTML style, as appropriate.

7. Click OK to return to the Export dialog box.

8. Click Save to export the HTML file and the graphic assets.

9. In your HTML editor, open the code editor.

10. Open the Fireworks HTML file in a code editor as well.

11. Using the comments (or suggestions in the next section) as a guide, copy and paste the appropriate HTML code into your HTML editor. Figure 12-5 shows Fireworks code pasted into GoLive 5's text-based HTML editor.

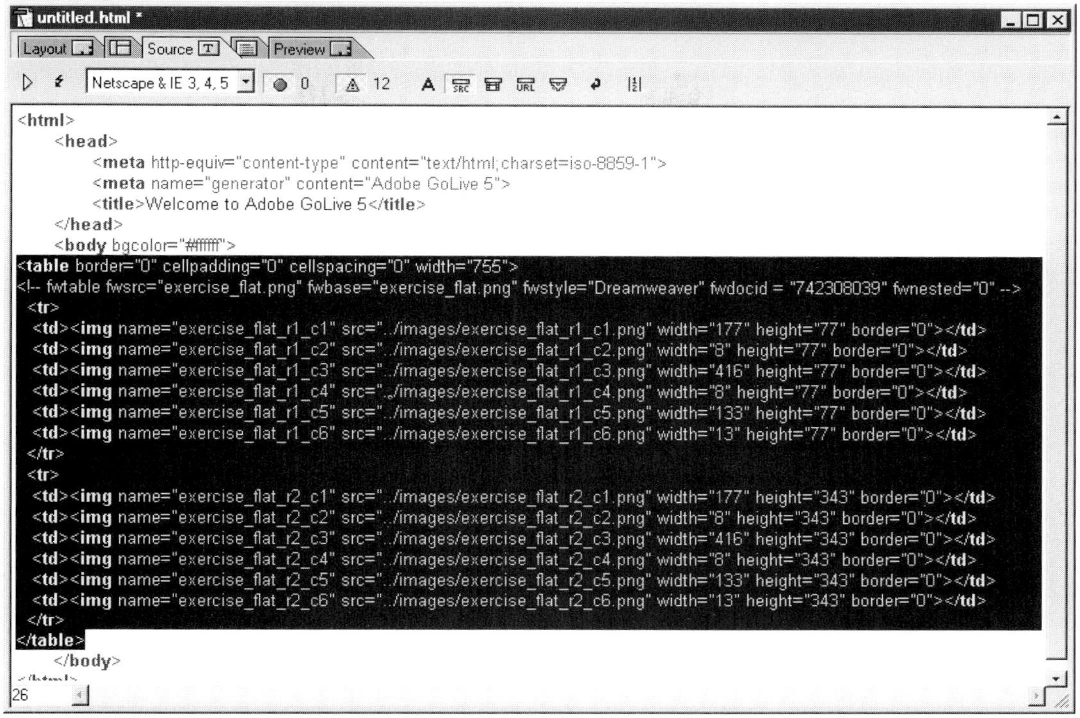

Figure 12-5 Fireworks code pasted into Adobe GoLive 5's HTML editor

Power User Strategies for Importing and Using Fireworks HTML

Unless you are completely new to HTML, attaching Fireworks HTML files to blank or simple HTML documents is quite straightforward. You copy in between the begin and end comments that Fireworks provides by default, and you paste in between the appropriate `<head>` or `<body>` tags.

In a realistic workflow, though, you will much more likely be bringing Fireworks elements—from simple graphics to pop-up menus—into already complex HTML files. "Complex" here simply refers to the fact that most page layouts are the result of elaborate (and often nested) tables. Bringing Fireworks HTML, which can also be structured with nested tables, into such documents can be a headache. In such cases, relying on the Fireworks comments can overcomplicate the process, forcing you to go in and significantly edit the Fireworks HTML from within your editor.

This section, in addition to showing you how to get Fireworks HTML into your editor, will provide some advanced techniques for getting the most out of Fireworks HTML. At its core is a distinction between two different kinds of HTML that you are likely to create in Fireworks: (1) entire page designs and (2) page elements, such as banners. Your page designs can be created right in Fireworks—we recommend it strongly. As for your page elements, *some* can be created in Fireworks, like graphics.

But (and here's the rub) you need to create many page elements in your HTML editor, for instance, text.

The problem is, then, that there is little chance for you to be able to do all of your HTML work in one location and bring elements into that document. You can create a page design in Fireworks, but you cannot paste an article from your word processor into it and mark it up. You could do all of the designing in your HTML editor, but you lose a key benefit of Fireworks (vector-based page layout), and anyway you will still have to import the HTML for all of your interactive graphic elements. In almost all cases, you will have to reconcile two different sources of HTML—Fireworks and that of your HTML editor. What's worse is that each of these sources may provide you with more than one HTML document to be reconciled.

The remainder of this chapter is divided into two sections. In the first, we will walk you through reproducing entire page designs into your text-based HTML editor. In so doing, we will temporarily set aside all interactivity and the robust features of the elements you create. In the second section, we will show you how to get your interactive elements back into the whole. Using this two-step process, you will get the most out of Fireworks—and along the way, you'll probably develop a new respect for Fireworks HTML.

Power Slicing: Design Tricks for Optimal Fireworks HTML

So far, we have devoted some time to discussions of slicing for optimization (for example, slicing images with photographic and clean line elements) and slicing for interactivity (creating rollovers and pop-up menus). However, there is another, rather underutilized strategy that you can use to help Fireworks generate optimal HTML code for your needs: slicing to create optimal HTML.

The Slice-Table Connection

Even before the possibility of interactivity or optimized graphics, slices in Fireworks always mean HTML tables. Anytime you slice a graphic in Fireworks, for whatever reason, Fireworks will reconstruct the sliced graphic using an HTML table (the single exception is if you export them as CSS layers, which is discussed in Chapter 13). This can work to your advantage.

Using Slices to Replicate Page Layout

If you have, as we have suggested all along, created your page design using Fireworks' vector tools, you might be wondering what the best way is to reconstruct your pages in your HTML editor. The fact that slices become HTML tables provides us with an easy way of creating this reconstruction.

The tricky part to all of this is that since slices can be used in so many ways, letting Fireworks just create the HTML from a complex file often does not really work. What you need is a way of isolating those slices that create the overall page layout from those slices that are used for other reasons, such as optimization or interactivity.

1. Create your whole page in Fireworks, using the vector tools to create areas for nav bars, and so forth. If you like, go ahead and create whatever interactivity and optimization slices you like—we are not going to do anything destructive here.

2. Export your file as a flat PNG (as opposed to a Fireworks PNG) with no HTML (or slicing). To do so, choose PNG-32 as the export format. Choose Images Only for the Save As Type; the HTML box becomes grayed out. Choose None in the Slices drop-down list. Since the generic PNG format does not support slicing, all of your optimization and interactivity settings will be lost in the exported version (but not in the Fireworks PNG, of course!).

 During export, be sure to save this file with a filename different from the main authoring file.

3. Close the source Fireworks PNG file.

4. Open the flat PNG file you created.

5. Use the Slice tool to draw slice regions on top of each of the elements that you would like to be in its own cell in the main HTML layout. If you have an image element that was sliced before, you can re-import it later as a nested table into an HTML layout area (`<td>` cell). But don't worry about such things at this point. Be sure that your regions are precisely over the corresponding page regions, that they do not overlap, and that you have covered the entire document.

   Here's where it gets fun. Some of these regions you are drawing will eventually have marked up text in them, while others will have graphics in them. The graphic regions will be updated with your real Fireworks slices and interactivity. But those regions that will have text will never have any graphics in them. For those areas that will eventually hold only text—say, your left navigation bar, which might use text links marked up with CSS above a dark-colored background, you do not want Fireworks to export a large solid-colored graphic! Fortunately, Fireworks allows you to export slices as text regions, too.

6. Click a slice that should eventually hold text, rather than a graphic.

7. In the Type drop-down list of the Object tab, choose Text, as shown next.

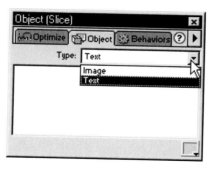

8. Continue in this manner until all of the slices that will become text cells are properly designated. You don't need to do anything for graphic cells—they'll export that way by default.

9. With your flat PNG resliced, it is time to export it as an HTML page layout template. Choose File | Export.

10. In the Save As Type drop-down list, choose HTML And Images.

11. In the Slices drop-down list, be sure Export Slices is selected.

12. Click the Options button to open the HTML Setup dialog box.

13. On the General tab, set your HTML Style to Generic.

14. On the Table tab (Figure 12-6), you should choose Single Table – No Spacers in the Space With drop-down list.

15. Also, check Use Canvas Color to fill the background color of the empty cells, and choose Non-Breaking Space in the Contents drop-down list, which will add a   to your empty cells so that browsers recognize them.

16. Click OK to return to the Export dialog box.

17. Click Save to export the HTML file.

If you open the resulting file in an HTML editor, you will see that you have a functioning skeleton of the entire page. You may still need to make some

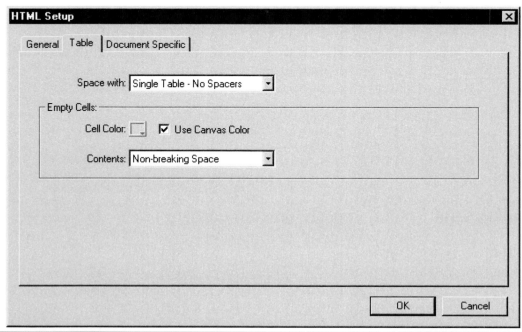

Figure 12-6   Table tab settings for creating basic HTML layouts

adjustments and tweaks—such is life with HTML. In particular, Fireworks tables tend not to use the `colspan` and `rowspan` attributes of table cell `<td>` tags. In a way, that is to your advantage, since it is easier to make an overly simple code more sophisticated than it is to tidy up overly convoluted code. Just make all of these tweaks before you move on to the next step. Your goal is to have a complete HTML layout page into which you can paste text and import interactive Fireworks elements. Be sure also to test in Netscape and Internet Explorer before moving on—at least one of them almost always finds a way to screw up something.

Next, we'll show you how to reintroduce your original optimization and interactivity slices.

Strategies for Exporting Complex Elements

Now is a good time to reinforce our key concept: Use the different HTML export options to isolate on the part that you are trying to export, whether it is the overall layout for the page or an interactive series of buttons within a banner. Don't try to do it all at once.

When bringing individual Fireworks elements into an existing HTML page, the golden rule is that you should always isolate your Fireworks elements into self-contained HTML pieces. That way, you can import them whole without disturbing the surrounding code.

The Problem: From Part to Whole and Back Again

As stated earlier in the chapter, Fireworks generates fully functional HTML files. However, when exporting individual elements (such as banners with nav bar slices) into target HTML documents, you don't need full HTML documents—just some pieces of them. That is, your goal is to go from a part (the element) to a whole (the target HTML document). But Fireworks generates whole documents as well.

So, if you export Fireworks HTML and do what the Fireworks comments tell you to do, you will wind up exporting a *part* (the graphic) as a *whole* (complete Fireworks HTML), and import a *whole* (the Fireworks HTML) as a *part* (of the target HTML document), and edit down the *whole* (Fireworks HTML) until it actually functions as a constituent *part* of the target *whole* (HTML document). Sound complicated? It is. And unnecessarily so.

There are a couple ways to deal with this. First, you could export each slice region individually. Second, you can export the entire document using nested tables, which will create tables around each slice cluster.

Solution 1: Exporting Slices Only

Using this solution, you export only selected parts of your Fireworks file, making it easier to separate and integrate Fireworks elements in the target HTML file.

1. Click to select one or more slices that you wish to export.

2. Adjust the Optimize settings as needed.

3. Choose File | Export to open the Export dialog box.

4. Choose HTML And Images in the Save As Type drop-down list. You need the HTML file to keep your interactivity and to reassemble your slices in an HTML document.

5. Click the Options button to open the HTML Setup dialog box.

6. Choose Generic as your HTML style in the HTML Setup dialog box.

7. Choose Single Table – No Spacers in the Table tab. Since you are exporting individual slices, rather than a complex file with many parts, you will benefit from a simple table.

8. Click OK to return to the Export dialog box.

9. Choose Export Slices in the Slices drop-down list. Below the Slices drop-down list is a series of check boxes.

10. Check Selected Slices Only. This is how you force Fireworks to ignore the rest of the document.

11. Uncheck Include Areas Without Slices to prevent Fireworks from picking up any of the document again. The final settings of the Export dialog box are shown in Figure 12-7.

12. Click Save to export.

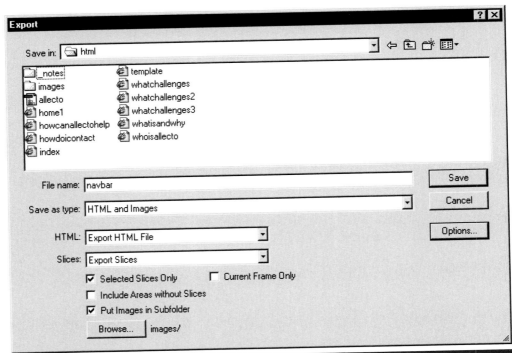

Figure 12-7   Final Export dialog box settings for creating basic HTML layouts

The result of this operation will be that Fireworks will create a functioning HTML document, that is, you can open the HTML file in a browser and see not only the slices, but also any behaviors attached to them (such as rollovers). However, the document will be empty except for the selected slices, making it ripe for importing into the proper place (usually a table cell in your overall table) in the target HTML document.

The following code listing shows the resulting HTML using this technique on a very simple file, with three slice regions with no additional frames or behaviors. The file was called "sliceTable.png" prior to export. Note that to accommodate the need to wrap lines of text, we used the ¬ character to indicate the continuation of a line. The ¬ character is *not* a part of the HTML code.

```
<html>
<head>
<title>sliceTable.gif</title>
<meta http-equiv="Content-Type" content="text/html;">
</head>
<body bgcolor="#ffffff" onload="" topmargin="0" leftmargin="0"¬
    marginheight="0" marginwidth="0">
<table border="0" cellpadding="0" cellspacing="0" width="171">
<!-- fwtable fwsrc="sliceTable.png" fwbase="sliceTable.gif"¬
    fwstyle="Generic" fwdocid = "742308039" fwnested=""0" -->
  <tr>
   <td><img name="sliceTable_r1_c1" src="sliceTable_r1_c1.gif"¬
     width="57" height="38" border="0"></td>
   <td><img name="sliceTable_r1_c2" src="sliceTable_r1_c2.gif"¬
     width="57" height="38" border="0"></td>
   <td><img name="sliceTable_r1_c3" src="sliceTable_r1_c3.gif"¬
     width="57" height="38" border="0"></td>
  </tr>
</table>
</body>
</html>
```

To move this code into a target HTML document, simply copy everything from the opening `<table>` tag through and including the closing `</table>` tag.

Solution 2: Using Nested Tables

There is a downside to Solution 1. If you create entire pages in Fireworks and you are ready to move multiple elements into your target HTML file, you will have to perform Solution 1 as many times as you have elements. What if you wanted to move an entire page design's worth of interactive and optimized Fireworks elements—without moving the page as a whole? If the target page is already set up, that is, you can't simply rely on Fireworks HTML to mock up the whole page, then you've got a chore. Or have you?

Recall that the golden rule of moving Fireworks elements into HTML documents is to isolate your elements into independent units. So, if your goal is to export several parts of a page design (such as the banner, a navbar, and an animation), you want to have Fireworks create code that will enable you to move each part into your HTML editor. What you want to avoid is the scenario described earlier, where your parts are exported as wholes and you have to go through some rigmarole to make them parts again. Instead, you want your parts to function as parts, and your wholes to function as wholes. Here's one way to do it.

Export Settings for the Nested Tables Method There are two major steps to this technique: configuring optimal HTML settings and then getting the HTML into the target document. In this first step, you'll configure Fireworks to export some workable HTML.

1. Open the source PNG file that contains the different elements.

2. Optimize and apply all appropriate settings.

3. Choose File | Export to open the Export dialog box.

4. Choose HTML And Images in the Save As Type drop-down list.

5. Choose Export Slices in the Slices drop-down list.

6. Click the Options button to open the HTML setup dialog box.

7. Choose Generic as the HTML style.

8. Choose Nested Tables – No Spacers in the Space With drop-down list.

9. Click OK to return to the Export dialog box.

10. Click Save to create the HTML file and all slices.

At this point, you have created a very complex HTML file that is probably unusable as a whole. However, like an old car, it is a gold mine for parts.

Getting the Right HTML into the Target Document Now you have your Fireworks HTML, and it's time to move your elements into your target document.

1. Open the just-exported Fireworks HTML file and the target HTML file side-by-side in a text-based HTML editor (which could include text editors within GUI applications).

2. Look in the Fireworks HTML file. Each of your sliced segments will appear in a nested table inside a cell of the main table. The main table does you no good, but the nested table is a self-contained element just begging to be copied and pasted. Figure 12-8 shows a portion of an HTML file with (only) the nested table selected.

3. Copy the selected portion.

4. Switch to the target HTML document.

```
<table border="0" cellpadding="0" cellspacing="0" width="590">
<!-- fwtable fwsrc="training_banner.png" fwbase="training_banner.gif" fwstyle="Generic" fwdocid = "1336093(
  <script language="JavaScript">
  <!-- hide
  if (document.images) {
  training_banner_r2_c1_f2 = new Image(87 ,28); training_banner_r2_c1_f2.src = "training_banner_r2_c1_f2.gi
  training_banner_r2_c1_f1 = new Image(87 ,28); training_banner_r2_c1_f1.src = "training_banner_r2_c1.gif";
  training_banner_r2_c2_f2 = new Image(141 ,28); training_banner_r2_c2_f2.src = "training_banner_r2_c2_f2.c
  training_banner_r2_c2_f1 = new Image(141 ,28); training_banner_r2_c2_f1.src = "training_banner_r2_c2.gif'
  training_banner_r2_c3_f2 = new Image(123 ,28); training_banner_r2_c3_f2.src = "training_banner_r2_c3_f2.c
  training_banner_r2_c3_f1 = new Image(123 ,28); training_banner_r2_c3_f1.src = "training_banner_r2_c3.gif'
  training_banner_r2_c4_f2 = new Image(140 ,28); training_banner_r2_c4_f2.src = "training_banner_r2_c4_f2.c
  training_banner_r2_c4_f1 = new Image(140 ,28); training_banner_r2_c4_f1.src = "training_banner_r2_c4.gif'
  training_banner_r2_c5_f2 = new Image(99 ,28); training_banner_r2_c5_f2.src = "training_banner_r2_c5_f2.gi
  training_banner_r2_c5_f1 = new Image(99 ,28); training_banner_r2_c5_f1.src = "training_banner_r2_c5.gif";
  }
  // stop hiding -->
  </script>
  <tr>
   <td><img name="training_banner_r1_c1" src="training_banner_r1_c1.gif" width="590" height="72" border="0"
  </tr>
  <tr>
   <td><table border="0" cellpadding="0" cellspacing="0" width="590">
     <tr>
      <td><a href="#" onMouseOut="MM_swapImgRestore();"  onMouseOver="MM_swapImage('training_banner_r2_c1'
      <td><a href="#" onMouseOut="MM_swapImgRestore();"  onMouseOver="MM_swapImage('training_banner_r2_c2'
      <td><a href="#" onMouseOut="MM_swapImgRestore();"  onMouseOver="MM_swapImage('training_banner_r2_c3'
      <td><a href="#" onMouseOut="MM_swapImgRestore();"  onMouseOver="MM_swapImage('training_banner_r2_c4'
      <td><a href="#" onMouseOut="MM_swapImgRestore();"  onMouseOver="MM_swapImage('training_banner_r2_c5'
     </tr>
   </table></td>
  </tr>
```

Figure 12-8   An interactive slice group has been nested inside its own table and selected here.

5. Find the cell in which you wish to place this table.

6. If appropriate (in most cases it is), remove all of the existing contents in that cell.

7. With the cursor between the `<td>` tags, paste the copied table into the cell.

8. Repeat with all of the nested tables until you have moved them all into the target document.

   The only remaining issue is the JavaScript. If your slice elements contain JavaScript behaviors, you will need the JavaScript to come into the target document as well.

9. In the header of the Fireworks HTML document, all of the JavaScript code should be between `<script>` tags. Copy this section, including the `<script>` tags, and paste it into the header of the target HTML document.

10. Finally, copy any JavaScript from the `<body>` tag of the source document, and paste it into the `<body>` tag of the target document.

Many JavaScript functions are called when the page loads and so are written into the <body> tag.

11. Save the target HTML document. (Need we remind you that backing up things before major changes like this is a good idea?) Then test it.

Assuming all of this worked, or that you have done any necessary tweaking to make it work, you now have a fully integrated HTML document. It has the precise layout (as much as that is ever possible in HTML) of the Fireworks page design, the functioning interactive and optimized elements, and regions where you can copy and paste in text from outside.

You can now use this document as a template for the rest of your project that uses these pages!

Summary of Fireworks to HTML Strategies

In summary, determine whether what you are exporting is going to be a part of the destination HTML, or whether the destination HTML is going to reconstruct the page layout as a whole. Use nested tables or single tables as appropriate to mark up parts or wholes, and ignore what the Fireworks comments tell you (or turn them off) and copy only what you need. By making the Fireworks HTML structurally resemble the target document, you ease the transition between them.

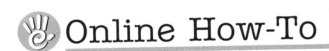 Online How-To

Using Slice Along Guides to Create Entire HTML Pages

This exercise uses a neat variation of the page layout replication technique outlined earlier. This one is a bit quicker, but also somewhat less flexible, so we recommend it for fairly straightforward page designs. The elements inside the pages can be as crazy as you want, but this technique will not work well if you have too many rows and columns in your page layout.

 GO TO THE WEB! For a free, self-paced interactive version of this tutorial, which includes video demonstrations and source files, visit www.expertedge.com.

Use exercise.png from the Chapter 12 folder. We will create a master HTML page reconstructed from the layout seen in Figure 12-9.

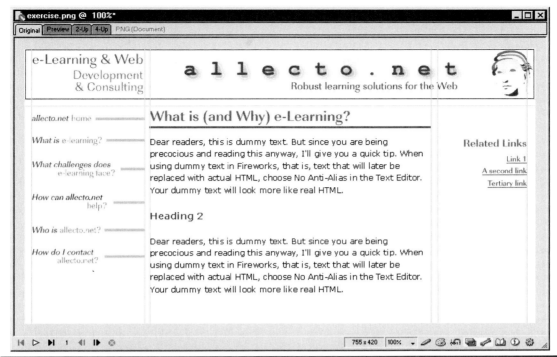

Figure 12-9 The original file (with web layer visibility turned off), from which we will reconstruct an HTML page

Get Your Bearings

Take a look at the file. Toggle visibility of the Web layer on and off to get a feel for the file. There are several slices already in place; some are image slices and some are text slices. These slices are there both for behaviors as well as for formatting. However, we need none of them for this exercise. As we did in the "Using Slices to Replicate Page Layout" section earlier, we are going to flatten this image.

Flattening the Image

To the flatten the image, follow these steps:

1. Export the file as a PNG-32, choosing Images Only as the Save As Type and None as the Slice type in the Export dialog box. Call the file **exercise_flat.png** to distinguish it from the current file.

2. Click Save. Fireworks exports a standard PNG.

3. Close exercise.png and open exercise_flat.png.

Redrawing the Guides

Our whole purpose of flattening the file was to get specific slicing information out of it. Of course, in the process, we also lost all of our guides. That's a bummer, because we are going to use the guides as a basis for creating HTML tables.

One by one, pull in guides from the rulers (be sure that View | Guides | Show Guides is selected) to mark areas where you would like columns and rows. Use the Zoom tool (or Table 12-2) to position the guides precisely; double-clicking a guide will bring up a dialog box that allows you to specify its position.

To save you some time, in Table 12-2 you will find the numeric values of the slices we did. Of course, you are welcome to experiment on your own. To enter a slice's position, simply double-click the slice to open the Move Guide dialog box, which allows you to specify a pixel position for the guide.

Certain browsers are notorious for being extremely finicky about tables, and if you specify table or cell widths and they do not add up perfectly, the table blows up. Well, not quite, but the display can be erratic. One of the causes for tables and their cells not adding up is that the cellspacing (and sometimes even cellpadding, depending on circumstances) attribute of the `<table>` tag adds extra width to each cell, which changes the width of the overall table. If you use the `<colspan>` attribute to change the number of columns in some rows, which then fudges the widths of the cells with cellspacing, certain browsers have a very difficult time rendering the tables properly.

One solution we have relied upon, with sighs of exasperation, is to specify both cellpadding and cellspacing as 0, which will at least simplify making cell widths add up to the table width total. Of course, then your elements will crash into each other. To avoid that, we put extra empty columns between real columns. These columns act like gutters. In this image, once we pulled out all the guides, we ended up with a file looking like Figure 12-10.

To clarify and reiterate, the two very narrow columns on the page are simply gutter columns to keep column content separate.

Alignment	Position
Vertical	177
Vertical	185
Vertical	601
Vertical	609
Vertical	742
Horizontal	77

Table 12-2   Guide Positioning to be Translated into HTML Table

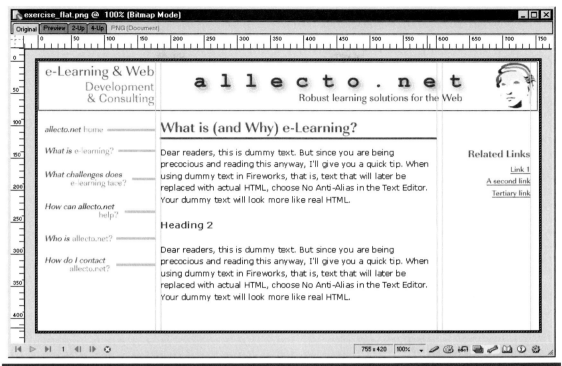

Figure 12-10   The slicing scheme that we chose

Reconstructing this into HTML

Next, we'll need to export this image, so we can convert the guides into slices:

1. Choose File | Export, to open the Export dialog box.

2. Choose HTML And Images in the Save As Type drop-down list.

3. Choose Slice Along Guides in the Slices drop-down list.

IDEA   If you store all of your images in a subfolder in your real site, check the Put Images In Subfolder check box. Name the subfolder the same as the subfolder you use—we usually just stick with the default, **images**. Then the Fireworks HTML will mirror your actual site, making integration that much easier.

4. Click the Options button to open the HTML Setup dialog box.

5. Choose Generic as your HTML style in the General tab.

6. In the Table tab, choose Single Table – No Spacers in the Space With drop-down list.

7. Click OK to return to the Export dialog box.

8. Click Save to export the page design to HTML.

If you open the HTML document, you should see the following code. Remember that the ¬ character simply means that a line is continued—it is not a part of the code itself. It should be much easier to read this in your code editor with word wrapping turned off.

```html
<html>
<head>
<title>exercise_flat.png</title>
<meta http-equiv="Content-Type" content="text/html;">
<!-- Fireworks 4.0 Dreamweaver 4.0 target. Created Sun Apr 15 21:01:08¬
   GMT-0500 (US Eastern Standard Time) 2001-->
</head>
<body bgcolor="#ffffff">
<table border="0" cellpadding="0" cellspacing="0" width="755">
<!-- fwtable fwsrc="exercise_flat.png" fwbase="exercise_flat.png"¬
   fwstyle="Dreamweaver" fwdocid = "742308039" fwnested="0" -->
 <tr>
  <td><img name="exercise_flat_r1_c1" src="../images/¬
   exercise_flat_r1_c1.png" width="177" height="77" border="0"></td>
  <td><img name="exercise_flat_r1_c2" src="../images/¬
   exercise_flat_r1_c2.png" width="8" height="77" border="0"></td>
  <td><img name="exercise_flat_r1_c3" src="../images/¬
   exercise_flat_r1_c3.png" width="416" height="77" border="0"></td>
  <td><img name="exercise_flat_r1_c4" src="../images/¬
   exercise_flat_r1_c4.png" width="8" height="77" border="0"></td>
  <td><img name="exercise_flat_r1_c5" src="../images/¬
   exercise_flat_r1_c5.png" width="133" height="77" border="0"></td>
  <td><img name="exercise_flat_r1_c6" src="../images/¬
   exercise_flat_r1_c6.png" width="13" height="77" border="0"></td>
 </tr>
 <tr>
  <td><img name="exercise_flat_r2_c1" src="../images/¬
   exercise_flat_r2_c1.png" width="177" height="343" border="0"></td>
  <td><img name="exercise_flat_r2_c2" src="../images/¬
   exercise_flat_r2_c2.png" width="8" height="343" border="0"></td>
  <td><img name="exercise_flat_r2_c3" src="../images/¬
   exercise_flat_r2_c3.png" width="416" height="343" border="0"></td>
  <td><img name="exercise_flat_r2_c4" src="../images/¬
   exercise_flat_r2_c4.png" width="8" height="343" border="0"></td>
  <td><img name="exercise_flat_r2_c5" src="../images/¬
   exercise_flat_r2_c5.png" width="133" height="343" border="0"></td>
  <td><img name="exercise_flat_r2_c6" src="../images/¬
   exercise_flat_r2_c6.png" width="13" height="343" border="0"></td>
 </tr>
</table>
</body>
</html>
```

Basically, everything between each of the <td> tag pairs is placeholder garbage, except perhaps the banner itself, which was static in the original. Once you re-export the real pieces from the Fireworks authoring file, you can paste them over the code between the <td> tags. Alternatively, if you are using a GUI editor, simply click each cell to select the graphic and press DELETE. You will be left with a basic page layout in HTML that is faithful to the Fireworks page design—just what you wanted.

To insert the original Fireworks nav bar, re-export the original file using Nested Tables, and paste the code in the left bar.

For text areas, including the gutters and any place you will place marked up text, delete the images (in a GUI editor) or replace the code with ** ** (the nonbreaking space character). In text areas, insert the actual text.

For the banner, you will need to use the colspan attribute to make the first row, currently split into five columns, a single cell, and to re-import the banner as a separate, whole image.

You will probably want to do some optimizing. For example, rather than slicing the banner, you might delete the three banner pieces. Once you have done all your tweaking, you have a basic page design ready to replicate throughout your site.

13 Fireworks and Dreamweaver Integration

Few software packages can boast the same level of integration that can be found between Dreamweaver and Fireworks. If you have both applications, you owe it to yourself to learn how to use them together. You will find that as your skills and projects grow more complex, Fireworks and Dreamweaver will grow with you. As you enjoy features ranging from the smooth transition of Fireworks elements into Dreamweaver, to Dreamweaver's ability to launch and edit Fireworks graphics in context, to Dreamweaver's more ambitious ability to control Fireworks via JavaScript, you will wish other software suites were this friendly to one another.

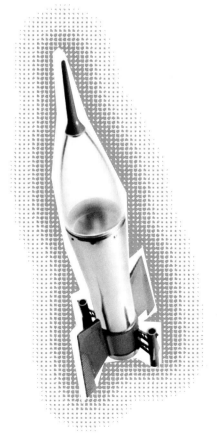

I f Fireworks and Dreamweaver are integrated properly, users should be able to go both ways: from Fireworks to Dreamweaver and from Dreamweaver to Fireworks. This two-way exchange is necessary because you will always need to make revisions. New information comes in, clients change their minds, you get a sudden inspiration, a new product comes out, and so on. But since different elements come from different sources, and (as we saw in the last chapter) integrating these elements properly in the first place was not necessarily easy, it is a boon to the workflow that Fireworks and Dreamweaver decided to get along.

If you are new to either of the programs or to working with them together, the "Basic Integration Techniques" section of this chapter will get you up to speed with techniques that gradually increase in complexity. By the time you are done, you will be able to do most of things you will ever want to do with the two programs.

But if you want to go a step further, to see how the two programs can be made to sing together, keep reading. The rest of the chapter points you toward some real-world solutions that'll have your clients' fingers twitching. We'll have you going from Fireworks to DHTML faster than you would have believed possible.

Dreamweaver and Fireworks Integration Overview

Now that we've whetted your appetite for some serious integration, let's first establish what we mean by integration, since you should know what is possible before you try to do it. Next, we'll give you an idea of how it works—which is the first step to taking advantage of the integration.

Kinds of Integration

Integration is an umbrella term covering a number of different processes, most of which are unrelated to each other, except that they involve manipulating some kind of content in both programs. This content can be actual files or even commands and processes. We'll cover the following types of Dreamweaver/Fireworks integration in this chapter:

- Importing Fireworks elements into Dreamweaver
- Launching and editing Fireworks elements from within Dreamweaver
- Updating placed Fireworks elements in Dreamweaver
- Using the two programs together to create special content that neither could create by itself
- Extending and controlling one application from within the other

Obviously, integration means much more than simply inserting objects from another application.

Understanding What Makes Integration Work

While it is not necessary for designers to know all of the underlying mechanics of what makes the integration tick, knowing some big-picture concepts may help you avoid shooting yourself in the foot. In addition, having a rough idea of what is going on behind the scenes will help conceptually pave the way into issues of extensibility (covered in the next chapter). That way, when you need to become a Fireworks super power user, creating your own custom commands, you'll have a running start.

Design Notes

One problem that Macromedia faced when planning Fireworks/Dreamweaver integration was that what Fireworks exported—GIFs, JPGs, and HTML documents loaded with JavaScript—was different from its own authoring files: the Fireworks PNG (with the metadata we have referred to in earlier chapters). Getting Dreamweaver to communicate with Fireworks authoring files, then, would mean going through the placed export files. But these exported files, unlike the PNG, are not proprietary (and cannot hold metadata needed for integration). Linking these diverse files to the authoring file from which they were generated became a key challenge.

Macromedia's solution was to create a system of *notes* that associate files exported from Fireworks with their source PNG files. When you export a PNG into a Dreamweaver site, a "_notes" folder is created in the same folder as the exported images. This folder contains a series of note files, one for each exported slice. Using them, Dreamweaver knows that a given GIF is actually an exported piece of a Fireworks PNG file. When you go to edit that slice from within Dreamweaver, you will have the option of editing either the exported bitmap slice itself or of returning to the source file and making the edits there, automatically re-exporting appropriate slices when you were done, so they are instantly updated in Dreamweaver.

This folder does not appear automatically upon export from Fireworks, unless you are exporting into a Dreamweaver site. If you just create a folder and export Fireworks HTML and graphics into it, there will not be a _notes folder. But don't worry—you can have one generated as soon as you try to edit an exported graphic in Dreamweaver. When you attempt to edit a Fireworks-exported image from Dreamweaver, if Dreamweaver can't find the source PNG, it gives you an option to find it yourself.

If you open one of these notes and look at the code, you will see that each note is a simple XML file, which identifies the source and provides info about the exported slice. The following listing is an example of one such note. There is a similar note for each graphic exported from the authoring PNG.

```xml
<?xml version="1.0" encoding="iso-8859-1" ?>
<info>
     <infoitem key="fw_source" value="/page_design.png" />
     <infoitem key="fw_slice_info" value="2a81fe8 2f3 1a4 0 d4 ¬
          b1 2f 0" />
</info>
```

Most of this happens automatically and behind the scenes. However, you do have some control, and with it the risk of tripping up the linkage created by the "_notes" file. Following are some tips to ensure that you do not inadvertently doom the linkage to failure.

Designate Fireworks as Your External Editor for Graphics Files
If you install Dreamweaver and Fireworks together, Fireworks will automatically be designated as the external editor. If it is not so designated, here's how to do it:

1. In Dreamweaver, choose Edit | Preferences. An extensive Preferences dialog box appears.

2. From the Category list on the left side, choose File Types / Editors.

3. In the lower half of the right pane, select a file type Extension, such as .gif, from the list.

4. Click the + symbol above the Editors list, and the Browse dialog box appears.

5. Find and select the Fireworks executable file, by default stored in C:\Program Files\Macromedia\Fireworks.

6. Click Open, and when you return to the Preferences dialog box, the file will be listed among the Editors.

7. If necessary, click Fireworks and then click the Make Primary button, so that Fireworks is the default editor. Note that you can have multiple editors for one file type. (See Figure 13-1.)

Do Not Remove the _notes Folder
You may be tempted to remove autogenerated folders from your site to keep it clean, but don't remove the _notes folder! Although the folder takes up space on your server, this space is minimal, and your users will never have to download these files.

Store the Source Fireworks PNG Within the Site
The best way to ensure that Dreamweaver can open the proper PNG file is if it is stored in the site (that is, within the folder designated in the Dreamweaver Define Sites dialog box). This also applies if you are working on a network drive; this way your colleagues can also benefit from Dreamweaver/Fireworks integration.

 Once you have a _notes folder and your source PNG is in your site, do not move the source PNG file (even from within the Dreamweaver Site Manager). Not only does this break the link established in the _notes files, but they also do not update, even when you re-associate the files in the Find Source dialog box (seen later this chapter, in Figure 13-6). The result is that you can no longer access the original PNG.

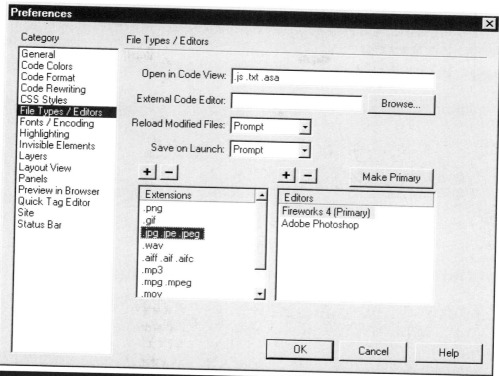

Figure 13-1 Making Fireworks the default editor for graphic file types is done through the Dreamweaver Preferences dialog box.

The Fireworks API

Notes are not the only means through which the two programs are integrated. On an even deeper level, both programs have compatible built-in extensibility features. Without getting into the gory details, Fireworks commands are processed almost exclusively through JavaScript functions. One powerful feature of integration is that Macromedia designed these functions to be available to Dreamweaver. Thus, Dreamweaver can send commands to Fireworks, invoking windows and features that enable users to make use of Fireworks tools without ever leaving Dreamweaver. After they are done, they can close these windows.

This relationship underpins much of the Launch and Edit tools. What is even more powerful is that users can extend the software themselves by writing their own extensions. Dreamweaver guru Joe Lowery, for example, has created extensions that take text entered into Dreamweaver and convert them into graphics with Fireworks styles automatically applied. His extensions, and hundreds of others, are available for free at the Macromedia Extension site: http://www.macromedia.com/exchange.

Although Macromedia makes its extensibility documentation available on the Web, comparatively little has been done in the area of Dreamweaver/Fireworks integration. This represents a tendency toward Fireworks' underrepresentation at Macromedia's extensions site and elsewhere on the Web. Admittedly, writing commands is not for the faint of heart, as some JavaScript programming ability is a must. That said, it is not quite as hard as it appears at first glance, and many commands can be created visually, without knowing the difference between a loop and an array.

CROSS REFERENCE → Fireworks extensibility, including writing commands, is covered in Chapter 14.

Basic Integration Techniques

The most common, and thankfully, easiest, integration tasks involve making minor changes to a file in one program without having to do reconstructive surgery in the other. For Fireworks and Dreamweaver, this is a two-way process. Most elements that you create in Fireworks can be edited directly in Dreamweaver, from the text on a button to the button behavior itself.

Importing Fireworks HTML

We devoted an entire chapter to moving Fireworks HTML into your HTML editor. We analyzed the code, interpreted the comments, and developed strategies for optimal transfer. Much (not all) of that goes out the window, though, if your HTML editor happens to be Dreamweaver.

Importing Fireworks HTML, which means the slice tables, slice layers, graphics, and behaviors, is as easy as clicking the Insert Fireworks HTML button on the Tools panel (see Figure 13-2) and pointing to the file in the Insert Fireworks HTML dialog box, which works like a simple Open File dialog box (see Figure 13-3).

Figure 13-2   Inserting Fireworks graphics (behaviors, and so on) is a click away.

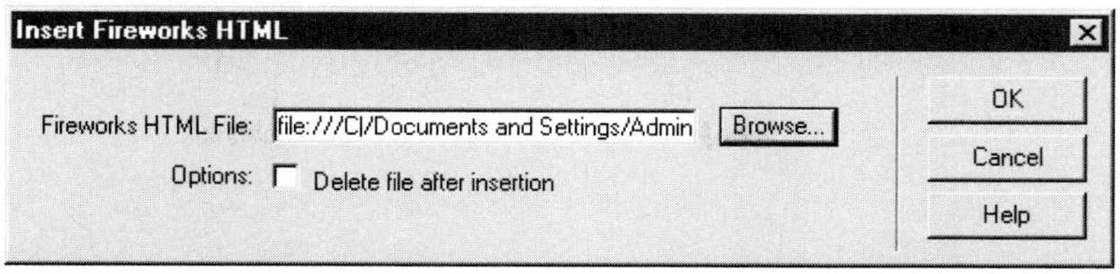

Figure 13-3   The Insert Fireworks HTML dialog box

This process imports only the necessary code to reassemble your slice tables and to make your behaviors function. The best part is that Dreamweaver knows where each of the elements is supposed to go, saving you from wrestling with code. And for you code purists out there, the only superfluous code (from a functional standpoint) is a comment that identifies the table as a Fireworks table.

Optimizing an Image Placed in Dreamweaver

As you well know by now, Fireworks has a lot of powerful tools for the creation of graphic content. But one of its standby abilities will always be its powerful optimization interface. One feature calls up the Fireworks Export Preview dialog box, allowing you to take full advantage of Fireworks' most advanced optimization interface—without ever leaving Dreamweaver.

1. In Dreamweaver, select the image that you would like to optimize.

2. Either choose Commands | Optimize Image In Fireworks, or simply right-click or COMMAND-click and choose Optimize Image In Fireworks from the context menu.

3. A modified Fireworks Export Preview dialog box appears (see Figure 13-4).

4. Optimize the image, using any of the tools in the Export Preview (including the options for scaling and exporting image areas).

CROSS REFERENCE ➔ See Chapter 8 to learn how to use the Export Preview dialog box.

5. When you are finished, click the Update button. Fireworks goes away and you are returned to Dreamweaver—with your new graphic already in place!

Note that you can use Dreamweaver's Optimize In Fireworks command to optimize any image, regardless of whether it was created in Fireworks.

IDEA If you have a page with many images and you need to keep the total page (including all its assets) under a certain number of KB, you can assemble all of the high-quality images on the page in Dreamweaver, and then choose which ones could bear a little more compression (don't forget that when an image is selected, its file size is displayed in the Properties Inspector), and optimize from there!

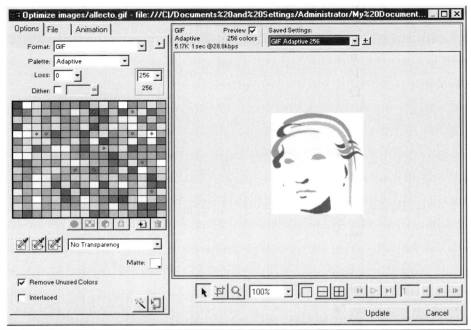

Figure 13-4 A modified version of the Export Preview dialog box appears when you choose Dreamweaver's Optimize Image In Fireworks command.

Unfortunately, if the image was created in Fireworks, the optimization settings will *not* be saved in the source PNG, since during this operation Dreamweaver does not attempt to associate the image with its Fireworks source, even if it has already done so. That means that if you later go back to the source and re-export, Fireworks will export at whatever settings it has for that image or slice. There is a silver lining to this limitation: since you cannot undo modifications made in Fireworks from Dreamweaver, you could theoretically get stuck with a badly optimized graphic. The source PNG is unaffected, though, so you can always go back to Fireworks and re-export with the original settings.

Editing Fireworks Graphics with Launch and Edit

Now let's assume that you have inserted your Fireworks designs in Dreamweaver and are in the process of developing the site when you discover that you put the wrong name on one of the buttons. Or you want to change the optimization setting of a slice, or resize an element within a slice. Use the Fireworks Launch And Edit option to modify any Fireworks graphic element or optimization setting. The only pause you should give is if you need to modify complex objects, such as tables/slices, which can be more complicated. We'll cover the more complex problems in the next section, "Modifying Tables and Other Complex Fireworks Elements."

Using Launch And Edit to modify placed graphics is impressively easy. The only tricky part involves a decision you will often be prompted to make on whether you wish to edit the selected graphic itself, or the source Fireworks PNG from which it was generated. In most cases, you will want to edit the source PNG where possible. That way, you will always have the most up-to-date graphics in both your authoring PNG and in your Dreamweaver page.

1. In Dreamweaver, select the graphic that needs to be changed.

2. In the lower half of the Properties Inspector (which you might need to make visible by clicking on the triangle pop-up button in the lower right corner), click the Edit button. If the image is already associated with the Fireworks source PNG, a Fireworks logo appears inside the Edit button (as shown here). Otherwise, the Edit button features a pencil-and-paper icon.

3. What happens next depends on a couple factors:

- If you are using the default Launch And Edit setting in Fireworks (in the Launch And Edit tab within Edit | Preferences, the When Editing from External Application drop-down list is set to Ask When Launching), you will probably see the Find Source dialog box (shown here). Choose Yes to associate the selected image in Dreamweaver with an original Fireworks PNG, or choose No to edit the bitmap itself (which will not affect the source PNG, if there is one).

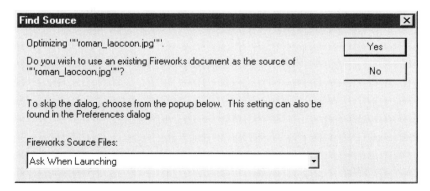

- If you are using a different Launch And Edit setting (in Fireworks' Preferences dialog box), such as Always or Never, you will go straight into Fireworks— to the source file or to the bitmap, depending on your setting.

- If you have already edited a given graphic associated with Fireworks using the Fireworks PNG method, you will probably also skip the Find Source dialog box and go straight to the Fireworks PNG source file.

4. One way or another, you are now in Fireworks and can make any desired changes. Notice that this is a special version of Fireworks. A special Editing From Dreamweaver bar appears in the document window (see Figure 13-5).

5. When you are finished, click Done. You will return to Dreamweaver. If Fireworks was not open before you began the launch and edit, it will close. If it was, your document window will be closed, but the application will remain open. In either case, your file will be re-exported and automatically updated in Dreamweaver.

Modifying Tables and Other Complex Fireworks Elements

Clicking a GIF slice and correcting a misspelled label or adjusting a drop shadow setting in the source PNG is pretty easy stuff. But what if you have created a page out of Fireworks slices—and you need to make serious structural changes? What if you need to modify a behavior? What if you need to add a hotspot or convert a hotspot to a slice?

Determining which approach to take can be tricky, because many of these elements can be handled right in Dreamweaver. You can edit tables in Dreamweaver. You can access most Fireworks behaviors from Dreamweaver. You can update URLs, edit hotspots, and so on. Of course, if you do, your Dreamweaver file no longer resembles the Fireworks file.

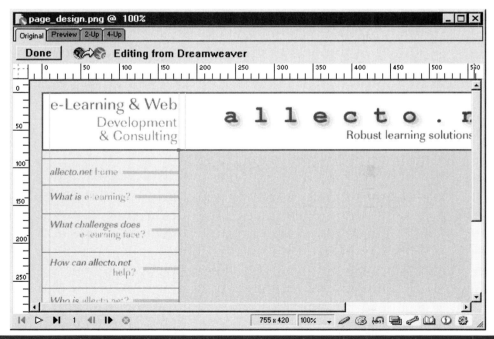

Figure 13-5   The Fireworks document window, when editing a file from Dreamweaver

Alternatively, you can go back to Fireworks, make the changes there, and re-export. But that may require a fair amount of tinkering in Dreamweaver to get things back to the way they were. The truth is, there is no easy answer to these questions. Fireworks/Dreamweaver integration is sophisticated enough to provide several solutions, but each has its limitations.

Fireworks-to-Dreamweaver Solutions

Perhaps the easiest way to modify a complex Fireworks element, such as a slice table, is to do it right in Fireworks. Most graphic assets, including slices, are created in Fireworks as vector graphics. You can easily scale the graphics and export, without having to wrestle with a whole bunch of `width` attributes of `<td>` tags. Other parts of the HTML (such as URLs and behaviors) are handled through panels and dialog boxes. In plain terms, by staying in Fireworks, you get the double benefit of having the same content in both Fireworks and Dreamweaver, while also doing all of your modifications in a GUI environment.

Using Fireworks' Update HTML

One nifty feature is Fireworks' Update HTML command, found in the File menu. It allows you to go into the Fireworks source PNG file, make changes, and with a single command, update the output HTML. Not only is everything automatically updated in Dreamweaver, but Dreamweaver also doesn't even have to be open! The next time you open Dreamweaver, you will see that your changes are already there.

1. Open the source PNG in Fireworks.

2. Update slice regions by dragging, scaling, adding, or modifying (such as changing graphic slices to text slices, optimization settings, and so on) your slices.

3. Update HTML attributes, such as URLs, behaviors, hotspot areas, and so on.

4. Modify text and images.

5. When you are finished updating the PNG, choose File | Update HTML. The Locate HTML File dialog box appears.

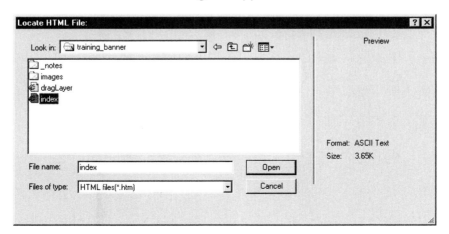

6. Navigate to the target HTML document and click Open. The Update HTML dialog box appears.

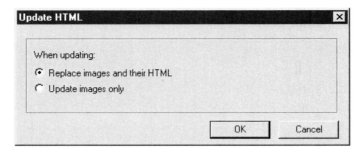

7. Select whether you wish to update images only or both HTML and images.

 Exporting HTML will overwrite existing tables in Dreamweaver. If these tables include HTML added after the fact in Dreamweaver—including any customizations or imported elements from outside of Fireworks—these assets will be lost.

8. Click OK to continue.

Exporting and Using Dreamweaver Library Items

Another great Fireworks-to-Dreamweaver solution is to export an item as a Dreamweaver Library item.

Understanding Dreamweaver Library Items
Dreamweaver *Library items* are modular bits of HTML code that may include embedded assets, such as images. Typically, Library items are used in large sites where certain elements have to appear the same in multiple places. Examples might include page footers, repeated navigation elements (with links), and copyright notices.

Library items are linked to the source file, which means that every placed instance of a Library item will be the same, cutting down on chances of error. In addition, when these items need to change—and we all know they will!—you simply edit the original Library item, make the change, and then you can update it sitewide. No more risky find and replace operations or (worse) opening each page one at a time and making the change there.

The value of Library items to Fireworks files is by now probably obvious. If you create a sleek tabbed graphic interface in Fireworks (as shown here) and disseminate it throughout your site, you know what will happen next. A new tab will need to be added, or an existing one, modified or removed.

Such is the ever-evolving nature of the Web. While there are tools that you can use, like Dreamweaver's find and replace and Update HTML, each presents significant limitations for this kind of work. The Dreamweaver Library item, as modularized HTML code, is the perfect solution.

Creating and Using Dreamweaver Library Files with Fireworks

Creating Dreamweaver Library items is very easy in Fireworks. You can select Dreamweaver Library Item in the Export dialog box. Fireworks then creates the necessary files. These include the HTML file that holds all of the contents, each of the graphic slices, and a _notes folder, containing the notes Dreamweaver needs to associate the exported slices with their source PNG.

1. Open the source PNG in Fireworks.

2. Bring up the Export dialog box. To export the entire file as a library, choose File | Export. Of course, you can also use the Export Area tool or export a selected slice (by checking the Selected Slices Only option in the Export dialog box).

3. In the Export dialog box, navigate to the Library folder within your Dreamweaver site (see Figure 13-6). If you do not yet have one, you will be prompted to create one in the next step.

4. Choose Dreamweaver Library (.lbi) from the Save As Type drop-down list.

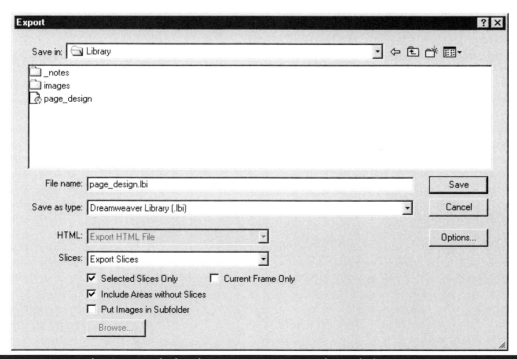

Figure 13-6 The Export dialog box, set to export selected slices as a Dreamweaver Library item

5. Click the Options button to set appropriate HTML settings. (See Chapter 12 for explanation of the options in the HTML Setup dialog box.)

6. Choose appropriate slice settings. In most cases, you will choose Export Slices in the Slices drop-down list, while the other options depend on the project.

7. Click Save.

Inserting Dreamweaver Library Items into HTML Documents
Once you have created and saved your Library item, inserting it into your Dreamweaver page is easy.

1. Open the target Dreamweaver page and the Library panel (Window | Library), seen in Figure 13-7.

2. Drag the Library item from the library onto the page.

Editing Dreamweaver Library Items that Contain Fireworks Elements
One key benefit of Dreamweaver Library items is their ease of updating. When the source file is Fireworks, there is an additional step, but it is straightforward enough.

1. With the Dreamweaver Library panel open, double-click the icon of the Library item you wish to edit. A new document window opens with the Library item in it.

 Do not attempt to edit any Library item from within a regular Dreamweaver HTML document—always edit from the source. Placed Library item instances are locked for editing. You can get around this, but if you do, you will only edit the individual instance, not the Library item itself, and you will not be able to update the changes sitewide. Always edit the source Library item itself, unless you have a particular reason for detaching it.

Figure 13-7   The Dreamweaver Library (Assets) panel

2. Make any changes within Dreamweaver that you desire. If you need to edit an image, you can follow the instructions from earlier in this chapter to inaugurate launch and edit.

3. When you are finished editing from within Fireworks, click the Done button to return to Dreamweaver. You have now updated your Library item, but not the placed instances throughout the site!

4. Click the triangle in the upper-right corner of the Library panel to open Dreamweaver's Library Options pop-up menu.

5. Choose Update Site. The Update Pages dialog box appears (see Figure 13-8).

6. Choose whether you wish to update the entire site or selected pages and press OK.

All of the tools discussed up to this point—importing Fireworks HTML, launch and edit, Update HTML, and export to Dreamweaver Library—have the benefit of enabling you to modify elements in both Dreamweaver and Fireworks. This means that if you go back to the Fireworks PNG at any point, it will be the same as what appears in the target HTML page(s). This consistency and flexibility is what integration is for.

Since Dreamweaver is an authoring application, you do have the power, of course, to forgo Fireworks and modify many elements right in Dreamweaver, without even dealing with Fireworks. We'll cover some of these options next.

Within-Dreamweaver Solutions

We should start by mentioning that the Launch And Edit and Optimize In Fireworks commands really belong in this "within-Dreamweaver" category. But what we actually mean here involves making changes to Fireworks documents in Dreamweaver, without invoking Fireworks at all.

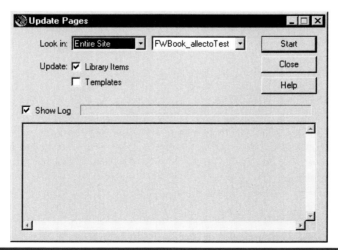

Figure 13-8   The Update Pages dialog box

This approach has a handful of advantages. Chief among them is that Dreamweaver is a powerful HTML authoring solution, as Fireworks is not. If you want to custom-write some JavaScript, modify behaviors, custom-write some tables, make use of DHTML layers, or apply CSS style sheets to table cells, you can in Dreamweaver. In addition, if in your workflow you like to have Fireworks generate a table that you then use as a starting point for customization in Dreamweaver's Code Editor, you can do it.

Another advantage is that Dreamweaver is a what-you-see-is-*almost*-what-you-get HTML editor (leaving room for Netscape's and Internet Explorer's inevitable surprises). Fireworks is a vector drawing application. It does a good job of converting slice regions to nested tables, but let's be realistic: they are frequently not workable as-is. What you hand-code in Dreamweaver is closer to what your end user will see than anything you could do with Fireworks HTML.

The bad news is that once you start customizing Fireworks HTML, you can cross a line, after which it can become difficult to modify elements from Fireworks.

Modifying Fireworks Tables in Dreamweaver

A new feature of Dreamweaver 4/Fireworks 4 is that Fireworks can actually pull tables that have been edited in Dreamweaver back in. That means that if you export Fireworks HTML, make certain changes to it in Dreamweaver, and open the file in Fireworks, your changes will be reflected in the PNG! Figure 13-9 shows a Fireworks PNG that was originally exported with a text slice. I later added some actual text to that text region in Dreamweaver. When I opened the PNG using Launch And Edit and selected the Text Slice in Fireworks, the text (along with HTML markup) I added in Dreamweaver showed up in Fireworks! Not bad!

But there are limitations to this new feature, welcome though it is. For one thing, you cannot make structural changes to the table—by merging two cells, for instance. Fireworks will simply say that the file has changed, and if you proceed, it will

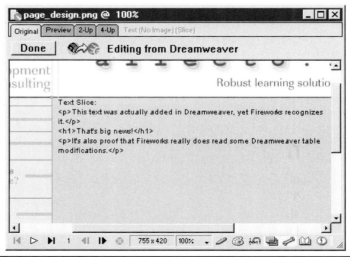

Figure 13-9   This image shows a Fireworks PNG that has been modified in Dreamweaver and reopened in Fireworks.

overwrite the Dreamweaver table. Another thing is that if you insert some non-Fireworks assets into a Fireworks table, such as a GIF produced in Photoshop, Fireworks will sometimes drop it out altogether.

The gist of this section is that if you choose to modify Fireworks HTML in Dreamweaver, you run the risk of breaking the link between the two and breaking down the two programs' integration features. More precisely, you do not actually break the link—it just becomes unusable from a practical standpoint, since one way or another, you will lose some of your work.

Modifying Interactive Fireworks Elements from Dreamweaver

An easily overlooked integration feature between the two programs is that Dreamweaver can natively read most Fireworks behaviors. If you add a Swap Image behavior to a Fireworks slice region, and you export the file along with HTML and import it into Dreamweaver, you will see the Swap Image behavior in the Dreamweaver Behaviors panel. Double-click the behavior and you can actually go in and modify it, as though it were a native Dreamweaver behavior. (You can even access and modify behaviors Fireworks elements exported as Dreamweaver Library items.) Note that Dreamweaver cannot read Fireworks pop-up menus.

Why would you want to modify a behavior? First, Dreamweaver has a more sophisticated library of behaviors (especially when you start piling on the extensions, such as the CourseBuilder extension). Second, you might create one asset in Fireworks that you use in multiple places in a Dreamweaver site. Perhaps you will need a behavior to work differently on a child level than it did in the parent level.

The disadvantage to this approach again is that if you apply a Dreamweaver behavior to a Fireworks element, Fireworks cannot work with the most up-to-date version.

IDEA If you find you need to use Dreamweaver-only behaviors with Fireworks graphics, just create the graphics in Fireworks without the behaviors. You can use the Frames To Files option of the Export dialog box to create a series of flat images. You can then import these into Dreamweaver and attach desired Dreamweaver behaviors. Should you need to modify the image in Fireworks, you can—without worrying about behavior compatibility.

Advanced Integration Topics

Due to the architecture of the two programs (discussed earlier in the section entitled "The Fireworks API"), the possibilities of Fireworks/Dreamweaver integration are nearly limitless. It should be possible, for example, to create a complex command that goes back and forth between the two programs more than once to create a sophisticated effect. One such technique has already been added to the repertoire: web photo albums. We'll also show you a handy technique that can have you building Fireworks-based DHTML applications in no time.

Web Photo Albums

Dreamweaver 3 shipped with an interesting tool for creating web photo albums (Commands | Create Web Photo Album). The command takes a folderful of images and creates thumbnails of each of the images—full-size, web-ready JPGs (or any other format you choose)—and then creates a thumbnails HTML page that links to each of the full pictures. The thumbnails are ordered alphabetically by filename.

Figure 13-10 shows a sample thumbnail page. To accomplish all of this, Dreamweaver calls Fireworks through its JavaScript API and performs the requisite batch processes to generate the two sets of images. Then it generates the page and links itself.

The option name might immediately conjure images of your friends' baby and/or cat pictures, but it has some business applications, too. Clearly an e-commerce site could benefit from a tool like this. You could also use it to create an online graphic-design portfolio with minimal fuss.

IDEA This tool can be used for more than simply end-user sites. You can use it to create, for instance, an online image repository for site developers. Illustrators and photographers can put all their images in a single folder, from which a web photo album could be made. Then the page designers have an easy all-in-one repository to browse and download appropriate graphics.

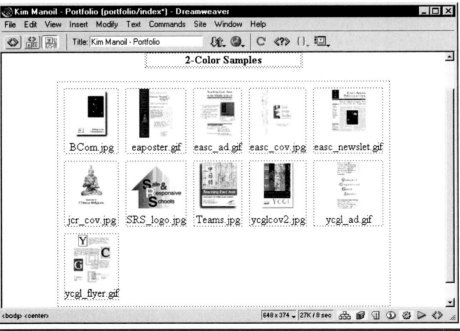

Figure 13-10   A thumbnail page created with Dreamweaver's Create Web Photo Album command

Creating a Web Photo Album is surprisingly easy.

1. Assemble a folder containing all of the images you would like to be in your photo album. The images can be of mixed type (GIF, JPG, JPEG, PNG, TIF, TIFF, PSD, or a mixture), and the folder need not be within the Dreamweaver site. Images with any other extension will be ignored.

 Avoid optimizing the source image folder before you run this command. You should use the original files—whether they are PNG, TIF, or PSD. Running the Create Web Photo Album command not only creates the thumbnails, but it also creates a new set of large images for the Web. If you begin with lossy compressed JPG files and run this command, you could end up applying lossy JPG compression to already compressed files, resulting in ugly graphics that aren't much smaller.

2. In Dreamweaver, choose Commands | Create Web Photo Album. The Create Web Photo Album dialog box appears (see Figure 13-11).

3. Fill out each of the fields of the dialog box, which is mostly self-explanatory. For the thumbnails, we generally recommend using GIF as the format. The only option that may be confusing is the Create Navigation Page For Each Photo check box at the bottom. Checking this option will create a separate HTML page for every single image, complete with Back, Home, and Next links. Unchecking the box will create a link to the image only.

4. Click OK.

5. After a few moments, an Album Created dialog box appears, and your photo album page appears.

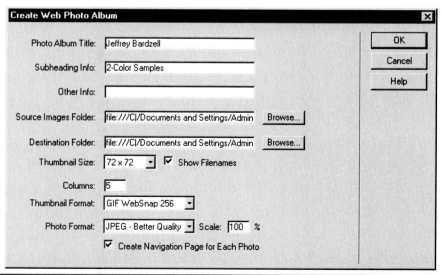

Figure 13-11 The Create Web Photo Album dialog box

We devoted a section to this tool not just to show you how to use it. This tool is also an inspiring model of what kinds of integrated commands can be created by making the two programs communicate via their respective JavaScript APIs. We hope to see more tools like this that take advantage of Dreamweaver/Fireworks integration—we'll be looking for you at the Macromedia Exchange!

From Fireworks to Dreamweaver DHTML, Using CSS Layers

Another quick technique that provides powerful results is to take advantage of the CSS Layers option of the Fireworks Export dialog box. This option saves Fireworks slices, frames, or layers as DHTML layers.

Layers are a comparatively new feature of HTML, though they have been around for several years. They allow you to create object-like container elements in HTML that can hold other content, such as text or images. Layers can be manipulated via JavaScript, creating interactive effects such as animation, visibility/invisibility, and drag capabilities. They are a key component of those features that together are referred to as DHTML—Dynamic HTML. Dreamweaver has several ready-made behaviors that you can use to easily manipulate layers.

 Layers (and DHTML in general) are only supported in 4.0 or higher browsers.

By saving individual Fireworks objects as CSS layers, you can create web pages that are just primed for all sorts of interactivity. In the "Online How-To" section next, you will use Fireworks to create a simple, interactive DHTML puzzle. Using the same techniques with minimal adaptation, you could build a drag-and-drop shopping application, navigation interface, or quiz.

Strictly speaking, this isn't a Fireworks/Dreamweaver integration topic per se, since you could export to layers and do the same kind of thing in, say, GoLive, but Fireworks and Dreamweaver work hand-in-hand so well here (with one hiccup—discussed next) that we had to throw it in.

One final note: You receive ample warning in any Fireworks documentation to avoid overlapping layers, since HTML tables can't handle them. When exporting to CSS, however, overlapping layers are not a problem. We haven't found much use for overlapping layers, but if you can, go for it—just remember to export as CSS Layers, rather than HTML.

Online How-To

Creating a DHTML Drag-and-Drop Puzzle

In this tutorial, you will create a DHTML puzzle from a single photograph (or other image). To do so, you take advantage of Fireworks' slicing and one of its advanced Export options: Exporting to CSS layers. From there, you open the resulting HTML file Dreamweaver and attach drag and drop behaviors to each layer. Figure 13-12 shows the unassembled puzzle as seen in a browser.

GO TO THE WEB! For a free, self-paced interactive version of this tutorial, which includes video demonstrations and source files, visit www.expertedge.com.

1. Scan or import an image into Fireworks. Touch up the image as desired.

2. Optimize the image, using the Optimize panel or the Export Preview dialog box. Be sure to choose a web format!

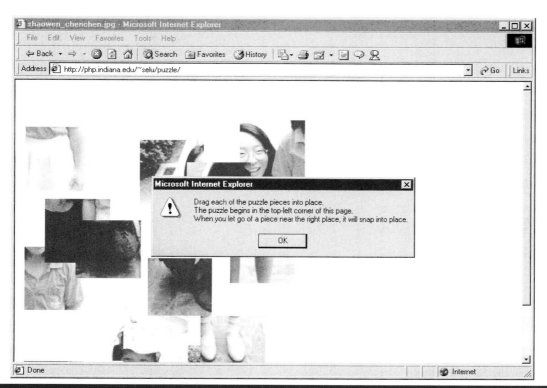

Figure 13-12   A drag-and-drop DHTML puzzle

3. Draw your puzzle pieces as slices over the image. They can be anything from a simple grid to carefully drawn puzzle pieces that are converted to slices. For this exercise we just drew a square grid by drawing out a 100×100 pixel slice and copying and pasting it until the image was covered (see Figure 13-13).

4. Choose File | Export to open the Export dialog box.

5. In the Save As Type drop-down list, choose CSS Layers (.html).

6. Click the Options button to open the HTML Setup dialog box.

7. Make sure that Dreamweaver is selected as the HTML Style and click OK.

8. In the Source drop-down list of the Export dialog box, select Fireworks Slices. You can check or uncheck the Put Images In Subfolder option as needed.

IDEA Make use of the Trim Images option if you are using this technique for a shopping cart application or for any other application for which you have created several discrete graphic elements.

9. Click Save to export the HTML.

Figure 13-13   A simple square slice grid

Moving Over to Dreamweaver

The Fireworks portion is finished, and the rest will be taken care of in Dreamweaver. We told you it was easy. The only problem is that there is a small hiccup in the process—no problem, we've got a work-around.

Dealing with a Small Bug

Here's the problem. If you try to import this Fireworks HTML into Dreamweaver by using Dreamweaver's Import Fireworks HTML command, you get an error message. Apparently, Dreamweaver doesn't recognize the exported HTML as Fireworks HTML. Of course, since Fireworks generates a whole and functional HTML file, you don't need to import it—you can use it as-is. If that is the case, you can skip ahead to the "Creating the Puzzle" section.

You're still reading. So you need to import this into an existing page? Well, there is nothing wrong with the HTML, and you chose Dreamweaver as the HTML style, so how come Dreamweaver doesn't recognize it? The answer has to do with the lines added to the head at the of the HTML document. Usually, when you export from Fireworks to Dreamweaver HTML, the following line appears somewhere in the head (with appropriate time and location information, of course).

```
<!-- Fireworks 4.0  Dreamweaver 4.0 target.  Created Fri Apr 06 ¬
    12:00:10 GMT+0800 (Taipei Standard Time) 2001-->
```

But when you export to CSS Layers, this line appears instead:

```
<meta name="description" content="FW4 CSS Layer">
```

A solution readily presents itself:

1. Open the exported HTML file in your code editor.

2. Delete the following line: `<meta name="description" contect="FW4 CSS Layer">`

3. In its place, insert the comment line above that begins `<!—Fireworks 4.0` ....

4. Save and close the file.

5. From the target HTML file, place the cursor at the desired insertion point.

6. Click the Insert Fireworks HTML icon in the Tools panel. Everything should now work as it is supposed to.

Creating the Puzzle

One way or another, you should be in Dreamweaver, with your Fireworks HTML imported and your image in front of you. Each piece of image will be in its own layer, but since none of them is on top of each other, you will just see the whole image with an apparent grid over it (see Figure 13-14).

Figure 13-14   The slices reconstructed in layers within Dreamweaver

To create the puzzle, you will need to add a Drag Layer behavior so that each slice can be dragged. You will also want to create a drop area, so that the pieces snap into place when the user lets go nearby. You might be tempted to drag the layers around and to create the initial arrangement of layers at this point, but avoid the temptation—we need to do a couple other things first:

1. The first problem is that Fireworks has given an arbitrary name to each of the slices. You'll need to identify each layer when you apply drag behaviors, so some more intuitive naming might help. If you can work with these, you can skip to step 4. For the rest of us, let's rename each layer. Click the layer to activate it.

 It can be very hard when working with layers to select the layers, as opposed to the images within them. But making a mistake here could prevent your file from working. Click the edges of each layer. (The cursor should appear as a four-way arrow.) When you have clicked, the first item in the Properties Inspector will be Layer ID. If the Properties Inspector's first element is something like "FW Image 3K," you have selected the image, so try again.

2. In the Layer ID text field of the first layer, replace whatever is there with **r1c1** and TAB out of the field to make sure the new name sticks.

3. Proceed in this manner until you have named all of your layers.

   Now, it is time to add the Drag Layer behavior. These must be applied to the <body> tag, not the layers themselves.

4. In the lower-left corner of the Dreamweaver document window, click the <body> tag.

‹body› ‹div› ‹img›

5. With the <body> tag selected, open the Behaviors panel (Window | Behaviors).

6. Click the + symbol in the upper-left corner of the Behaviors panel, to open the Behaviors pop-up menu.

7. In the Show Events For option at the bottom of the menu, make sure that 4.0 And Later Browsers is selected.

8. With the <body> tag still selected, click the + symbol again and choose Drag Layer from the drop-down list. The Drag Layer dialog box appears.

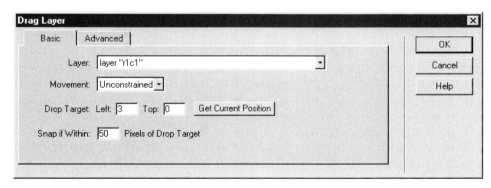

9. In the Layer drop-down list, you will see all your layers listed. Good thing we renamed them! Leave the first one selected.

10. Leave the Movement setting at its default, Unconstrained. You only use the movement option when you want users to be able to drag within a defined area only.

11. The Drop Target is the "correct" final position. Since you did not scramble your images, you can click the Use Current Position, which will enter the correct values automatically.

12. You can leave the Snap If Within setting at its default, 50 pixels.

13. Click the Advanced tab.

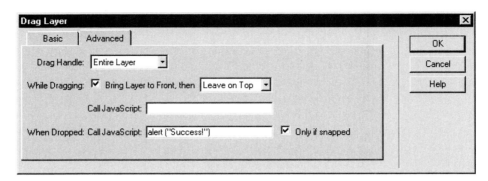

We are not going to do anything in this tab for this example. However, if you wanted the user's dropping the layer into the Drop Target to trigger an event, you could enter a bit of JavaScript in the last text box. For example, typing `alert ("You have moved the layer to the correct location.")` in the last text field will cause a JavaScript pop-up message to appear. Of course, you can use this to call more sophisticated functions, but for our example, you can leave this tab as-is.

14. Click OK to continue. You have added the ability to drag to the first layer. You will need to repeat steps 8–14 for every layer you have. Just be sure to select each layer's name in the Layer drop-down list; if you miss one, it will not drag. When you finish, you should have as many Drag Layer behaviors as you have layers.

15. Before you start scrambling your layers, you should do a Test Page (F12) and try to drag every layer. If something doesn't work, now is the time to troubleshoot. Most likely you didn't select the layer properly in the Layer drop-down list of the Drag Layer dialog box.

16. Once it all works, return to Dreamweaver and drag those layers all over the place!

17. Save your file.

Finishing Touch

As an optional feature, you can provide a JavaScript pop-up box with directions that appears when the page loads. That way, your user has some idea of why the page looks like the inside of a breakfast burrito.

1. With the `<body>` tag still selected, click the + symbol in the Behaviors panel.

2. In the Behaviors pop-up, choose Popup Message. The Popup Message dialog box appears.

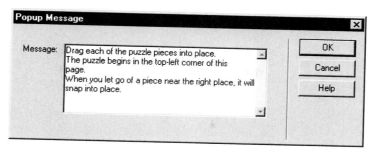

3. Enter the following in the text area, using hard returns at the end of each line. (Dreamweaver will insert a JavaScript paragraph break character \r for you.)

```
Drag each of the puzzle pieces into place.
The puzzle begins in the top-left corner of this page.
When you let go of a piece near the right place, it will
snap into place.
```

4. Click OK. The behavior is added to the Behaviors panel.

5. Save your file and test it in a browser. It's a real puzzler!

Using Fireworks to Build a Front-End for Database-Driven Sites

By Stephen Voisey

Not so long ago, all I did was design web pages. I used Fireworks to design and export the graphics, and then Dreamweaver to create the HTML and pull it together. I was always happy until it started to get difficult. I was never a coder, and I never imagined that I could be. This perception was completely changed when I took on a new position as a web developer.

I've never enjoyed my work more! Why? Because coding opens the doors to designs I've always wanted to do. I discovered that code is not simply logical and analytical; it also empowers creativity. Databases especially create some unique opportunities: not only are they extremely powerful if applied to a problem, but as you'll see soon, they also can alter designs depending on the data without the need for lots of DHTML.

If you are a web designer, there are several good reasons why you should start coding and implementing databases. Although encompassing a range of skills takes time and dedication, the end result to your creativity (not to mention career) is significant. People who can design and code are rare and often end up as web managers because of their wider experience.

Why Use Server-Side Code?

Server-side code overcomes a number of limitations with client-side code, and integrating the two can result in powerful web pages. The advantage of server-side code is that you can perform functions *before* the processed page is sent to the client, which means that your scripts can create customized content on-the-fly. Examples of server-side code languages are Active Server Pages, Java Server Pages, PHP, ColdFusion, or the old, but still popular, Common Gateway Interface (CGI). Each of these languages requires special extensions on web pages, so rather than the .htm extension, you will now see .asp, .jsp, .php, .cfm, .pl, and so on.

Because you can change the code before a client is sent a page, you can use information collected from the client in coordination with your database to modify, on the fly, how a page should look. You can, in short, change graphics depending on the data collected from the end user.

Case Study: An Intranet Application

The following example involves a page from my company's intranet. It was created with a combination of Fireworks, Dreamweaver, Microsoft SQL, Active Server Pages,

JavaScript, and Cascading Style Sheets. More than a mouthful, you'll agree, but I'll only be concentrating on how Fireworks was used to make the data look great and provide functionality, as well as touching on how the database was used to change the appearance of part of the design.

Overview

Before I go into how this page was created, let's take a quick look at the page (see Figure 13-15). All of the graphics were created in Fireworks; however, the text is pulled from a form and the database also controls whether graphics (such as the sticky note) are displayed.

This page is a part of an application that allows the sales folks to review database records. They arrive at this page after selecting an individual record from a page that lists all of the records in the database. This page is essentially the detail page, though it also allows them to take action with the record. Whether they take action or not, automatic tracking shows if the record has been previously viewed, and by whom. This is useful information for the managers and the team, so they don't inadvertently contact a client twice.

The data on the page is exactly the same data that the user filled in when she or he registered to download our software, minus user name and password. It also indicates which browser was used, which is always useful.

Building the Application's Graphic Elements

Working with a database means that your design in Fireworks has to correspond with the data. Although you can do the design first, and then do the database, it's normally the other way around. Because the database was already built, it was just a case of deciding how I was going to format the data.

I liked the idea that this was presented on a clipboard (shown in Figure 13-16). The clipboard is a natural metaphor, because it's something people already know how to interact with. In my other "Fireworks in the Real World" (see Chapter 5), I described how the pencil and mug were created, and the clipboard was no different; it was all done with Fireworks.

I started from the back, building the wooden board and the metal clip with the standard vector tools. I then added in the paper. This in turn is textured and has a slight color gradient.

With the clipboard finished, I needed to lay out the text that would describe the fields where the data would finally appear on the web page. I typed in the descriptions for each row of data, and I used a clear script font to give it that real-world feel. I then lined up each row. I also created a customized stroke style to look like a pencil, which is used to underline where the fields would later be placed. I used Modify | Align | Distribute Heights to make sure the text and lines were evenly distributed across the page. I also broke the fields into sections, using transparent blocks of color to make them stand out.

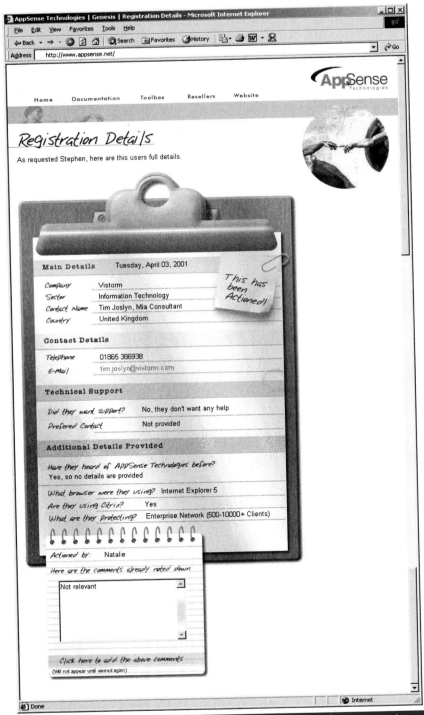

Figure 13-15   The completed page from our example. All of the graphics were created in Fireworks.

Figure 13-16 The clipboard was designed entirely in Fireworks.

Finally, but not least, the little notebook was created; the ring binds are just stroked circles with an inner bevel on them. This is used on the page for the form where users can add what actions they've taken.

Now here's the interesting part: the image is exported as one big graphic. The only things that are separate are the button at the bottom of the page and the sticky note. I know what you're thinking! Yes this *is* a large file size, but it's only going to be used over the fast internal network, so download time is not an issue.

Now you may be wondering how I managed to get all the data outputted through the HTML page to line up with the graphic. This is a lot easier than you might think. I used Cascading Style Sheets (CSS) code to place the graphic behind the table. This gives you total freedom. The graphic does not interfere with laying out the table or adding forms, or with dropping the database fields into place.

Because the image isn't moving, or being held in place by other graphics (which might be the case if you cut it up and have it in foreground along with the data), it's easy to align the database data to the design. I kid you not! There are no shims, and other than the CSS to get the image in the background, there is no coding involved.

I wanted to make the sticky note change depending on the tracking status of the record. If a record has never been viewed before, the user doesn't see a sticky note. However, if it has already been viewed, or even actioned, the sticky note will indicate as much (see Figure 13-17).

Figure 13-17 Depending on the status of the record, a different sticky note appears.

To make this work, I created the sticky notes in Fireworks and saved them as two GIFs. I then used the server-side ASP code to look at the database record and write some HTML into the page, depending on what it says. In pseudocode, the logic is something like this:

If record status = 0, then don't add any graphic.
If record status = 1, then add `<img src="viewed_post_it.gif">` into the HTML code.
If record status = 2, then add `<img src="actioned_post_it_gif">` into the HTML code.

Naturally there's more to it than this (such as adding the tracking code), which is beyond the scope of this short piece, but in all, this page took just over a day to build.

Conclusion

If you cannot write ASP (or its equivalent), don't forget that Dreamweaver UltraDev will do a lot of the hard work for you. However, if you want to get your hands dirty (and the clever stuff always requires that you do!), your first stop is, of course, the Web. There you will find ample help, from tutorials to working source code. You'll have to decide which languages you'd like to learn—they all have their merits.

A final recommendation: before you embark on learning any server-side code, I'd recommend getting to know CSS and JavaScript inside out first. This also makes learning the server-side code easier. Once you get to a certain point, there isn't a great deal of difference between the languages, and you can apply your skills to new languages, databases, and technologies. Whatever you decide, good luck, and happy coding!

14 Automating and Extending Fireworks

When you first considered Fireworks, you looked at the package and read about all its features. You read that it had creative vector drawing tools, behaviors for interactivity, and a powerful optimization interface, and you imagined what you could do with those tools. But what if the back of the box had said that with a single keystroke, you could put your company's logo (not *a* company's logo, but *yours*) in the proper position at the right size as soon as you created a document? What if it said that you could drop button effects that *your* design department had created, with a single mouse click in any document? What if it said it came with a visual interface that created your company's signature animation across the number of frames you specified? In short, what if, in addition to a powerful set of features that enabled you to create diverse and beautiful graphic content, Fireworks had been custom made for your office, with your logos, tools, and effects built right into the software?

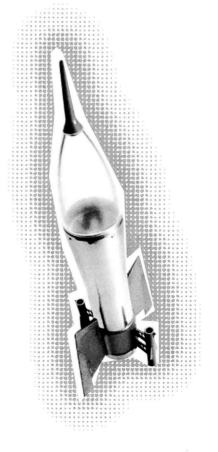

Fireworks has—and has had for years—several tools that allow you to create this kind of functionality. Some are as simple as filling out an easy wizard, while others are as complex as programming in a text editor. Macromedia created an open architecture that allows its users to extend and customize its application, to transform Fireworks from a great product with mass appeal to a greater product that was made just for you.

Some of its tools are visual, meaning that you don't have to write a word of code. We'll show you how to use some of those in this chapter. But the really good stuff is a bit harder and generally requires you to be somewhat conversant with JavaScript.

Unfortunately, it seems that few designers, even many power users, bother with some of these advanced capabilities. Perhaps people learn to work with what's already there, even if it is not ideal. Perhaps some designers are intimidated by programming. Perhaps there is little practical documentation. In spite of Macromedia's freely distributed 188-page PDF on the topic, *Extending Fireworks,* many designers simply don't know how to make the most of Fireworks. Certainly most of the third-party Fireworks books to date have not covered this topic.

Macromedia's *Extending Fireworks* is unreadable to most designers. It contains ample information about the functions and the guts of the program, including the Fireworks application programming interface (API), its Document Object Model (DOM), and its custom "functions." Unfortunately, it neither comes with a tutorial nor helps nonprogrammers know where to start. That is not to say that *Extending Fireworks* is no good; it is a fantastic document. It's just that it assumes the reader understands JavaScript and principles of programming. Yet many of Fireworks' most enthusiastic users are designers who do not understand programming.

But whether or not they have had a formal or systematic introduction to JavaScript, few designers today are insulated from JavaScript. How many have dabbled with it, made simple changes to it, or figured out how an easy script works, even if they could not have written it without help? How much programming does someone need to know to be able to work productively with some of these tools? Not that much.

Designers—this chapter is written for you.

By following the hands-on tutorial in this chapter, you will be able to write your own, usable Fireworks commands in JavaScript, even if you don't know JavaScript. If you are relatively new to programming and JavaScript, you will get a bit of a crash course in it, see it in action, and code some yourself. And you will know what is going on when you do it. If you are already conversant with JavaScript, you will learn how to apply that knowledge to programming Fireworks, in particular. Either way, both you and your software will become more powerful—and isn't that what it's all about?

Enough of the pep talk. It's time to begin.

What Does "Automating and Extending Fireworks" Mean?

By now you should have a pretty good idea about what this chapter covers, but some definitions never hurt. *Automation* refers to creating processes that perform a given task on multiple objects simultaneously, without the need to do so individually. *Extensibility* refers to a program's ability to grow or to be applied in ways unforeseen at the time of its creation.

Introducing Automation

Fireworks has made many automation tasks easy. Let's take an example. One task just begging for automation is the replacement of one URL with another in all of the images throughout the site, whether the URL is embedded in a hotspot or slice. Fireworks provides multiple ways to accomplish this task. It can be done in the URL panel, through Find and Replace, and/or through the Project Log. Some of these you have already encountered in other chapters.

There are two primary interfaces for automating Fireworks: Find and Replace and Batch Processing. Though both are used to modify multiple items all at once, they generally operate at different levels. Use find and replace to modify a page element in multiple locations, such as a font face, a particular color, or text string. Use batch processing to modify whole files, such as their dimensions, optimization settings, filenames, and so on. The only part that complicates this clean division is that batch processing has a full-featured Find and Replace interface within it, which allows you to conduct a find and replace operation in the midst of several other commands.

Introducing Commands and Extensibility

Whenever you do something in Fireworks—open a new document, create an oval, apply a drop shadow to a text block—you are using a command. In a GUI environment, commands are usually invisible, but they are there nonetheless. For instance, if you use the Paint Bucket to apply a new fill color to an object, the following is the command that happens behind the scenes:

```
fw.getDocumentDOM().applyCurrentFill(true);
```

Even if you don't know any JavaScript, you can probably make a good guess as to what this code says, especially if you know that the first part, `fw.getDocumentDOM()`, simply means "apply the following command to any selected objects within the active Fireworks document."

Understanding what commands are, then, means little more than knowing that commands are what happens behind the scenes when you cause some event. The significance of this for web developers is that Fireworks provides a few ways for you to create custom commands—thus allowing you, the world's greatest expert in how *you* use Fireworks, to extend and tailor the program's capabilities. That is what extensibility means in this context.

Later in this chapter—in fact making up a good portion of it—is an extended hands-on tutorial with two key learning goals:

- To teach you different ways to work with commands: visually through the History panel and "the hard way," by writing scripts in a text editor

- To teach you how to extend your own knowledge of commands; or, in other words, to teach you how to learn commands once you have completed these tutorials.

These goals may sound ambitious and, if you are not a programmer, you may be thinking that it will be beyond you. Nonprogrammers will be happy to know that with the right strategies, you can be very effective with commands just by faking it.

Automating Fireworks

Now that you have a better conceptual idea of ways to use Fireworks' built-in automation and extensibility to enhance your workflow, it's time to dive in. As mentioned earlier, there are two interfaces dedicated to automation: Find and Replace and Batch Processing.

In addition to these, of course, there are lots of ways to automate tasks—replacing URLs in the URL panel, using styles, and using the library are all ways of deploying automation. Just about anything you do twice in Fireworks could have been done through some automation tool or other. Because of the enormous productivity gains that they can effect, automation tools are well worth their time to learn.

Find and Replace

Find and Replace (Edit | Find And Replace, seen in Figure 14-1) works in Fireworks much like it does in other graphics programs. It allows you to search in multiple places (selection, frame, file, Project Log, specified files) for different categories of object (text, font, color, URL, non–web safe 216). Because of Fireworks' object orientation, finding and replacing is quite robust.

Since we devoted time to Find and Replace (and the Project Log) elsewhere, we won't repeat it all here. Instead we'll leave you with the screen shot in Figure 14-1 and the following cross-reference.

CROSS REFERENCE → Find and Replace is discussed in detail in Chapter 3.

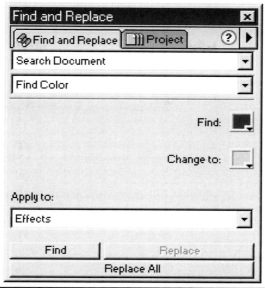

Figure 14-1   The Find and Replace panel

Using Batch Processing

Batch processing is a feature that allows you to perform from one to a whole series of commands on a group of files that you define. With options for backing up files and saving batch processing scripts, this powerful tool can make a minute's work out of a tedious and time-consuming task. Let's look at a real-world example.

Recently, Jeffrey was developing a corporate newsletter with a segment introducing new employees. He was given 60 digital images that had been taken from different cameras at different resolutions. In the end, each picture needed to be a bust fitting into a 122×122-pixel square. Some pictures were close-ups already, while others had been taken from a distance.

Fireworks provided a great set of solutions. Jeffrey opened each picture and cropped the images into square regions around the faces of each of the new employees—the square's dimensions were determined by how close the person was to the camera. He used the Xtras | Adjust Color | Curves option to improve the coloring of each of the images. He then exported each image as a flat PNG. When he was done, he had 60 square PNG images of all different sizes. Using batch processing, he applied a JPG optimization setting (selected by optimizing a handful of representative images) to each image and scaled each one to 122 pixels. Each image therefore needed four steps: it had to be cropped, adjusted for color, optimized, and scaled. In two minutes, batch processing did half the work. The other half of the work took over an hour.

NOTE There was a bug in the Batch Processing interface in the originally shipped version of Fireworks 4. Registered users can download a free update from Macromedia. This update, among other things, fixes the batch-processing bug.

Taking a look at the existing commands (see Table 14-1) in the Batch Processing interface will probably immediately give you some ideas about what you could do with it. Remember that you can perform as many of the commands at once as you need. You don't have to optimize in one batch and scale in another.

The Batch Processing Wizard

The Batch Processing interface in Fireworks 4 is different than it was for its predecessors. It now uses a wizard interface.

1. Close all open documents. This is optional—you can include open documents—but we find it easier to keep things straight if no files are open.

2. Choose File | Batch Process. The Batch dialog box opens (see Figure 14-2).

3. Navigate to the folder in the top window, and use the Add or Add All buttons to build the list of files you want to process.

Option	Description
Export	Choosing Export actually re-exports the document using the document's optimization settings.
Scale	Scaling resizes and resamples the image (replicating Modify | Image Size).
Find and Replace	This brings up a special Find and Replace interface for batch processing, which works much like the regular Find and Replace dialog box. The main difference is that you cannot batch-replace bitmap files (since there are no objects to modify).
Rename	This command allows you to rename files, including adding prefixes and/or suffixes to filenames.
Commands	The Commands list pulls in all of the commands listed in the Commands menu. Some of these can be quite powerful, such as converting all images to grayscale. Some don't make a lot of sense, such as batch processing settings for panel layout. Just remember that since all commands are available, you can custom create commands and execute them on multiple files through batch processing. Now that's powerful!

Table 14-1   Summary of Batch Processing Commands

1. Select source file(s).   2. Add them to the file list.

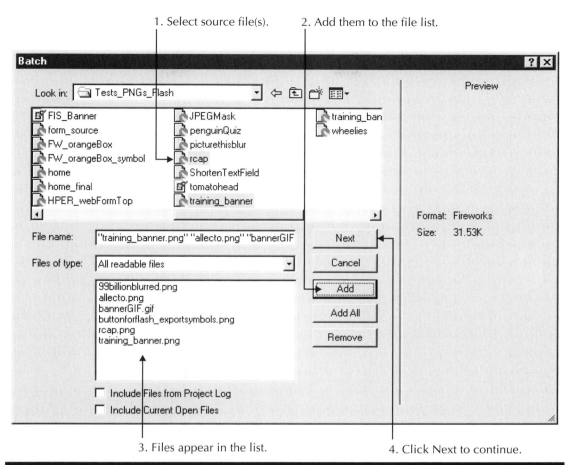

3. Files appear in the list.   4. Click Next to continue.

Figure 14-2   The Batch dialog box, first screen

NOTE You can add files from multiple folders, even pulling in files from different places on a network.

4. Click Next to advance to the screen where you choose which action(s) to apply to these files. The second Batch dialog box screen appears (see Figure 14-3).

5. Select an action from the left pane, and click the Add button to put it in your batch script. If needed, several options that allow you to enter parameters appear in the lower part of the window.

6. Enter the parameters.

7. Repeat steps 4–6 until you have all of your actions entered.

8. If needed, use the Up and Down arrows in the upper-right corner to change the order of your actions.

9. Click the Next button to advance to the third screen of the Batch dialog box (see Figure 14-4).

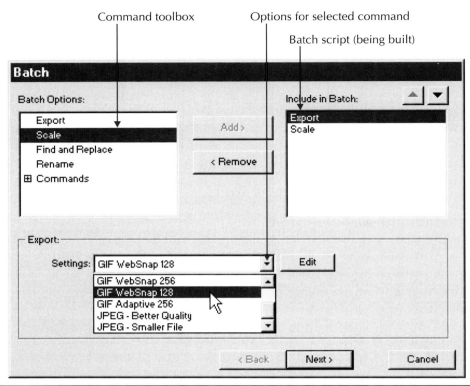

Command toolbox   Options for selected command

Batch script (being built)

Figure 14-3   The action-building screen of the Batch Processing interface

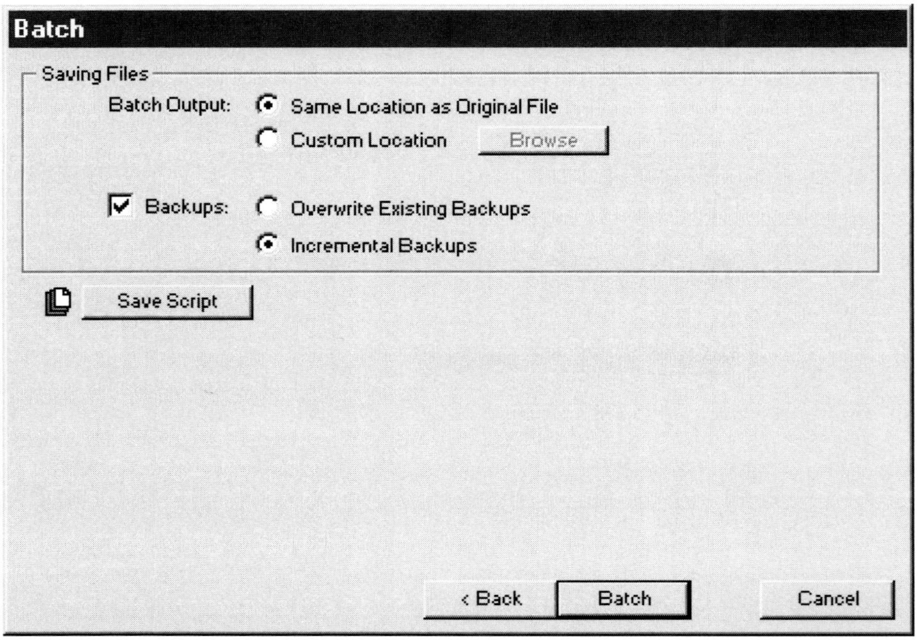

Figure 14-4   Screen 3 of the Batch dialog box

10. Choose where you want the output files to go. We strongly recommend that you do not overwrite your existing files! If you put files in the same folder, you should create backups. Alternatively, you can create a new output folder, and your original files will be unaffected. But if these are live web files, the links will still point to the old files.

11. Click the Batch button to run the batch process.

Creating and Using Scriptlets

One of the options in the third screen of the Batch dialog box allows you to save a script. Use this if there is a batch process that you tend to use a lot. Rather than rebuild it every time you need it, you can simply activate the script and choose the target files—Fireworks will do the rest.

When you click the Save Script button, you will be prompted to save the file. You can save it wherever you like—we usually keep batch scriptlets in the folders with the projects for which they were developed. One nice thing about scriptlets is that they are cross-platform, so you can share your batch scripts with all your colleagues.

 Batch scriptlets can be stored in the project file on your intranet (discussed in Chapter 3), which contains symbol libraries, master designs, and so on.

When saving, be sure to append the .jsf extension (it should appear by default). In the Save dialog box, Fireworks identifies this extension as a batch processing script. However, .jsf is actually the extension for any custom Fireworks JavaScript. You will use it for all of the command scripts you write.

Once you have created them, Batch scriptlets are easy to use:

1. From within Fireworks, choose File | Run Script, or alternatively, you can double-click the script's icon in your operating system. The Files To Process dialog box appears.

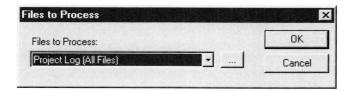

2. Choose one of the options from the drop-down list, or click the "…" button to activate the Open dialog box, through which you can build your own file list.

 If you run a script on an open file, it must have been saved somewhere first; if it is a new, untitled document, you will get an "internal error" alert and the script won't work.

3. Click OK. The Batch Progress dialog box appears to provide feedback.

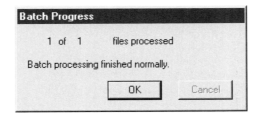

Taking Command of Fireworks

This section introduces some JavaScript basics and contains an extended tutorial with exercises that guide you through the process of creating command scripts. First, let's talk a bit about the potential of commands. Commands can be a great boon to productivity, because they can be used for automation. You can use them to customize your work environment. You can also use commands for artistic effects. One of the scripts that you will learn in this chapter, called Twist and Fade, is used for artistic effects. In this way, programming can be a part of the artistic process—not just a productivity-enhancing tool. Commands can therefore be used to manipulate objects in novel ways as well as to put a series of smaller operations all in one command.

Once commands have been created, there are a couple ways to use them. When saved in the proper folder (Fireworks | Configuration | Commands), commands will appear in the Commands menu in Fireworks. You can also assign them to keystrokes. Assigning commands to keystrokes can save you a lot of time, not to mention the relief to your carpal canal.

Learning How to Learn Command Scripts: A Strategy Guide

Creating commands and customizing your application are advanced tasks. For nonprogrammers, they are daunting ones. But there is a way to learn, a way to go from wherever you are now to the point where you can write simple scripts. If you can't program, this won't teach you how to program. But it will help you learn how to experiment, and through experimentation, learn.

Fireworks offers two fundamentally different ways of creating commands. The first is through the History panel. The second is to write them yourself. But there is a connection: what you do in the History panel actually writes code just like the code you would write yourself. That means that if you had access to the code generated by the History panel, you could create commands visually to generate some models, and then you could modify the models and eventually emulate them to write your own script.

In fact, Fireworks *does* give you direct access to the JavaScript code behind every action you take onscreen.

1. Do a few actions in Fireworks, such as draw out a rectangle, delete an object, or change a color.

2. Click to select one or more actions in the History panel (see Figure 14-5).

3. Click the Clipboard icon in the lower-right corner (beside the Trash icon) to copy the command to the Clipboard.

4. Choose Edit | Paste in the text editor of your choice. Some Fireworks JavaScript appears.

Deciphering this JavaScript—and you are aided by the fact that you know what it does—should give you an idea of how things work. You can begin to tweak existing command scripts that you download from the Web, and you can eventually start to put different ones together. With some patience and Macromedia's *Extending Fireworks* by your side, who knows what you'll develop?

We provide this overview of the learning process not to teach you how to do commands—the remainder of the chapter will do that—but to give you an angle from which to read the rest of the chapter. The tutorial in this chapter will use an approach very similar to the one outlined here. Following it in order will not just teach you how to write the command scripts included, it will teach you how to begin writing command scripts of your own.

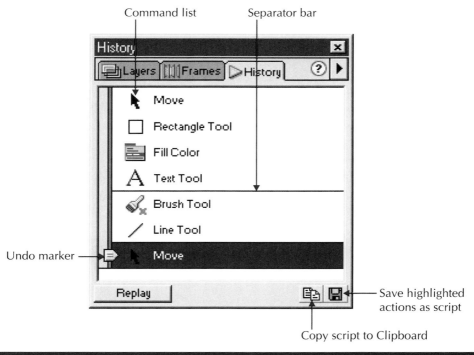

Figure 14-5   The History panel, with a Move action selected

Interpreting Dot Syntax

It is also worthwhile introducing you to the basic structure of JavaScript syntax. "Syntax" is term borrowed from grammar, and it refers to the proper ordering of the constituent parts of a sentence, or in this case, line of code. JavaScript has a very distinctive syntax, and it is very easy to read, if you understand its basic principles.

Understanding JavaScript dot syntax is also increasingly important for web developers, not just because of the prevalence of JavaScript on the Web, but also because many Macromedia products use it. The APIs of both Fireworks and Dreamweaver are written in JavaScript. This means that whatever you learn here about writing commands for Fireworks will also work in Dreamweaver. Another key point is that the new Flash 5 ActionScript is based on the standard from which JavaScript was written. Flash 5 now makes extensive use of JavaScript syntax. So a little work here will pay heavy dividends.

So what is dot syntax? *Dot syntax* is a standardized way of identifying elements in code. You might think of it as an addressing system. Let's examine the following piece of code, which was created when a blue stroke was added to a rectangle:

```
fw.getDocumentDOM().setBrushColor("#000099");
```

The line is broken into several parts. The dots in the line separate different components. Where we would say in English, "apply a blue stroke to the selected rectangle in the document," JavaScript would say something like this: "To the rectangle, apply a stroke (of the following color: #000099)." Sometimes this kind of paraphrasing can help nonprogrammers work with code, if they take a moment to break it down into its constituent parts.

As stated earlier in this chapter, `fw.getDocumentDOM()` tells Fireworks to identify the selected element in the current document—and apply whatever follows to it. The presence of the parentheses indicates that the line of code is a *function,* which is a bit like a verb in programming. This verb tells Fireworks to figure whatever has been selected in the current document. Parentheses can be empty, as they are in this case, when there are no *parameters* (related pieces of information) to pass.

The second half of the preceding code listing is the portion after the period, which contains another function: `setBrushColor()`. It should be easy enough to figure out what this one does. The one thing we do want to point out is that this time, the parentheses are not empty. Inside is a string of numbers, `#000099`, which, as a designer, you probably recognize as the hexadecimal number for a certain shade of blue.

Items by themselves followed by periods are usually *objects,* which are kind of like nouns. Items followed by parentheses are usually *methods* (or functions, which are custom methods), and they work like verbs. The items in parentheses, usually comma delimited, are the parameters (or options) of the method; you might say these are adjectives. Parameters are often the easiest to spot because they correspond to options visible in the GUI interface. Try typing a text block in Fireworks, changing a couple of the text parameters (font, and so on), copying that action to the Clipboard, and pasting it into a text editor. You will see font, leading, color, tracking, and other information embedded in the code that you just saw in the Fireworks text editor.

Let's look at a Flash example. The following code listing comes from Chapter 10, where we added a script to a button that advanced a movie clip's timeline to a certain label.

```
QA.gotoAndStop ("answer");
```

The movie clip was called QA, the label was "answer." Attaching the method `gotoAndStop()` directly to the name of the object affected tells the script exactly what to act on, even though the script is attached to a different object altogether. By passing the parameter in the same line, we have a compact method for sending commands to objects having different addresses.

Tutorial: Creating Command Scripts in Fireworks

Before we begin, we would like to say a word about the tutorial. As we were planning this chapter, we decided to ask our friend Stephen Voisey to write up a small tutorial on writing scripts for the Fireworks API in a text editor. We asked him to write something that designers rather than programmers could follow. We also suggested that his piece be about five pages. Stephen came back with the most comprehensive, user-friendly tutorial we have ever seen on the topic of creating commands. Needless to say, it was also a lot more than five pages. So, though all we originally wanted was a tutorial on writing scripts in a text editor, Stephen's tutorial turned out to be quite a bit broader. Its six exercises cover creating commands using the History panel, limitations of the History panel, modifying existing scripts, writing scripts from scratch, assigning commands to keyboard shortcuts, and finally, organizing commands. Out went the original chapter outline! Since his tutorial is so empowering and cogent, we have decided to go with his full tutorial as it is, rather than break it up into pieces.

We are very grateful to Stephen for this outstanding contribution.

Introduction

The mere mention of scripting or programming to most designers induces a change of facial color and instant loathing.

However, this tutorial will show you how easy Fireworks command scripts are to create. In fact, what's great about command scripts is that you don't have to write any code or understand programming to create them. There are limitations to this approach, but you shouldn't let that stop you. This tutorial will show you how to open, edit, and write Fireworks command scripts.

Command Script Basics

Command scripts are just a way of telling Fireworks to do something—change an object's size, apply a fill color, add a new frame, and so on. Fireworks already has several command scripts for you to use. You might like to explore these commands in Fireworks now; they are located in the Commands menu.

Let's take a quick example:

1. Create a new document.

2. Choose the Commands | Creative | Apply Picture Frame command script.

3. When prompted, enter the width in pixels.

This command script creates a wooden frame around your new document—clever, huh? It's just the beginning!

You can create commands from almost everything you do in Fireworks, because scripts power almost everything you do in Fireworks. When you draw a square box, Fireworks uses scripting language to create it in the document. When you change its color or add a drop shadow, it's all Fireworks' scripting behind the scenes, interpreting your actions into script code that is then displayed as the graphics (as shown next).

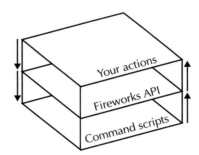

For simplicity, this tutorial will call command scripts, simply *scripts*. We will call saved scripts *commands*.

What Can I Do with Commands?

It's possible to get scripts to do a number of different things within the Fireworks environment, but since it's primarily a web graphics environment, the scripts you'll want to create will be of a graphical or timesaving nature. Although you can use Fireworks scripts to liaison with Dreamweaver, that is an advanced subject this tutorial won't be covering. But this tutorial will certainly point you in the right direction.

Here are some of the things you could do with a script:

● Instantly import common graphics, such as logos or images

● Create cool graphical and animation effects

- Get Fireworks to re-create required graphics
- Format your objects to a predefined format (similar to creating a style, but these can be assigned to a keypress, unlike styles)
- Change all slices to predefined export settings
- Create commonly used text at the font and style required
- Transform objects consistently to preset ratios/settings
- Create new documents preset at web friendly sizes
- Streamline and integrate processes between Fireworks and Dreamweaver (and vice versa)
- Create predefined export routines
- Add useful tools to Fireworks
- Speed up your workflow within Fireworks by scripting processes you use often

Scripting addresses the needs of web designers, helps automate repetitive tasks, allows you to enhance Fireworks' basic offering of tools, and can save essential time.

The following exercises will take you through the most immediately useful parts of scripting in Fireworks, working with graphics and streamlining your workflow.

The History Panel and Creating Commands

The easiest way to create commands is visually, with the help of the History panel. The History panel keeps track of all your actions. You can select a set of actions and export them collectively as a single command. This is much like recording a macro in a word processor. It has its limitations, but when it comes to creating powerful commands with no knowledge of coding, it can't be beat.

Exercise: Your First Command—Instantly Importing Graphics

Often, web sites use common design themes and have similar graphics throughout a web site. As a web designer, you may find yourself using the same graphics over and over. If this is the case, more often than not you will be opening or importing graphics into your current document. This chore can become very repetitive, and you always run the risk of altering the original graphic by accident.

In this exercise you'll see how creating a script can allow you to import graphics instantly without having to resort to coding.

1. Start a new document with ample space to work in.

2. Open the History panel (Window | History). It's from this panel that scripts can be saved as commands. We will be using the History panel extensively throughout this exercise, but at present it should be completely blank.

3. Now we will import a graphic. For this exercise, let's use the clock, which is contained in the Fireworks Samples folder. Choose Insert | Insert Image, locate the Clock.png graphic on your computer (it should be in the Fireworks\Samples folder), and click Open.

4. The mouse cursor changes to a corner shape, allowing you to place and drop the file. Do so anywhere in your new document. The image appears within your new document (and is a testament to Art Deco).

5. Take a closer look at the History panel, and note that this insert has been named "Import."

6. It's now a simple case of saving the History item as a command. Select the Import item in the History panel.

7. Choose Save As Command from the History panel pop-up menu (as shown here). The Save Command dialog box opens.

8. For simplicity's sake, just type in **Clock**; you will learn how to delete this and organize your commands later.

9. Congratulations, you've created your first command script! But now it's time to see it in action. Close the document without saving it, and start a new blank document of the same proportions as the last.

10. Go to the Commands menu, and you'll see "Clock" at the top of the list. Click it.

11. As you may have already guessed, the clock is instantly imported into your new document.

There are a few important things to note here. First, look at the History panel, and you'll see it says "Command Script" instead of "Import." Second, the clock has been imported into the *exact* position you originally placed it when you imported it in the other document. This demonstrates that the History panel is extremely faithful in copying your actions, but this could lead to an unfortunate side effect—on smaller documents, your command would import the image out of sight! Finally, and most importantly when importing external images and saving them as scripts, be aware that your script refers to the location of the image at the time of your import. If you rename a file or move it, your script will effectively be broken, and you will receive an error message when you try to run it.

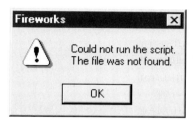

If this occurs, you have two choices, either re-create your script and save it over the old one, or manually edit the script file to change the location manually. It is toward this subject we will be progressing.

Limitations of the History Panel

While the previous exercise was very easy and demonstrates how you can create a number of simple commands to fit your requirements with the History panel, at some point you will also encounter its limitations.

Exercise: A Dubious Command

The following exercise will expose these problems—and show you how to deal with them:

1. Start a new document with ample space to work in.

2. Draw a simple rectangle filled with a color of your choice.

3. Select the Pointer tool from the Tools panel, and resize your rectangle bigger by dragging one of its corner points.

The History panel clearly shows the rectangle being created, and below that it shows the Modify Rectangle step has just been performed. What's important to spot here is the line between the two items (see Figure 14-6). Let's see what happens when we try to save these steps as a command.

1. To select more than one step, either hold down SHIFT and click from the first step to the second, or click the first one and then hold down COMMAND or CTRL to click on the second step. In this way you can highlight steps that are not in sequential order and save them as one command, ignoring steps in between.

Figure 14-6   The black line between two actions indicates trouble when creating a script from actions before and after it.

2. Now save these steps as a command from the History panel Options menu as before.

3. Uh-oh! A warning message has appeared.

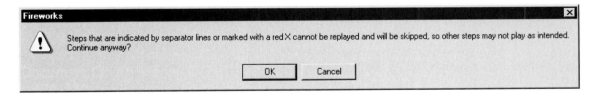

Obviously, there are some things the History panel simply cannot guarantee to save correctly for one reason or another.

Just because you're getting the warning doesn't mean you shouldn't save the command to see what happens. Exploring the History panel's limitations is an excellent way to understand how the Fireworks architecture operates beneath the surface.

1. Click OK on the warning message, and save the command as **Testing**.

2. Let's delete the existing rectangle so we have a clean sheet to work from.

3. Run your Testing command.

4. Surprisingly, despite the warning, the command runs fine. It simply creates a new rectangle and then alters it to the size you changed it to originally.

Exercise: The Command that Failed

For the benefit of experience, we will quickly create something that cannot be saved as a command:

1. In the same document, delete the new rectangle.

2. Select the Pencil tool, and get creative and draw some squiggles.

3. Take a look at the History panel again, and you'll see the icons now have *X*s through them. Not only can you not save these as a command, but you also can't even replay the steps or copy them.

4. Click on that single step in the History panel, and try to save it as a command.

5. You will get the same warning message as before; however, you will not be prompted to save the command.

The main tools that *cannot* be scripted are as follows:

- Brush and Pencil tools
- Rubber Stamp tool
- Freeform tool
- Path Scrubber tool, both Additive and Subtractive
- Redraw Path tool

Paths created with the Bezier tool will script without any problems.

NOTE If you try to save a command that includes several steps, including a red *X*, all the steps will be saved, except the red *X* ones.

While this exercise shows you the limits of the History panel, please don't be afraid to explore. However, as you will soon find out, some things are simply impossible to do from the History panel alone.

Manually Editing Command Scripts

Unlike other graphics software, Fireworks does not use a proprietary scripting language; it uses JavaScript. JavaScript is used extensively on the Web, and you may already be familiar with it. We'll be keeping these exercises simple, so don't worry if you aren't familiar with JavaScript.

Exercise: From History Panel to Command Script

Fireworks has its own unique flavor of JavaScript. It is different from that used by web browsers, but follows the same common syntax and rules. What makes it different is that it has its own unique Document Object Model (DOM), which allows you to interface directly with Fireworks. It's easier to see in action than to explain, so let's dive in:

1. Start a new document with ample space to work in.

2. Draw a rectangle.

3. Change its color and add a simple drop shadow. You will now see three steps in the History panel.

4. Highlight them all and save them as a command called **Openme** (see Figure 14-7).

   Now it's time to open this file outside of Fireworks to see what the script actually looks like. The file is just plain text, so a basic text editor such as Notepad or SimpleText will work perfectly. You can also use HTML/text editors such as HomeSite or BBEdit. We generally don't recommend using something like Word, which will more than likely add its own code to the script, effectively breaking it.

5. Launch a text editor.

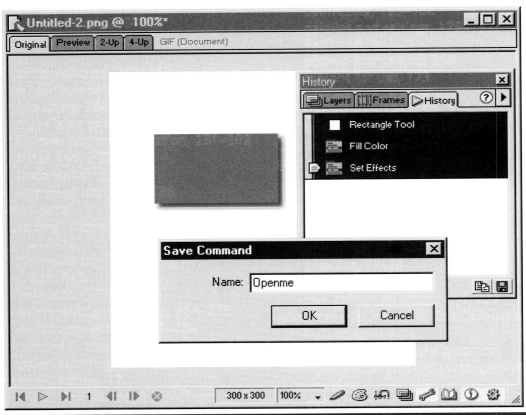

Figure 14-7   Create a script called "Openme."

6. The command that you have created has been saved within the Fireworks\Configuration\Commands folder. All commands are saved here when you save them with the History panel. If you want to add commands you downloaded from the Internet, place them in here.

NOTE The Fireworks folder's location can vary depending on where you installed it on your system.

7. Having found the folder doesn't always mean you can see the command script files. Because the files are unique to Fireworks, they have their own extension, .jsf. Depending on the editor and your system, you may have to choose View All File Types to see them.

8. When you've opened the Openme command, you will see at least three lines of text. (See Figure 14-8—note that we have turned on Word Wrap and placed an extra carriage return between each line of code for legibility.) Let's go through each line to explain what they are doing.

Each line starts with:

```
fw.getDocumentDOM()
```

This is the first part of almost all the lines you'll see when viewing scripts. It tells Fireworks to use the current document to perform some actions. You may recognize the letters "DOM" that were explained earlier as the Document Object Model. Essentially then, this line says "Hey, Fireworks, I want to use the current document to do something."

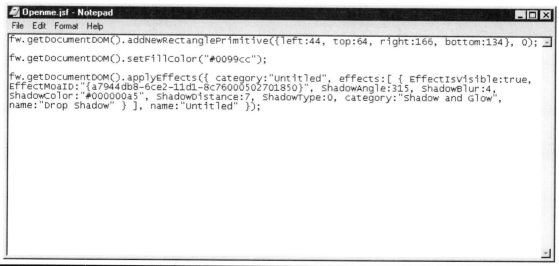

Figure 14-8 The script as it appears in Notepad

The first line continues with more code. (Remember that the ¬ symbol is simply where the line wraps to fit the format of this book. It is not actually a part of the code.)

```
fw.getDocumentDOM().addNewRectanglePrimitive({left:44,¬
 top:64, right:166, bottom:134}, 0);
```

Immediately following the first request, this is what is called a *function.* This particular function, `addNewRectanglePrimitive()`, simply adds new rectangles at the pixel locations specified in parentheses.

The next line is even more straightforward:

```
fw.getDocumentDOM().setFillColor("#0099cc");
```

Yet again, the line starts by telling Fireworks that it wants to do something with the current document. Then it's saying to set the rectangle's fill color to #0099cc.

The next line is much longer than the others. This is because it is the Drop Shadow effect we added. Because effects have lots of parameters you can change, such as angle, distance, and blur, these settings have to be taken into account by the script.

```
fw.getDocumentDOM().applyEffects({ category:"Untitled", ¬
 effects:[ { EffectIsVisible:true, EffectMoaID:" ¬
 {a7944db8-6ce2-11d1-8c76000502701850}", ShadowAngle:315, ¬
 ShadowBlur:4, ShadowColor:"#000000a5", ShadowDistance:7, ¬
 ShadowType:0, category:"Shadow and Glow", name:"Drop ¬
 Shadow" } ], name:"Untitled" });
```

After all that, you might be wondering what is the point of editing the script. This is just text that the History panel has created, but in the next exercise you'll be creating a script from scratch that creates a special graphical effect that would otherwise be impossible without coding the script yourself.

Writing Scripts from Scratch

Now comes the more challenging part: composing your own scripts. In the exercise that follows, you will write your own script from scratch. As you go along, the code will be explained step-by-step. The script you will write, Twist and Fade, can be used to create an artistic effect that would be very difficult to draw by hand. The best part is, since you have already gotten into the code in the previous exercise, most of it will be familiar to you.

Exercise: Creating a Special Effect with a Script, Part 1

Even interesting scripts like this are so simple; with just ten lines of code you can create the special effects seen in Figure 14-9!

Figure 14-9   These effects were all created through scripting.

The command discussed in this section is available at the book's web site, but we recommend you type in the code yourself, just to get the hang of it.

1. This time we won't be starting in Fireworks at all. Instead, create a new clean sheet in your text editor.

2. We will go through each line one at a time. Type them in after reading the explanation.

```
var fwDOM = fw.getDocumentDOM();
```

This line saves you some time typing the rest of the script. In this script, each line starts with `fw.getDocumentDOM()`, but it's pointless writing it out repeatedly. So we created a variable, `fwDOM`, which simply refers to the full string. That way, whenever Fireworks sees the variable, it will know to substitute the actual function. It saves us some time typing, plus this method reduces the chance of typos. In scripts, one wrong or missing character can break the script. At the end of the line is a semicolon. Make sure to include this when it appears in the example, and then press ENTER or RETURN to start a new line.

The next line of code queries the user. (Note again that you should not type the ¬ symbol into your code.)

```
steps = prompt("How many steps would you like the pattern to ¬
  repeat? (1-50)","7");
```

This line is important, because it provides interaction between you and the script, without having to edit it each time. When the script runs, you will be prompted with the question in quotes.

```
fwDOM.setOpacity(10);
```

We'll now start to use the shortcut variable we typed in earlier, fwDOM. Make sure you match the case letters, as JavaScript is case sensitive. The setOpacity(10) function changes an object to just 10 percent opacity.

```
for(i=0;i<steps;i++) {
```

Now this line introduces a bit of programming. It is a for loop. Loops will continue to do a series of commands over and over until a certain condition is met. This is necessary because we are allowing the user to type in the number of steps, or *iterations*. So, in essence this line says that as long as the loop iteration is lower than the total number of steps, process all of its actions and add one to the loop number. It will keep going until the loop number (stored in the i variable) reaches the number the user entered into the prompt. When it does, the loop will break and the script will skip to the end.

```
fwDOM.duplicateSelection();
```

This line duplicates whatever object(s) are selected when you run the command. The duplicate is moved ten spaces down and right, which is why we need the following line:

```
fwDOM.moveSelectionBy({x:-10, y:-10}, false, false);
```

This line, as it suggests when you read it, moves the duplicate back to where we want it for the special effect to work suitably.

```
fwDOM.setOpacity(10);
```

This is the same line as earlier; this time it's formatting the new duplicate we've created. So are the next two lines.

```
fwDOM.scaleSelection(0.87, 0.87, "");
```

This one scales the object down to 87 percent of its original size on each axis.

```
fwDOM.rotateSelection(10, "");
```

And this line rotates the object by 10 degrees clockwise.

If you have been counting carefully, that was the ninth line. The tenth and last line is the hardest:

```
}
```

It's just one little curly bracket to finish with and you're all done! The final script should look exactly like this:

```
var fwDOM = fw.getDocumentDOM();
steps = prompt("How many steps would you like the pattern to ¬
 repeat? (1-50)","7");
fwDOM.setOpacity(10);
for(i=0;i<steps;i++) {
fwDOM.duplicateSelection();
fwDOM.moveSelectionBy({x:-10, y:-10}, false, false);
fwDOM.setOpacity(10);
fwDOM.scaleSelection(0.87, 0.87, "");
fwDOM.rotateSelection(10, "");
}
```

Exercise: Creating a Special Effect with a Script, Part 2

After all your hard work, it's time for the fun part, to save your work and try out your new command:

1. In your text editor, save your command as **Twist and Fade.jsf** in the Fireworks\Configuration\Commands folder, and make sure you include the .jsf extension, even on Macintosh machines.

2. Launch Fireworks, if it's not already open.

3. Start a new document with plenty of space to play with.

4. Now draw an object. It can be anything—rectangles, squares, ovals— they all work. You can even apply your script to text or Bezier paths—any type of object.

5. As soon as you've finished drawing your object, go to the Commands menu and run your new command, Twist And Fade.

6. As you've programmed it to, your command prompts you for the number of steps you'd like to take. Type in a number and then click OK.

7. Away your script goes. If you got it all right, you should have a nice special effect. If you got it wrong, Fireworks will display an error, or nothing will happen. Don't despair, check your code again; most likely it's a missing bracket, quote, or semicolon. It's essential to get little things like that right. If you still can't get it to work, download the final command from the book's web site, and place it in the Commands folder.

IDEA Try selecting more than one object, and some interesting effects occur. Also, don't forget that your objects can be formatted with fills and live effects before and after you apply the command.

Assigning Commands to Shortcut Keys

There is one significant advantage to Fireworks commands that we haven't told you about yet, but it is the greatest timesaver of them all.

Commands can be assigned shortcut keys!

Based on the first exercise, you could import your company's logo, save it as a command, and then assign it to a shortcut key. Imagine bringing in the logo just by pressing OPTION-L or ALT-L!

Exercise: Assign Your Command to a Shortcut Key

As with most things in Fireworks, creating or changing keyboard shortcuts is simple:

1. Choose Edit | Keyboard Shortcuts. The Keyboard Shortcuts dialog box appears (see Figure 14-10).

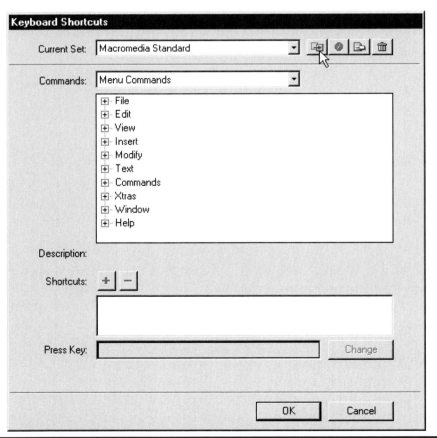

Figure 14-10   The Keyboard Shortcuts dialog box

2. The first thing you need to do is duplicate the Macromedia Standard settings. You are not allowed to alter these, so a duplicate is required. At the top of the dialog box are some icons—the first one on the left is the Duplicate icon (shown here).

3. The Duplicate Set dialog box appears, asking you to name your new set. For simplicity, call it **My Settings** and click OK.

4. Now that we've got our own set of keyboard shortcuts, you can add, change, and delete keyboard shortcuts as you wish. All we want to do at present is assign the Clock command we did earlier to a key. The tree hierarchy in the main box shows all the menu items. Click the + symbol next to the Commands menu.

5. When it expands, you will see all the commands you've created in the exercises, including Clock. Select Clock and click the + symbol near the bottom of the dialog box.

6. You now have to hold down the key or keys that you want the command to be assigned to. Hold down OPT-C or ALT-C; this is normally available, unlike most of the keys using COMMAND or CTRL, which will already have been assigned by Fireworks.

7. It's important you click Change to complete the request, before finally clicking the OK button at the bottom.

8. Now that you're back in Fireworks, make sure you have a document open and press your shortcut key. The Clock command will instantly run. You can assign keys to as many commands as you like.

Renaming, Deleting, and Organizing Commands

If you decide to experiment with commands, you may find that you've got a long list of unwanted or unorganized commands.

It's very easy to delete commands; there is an option at the top of the Commands menu, which you may already have noticed, called Edit Command List. Clicking this brings up a dialog box (see Figure 14-11) allowing you to rename or delete your existing commands.

You can organize commands into submenus by placing them in folders inside the Commands folder in the Fireworks\Configuration\Commands folder. Just create folders and drag commands into them. Be aware, though, that you can only have one level of subfolders. If you place a set of folders within one of the Fireworks subfolders, Fireworks will ignore them.

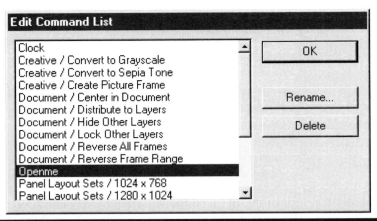

Figure 14-11 The Edit Command List dialog box

About the Tutorialist

Stephen is a webmaster for an up-and-coming software company called AppSense Technologies, based in Manchester, England. His experience sweeping a factory floor several years earlier inspired him to bigger and better things and set him on a path that eventually led to computers, and finally, to training and web design. For the last year, Stephen has been combining his design skills with his programming and database repertoire. When not coding or designing, he enjoys traveling and philosophy.

Where to Go from Here

There are several things you can do at this point to continue improving your ability to extend Fireworks. First, you should download the free PDF *Extending Fireworks* at the following URL and follow the extensibility links:

http://www.macromedia.com/support/fireworks/

Second, it would be worthwhile to download scripts that others have written. These will not only give you some examples to work with, but they also will inspire your creative juices. Several were created just for this book, and they are available at the book's web site.

In addition, several third-party sites offer Fireworks commands, including the following:

http://comharsa.com/firefaq/

http://www.massimocorner.com/

http://www.phireworx.com/

http://www.projectfireworks.com/

Of course, to write commands for real, you will be well served if you learn JavaScript. No one would learn JavaScript just to write commands in Fireworks, of course. But JavaScript is such an important web skill that your skills in it will inevitably increase. And once they do, don't forget that you will be, among other things, well equipped to write commands in Fireworks and Dreamweaver.

Learning JavaScript for the first time is like walking up a hill, only to find it suddenly flattens out into a plateau. Once you've gone up the initial learning curve and learned the essentials, it suddenly gets a lot easier. It is a consistent, object-oriented, and relatively simple language to learn.

Above all, as with all software (and most things in life)—just play, experiment, and explore. Most great ideas began as "what-ifs." Becoming a more powerful user is often merely a matter of trying those tools, dialog boxes, and menus that you don't usually open. The end of a book, even an advanced graphics software book, is always just a beginning.

Index

P

INTERNATIONAL CONTACT INFORMATION

AUSTRALIA
McGraw-Hill Book Company Australia Pty. Ltd.
TEL +61-2-9417-9899
FAX +61-2-9417-5687
http://www.mcgraw-hill.com.au
books-it_sydney@mcgraw-hill.com

CANADA
McGraw-Hill Ryerson Ltd.
TEL +905-430-5000
FAX +905-430-5020
http://www.mcgrawhill.ca

GREECE, MIDDLE EAST,
NORTHERN AFRICA
McGraw-Hill Hellas
TEL +30-1-656-0990-3-4
FAX +30-1-654-5525

MEXICO (Also serving Latin America)
McGraw-Hill Interamericana Editores S.A. de C.V.
TEL +525-117-1583
FAX +525-117-1589
http://www.mcgraw-hill.com.mx
fernando_castellanos@mcgraw-hill.com

SINGAPORE (Serving Asia)
McGraw-Hill Book Company
TEL +65-863-1580
FAX +65-862-3354
http://www.mcgraw-hill.com.sg
mghasia@mcgraw-hill.com

SOUTH AFRICA
McGraw-Hill South Africa
TEL +27-11-622-7512
FAX +27-11-622-9045
robyn_swanepoel@mcgraw-hill.com

UNITED KINGDOM & EUROPE
(Excluding Southern Europe)
McGraw-Hill Education Europe
TEL +44-1-628-502500
FAX +44-1-628-770224
http://www.mcgraw-hill.co.uk
computing_neurope@mcgraw-hill.com

ALL OTHER INQUIRIES Contact:
Osborne/McGraw-Hill
TEL +1-510-549-6600
FAX +1-510-883-7600
http://www.osborne.com
omg_international@mcgraw-hill.com